Open

0 Rebecca Merlic

Verlag für moderne Kunst

Enter

TheCityAsAHouse
...How the Network of 即席 Spaces Abolishes the Private Apartment.

SOKUSEKI: 即席
...you can choose 即席台所 (SOKUSEKI DAIDOKORO) or 即席キッチン (SOKUSEKI kitchen) I think.

We put 即席 before words when it becomes easy or fast or both. It means “instant”...

MAYUKO

Home

In the following essay I erased the private home and focus on my individual life without renting a private apartment.

A building is not a building. A building—in the sense of walls, floors, empty spaces, rooms, materials etc.—is only the outline of a potential. It is only made relevant by the group of people for whom it is intended.

I am one of them.

Rebecca Merlic

As humankind awaits the point of no return concerning climate change or the depletion of resources, the timeframe of the changes differs among the scientific community. Architecture has to provide solutions for a new and problematic era of living on the planet. Seeing the point of no return and facing the challenge for housing architecture, a new nomadic sense of living can provide a new solution. It can have an ecological, economical and psychological impact on the individual human and the world we live in. In the following essay, a subjective form of writing is used to guide through a vision of a city called Tokyo, reorganized through the experience of a female, thirty-year-old, European human.

Vast amounts of pictures, sounds, videos and 3D Sscans are organized as environments in the form of a visual novel and used by the artist as stimuli triggering recollection, thus allowing her to compose an impromptu narrative. Consuming my work enables the user to be at home without being bound to a physical space. It is a speculative exploration of the possibilities offered by abolishing known forms of habitation and should be understood as an attempt to repossess a certain amount of private space while suggesting the limitless forms of comfort abundantly available. Above all, I see women underrepresented in media art and would like to include this in my agenda.

While the pandemic has brought structural injustices and systemic injustices more into focus, digital virtual art has moved more into the spotlight, especially in the field of art and technology, I feel it is my calling to build networks of support that focus on the marginalized. I want to create opportunities by interweaving new technologies and co-creative processes for interdisciplinary collaboration with personal stories at the center. One could say that media art is an expression that constantly renews its own genre, with a tautological definition of media as the art of thinking about media. Some of what is (or could be) called media art today has in many ways become more firmly established in society. For me and my work, the future of art lies primarily in working with virtual political spaces that address issues such as gender, biopolitics, feminism, social inclusion, migration and class difference. I also see the testing of technological boundaries as a strong focus of my future work.

Experimenting with tracking and scanning the body working on the topic of glitch. I believe the world is a better place with more creators in it. The future of media-art creation is real-time, delivering everyone unprecedented artistic freedom. I want to create, iterate, collaborate, in real-time, to bring artwork interactively to humanity.

For me, the future of life lies in merging the knowledge of computer games and translating it into experiences for the body. Huge amounts of images, sounds, videos and 3D scans are organized as environments by making use of digital tools and computer programs, in the form of a visual novel, in a game engine to create experiences. For years I have been working with different computer programs and now I have found a cinematic tool, the game engine Unity. This is a tool that has been developed for the creation of digital worlds in computer games in which humans can move freely.

Comment
Feb 19, 2020

By
Mag. Dr. Andreas Spiegl

Academy of Fine Art, Vienna
Institut für Kunst- und Kulturwissenschaften

Reading Time:
02:00 Min

Rebecca Merlic's animation is based on a stay in Tokyo during which she decide- not to take an apartment for a month and to distribute and manage her daily life—from sleeping and eating to personal hygiene and communication—using the infrastructure available in the city. Instead of using an apartment with different rooms and functions, she encountered the city itself as an apartment whose rooms were spread out over the entire city. Sentos are the bathhouses that replaced a bathroom, Konbinis fulfilled the function of a kitchen with a lounge, and the capsules in Love Hotels took the place of a bedroom. As an architect, Rebecca Merlic thus "designed" the model of an urban-living and working space for a life without ownership and claims to ownership. Her smartphone alone was necessary to organize the search and selection of the respective urban infrastructure. The former coherence of different spaces in an apartment condenses into telematic space that can be updated as temporarily as contingent in the city. The former home of one's own is condensed into a smartphone, which now makes it possible to compile the idiosyncrasies of everyday demands anew and configure them individually on a daily basis. Giving up one's home also means the possibility of taking advantage of the largest and most variable of all homes.

The animation, using Unity's game engine, sketches the visual narrative of a life without a home—the possible everyday life of a population without a fixed residential address that reconfigures itself every day and reassembles itself again and again throughout the city. Merlic's "TheCityAsAHouse" enables virtual immersion in a future everyday life. Merlic has succeeded in recognizing an architectural tool in the smartphone taking housing and urban planning into its own hands, able to adapt and correct it as required. In this sense, the "Visual Novel" also tells a second story, as utopian as it is dystopian, which no longer asks how and where "smart" information technologies can be integrated into everyday life, but how a life can look like, which begins by getting an idea of this everyday life in advance, in order to then decide which images to put into practice.

Comment
Oct 13, 2020

By
Mag. arch. Dominik Strzelec

Academy of Fine Arts, Vienna
IKA

Reading Time:
02:00 Min

TheCityAsAHouse is an interactive installation built around the theme of Sokuseki meaning "improvised", "instant", "ad-lib." An artist sitting on the tatami mat in front of a screen uses a game controller to navigate the forking paths of her past experience living in Tokyo without a permanent place to stay. Rebecca Merlic's work is about being at home without being bounded. As a speculative exploration of the possibilities of abolishing known forms of habitation understood as an attempt to possess certain amount of private space, it suggests appreciating the limitless forms of comfort abundantly available in the contemporary metropolis.

The transient qualities of such state of being are foregrounded by the contrast between saturated multimedia landscapes and the presence of the artist herself, making it clear that human experience cannot be shared no matter the amount and sophistication of representational material. Allowing the audience to take their own path through the novel further emphasizes this incommensurability.

The work beautifully and maturely abstains from ideologically biased, one-sided critique of contemporary precarious living condition: skyrocketing property and rent prices, an unstable job market and uncertain relationships. Instead, it proposes fearlessly embracing and cultivating the here and now of the digitally mediated self as an alternative to desperately seeking stability in permanent, inert, recurring order of anything that can be owned. With a sense of admiration.

By
Manuela Hillmann

Curatorial Fellow Haus der Kunst, München, Founder & curator vent-gallery Wien/München, Founder notanotherwhitecube, Hohenbrunn

Reading Time:
03:05 Min

Urban portraits of large cities are usually an ode to verticality, consisting of magnificent views of the sprawling city, mimicking the frantic pace of daily life with rapid rhythms that make one dizzy. Critiques of social forms and the circumstances of life that becomes visible in a big city, are also often conceivable. Periodically, these concepts make one think of crowds, but not of the individual lives of real people.

In this sense, Rececca Merlic's TheCityAsAHouse proffers a different perspective. The multimedia work marked her graduation in Fine Arts and Architecture at the Vienna Academy of Fine Arts in January 2020 and is also the starting point of a consistent body of work that embodies the artist's curious mind and irrepressible creative urge.

When the artist was thirty years old, she explored the metropolis of Tokyo for two months without a fixed abode or any possessions other than a few pieces of clothing and her mobile phone. Seeking to redefine the concept of a house as being based on its functions, Merlic draws upon the public structure of the city: the Sento becomes a bathroom; the Konbini a kitchen; the capsule hotel a bedroom; and the park a place of retreat. In her work, Merlic creates a dynamic connection between the infrastructure of Tokyo and the needs of her daily life, which she then transforms into a floating island whose appearance is constantly in flux. The result is an invisible structure that sheds light on a possible future of urban life, focusing on a collective togetherness. In order to generate this, the artist questions her own conventions, crossing her own boundaries and detaching herself from traditional ideas of living: broadly speaking about (female) emancipation.

Conceived in the style of a visual novel, the work creates a mysterious urban setting across four chapters. Through this, Merlic transforms into a modern nomad who creates her living space in a flexible and sensitive way by entering a symbiosis with the city. This is accompanied by a complex soundscape consisting of the artist's narration, original sound recordings from Tokyo, and acoustic interventions by Austrian sound artist Manuel Riegler. TheCityAsAHouse thereby represents a unique example of the courage with which Rebecca Merlic moves along and beyond her personal limits in her artistic work, leaving her safe spaces to question and redefine existing structures.

I met Rebecca shortly before she left for Tokyo and was able to deepen my understanding of the work in the winter of 2019/2020 when we shared a flat in Vienna for a few months. During this period, Merlic was working on the finishing touches of TheCityAsAHouse. In both her living and working, Merlic often puts her own comforts and demands to one side in order to explore her surroundings with an alert sensitivity. She then rapidly translates her observations into impressively large-scale projects. In doing so, she does not get stuck in the realization, but rather is able to spontaneously respond to questions that arise in the process, thus able to adapt her works during their implementation.

In conclusion, TheCityAsAHouse is an impressive portrait of Merlic's love for Tokyo, told with an attentive female gaze from the perspective of an emancipated young artist at the beginning of a promising career.

A visual novel or a artistic realization of an experiment

Rebecca Merlic Meets Gustav Klimt—The Image of Women Then and Now

On April 28, 2022, the Ars Electronica Center in Linz organized an event at which Rebecca Merlic and I were able to introduce an attentive audience to the contrasting artistic positions of Gustav Klimt and Rebecca Merlic. We took advantage of Deep Space 8K's sixteen-by-nine-meter video wall, which certainly allowed for a visually brilliant presentation. The high-resolution Gigapixel images of Klimt's paintings created by Google Arts & Culture for the new digital Klimt presentation "Klimt versus Klimt," that I co-curated, were available to me, and Rebecca showed her impressive videos and film stills in the monumental Cinemascope format.

Our theme was the image of women in Gustav Klimt's time and today. As is well known, Klimt's image of women was strongly influenced by a predefined understanding of roles, which allowed women hardly any room to maneuver. Only slowly and with many personal sacrifices did strong female personalities manage to break away from these roles and demand their own rights. Klimt, however, never questioned the traditional understanding of roles in his portraits of women. He painted women largely as passive representatives of a financially privileged society, intended to convey serenity, dignity, and above all beauty.

The difference between this and Rebecca Merlic's portrayals of women could not be greater. Her representations of women, which she creates exclusively with the help of digital means, are by no account limited to a mere visual and aesthetic experience, but possess an important socio-political relevance. In her project GLITCHBODIES, for example, Merlic worked co-creatively with over 47 protagonists, all strong, emancipated and activist women from Vienna, Berlin, Hamburg, Munich, Zagreb and Bangkok. She has developed close contact with each of those involved in the project over the course of the collaboration, and networking among the protagonists was, and is, also a major concern of hers. "My art is meant to reposition ways of thinking that are still tabooed and persecuted in our society, and in doing so, I hope I can contribute something to the discourse of women's portraits," says Rebecca Merlic in the Ars Electronica Blog of 4/26/2022, which was quite magnificently created by Shirin Darwish.

As different as the artistic results of Klimt and Merlic are, in both cases the works present themselves as the result of a strikingly long working process. In Klimt's case we know how many months, sometimes years, he worked on a single painting, how much attention he paid to the composition and drew numerous studies for it. And with Merlic, the main focus of her work is in creating entirely new art productions based on advances in digital technology. World-building and using computer games as a medium in art, for example, are exciting, ongoing processes for her. And each task involves intensive collaboration with her models and protagonists, as in the video works MOTHERLAND or in the works for the series KLITCLIQUE.

There is, however, one immediate commonality between Klimt and Merlic, namely their affinity for Japanese culture. We know of Klimt's extensive collection of art from East Asia, of his enthusiasm for Japanese kimonos, the patterns of which also appear in many paintings of women. Klimt, however, never visited Japan himself. Merlic, on the other hand, visited Japan frequently and for longer stays each time. According to her own statements, her studies at the Tokyo Geidai under Atsushi Kitagawarasan were one of the most exciting times for her.

By
Helen Starr

Curator, Cultural activist, Commissioner &
Founder of the Mechatronic Library

Rebecca Merlic's work is a powerful tool to re-conceptualize what a CityAsAHouse may mean within the context of Audre Lorde's beautiful quote: "I am my best work—a series of road maps, reports, recipes, doodles, and prayers from the front lines." By Audre Lorde (Zami: A New Spelling of My Name. Berkeley, CA: Crossing Press, 1982.)

After her studies at Tokyo University, Rebecca changed the very form of her previous lived experience by eating, working and living exclusively in the publicly shared buildings of Tokyo's neon-lit, fast-paced cityscape. These communal spaces, activated by the tap of a card, formed a sprawl interconnected by temporal travel rather than conventional doors, thus transmuting the entirety of the city into one expansive dwelling. Much like nomadic individuals who perceive vast, starlit landscapes as their abode, Rebecca harnessed the power of her smartphone as a compass, a guide to real-time information on bathhouses, love hotels, and ramen shops. And as Rebecca travelled through the permeable borders of Tokyo, she transformed into a chattel person.

In the Caribbean, we have, a type of house which moves according to the needs of the land's resources. Known as the "chattel house," it is a traditional style of housing that is commonly found in Trinidad and Tobago.The term "chattel" refers to movable personal property, and the name "chattel house" stems from the historical context in which these houses were built by enslaved Africans who were not allowed to own land.

As a result, they developed a unique architectural solution by constructing houses that could be easily dismantled and moved when necessary. This mobility allowed them to maintain a sense of ownership and control over beautifully crafted living spaces teeming with memories and mementos. And, it fit well into the culture of the indigenous people where entire villages moved to allow the land to replenish itself with their left-behind, rich, human-made compost known as "terra preta de indio" or "the black soil of the Indian."

A house, and a group of houses which expand into a city, serves the ecological purpose of demarcating boundaries to delineate resources. Rebecca's radical work challenged the very concept that necessitates this boundary and incorporates the metaphysical notions of Lorde's the "I" as a bounded vessel which contains our experiences, struggles, and aspirations. We, they both seem to be saying, can become our own home with personal histories and accumulated wisdom which we carry through our lives like the House of Baba Yaga which roamed the land on chicken legs.

Rebecca's smartphone captured her memories of these spaces along with data about her emotions and wellbeing. She expanded her consciousness into an interactive virtual realm, replete with evocative reminiscences of ramen shops, public baths, capsules, and love hotels—a tapestry of locales encompassing both Wi-Fi-infused havens and places unburdened by the obligation to consume, where one could simply "be." Created using the Unity open-source game engine, the result manifests as an exquisitely rendered virtual world, inviting exploration and offering glimpses into an alternative, less extractive mode of existence. Rebecca, by opening this portal, serves a poignant reminder that magical and sustainable ways of treading lightly upon the Earth have existed and persist.

With the legacy of climate change now upon us, we may all one day become nomadic by inheritance. Hope.

By
Michaela Wimplinger

Special Projects,
Ars Electronica

When I first saw Rebecca Merlic's interactive work TheCityAsAHouse in 2020 as part of the Marianne.von.Willemer jury meeting, I was very impressed by her courage to carry out this project alone in Japan. Not only the presentation and content of the visual narrative were convincing, but also and especially the powerful approach of the artist. The versatility of her work stems from her expertise situated between the analog and the digital, as well as her architectural approach.

I finally got to know and appreciate Rebecca in person at the press conference and award ceremony for the Marianne.von.Willemer Prize for Digital Media at the Ars Electronica Center. Her positive and enthusiastic nature inspired me from the very beginning and distinguishes her as an artist, but also as a person. This encounter gave rise to the idea of making her work the focus of the exhibition "hosted by AEC" at Bildraum 07 in Vienna. Rebecca's art is capable of being effective—I consider her examination of gender roles and gender identities in particular to be significant. That's why we also invited her a year later for a special project to present her transcultural, artistic investigations in the unique setting of Ars Electronica Deep Space 8K. Here, too, the focus was on an intensive exploration of the theme of intersexuality through the means of bodies.

In this project, for example, she deals with prejudices and stigmata in the context of transidentity. Here, too, she finds a captivating expression for her concerns. Rebecca thus continuously sends a "message" that impresses me and that I consider particularly valuable. For the future, dear Rebecca, I wish for many more of your powerful and inclusive works—no matter if solo or collaborative. For you, I wish only the best —and for everything that may come. And for us, I wish for many more encounters and exciting collaborations together.

Rebecca Merlic creates virtual worlds, not as a copy or mimicry of reality, more as a digital translation of world descriptions. She finds world possibilities. To this end, she builds virtual spaces and situations that can be experienced interactively, not merely as portals from the real to the digital world, but as portals into spaces of thought and options that can only be discovered in the fluid negotiability of virtual worlds.

In her works she does not just show us a virtual world, nor does she simply take us traveling along, she sends us on a journey. On a classic odyssey, on which we must/are allowed to orient ourselves in the world possibilities that she opens up with her work—always on the threshold of voyeur, viewer and protagonist.

The glitch, the small errors in digital images and programs, which she often uses as a stylistic device, go far beyond chic decor or aesthetic play in her art worlds and refer to the breaking points of our time, in which we are just beginning to feel comfortable with digital and virtual twin realities. They stand for the vulnerabilities, the fragility of human existence and the glaring differences between appearance and reality in the "brave new worlds" of the tech industries.

Does her work being shown on screens make her a media artist, or is she a visual artist? Is she not rather creating sculptures? Is she an architect who builds 3D worlds with geometric models, an urbanist who analyzes the social textures of global metropolises? Is she an anthropologist of a new human image, of digitally networked societies and cultures? Does her use of controllers and game engines to interact with her artworks make her a game designer or is she a screenwriter and author? These are rhetorical questions, of course, but Rebecca Merlic is an exceptional artist who manages to combine all these options as very few do. She prototypically represents artists who are networked with the plurality of our world. A James Joyce of the 21st century, who writes the odyssey of our time, not with a typewriter but with all available means of our time. Not only by her outstanding works, but especially by her consequently "non-disciplinary" way of working, Rebecca Merlic is one of the trend-setting artists of our days.

Interview | By | Ars Electronica | Reading Time
Oct 16, 2020 | Katia Kreuzhuber | | 06:00 Min

Rebecca Merlic, who yesterday was awarded the Marianne.von.Willemer Prize for Digital Media 2020 at the Ars Electronica Center and was already represented at the Ars Electronica Festival 2020, has abolished the private apartment: After her studies in Tokyo, she decided that living, working and eating can also take place in public spaces. As a young, caucasian, heterosexual young woman, she no longer needs private spaces in the future; she makes the city her own. Everything she needs is there: ramen stores to eat, public baths to wash and relax, together with other people, capsules or love hotels where you can sleep cheaply and places with wifi and no obligation to consume where you can stay. She collects the experiences she had during these two months in Tokyo with her smartphone, she collects data about her health, about her location, makes 3D scans and pictures of herself and writes a diary. This results in the work TheCityAsAHouse, a visual novel, created with the open-source game engine Unity, that opens up a digital space for the human user in which he or she can relive the created experiences and open up new spaces. We wanted to learn more about this possible-future-oriented project and talked to the artist about the loss of security, the concept of home and plans for the future.

Making the City Your Own

Imagine giving up everything:

RM **Your bed, your kitchen your bathroom, your apartment. From now on you live, eat and sleep in public space.**

What do you associate with the person Marianne von Willemer and what does it mean to you to receive a prize that bears her name?

RM **I did some research on her after the call for entries and find her story very tragic. She was married relatively young, her work was not recognized, or rather her success was credited to others in her place. I was surprised by the role she played in literature because she was never recognized for it.**

Where did the work TheCityAsAHouse originate? What was the idea at the beginning of this exciting project, what thoughts did you have before you started this "experiment"?

RM **On the one hand, I was inspired by my encounters with young Japanese women, some of whom already live like this—not as much as I have, but once or twice a week. On these days they don't return to their parents' house, they rent something in the city and stay there overnight because they don't have to explain themselves and are much more free. On the other hand my own living situation—I moved very often when I studied in Tokyo because it is very difficult to rent apartments, especially for foreigners. That's when I realized that I pay 1,000 Euros for an apartment in which I only sleep six hours, because otherwise everything is transferred outside, into the public space.**

"Young women in Japan already live like this in some cases (...). They rent a room in the city once or twice a week, they don't return to their parents' house because they don't have to explain themselves there and are much more free."

What does home mean to you, the concept of home?

RM **Because I grew up with Croatian roots in Germany and moved around quite often as a child, there is no permanent home for me. My more unstable lifestyle as a child, which probably also made it easier for me to give up this "home" and look for its functions in an urban context. If you abstract it, reduce the home to certain functions, you can find a home anywhere.**

After all, these "own four walls" offer most people a great deal of security. What does one replace this security with when one throws everything overboard?

RM **It's actually all fiction. When you rent an apartment, you can break it down into its functions, you can calculate the value per day. Even if you buy a house, on credit, it is a fiction of ownership that you may never pay off. Six days a week it is a liberating feeling: on these days you don't need the security because you feel freer. The other day, because of my childhood upbringing—even though this day has no meaning in Japan—was Sunday. On this day I wanted to surround myself with emotional objects to which I, or other people, have an emotional connection. I think that is what makes a home. It is an archive of a life that you have accumulated. One could produce such archives to replace this thought.**

Have you returned to the same places? Have you slept in the same capsules, eaten in the same restaurants?

RM **Yes, sometimes. Yes, when I had interactions with people. So in the ramen store where I often went, the food was cooked by the owner and the capacities were very small, so it was very personal and familiar. Sometimes I built up very nice relationships, despite language barriers, then I drove halfway through the city to eat there again.**

So you create patterns yourself?

RM **Yes, although interrupted from time to time, depending on the day of the week etc. On weekends I sometimes drove to the countryside because the rent for overnight stays is adjusted daily. They are oriented to the market, so the same capsule can cost sometimes 25, sometimes 100 euros per night. So, on the weekends I often went to the country or stayed overnight with friends.**

How do you live now and can you imagine to live like this in the long run?

RM **I can imagine it very well and sometimes I miss it too! I live together with my partner now, but I often change my studio, rent a room where I can stay overnight, so I don't always have to return to the same place. It means a certain freedom and inspiration for me. I would like to try the same thing in Vienna, but I'm afraid it would be very one-sided because there aren't so many different possibilities.**

What makes Tokyo different from a city like Vienna or Linz?

RM **There are places there that I have declared as kitchen, bedroom, bathroom extension. It was never about homelessness because I would never dare to say anything about this feeling. It was more about living a free, hedonistic lifestyle and to make use of the capitalistic lifestyle, which is much more pronounced there than in Europe. For example, I spent a lot of time in supermarkets, I worked there, there was internet and a toilet, and you didn't have to consume anything. That's more difficult with us—there are few places that offer consumption but don't demand it.**

But still only a few use these places the way you used them?

RM **I think so, partly. But I think that in Tokyo there is no public space anymore, but it's the other way around, private space is in public space.**

Are there any follow-up ideas, a follow-up project that you have planned?

RM **I would like to go back there and see how it would be possible under corona conditions. At the moment it is not yet possible to immigrate, but in January I hope that it will be possible.**

Chubgirl
Gem
Ken Fukuda
Kodai
Kobei
Manabi Fukuda
Mayuko
Me, I
Midori
Miyamoto
Oba-Chan Matsuzaki
Raku
Ryo
Ryota
Takashita
Unknown
Milkman
Ryuji

Thanks to all people who helped me

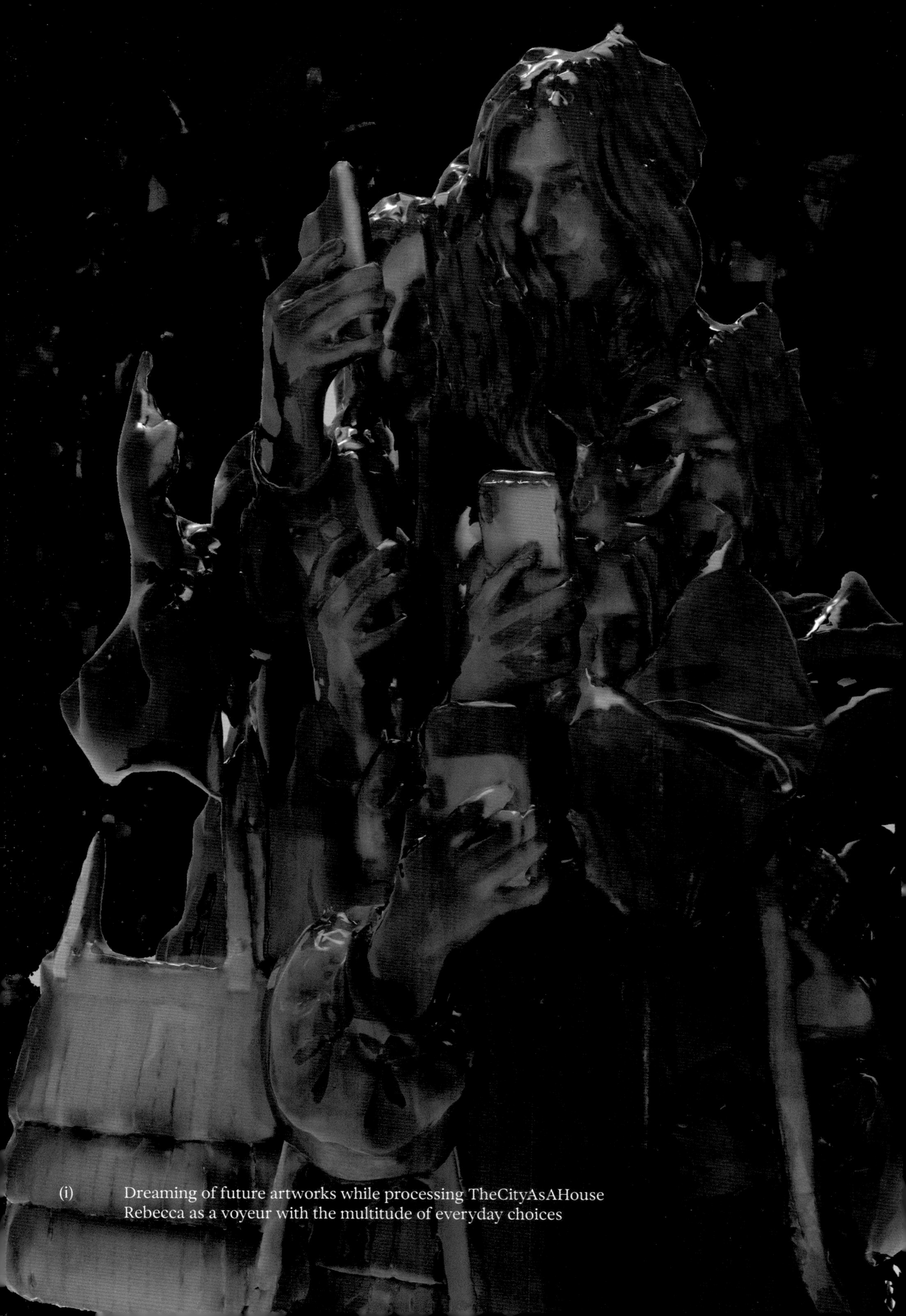

(i) Dreaming of future artworks while processing TheCityAsAHouse
Rebecca as a voyeur with the multitude of everyday choices

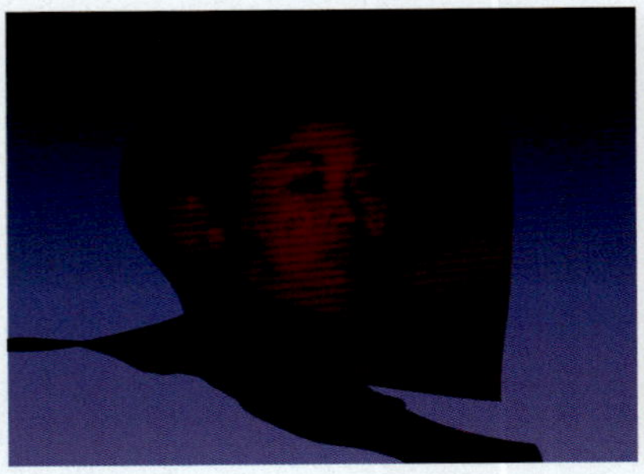

CLUBGIRL

FOV: 60 FPS: 58.8
BO_RENDERING

Current Mesh: RIU

Vertices: 34,960 (696,840)
Faces: 69,576 (1,336,389)
Selection: v: 0 f:0
VQ VC

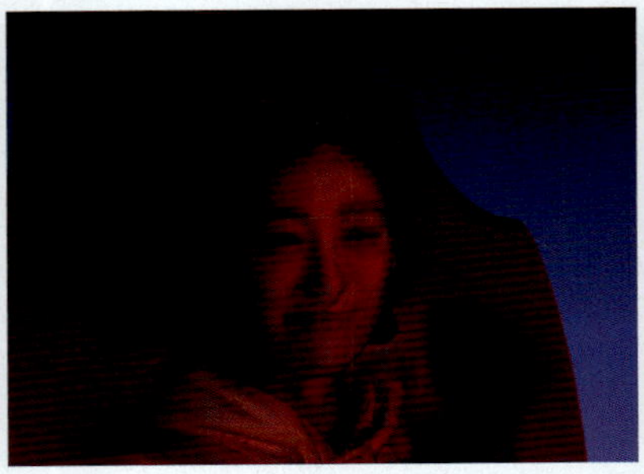

GEM

FOV: 60 FPS: 67.1
BO_RENDERING

Current Mesh: GEM

Vertices: 66,435 (696,840)
Faces: 132,611 (1,336,389)
Selection: v: 0 f:0
VQ VC

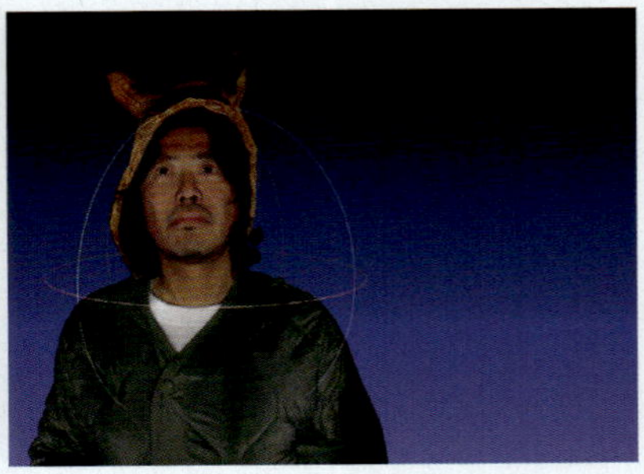

KEN FUKUDA

FOV: 60 FPS: 61.7
BO_RENDERING

Current Mesh: Ken02.obj

Vertices: 467,906
Faces: 935,800
Selection: v: 0 f:0
FC WT

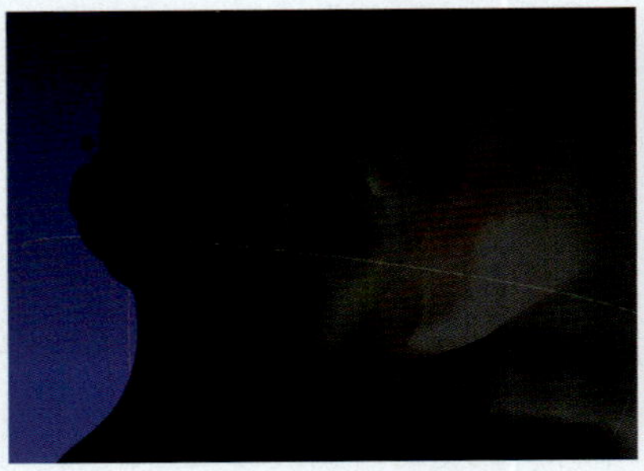

KODAI

FOV: 60 FPS: 66.7
BO_RENDERING

Current Mesh: KODAI

Vertices: 53,780 (353.375)
Faces: 107,387 (651,706)
Selection: v: 0 f:0
VQ VC

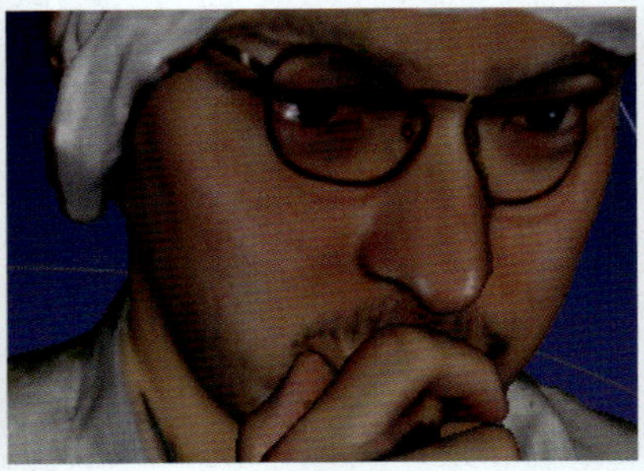

KOHEI

FOV: 60 FPS: 62.5
BO_RENDERING

Current Mesh: Koheio1.obj

Vertices: 445,035
Faces: 890,078
Selection: v: 0 f:0
FC WT

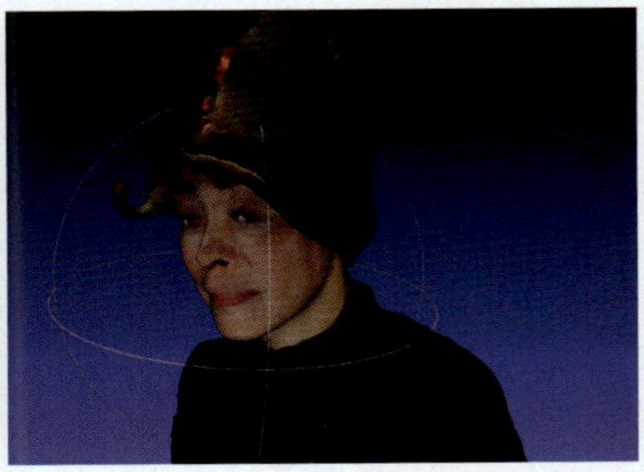

MANABI FUKUDA

FOV: 60 FPS: 88.5
BO_RENDERING

Current Mesh:
Minari Fukuda 03 HUT
Vertices: 463,520 (931,426)
Faces:927,060 (1,862,860)
Selection: v: 0 f:0
VQ VC

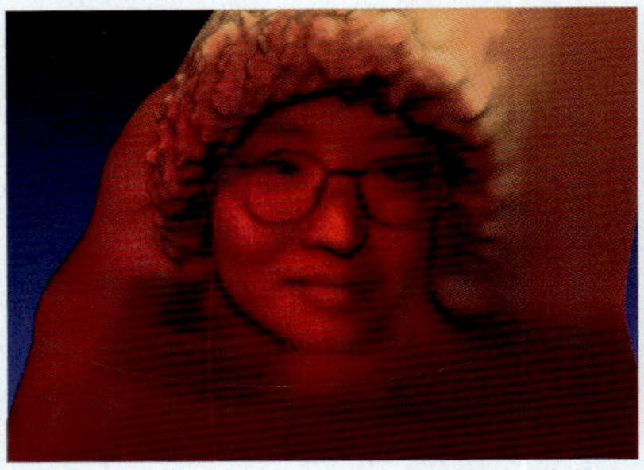

MAYUKO

FOV: 60 FPS: 53.2
BO_RENDERING

Current Mesh: MAYU

Vertices: 45,410 (696,840)
Faces: 90.571 (1,336,389)
Selection: v: 0 f:0
VQ VC

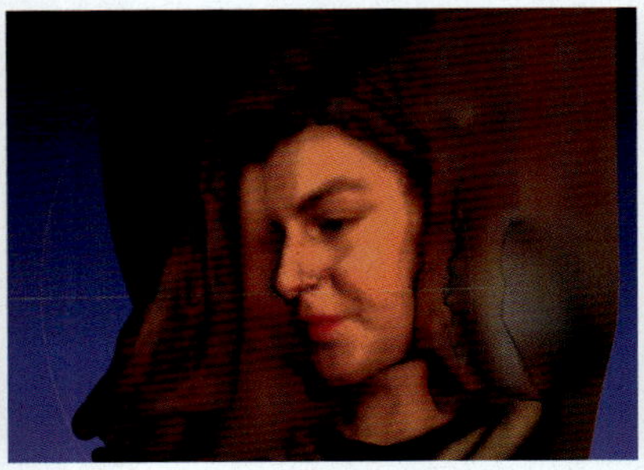

ME

FOV: 60 FPS: 68.5
BO_RENDERING

Mesh: REBI.plv

Vertices: 86,621
Faces:173,075
Selection: v: 0 f:0
VQ VC

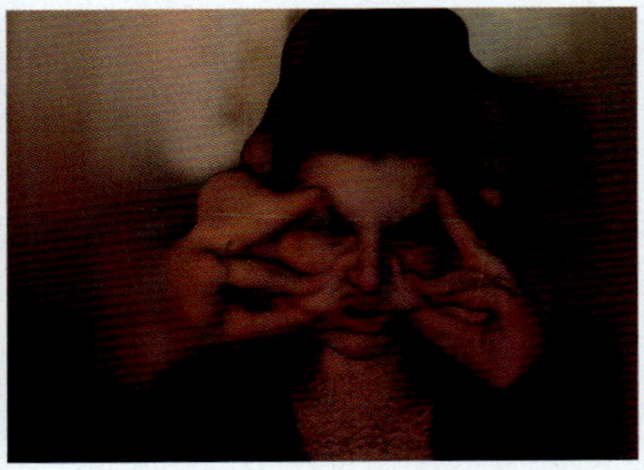

ME

FOV: 60 FPS: 82.6
BO_RENDERING

Mesh: REBIMOnster.obi

Vertices: 43.144
Faces: 86.140
Selection: v: 0 f:0
VQ VC

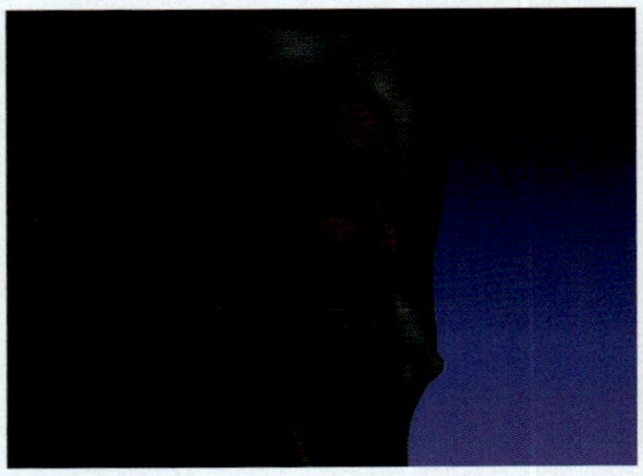

MIDORI

FOV: 60 FPS: 62.9
BO_RENDERING

Current Mesh: RIU

Vertices: 27,078 (696,840)
Faces: 53.955 (1,336,389)
Selection: v: 0 f:0
VQ VC

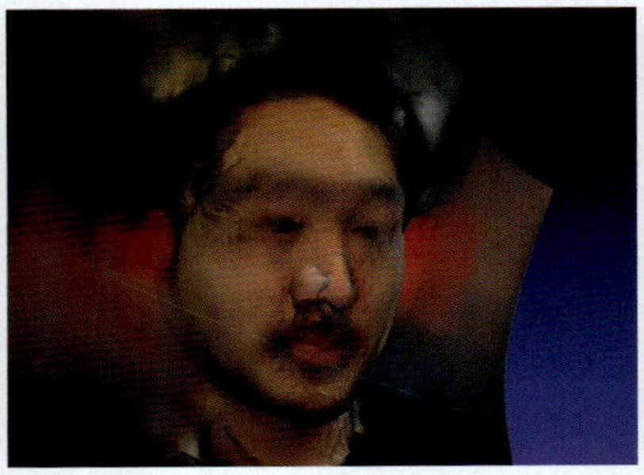

MIYAMOTO

FOV: 60 FPS: 57.1
BO_RENDERING

Current Mesh: MIYAMOTO

Vertices: 22,875 (696.840)
Faces: 45,598 (1,336,389)
Selection: v: 0 f:0
VQ VC

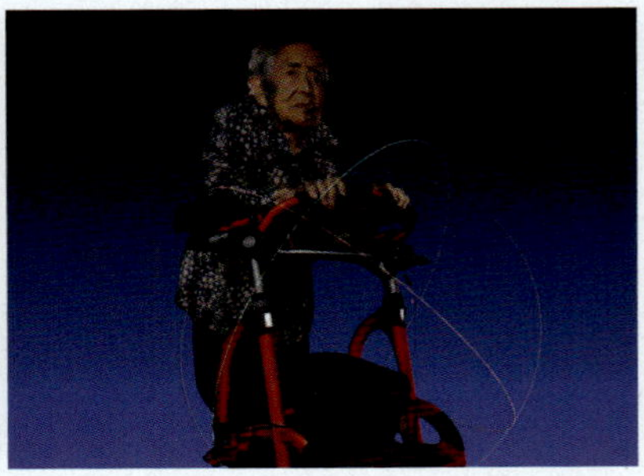

OBA-CHAN MATSUZAKI

FOV: 60 FPS: 61.3
BO_RENDERING

Mesh: OBA-CHAN–standing.obj

Vertices: 1,319,942
Faces: 2,639,964
Selection: v: 0 f:0
VQ VC

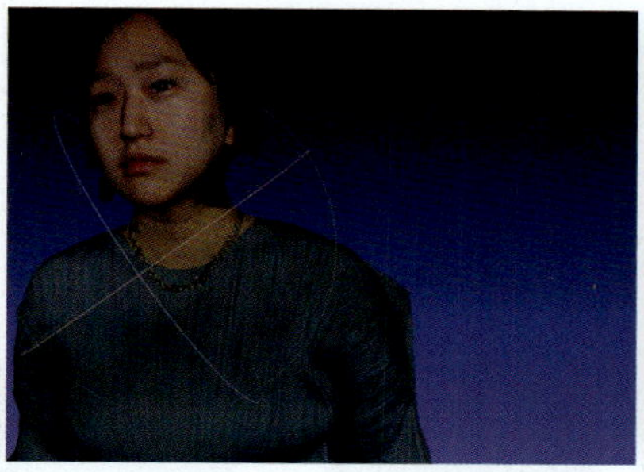

RAKU

FOV: 60 FPS:2.1
IMMEDIATE MODE
RENDERING

Mesh: Raku01.obj

Vertices: 1.826.152
Faces: 3,652,324
Selection: v: 0 f:0
FC WT

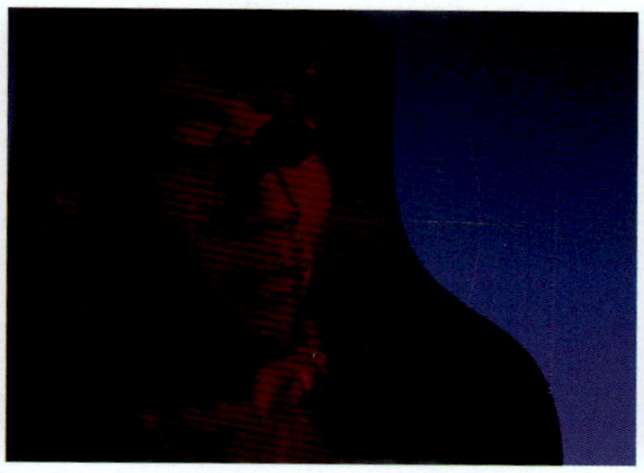

RYUJI

FOV: 60 FPS: 59.9
BO RENDERING

Current Mesh: RYUJI

Vertices: 48,530 (135,151)
Faces: 96,885 (269.963)
Selection: v: 0 f:0
VQ VC

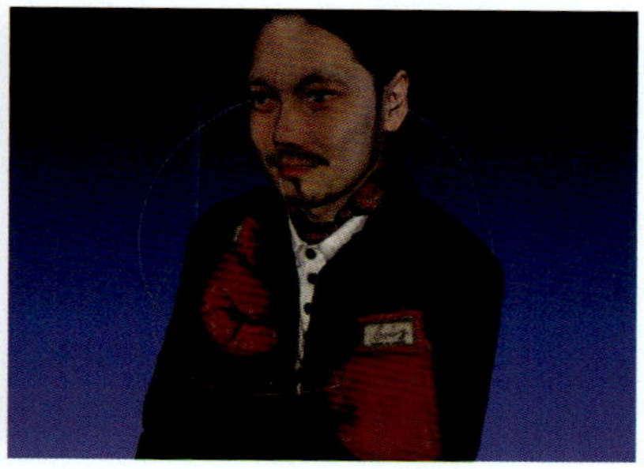

RYO

FOV: 60 FPS: 1.8
MIXED RENDERING

Current Mesh: Ryo01

Vertices: 1,657,150 (2,588,576)
Faces: 3,314,308 (5,177,168)
Selection: v: 0 f:0
VQ VC

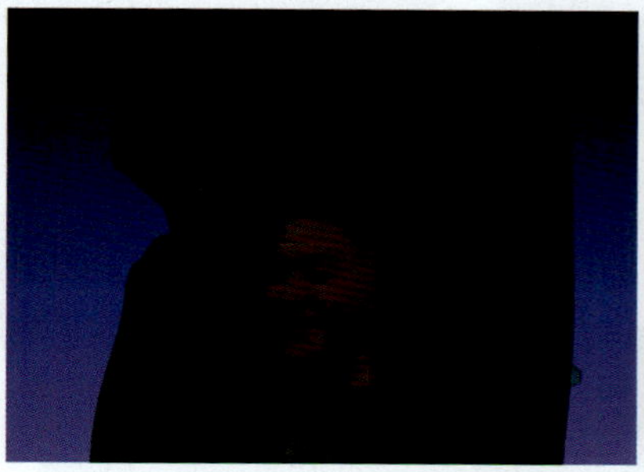

RYOTA

FOV: 60 FPS: 58.8
BO_RENDERING

Current Mesh: RYOTA

Vertices: 27,499 (353,375)
Faces: 54,790 (651,706)
Selection: v: 0 f:0
VQ VC

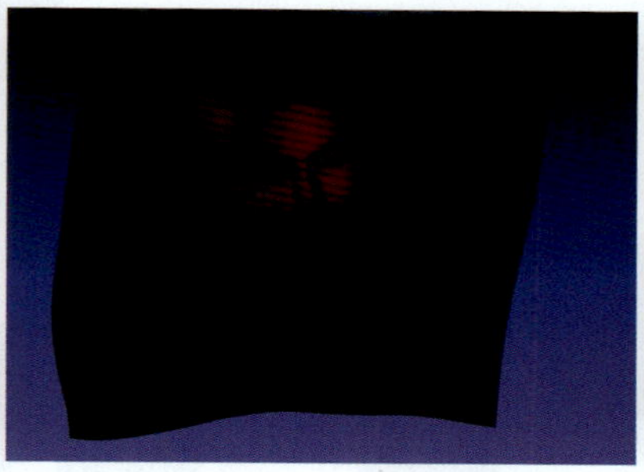

TAKASHITA

FOV: 60 FPS: 59.9
BO RENDERING

Current Mesh: TAKASHITA

Vertices: 44,781 (353,375)
Faces: 89,347 (651,706)
Selection: v: 0 f:0
VC

UNKNOWN

CLFOV: 60 FPS: 55.2
BO_RENDERING

Current Mesh: OMAR

Vertices: 16,799 (696,840)
Faces: 33,363 (1,336,389)
Selection: v: 0 f:0
VQ VC

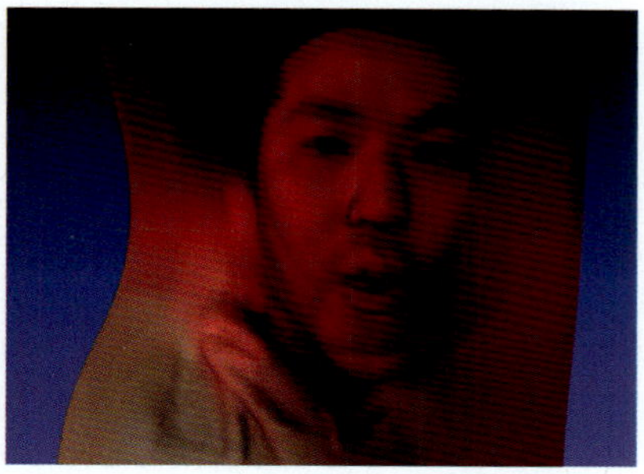

MIKMAN

FOV: 60
FPS: 82.0
BO_RENDERING

Current Mesh: MIKMAN

Vertices: 27.499 (696.840)
Faces: 54,790 (1,336,389)
Selection: v: 0 f:0
VQ VC

Ab
TheC
A
Ho

Part I

out
ityAs
use

In the visual novel TheCityAsAHouse I erase the private home and focus on individual life without renting a private apartment.

A visual novel—experiment of a caucasian European thirty-year-old human living in Tokyo over a period of time without inhabiting a private apartment. My smartphone is my only property, my organizer. No need for private space in the future. A conservative private space consists of rooms in which to sleep, wash, eat, for delight and storage. I used to live in an apartment in the past. The conservative apartment had four rooms. A bedroom, a living room, a bathroom, and a kitchen. I sleep in public spaces. In the train, in the love hotel, in the capsule, in the Anime Café, the book and bed, the nine hours, or at the workplace. The bedroom is abolished. No more cooking. The infrastructure of the so-called *konbini* and affordable food in restaurants, fast-food restaurants and street food stalls is abundant and an integral part of Japanese everyday life and culture. The bathroom is abolished. Bathing is carried out in public spaces. In so-called *sentos*. Bathhouses are not only meant for cleaning, but also for your wellbeing, beauty, and health. The bathroom is abolished. TheCityAsAHouse is a new strategy of dissolving one room after another. It is a liberation. We don't have to own or pretend to have property anymore. In 1903, Hermann Muthesius said: "Japan is in many respects the country that comes closest to one's dream of paradise." Dissolving the private liberates creates new forms of society. In the history of pre-modern Japanese housing, the concept of *puraibashii* (privacy) was alien and it was unknown to the general population during the Meiji restoration. Pre-industrial Japanese households were "fluid" spaces with virtually no privacy. The current situation in Tokyo allows for the emergence of a turbo-dense, capitalism-driven space generator for satisfying one's personal desires and needs. The question is whether the in-between spaces, the decentralization, as well as networked and digitalized urbanism, make it possible to live without private spaces altogether. Is a new form of nomadic living not only being constructed in digital and virtual spaces, but also in concrete spaces? Will this lead to the alteration of the city's skyline and the creation of ruins of property? What will happen to these spaces should they become obsolete? Shifting privacy in non-domestic spaces can lead to different architectural consequences. The space left by this shift can provide new space for more and different infrastructure, which can add value for society. The resulting developments are drien by technology, money, and societal needs. TheCityAsAHouse depicts an illusion of private ownership of a place we call home and transfers it into the cityscape where the human occupies a certain amount of space while moving or resting depending on time and need. What does it mean to be freed from the urge of craving a nest? The CityAsAHouse is a strategy of successfully surviving with-out being dependent on the housing market. Let us use this system and reinterpret what it means to live with-out a home. It is a proposition of a new form of society. A new form of living. The next self-improvement of humanity or going back to our roots. TheCityAsAHouse is a visual novel built with the game engine Unity to open up digital space for the human user to relive the created experiences and open up new ones. We must think of a city as a complicated construction of various and diverse networks. The instant or 即席 Places I discover are pearls on a chain, chains which multiply and autogenerate themselves. No complete overview can be given. The device which we carry with us every day provides glimpses based on pure hedonistic preferences and previous encounters with the 即席 Rooms we have chosen to visit. Data can provide the information; the network system needs to develop itself.

Architects build enough.

Building sites must be divided, reused, refunctioned, redesigned to provide a more sustainable view on city planning. By taking this one step further and abolishing the private apartment and using the functioning city's networks to gain more experiences, a new kind of digitalized city can evolve. The ridiculous housing market would crash and make place for a new economy of experiences favored by millennials and Generation Z. Digital natives spend their time using devices to flee from the real world. It is time for architects to use the digital to design a new cityscape for the future.

TheCityAsAHouse

Spe
TheC
A
Ho

ces
ityAs
A
use

2 即席 Spaces The Bathroom is Abolished

Sento 銭湯

The 即席 Bathroom can be seen as a place, that deals with more than just the hygiene of the body, it addresses the cleaning of the soul. Recharging energy which is lost while living 24 hours in Tokyo. The 即席 Bathroom is a concept of removing and abolishing all bathrooms in the private apartment and embedding them in the city network. The 即席 Kitchen type of *konbini* can also function as a bathroom in terms of creating a network of toilet facilities all over the city. In *konbinis* the use of the toilet unit does not require consumption. Every so-called *konbini*, a kind of supermarket, has several functions to serve humans. They offer free internet access, designated smoking areas, work stations, as well as toilets. The use of the toilet is allowed to everyone and is free of charge. This offers a network of privatized public sanitary units which can be used by every human. Bathing takes place in public spaces known as *sentos*. These bathhouses are not only used for cleaning the body, but also for wellbeing, beauty and health. This is an accepted and loved convention which permeates society while transcending generational, social, economic and geographic barriers. Any private bathroom is superseded by the *sento*. A relict from the past still in strong use today as the 即席 Bathroom of a new social life. Taking a bath in the *sento* compared to one in a private apartment requires the human to move through a sequence of spaces with different functions and rules. It also means removing your clothes protecting you from the outside world.

Standing in front of the koi-sign
made out of textile which is moving in the wind.
Bowing and taking a small step to enter the locker area.
The entrance.
Taking off my shoes and stepping up to the bandai.
The old lady is sitting behind it, smiling at the gaijin.
I pay 360 yen and fifty for the towel.
Soap and shower are included.
No baggage needed.
After stripping off my clothes
in the dressing room, I store them in a locker with a wooden key.
I enter the bathing area.
The bathing area.
I can feel the steam rising
from the three hot tubs in the back of the room.
After taking an oke 即席and a stool I head to an empty karan 即席.
It is a small place with a mirror
and two faucets.
I observe my naked body in the mirror
in front of me.
The three different tubs are steaming
like ramen soup
waiting for my clean self to enter.
I am scrubbing my skin
with the collective soap
from the huge dispenser
in the middle of the room.
The faucets are placed in front the mirrors which are arranged in a line.
Cold and hot water mix
to a perfect temperature in the oke.
I hear water splashing down the tiles.
The whole room is tiled in pastel colors.
I am filling the bucket first with cold
then hot water.
Splashing it on my soap-covered body.
Again, I examine my body in the mirror.
Fully exposed, I do not look at the other naked patron next to me.
The women are examining
my steps of cleansing.
Everyone is concentrating on their own ritual.
Only your clean self
is allowed to enter the tubs.
Rubbing my skin with soap again.
Washing my hair thoroughly.
Combing through it with my fingers.
Splashing water on my naked self again.
Splashing sounds every couple of minutes.
Combined with the bubbling sound
of the hot water from the tub.
Almost like music.
Everywhere.
The tub awaits me to enter.
The hair must be kept up as not to touch the shared water.
Finally, your clean self is ready to enter
the hot tub.
First, I drip some water from the tub on my body.
Sitting on the edge of the tub with only my legs in the water to adapt.
Looking at the tiled room-high Mount Fuji painting on the wall.
I feel the warmth.
The heat is rising through my body.
It's eight o'five.
Now I'm sitting in the hot water.
Purifying myself.
The old lady next to me talks in Nihingo.

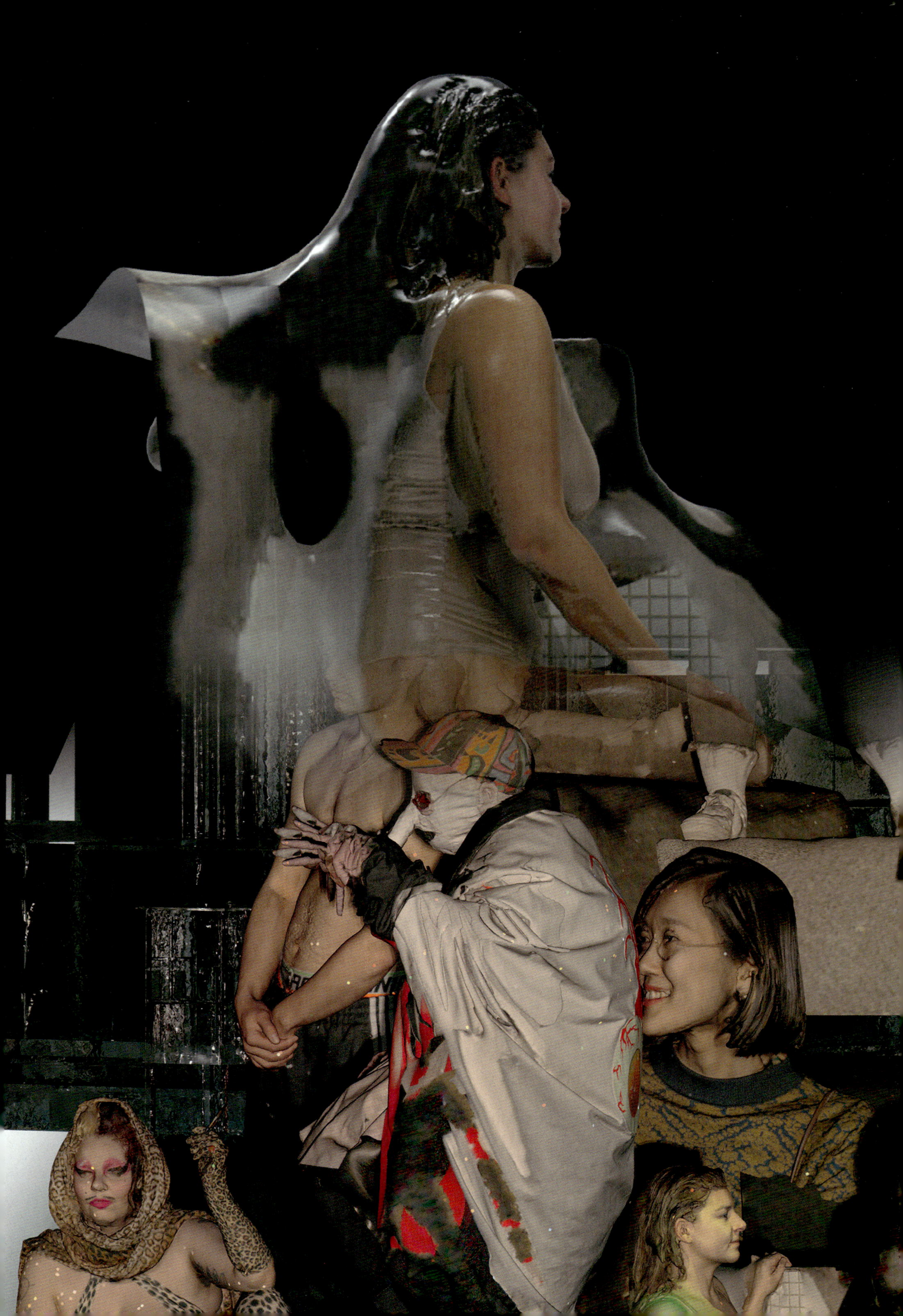

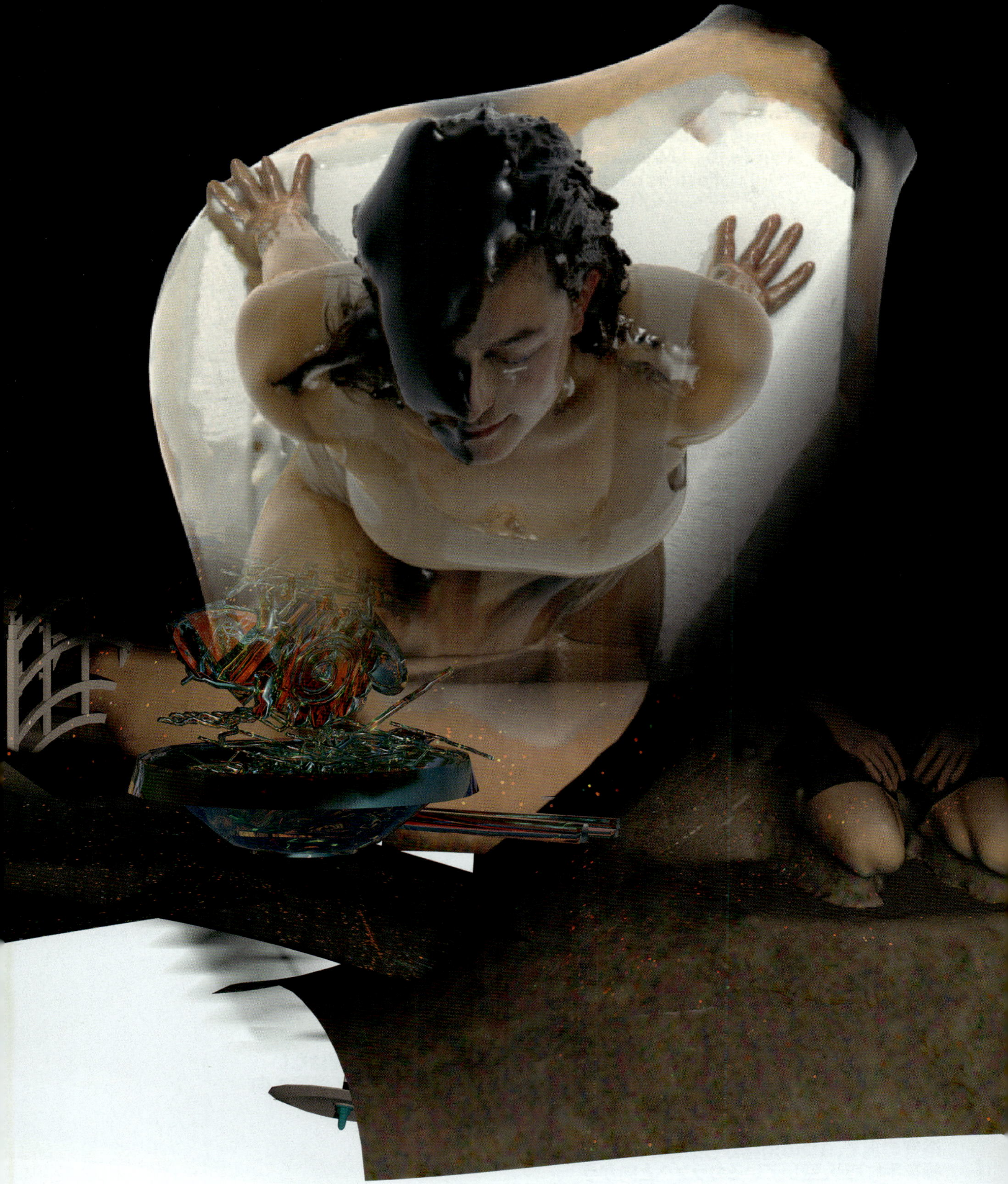

(i) Dreaming of future artworks while processing TheCityAsAHouse showing body scans of Annemarie Arzberger, Susie Flowers, Ari Ban and Suchart Wannaset.

I smile.
She smiles back.
Now she tries to speak English, she married an Englishman thirty something years ago.
I am looking at Mount Fuji again.
I'm thinking about work and home.
Washing myself clean from my sins.
I see my red body in the mirror now
and decide to dive into the ice-cold water.
The light is bright.
I can see every mark on my body.
I sit in the cold water.
Feeling needles everywhere.
My body adapts again.
I feel like taking another turn
in the hot brown water.
After four cycles I stop.
I go back to the faucet
where I left my stool and sit.
Filling up the bucket with hot and cold water.
Mixing it with my hand.
Splashing it on my body. Again.
I wait until my body is dry to enter the dressing room again.
The old lady from the bandai is smiling at me.
I put cream on my dry skin and dry my hair.
I put on my clothes.
"arigatou gozaimasu どうもありがとうございます",
"doumo"
I bow to the old lady
Take my shoes from the locker.
I open my umbrella and enter the rainy dark.
I feel relief.
I feel the skinship.
I want to sleep.

Sento (JAP)

銭湯:
風に揺れる暖簾の前に立つ。
小さな階段を上がり、暖簾をくぐり下駄箱へ行く。
入り口
靴を脱いで番台へ進む。
おばさんが座っていて、外人へ微笑みかける。
私は入湯料360円とタオル代50円を払う。
これには石鹸とシャンプーも含まれていて、荷物を持ってくる必要はない。
脱衣所で服を脱ぐと、それらをロッカーにしまい木製の鍵を締める。そして浴室へ向かう。
浴室
浴室の奥で、3つの浴槽から蒸気が立ち昇って行くのが感じられる。
桶を手に取り、空いているカランへと向かう。
それは二つの蛇口がついた小さなスペースで、私は鏡の前で自分の裸を観察する。
3種類の浴槽は、まるでラーメンのスープのように湯気立ち、
綺麗な私の体が入っていくのを待っている。
正しい石鹸を浴室の真ん中にあるディスペンサーから取り、泡立てて肌をこする。
蛇口は鏡の前に整列し、桶の中で冷水と熱湯を混ぜて、適温にする。
水がタイルにはねる音が聞こえる。

浴室はパステルカラーのタイルで覆われている。
桶を冷水で満たし、次に熱湯を加える。
泡でいっぱいになった身体にかけて、泡を落とす。
もう一度、鏡の中の自分の身体をくまなくチェックする。
とても無防備な状態だ。私は絶対に隣の客の裸をみない。
女たちが私が身体を洗う様子をチェックしている。
みな自分自身の儀式に集中している。
身体を洗ったものだけが、浴槽に入ることを許されているからだ。
再び石鹸で身体をこする。髪を徹底的に洗う。
指でそれらを混ぜ合わせる。
首に再びお湯をかける。
毎分、皆がお湯を身体に打ちかける音が響く。
泡立てる音と、浴槽のお湯の音、それらが組み合わさって、ほとんど音楽のようだ。
そこら中で音楽が奏でられている。
浴槽が私を待っている。
髪はお湯に浸からないように結い上げられ
ていなければならない。
やっとお湯に浸かる準備が整ったというわけだ。
湯に慣れるため、湯船の縁に座って、両足だけをお湯につける。
部屋の高さいっぱいにペイントされた富士山を見上げる。
温もりを感じている。
暖かさが身体に昇ってくる。
8時5分だ。
湯船の中に座る。
身を清める。
隣のおばあさんが日本語で話している。
私は微笑む。
彼女も微笑み返す。
彼女が私に英語で話しかけようとする、
三十数年前、彼女はイギリス人と結婚していたという。
再び富士を眺める。
私は故郷と仕事のことについて考える。
私は私の罪を洗い流す。
鏡の中の赤く上気した身体を見て、水風呂に入ることを決める。
光は明るい。
身体の傷跡全てを見ることができる。
水風呂の中に腰掛ける。
全身を針で突き刺さされるようだ。
そしてまた身体が慣れていく。
もう一度茶色の湯に浸かろうかという気持ちになってくる。
私はこれを4周繰り返した。
カランに戻り、腰掛ける。
番台のおばさんが私に微笑みかける。水気を落とした肌と髪にクリームを塗り、服を着る。
ありがとうございます。
どうも。
お辞儀をして、靴を手にとる。
傘をさして、雨降る闇に入っていく。
安心した気持ちになっている。私は人とのふれあいを感じている。眠りにつきたい。

2 即席 Spaces
The Kitchen is Abolished

Focusing on the heart of the home, the 即席 Kitchen, we begin with the most nurturing and important room of the apartment. The Kitchen is abolished. Cooking and eating take place in various locations throughout the city. If we imagine the kitchen is lost and implemented as a network of various kitchens in the cityscape, we can ensure more sustainability if some factors are true. Research suggests that if a restaurant, also known as the 即席 Kitchen, serves more than 1,800 meals a day of just one or two kinds of dishes it is more sustainable for the environment compared to every customer cooking their own meals at home. This raises the question if a network of kitchens would work in present times. 即席 Kitchens can be found in places like *konbinis, izakayas,* ramen bars, udon shops, fast-food chains, third-wave coffeeshops, food service operators, sushi and so-called family restaurants. These spaces create an intimate atmosphere between humans and their food. It is a sensual, exciting, glazed, satisfying, nurturing experience, which can also be lonesome, contiguous, bonding. The 即席 Kitchen can be found everywhere in the Japanese capital. Different spaces can transform into, and be used as, a 即席 Kitchen and ensure that the human user does not have to prepare the meal themselves. In some cases just a finishing touch is needed, and people can sit and enjoy a meal, alone or in company depending on the social relations of their lives. One kind of a network of 即席 Kitchens is the *konbini*-network. One *konbini* in the metropolitan area of Tokyo serves around 1860 residents. A *konbini* is a variety of supermarket which includes more functions than just buying products and ingredients. It begins with its visibility throughout the city. The konbini is not only a food service operator, providing the user with everything s/he needs for surviving 24 hours in Tokyo. The *konbini*-network serves as lunch table, bookstore, post office, copy shop, working space, wifi-provider, restroom, wardrobe, tobacco stand, coffee shop, bakery, refectory, one social interaction of the day and, of course, as a kitchen. The sliding doors and the neon sign, which illuminates the name of the chain of *konbinis* like Lawson, 7-Eleven and Family Mart, greet the customer with a short and friendly electronic jingle. In front of the shop, an umbrella stand accommodates many umbrellas on a rainy day in Tokyo. Similar to your own apartment, you do not want the floor to get wet unnecessarily. You squeeze your see-through rain protector between all the others in the stand.

It is impossible to find the same umbrella you came with after you exit the store. It is a personal and almost compulsory exchange of goods, which does not even occur to most people since an umbrella can be bought in every konbini for around 500 Yen. You stick it in and when you exit you take another person's umbrella. I hold the umbrella handle in the same place as someone else has already done before. It feels like touching someone else's hand without knowing the person. Concluding in touching one another. The entrance area provides the self-service area with coffee and machines for hot drinks, a water heater and microwaves. You pass through the aisle offering cosmetics and underwear. When the salarymen have spent a night at the love hotel and they need fresh underwear and a toothbrush. Or the schoolgirl stained her shirt while eating lunch at the ramen shop and wants to buy another one for afternoon classes. Small packaged snacks are provided in another aisle. Hundreds of different kinds of cans and bottles aim to quench the thirst after a long day. Finally, the single portioned meals are offered hot and cold, however you prefer them, to eat in the eating area where you can work as well as transform it into your safe space. When I wandered the city without having a private apartment, I stopped in a *konbini* and stayed there for some hours, sitting at the working area and looking at the people coming in, fulfilling their needs and exiting again. In two-to-five-minute periods. I just sat there and thought about where to go next. Sometimes using the bathroom or buying a bottle of tea. Surfing the internet in the search of a new home I can afford and which can fulfil my needs again. Architecture is all about telling stories...

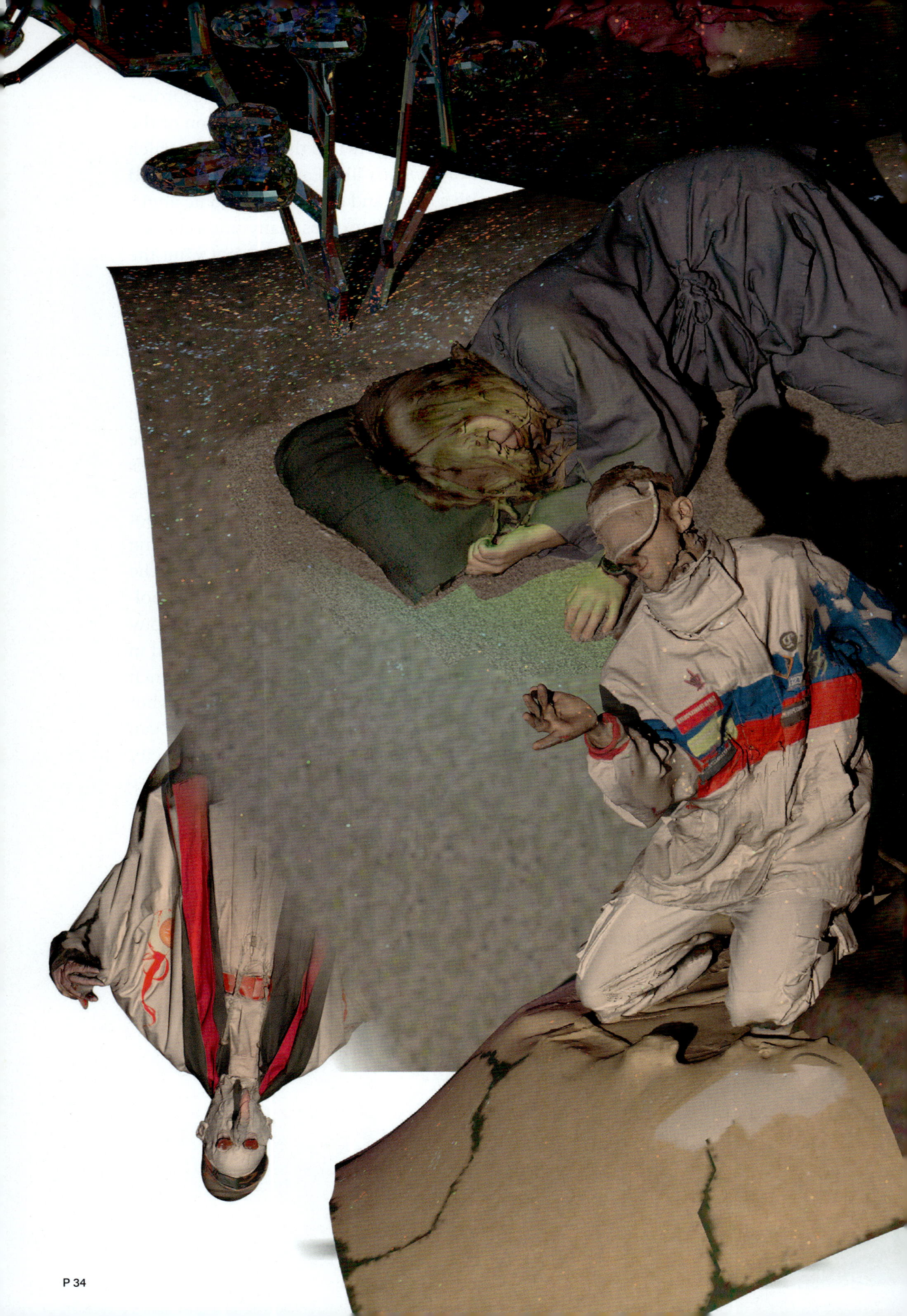

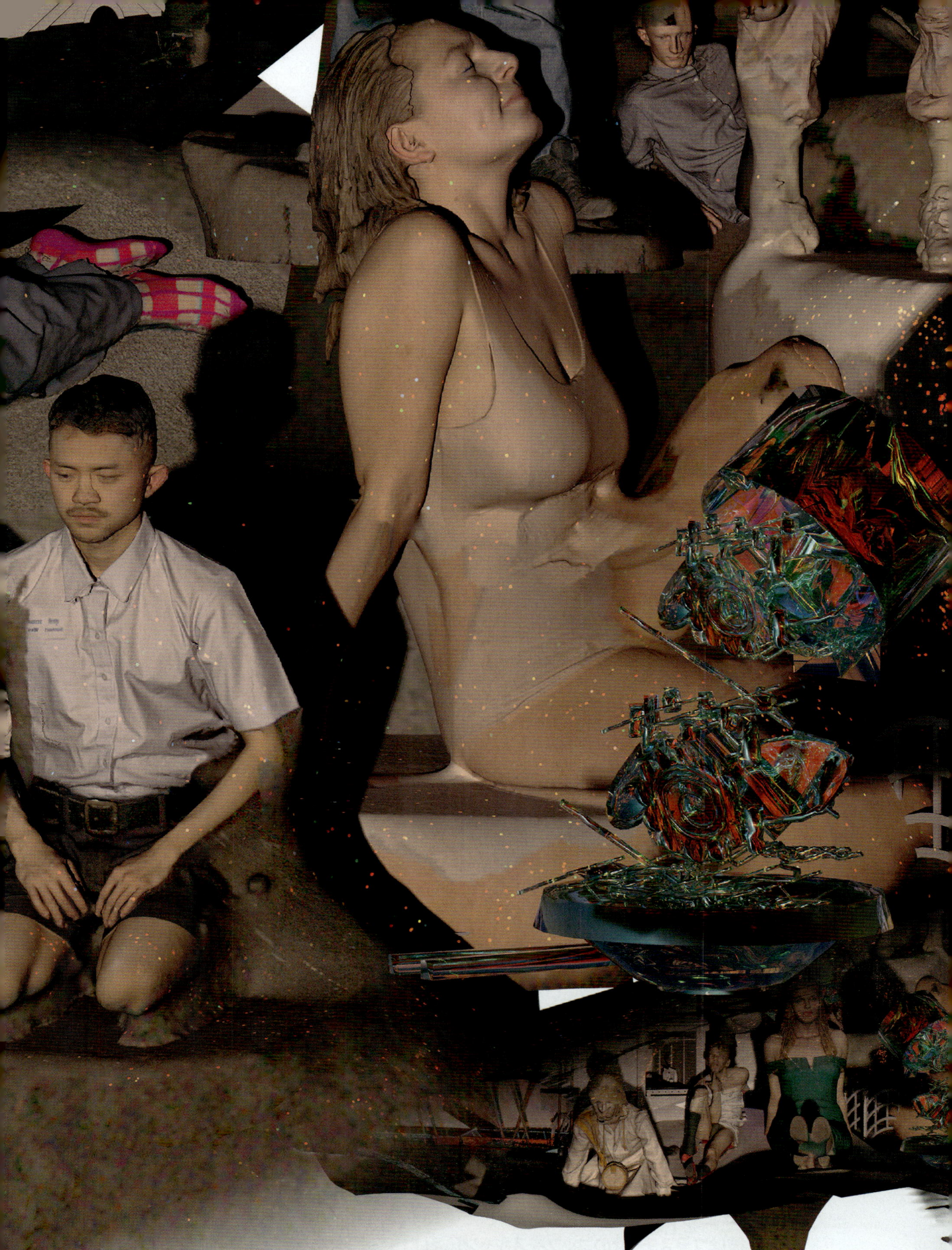

(i) Dreaming of TheCityAsAHouse while portraying Harald Stojan, Suchart Wannaset and Annemarie Arzberger. And Hans Schmidt in the right top corner.

Standing in front of the Family Mart sign.
I am tired.
It's nine.
The sliding doors open.
I enter.
Passing by the copy machine
and the slim working tables with
charging stations.
I hear the shop workers yell:
お次の方どうぞ! Otsugi no kata douzo!
One hundred different cans are looking at me.
I stand in front, of the fridge.
Which triangle should i take?
I choose the one with sake inside.
The mori is wrapped in extra plastic.
I step into line. In front, five salary men.
waiting
in line.
少々お待ちください.
It's my turn now.
The young man behind the counter looks me in the eyes.
Smiles.
I smile back.
He says:
お待たせいたしました.
Omatase itashimasita.
Hai.Hai.Hai.Hai..
„One HOT kōhi please“
He scans a plastic cup.
I pay five hundred forty yen.
I take my plastic bag
with the onigiri inside and the cup.
Move forward to the coffee machine.
I press some buttons.
Hot brown water floats into my cup.
I leave the store.
They yell again in a choir.

Sento (JAP)

私はファミリーマートの看板の前に立っている。
私はとても疲れていて、時刻は9時だ。
自動ドアが開き、私は中に入る。
コピー機を通り過ぎ、充電器とイートインのコーナーを通り過ぎる。
お次の方どうぞ!
店員が叫ぶのが聞こえる。
100種類もの缶飲料が私を見ている。
私は冷蔵庫の前に立ち、どれを選ぼうか?と考える。
私は酒が入った飲み物を選んだ。もりはプラスチックで包まれている。
私は5人のサラリーマンが待つ列に並んだ。
待っている。
列で。
少々お待ち下さい。
私の番が来た。カウンターに立つ若い男が私の目に向かって笑いかける。
私も微笑み返す。
彼はお待たせいたしました。という。
はい、はい、はい、はい、、、
ホットコーヒーを下さい。
彼はプラスチックのコップをスキャンし、私は540円を払う。
おにぎりとコップが入った袋を手にとり、
コーヒーマシンの前へといく。
いくつかのボタンを押すと、熱い茶色の液体が私のカップに注がれて行く。
わたしは店をあとにする。
彼らがまた叫び、合唱している。

KONBINI
コンビニ

THE UMBRELLA STAND
—As an Intimate Relation to a Stranger

In front of every shop an umbrella stand always contains a lot of umbrellas on a rainy day in Tokyo. Like in an apartment, you don't want the room to get wet. You squeeze your see-through rain protector in between all the others in the stand. It is impossible to find the same umbrella after you exit the store. It is a personal exchange of goods.

An umbrella which can be bought in every konbini for around 500–600 Yen. You stick it in and when you exit you take another person's umbrella. I hold the umbrella handle in the same place as someone else has already done it. Like touching someone else's hand without knowing the human. Feeling the touch. What a nice personal touch without knowing.

THE COUNTER

On the left you can see a big counter containing several gadgets. Behind it the greeting and friendly staff, sometimes gaijin are woring there. They are paid less than the Japanese, I heard. It is an easy start when you move to Tokyo. The Japanese you need to know is basic and you don't need much training and education before-hand. Some employees greet you with an accent. The counter is 60 cm deep and at least 200 cm wide. It is made from materials dating back to the time of the bubble economy.

THE SELF-SERVICE AREA

The self-service area functions as a 即席 Kitchen in a way. You buy your 即席 Meal and prepare it with the microwave or the hot water cooker. You can enjoy your meal in the table-and-stool-prepped area or simply take it outside in front of the store to eat it and then walk away. It is impolite to eat while you walk. You prepare your own coffee like in a private kitchen, just buying the cup before. Even iced coffee cups are available, which is lovely.

THE HOT FOOD CONTAINER

If you imagine the *konbini* acting like a 即席 Kitchen of your private apartment, the hot food container is the pot your grandmother used to cook you soup. It is a container made from glass to see the goods. Heating up several small pocket dishes you mix and match to feed your hunger. It stores my favorite bun, the pizza man. The pizza man is a big fat dumpling filled with fake cheese and tomato-sauce.

HOME FOR THE ELDERLY AND THE SINGLES

Since a *konbini* serves almost every kind of food in one-person sizes, it is a perfect and reasonable place for singles to go who don't bother to cook for more than one person. It is a home for the elderly, in my opinion, where they purchase a meal and heat it up in the 即席 Kitchen aka the microwave and enjoy it at the 即席 Kitchen table near the entrance of the konbini. Maybe they gather together.

THE MICROWAVE

The microwave is part of the 即席 Kitchen inside the *konbini.* Individ-uality of the "konbinity". The franchise system of the *konbini*-network allows the owner to fill the store with individual items you want to sell. Since I am a smoker, I loved one Family Mart on my way from the "Shinjuku" station to Yotsuya-sanchome. They had a variety of European tobaccos and papers and filters and a funny way to decorate the store. There were a lot of framed pictures of Jポップ J-Poppu-stars and Jamaican-style flags and posters. The owner was very young and reminded me of my Japanese hippie friends. So this was the *konbini* I went to the most. After work I used the Yama-note-line from Meguro-ku to get out at Shinjuku-Station to take a forty-minute walk to Yotsuya. It was my time to think about my workday and have a small beer before going to sleep. And also, to make some steps to have a better sleep. Sometimes I connected to its Wi-Fi and called my friends and family while enjoying a cigarette in the smoking area.

RECYCLING MACHINE

Recycling is a huge topic in a waste producer like the city of Tokyo. You recycle everything. If you don't stick to the rules you even get your trash delivered back to you. So every *konbini* provides several bins for recycling. For every part of the product. Even bottle caps are recycled in their own specific container.

THE SLIDING DOOR

The sliding glass door next to the *konbini* sign opens up when you approach the store, sucking you into the cold or warm air, depending on the weather conditions outside. It provides a shelter for consumerism. The light conditions resemble an emergency room, ready to operate on the human body.

THE WORKING AREA

It provides a place to sit and look out of the window to look at people passing by in the busy streets. It provides Wi-Fi, a copy machine, a fax, a post office, and electricity. Materials like paper and pens, as well as chargers, can be bought at the store. The Wi-Fi is free as you pay with your data. Login is needed beforehand. The working table is 145 cm high, and chairs are fixed. You can use it as a kitchen table and enjoy your 即席 Cupnoodles, but also sit and work or read magazines you bought. Men standing next to the newspaper stand looking at all kinds of magazines.

THE NEWSPAPER STAND

The newspaper stand functions as a library. You can see humans standing there reading almost through one third of the manga before purchasing it. Or never purchase it at all. Moving from *konbini* to *konbini* always reading a bit until the end. Some of the magazines and mangas have a rubber band around them to let you know that you are not allowed to open them.

THE BATHROOM

In one corner of the *konbini* there is a toilet. It is free to use for anyone without having to consume anything. The *konbini* toilet network provides free toilets around the city. You enter a *konbini* to use the toilet. It is part of the toilet network of Tokyo. Every human needs a toilet to live in the city.

Facts

ARCHITECTURAL AND SPATIAL ELEMENTS OF THE KONBINI

Another kind of 即席 Kitchen is the ramenshop. The average distance between two 即席 Kitchens is less than a few meters. There are approximately 7,100 ramen shops in Tokyo. The ramen shop is different in its functionality from other 即席 Kitchens like the *konbini*, a kind of convenience store, which satisfies your daily needs or the *izakaya*, which can be seen as the 即席 Living room as well. Cooking and eating take place in various locations throughout the city at places like *konbinis, izakayas,* ramen bars. The spaces create an intimate atmosphere between humans and food. It is a sensual, exciting, glazed, satisfying, nurturing experience that can make you feel lonesome, contiguous, accompanying, bonding. The floor plan of a ramen shop is divided into two parts, which are usually separated by a counter, separating the cook from the user and forms the main element of the room. The separation is in most cases not complete, since the raised seats provide a visual communication between the caregiver and client. The human using the ramen shop as a kitchen does not know what is behind the counter. Does not know what is hidden in the cupboards. Does not know what the ramen cook is wearing until s/he turns his/her back. Does not know every ingredient in the meal and where it comes from, if it is bought in a big supermarket or a small back alley market. Does not know when the base of the soup began to simmer or whether it simmered for 52 hours, 24 hours, or just for 8 hours. The secret ingredient which makes every ramen in Tokyo different is, of course, secret. There are many secrets which can be uncovered if the person behind the counter chooses to reveal them. Or is not cooking in your personal kitchen the secret ingredient? The mystical thing about the 即席 Kitchen might be all the things you don't know about it. It feels like a setting of architectural elements visible only to the human sitting in front of the counter. The mind of the human looking at the architectural element is also important. Every human will have a different perception of things and will decide for themselves if this 即席 Kitchen is his/her 即席 Kitchen. The ramen shop my human mind chose is close to a rather small train station, frequented daily, especially late in the evening, to get some comfort and interaction before going to sleep.

I enter the ramen shop.
Bowing down not to touch the fabric.
I feed the machine with money.

I can't decide...
The machine vomits my money back.
Like a drunk salary man.
I put it back again.
And quickly decide.
Spicy miso
The ramen cook looks at me.
He smiles.
He remembers me.
I was there a couple of nights ago.
I ordered beer.
We laughed.
I was a funny girl to him.
Then he asks me if I want rice.
I'm shaking my head.
Of course I can't eat rice and ramen.
I'm a small woman.
The soup is bubbling in the back.
All the little feet moving in the thickening broth.
How far did they walk before
they ended up in the pot.
Cooked for more than twenty-four hours.
It's no fast dish to prepare.
The soup is cooking forever.
But they serve it within minutes.
Salary men are sitting right and left of my body.
Slurping the soup.
Very sexual sound somehow—I think.
The water for the noodles is steaming in the back.
Covering the open kitchen with a curtain.
He's quick.
Every step is prepared.
Carefully he puts the extra cilantro on top of the bowl.
I am glad that we know each other.
I feel like he's taking care of me.
I feel like a mess.
I almost finished it all.
You shouldn't 't eat the soup they say.
Too much grease.
But isn't that the best part?
It's very spicy for a Japanese dish.
Sumimaseeeen...
すみません/済みません
I ask for a bib.
Now I can start without regret.
and without ruining my clothes.
I start to slurp.
The salarymen stop their ritual and look at me
They didn't expect me to make that sound.
A Sound which tells Yamamoto-san
that I appreciate his effort.
He takes care of us all.
After a long day.

RAMEN SHOP

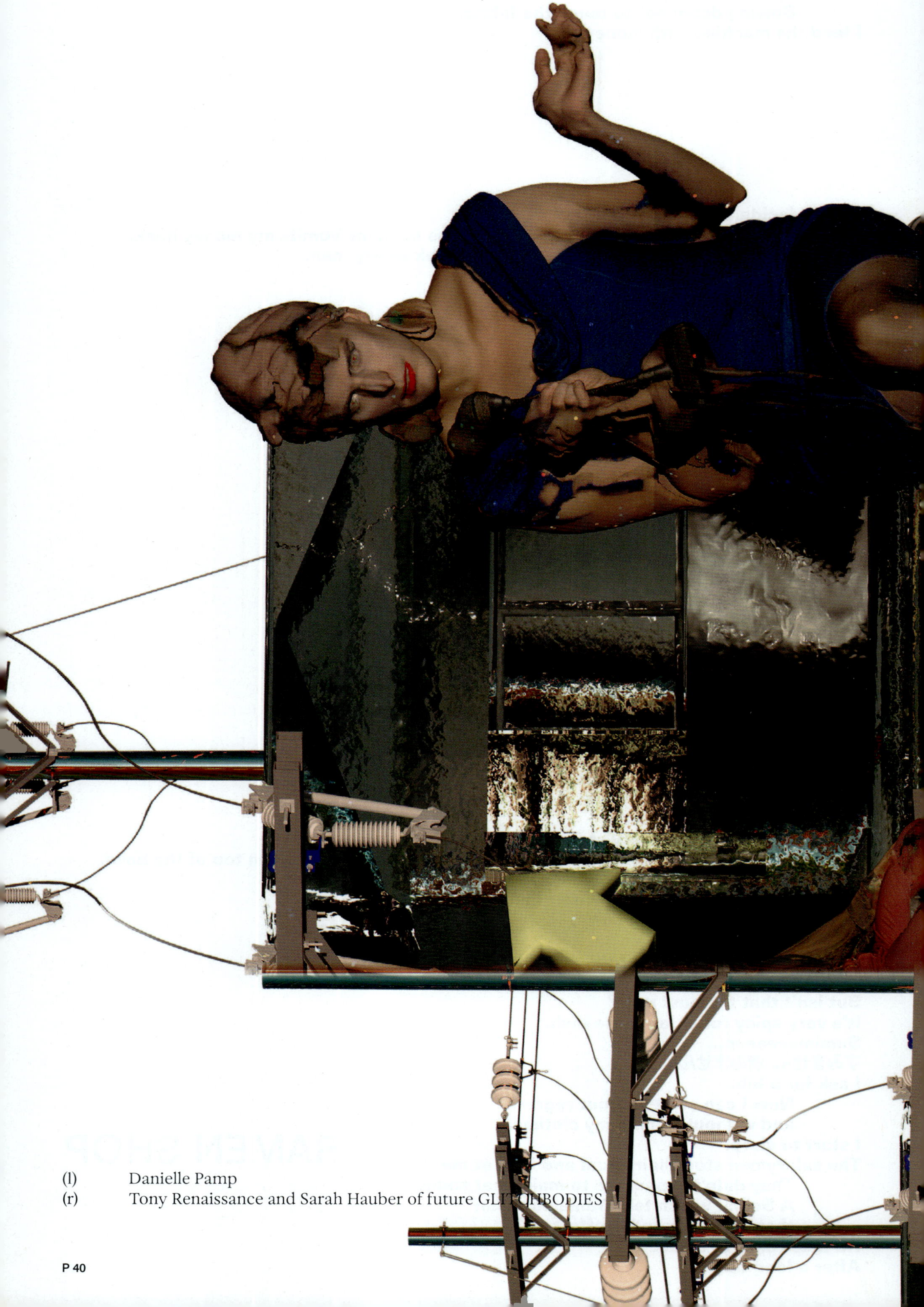

(l) Danielle Pamp
(r) Tony Renaissance and Sarah Hauber of future GLITCHBODIES

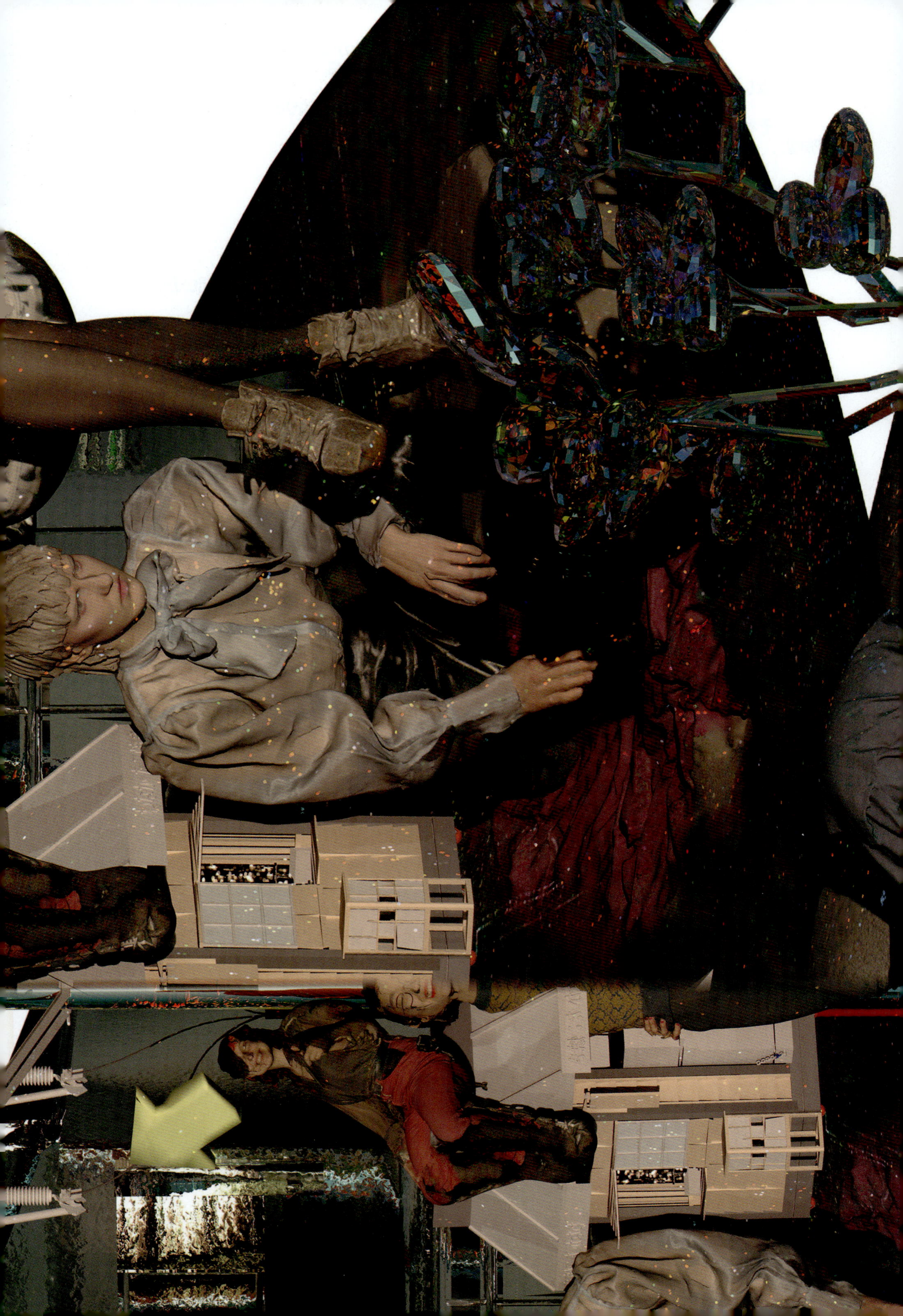

ラーメン屋に入る。
のれんを触らずに、お辞儀しながらくぐる。
券売機にお金(餌)をやる。
決められない。
券売機は酔っ払ったサラリーマンのようにお釣りを吐き出す。
それらをもう一度入れ、急いで決める。
辛味噌。
店員が私を見ている。
彼は笑う。彼は私を覚えているのだ。
私は何日か前の夜も、ここにいた。
私はビールをオーダーした。
彼は笑う。
私は彼にとって面白い女の子だったようだ。
そして彼は私にご飯はいるかと問いかける。
私は首を横に振る。
もちろん私は小さな女の子だ。
ご飯とラーメンを同時には食べられない。
小柄な女性なのだから。
スープが奥でグツグツと煮えている。
全ての小さな足たちが濃厚魚介だしスープの中で動いている。
彼らはどれほど歩いたのだろう。
鍋の中で終焉を迎えるまで。
24時間以上調理されている。
準備を考えると、これは全くもってファストフードなんかではない。
スープなど永遠に調理される。
しかし彼らは数分でよそって出してしまう。
サラリーマンが私の身体の右と左に座っている。
スープをすする。
私はなんとなく、それは性的な音だと思う。
麺を茹でるための水が奥で湯気立っている。
カーテンがオープンキッチンを覆っている。
彼は素速い。
全ての段取りは準備されている。
注意深く、彼はラーメンの中央にパクチーをのせる。
私はお互い知り合いだということがとても嬉しい。
私は彼が私を気にかけてくれているように感じる。
私はめちゃくちゃな気分だ。
私はほぼ完食した。
彼らはスープは飲んではだめだと言う。
あまりにも脂が多すぎると。
でも、スープが一番でしょう?
一番アツい日本料理。
すみませーーーん 私はエプロンを頼んだ。
これで服を汚して後悔しなくて済む。
スープをすする。
サラリーマンは食べるのを止めて私を見る。
彼らは私が音をたてて麺をすするのを予想していなかったのだ。
この音は山本さんの努力に感謝を伝える音なのだ。
彼はみんなを気にかけてくれている。
永い一日の後で。

ラーメン屋

ARUGAMAMA

Arugama (JAP) **I enter the shop of an elderly lady.**
Arugamama.
The granddaughter rushes towards me and
shows me my place.
With a question.
Okuchai or mizu-des?
おくちゃいおｒみずーでｓ?
Okuchai.
I look deep into the menu and hear the melody.
A woman with two little girls enters the shop.
The old lady behind the kitchenette
is delighted with the little ones.
A loud kawaiii
breaks through the elevator melody.
A loud laugh from all involved follows.
I feel good.
No one coughs because of my presence.
I call すみません Sumimaseeeeeen through the room
"Hanbāgā se to de koza ima s edo
...onsen tama go de s"
I try.
A young man enters the room and sits down at the counter.
Ordering the same.
I'm waiting for the seto and feel happiness.
I often come here
when I want a self-cooked meal in peace.
Hans comes along.
Sometimes.
We often have Sunday meals in such quiet,
warm places.
I realize why I do not long for Europe.
This quiet atmosphere can often be found in a
bustling city like Tokyo.
It is enchanted.
I stop with the kitsch.
And enjoy my seto.
Hanbaga with rice and small salads, egg and pickles.
I put on my jacket.
Go to the cash register.
Pay 880 yen.
And bow.
I leave Arugamama
...

A laugh! A shout!
My hunger is satisfied
My wellbeing too.
ARIGATO GOZAIMAS!!!!

Arugamama (JAP) **私は、"あるがまま"というひとりのおばあさんの店に入った。**
在るがまま。
おばあさんは急いで私の元へやってきて、こう聞いた。
お茶ですか、水ですか?
お茶をください。
私はメニューによく目をとおし、メロディーに耳を傾けた。
一人の女性が小さな女の子二人と店に入ってきた。
おばあさんがキッチンの奥から女の子たちに挨拶する。
かわいくって大きな笑い声がエレベーターの音楽を遮る。
素敵な気分だ。
誰も私がいることで咳払いをしたりしない。
私はすいませーーんと声をあげた。
ハンバーガーセットでございますね、えっと、温泉卵です。
試してみよう。

あるがまま

若い男が入ってきて、カウンターに座ると、同じものを頼んでいる。
私はセットを待ちながら、幸せな気分でいっぱいだった。
私は手づくりの料理を食べたくなると、よくこの場所にくる。
ハンスも時折私と来た。
私たちはしばしば、この静かな、暖かい場所で日曜日の昼を食べた。
私はなぜヨーロッパをこがれることがないか、分かった。
こういった静かな雰囲気を持った空間が、とてもにぎやかな街東京でもよく存在する。
私はキッチュになるのをやめた。
ハンバーガーとライス、小さなサラダ、卵とピクルスのセットを楽しんだ。
私はジャケットを羽織りレジへ向かった。
880円を払って、お辞儀をし、”あるがまま”をあとにした。
笑い声！叫び声！
私の空腹は満たされ、よい気分になった。
ありがとうございます！

UDONSHOP MARUGAME SEIMEN
うどん屋丸亀製麺

It's lunchtime.
I step out of the office and walk the streets.
The sliding doors opens.
I step into the line of humans waiting in front of the big steaming pots.
the raw noddles are thrown into the bubbling water.
Taking a bath in an ice-cold one afterwards.
Like sento
being rinsed.
The floor is wet.
Several humans are behind the counter.
wearing rubber boots.
I hold the tray.
Waiting for moon viewing noodles.
I skip the fried and pay at the counter.
I am searching for a free spot.
I am sitting in front of a human without seeing his eyes.
I mix the raw egg with the hot udon.
I let the egg stagnate.
I slurp one after another without biting of.
I take a sip from the free water.
I am finished.
I'm out.
people are passing through me.
お昼時だ。
私はオフィスをでて通りに出る。
自動ドアが開き、私は人々が鍋の前で待つ列に並ぶ。
生麺が沸騰して泡立つ鍋に投入されていき、その後水風呂に入れられ、洗われていく。
まるで銭湯の様に。
すすがれてゆく。
床は濡れている。何人か長靴を履いた人がカウンターの奥で働いている。
私はトレーを手にし、月見うどんを待っている。
私は揚げ物のコーナーをスキップして、レジでお金を払った。
私は空いている席を探し、一人の人の前に、彼の目を見ずに座った。
生卵を温かいうどんに混ぜた。
私は卵をだしの中にとどめておき、
うどんを噛み切らないように次から次へとすする。
無料の水を一口飲み、食事を終えた。
店をあとにする。
人々が私を通り過ぎてゆく

Udonshop (JAP)

'jesi dobro?
Fališ mi. 🤍' (message from Maja)
Nisam dobro.
Sjedim u predivnom i prefinom yakitori restoranu
And I wish to press my face against the hot coal.
Then I just drink more shochu.
The girl next to me is here with another 20-year-older guy.
I am sitting and eating.
For 54 minutes.
She didn't say a word.
Yet
Maybe he is divorced
or maybe it is just the affair,
It is a fancy place for yakitori.
Very indeed.
So maybe she will be the second wife.
He is looking at me now.
Like he knows what I am writing.
One quick guilty look.
Or maybe because I am drinking hard liquor.
Idk.
She wants to pay.
Suddenly.
He is not letting her.
Maybe because he looked at me.
I am going for a cigarette.
She left.
He left too.
The store's name was fuku.

Udonshop (JAP)

できることなら炭に顔を押し付けたい。
そしてもっと焼酎を飲んだ
私の隣にいる女の子は20以上年上の男性と一緒だ。
私は座って食べて
分が過ぎたけど、
彼女は一言も喋らない。
未だに。
おそらく彼は離婚しているのだ。
或いはただの浮気か。
そこは高級な焼肉屋さん。
なるほど。
きっと彼女は二番目の妻になるのでしょう。
すると彼は私を見た。
私が何を書いているかわかったのか。
ちらっと一回だけ。
それか私が強いお酒を飲んでいるからか知らないが。
彼女は唐突に会計をしたがったが
彼はそうさせなかった。
おそらく私が彼を見ていたからだと思う。
私はタバコに席を立った。
彼女が去り、
彼も去った。
店の名前は福という。

IZAKAYA
居酒屋

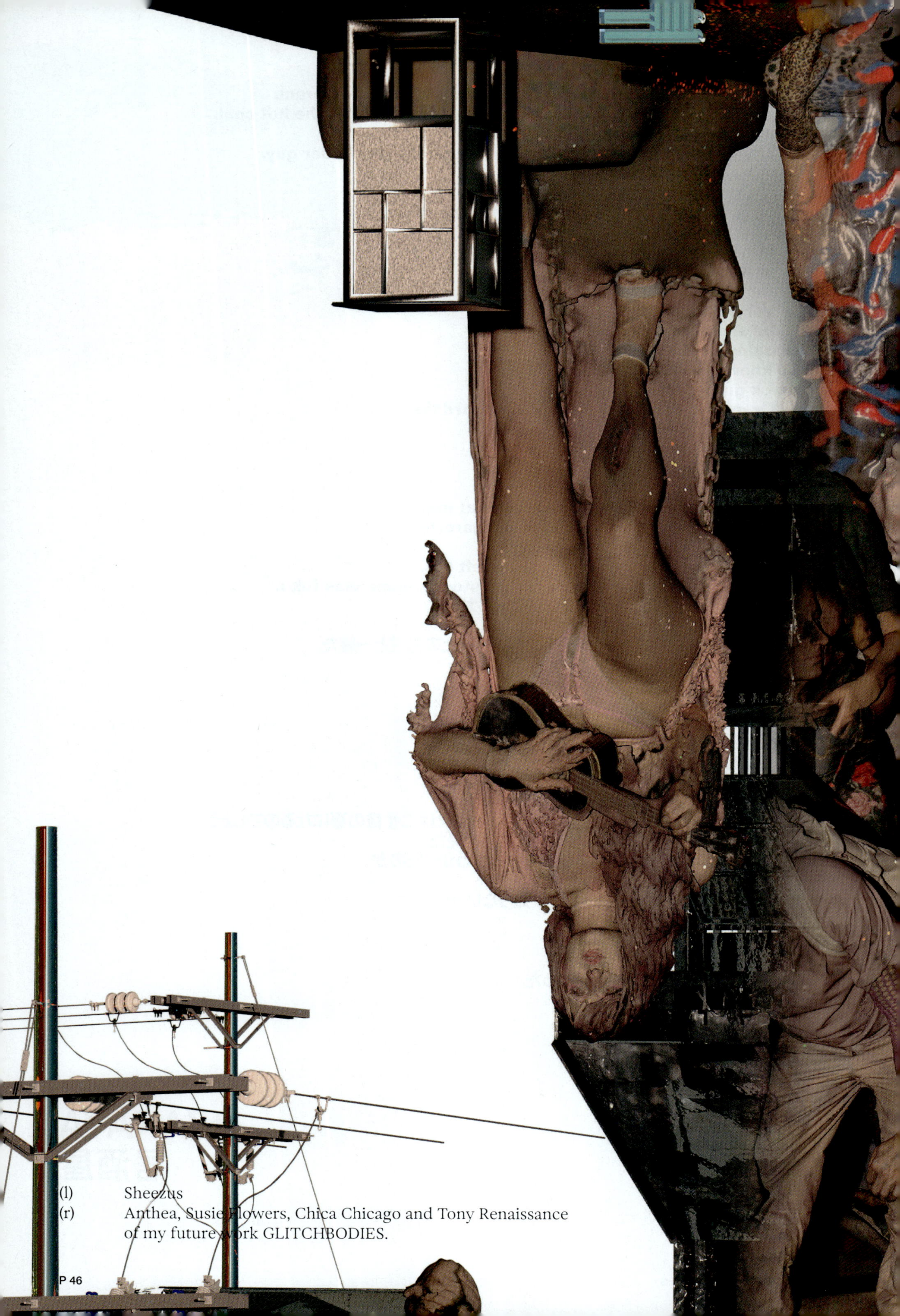

(l) Sheezus
(r) Anthea, Susie Flowers, Chica Chicago and Tony Renaissance of my future work GLITCHBODIES.

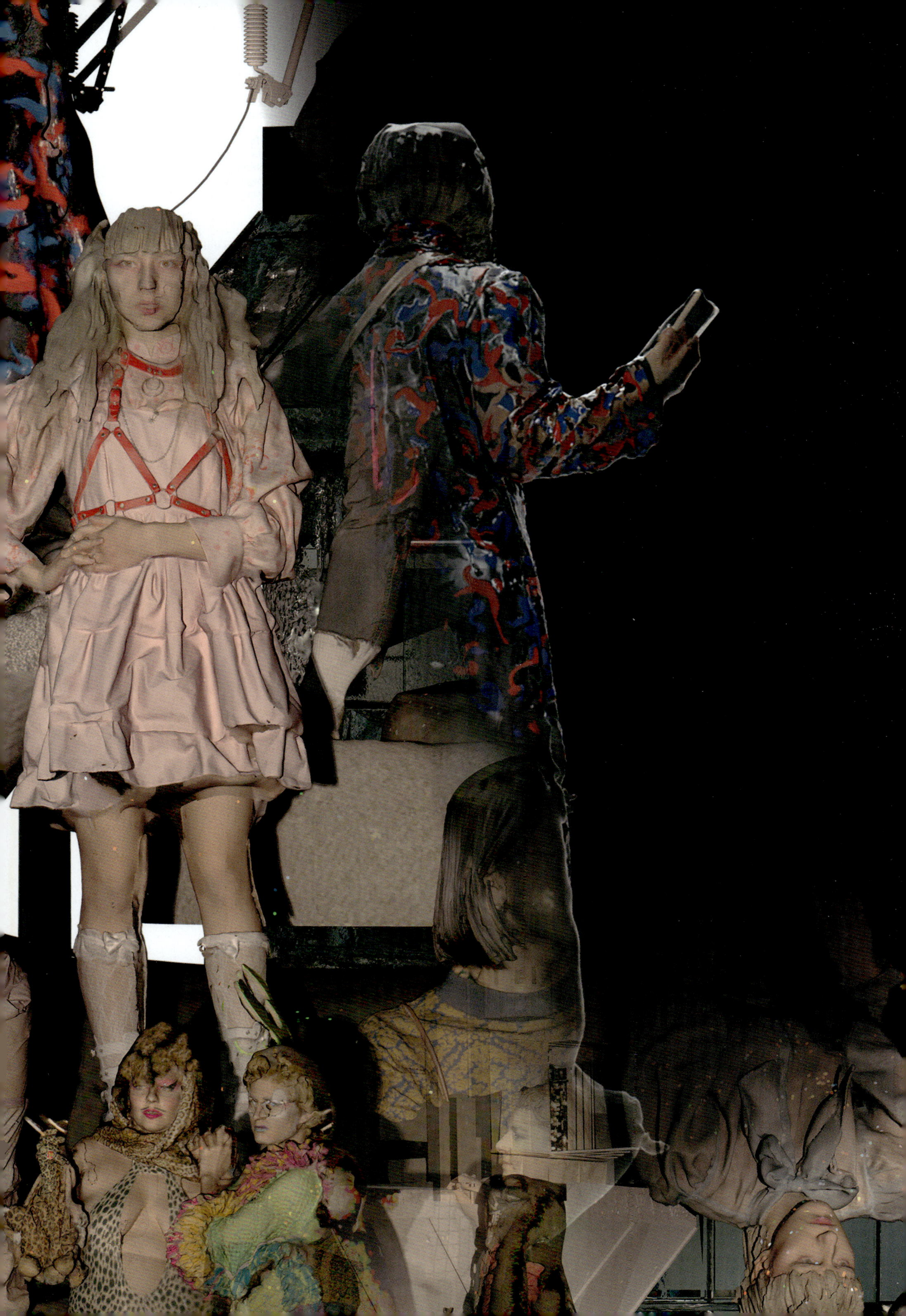

IZAKAYA (Izakaya Story)

The "safe zone" is created by the satisfying pleasure food brings to the body and mind. Food creates an invisible bubble-like space around every table in an *izakaya*. This invisible bubble is, in my mind, part of the living room in a conventional apartment. What defines this space is the bubble created by sounds and the smell of food dispersing over a 30 to 50 cm border between each table. People's laughter becomes louder and louder the longer you sit in an izakaya. An invisible room forms and creates privacy which can be shared with other guests as well. Even going to an *izakaya* by yourself makes you feel like being in someone else's living room. While awaiting the arrival of the delicious food your body craves after a long day at work, the restaurant owner takes over the role of your grandmother when you were young. There was this one *izakaya* I used to frequent while spending time around Shimokitazawa. It was known for horse meat and the thing I liked the most was ordering a small portion of ramen and dumplings along with a Yuzu sour. I would go there after work, often alone and sometimes in the company of friends, chatting about my day at work or architecture topics or talking about our private lives. After some Yuzu sour and food, I would go to a bed I chose for the night, feeling happy and glad having taken the journey to Shimokita. When I visited the *izakaya* alone, I would sit on the counter, first order a drink and enjoy a rolled cigarette.

FAMILY RESTAURANT (Arugamama Story)

Food not only keeps the human body fueled with nutrition and power, it also has a big role in sustaining the mental state and producing social interaction. A restaurant like an izakaya not only replaces functions of the living room, it even has considerable benefits for the human. Maiko Arrieta Aoki points out, in her essay about food and the feeling of home, that going to the same places, like an *izakaya,* creates a safe zone for her in the craziness of Tokyo.[1] Routine, and the repetition of visiting an *omoiyari,* can create a place like home. This place was Arugamama for me. Another 即席 Kitchen is the family restaurant. In addition to low-cost dishes, it also offers a familiar atmosphere and is usually handed down from generation to generation. The dishes are usually offered as a set and consist of a small main course of fish or meat, salad, a miso soup, a few anchovies, pickled vegetables and an egg and green tea. The following is an experience of an individual in a family restaurant named Arugamama. It is made visible through signs. The city is covered in signs. They make the networks visible if you can read them. A maze of signs, you cannot read. You make it readable by Google Translate. Or you experience the place to know its purpose. I enter the shop of an elderly lady.

Abolishing the kitchen as the heart of the home at first. By using the networks which are everyday freshly generated.

I am tired of writing anymore.
Sitting in an old kohi shop.
Choosing the delicious blend.
Couples surround me.
Whispering to each other.
すごい (Sugoi)! ne—
I hear the shout.
I am asking myself if they will marry.
Or take the last train instead.
Wagner is playing in the back.
For the atmosphere I suppose.
Looks like a Viennese coffee house.
Japanese style.
Low ceilings but same cups.
Just smaller.
I close my eyes and listen.
Trying to hear the voices of one of my homes.
Enjoying this pleasure of simulation.
The play.
The taste is strong.
The smell reminds me of home.
Tristan und Isolde.
I pay 950 ¥en and leave into the green.
私は書くことにうんざりしている。
古いコーヒー屋に座っていて
デリシャスブレンドを選んでいた。
カップルが私を囲んで
耳打ちし合っている
すごい (Sugoi)! ne —
すごいねー!!
私は叫び声を聞いた。
私は心の中で、彼らは結婚するか
それとも終電に乗るか、と問いかけている。
店内にはワグナーが流れている。
雰囲気から察するに。
そこは日本スタイルのウィーンの珈琲屋さんの様だ。
天井は低いけれど、同じカップで。
ただ全てが小さいだけだった。
私は目を閉じて耳を澄ました。
故郷の声を聞こうとしていた。
その疑似体験の喜びを楽しんだ。
演奏。
その味はとても強くて。
香りが私に故郷を思い出させる。
トリスタンとイゾルテ
私は950円を払って緑の中へ去っていった。

KOHI SHOP
フラ カフェ

The 即席 Kitchen connects with all the other 即席 Kitchens and creates a network that provides a more sustainable, ecological and economical situation of the human living in the city after the point of no return. A city is assembled by a network of experiences or, better to mention, a network of experience providers. Tokyo creates a network of spectacles and foggy confusion. You have to track your movement and inhabitations of the spaces by devices to recall your time spent there. Due to tracking everything you do and consume in the city, you create a digital self, that can predict the behavior of the Tokyoites. The network doesn't have to be planned by individuals. Guidelines and rules extracted from tracked data can provide the information the network system needs to develop itself. Architects build enough. The built space has to be divided, reused, refunctioned, redesigned to provide a more sustainable view on city planning. We have to create experiences and situations, moments of which the monotony of capitalist everyday routine may be disrupted by using already built spaces instead of building new ones. Architects build enough. In the following the individual has to use devices to wander throughout a city to allow oneself to meet new humans and places, to recognize the spectacle and subvert it. Capitalism must be redefined in the case of pure survival resulting into pleasure for every human.

3 即席 Spaces The Bedroom is Abolished

9H CAPSULE

The 9h capsule is one of the most convenient places to stay overnight. You book online for a good price depending on the time and location you wanna stay. You get a package of everything you could possibly need for an overnight stay, even pajamas and hygiene products and slippers. It functions like a uniform for everyone who stays with you. Feeling like in an episode of Star Trek when you enter the collective bathroom in the morning, everyone has the same futuristic outfit. Getting the key from the counter, a.k.a. the application on your phone, is the key. You can open the locker next to the bath facilities and change there. You are not allowed to enter the sleeping area with your street shoes. Almost every capsule has a view to the outside. The facade is made out of glass. It is almost like sleeping outside yet being inside. A comfortable capsule which functions as a womb. No feelings of claustrophobic nature are detectable. It nurtures your tired body with sleep. The capsule itself has different options. You can arrange the temperature and moisture, as well as a wakeup service. You can charge your telephone and listen to calm music to fall asleep. You can stay less than nine hours. You can rent it in the afternoon just for two, to get a little rest after you spend some time in the city. Every capsule hotel has a different theme. 9h & Run gives you sports clothing as an extra to take a run before you sleep in the garden of the Tokyo Imperial Palace. Or the Capsule and Sauna where you enjoy wellness and wellbeing achieved by useing the exotic thing called "sauna." The concept is always exploring new kinds of capsule hotel themes.

LOVE HOTEL

You wander around the Shibuya mountain, where all the love hotels are located, in need of a place to sleep or rest or feel pleasure or sing. The streets are not linear, the structure of love hotels grew organically in the heart of the night district. Surrounded by *izakayas* and bars and sex shops. A place where you can rent acoustically isolated rooms with a luxurious bed and luxurious bathroom. You pay by the hour or two or six or the whole day or night. The rooms provide a TV, playstation, karaoke booth (sometimes), shower gel, shampoo, conditioner, razor, cotton swab, lubricant, comb, toothbrush, toothpaste, mini-fridge with alcohol and water and snacks, a whirlpool, mirrors, decoration in different themes. You go there with your partner or lover or friends to have pleasure time like you would in a private bedroom. It is a space in the middle of the pulsating city to provide you with quietness and let yourself be isolated and left in peace. Like a temple or a shrine or a church, but you can do what you wish. The entrance is different from that of a normal hotel. It is divided into two sections. A left and a right entrance divided by a wall as a privacy protection. Nobody knows if you exit alone or together. The hallway is usually very narrow. You take an elevator to get to the right floor and room. Waking up in a love hotel is unusual. It feels weird. The windows are covered with more privacy protection and the room is dark. There are so many buttons you can press to play different kinds of music or generate different light situations.

MANGA KISSA

A manga kissa is a small space equipped with a computer with internet access and an office chair or other seating opportunity. You have access to shared hygiene facilities and kitchen elements and a manga library. The extra features depend on the manga kissa you are visiting. Being alone in manga kissa freeing individual human providing intimacy augmented through digital space, showing the benefits of the bourgeoise thinking of European heterotopian view of the need of a private apartment. The elements of a manga kissa. The Counter: You order the plan in relation to your needs for your stay at the manga kissa. You take the elevator to your floor, since manga kissas are different in architecture but it happen to be narrow, multi-story buildings. You walk the narrow aisles to your box number, since it is not a closed room but more an open box where the roof is missing. You hear kissing and whispering. You enjoy your stay entering the digital or reading or whatever is allowed or maybe not allowed but quiet. You can go to the smoking area box inside the building to have a cigarette. After the booked hours are spent you leave the building.

THE GALLERY

Imagine you can sleep in an art gallery. You enter a small wooden area that is a 即席 Kitchen during the morning, and serves as the gallery's reception in the afternoon, and then turns into a 即席 Living room in the evening. The ground floor exhibits Japanese and international artists in the interior space as well as in the courtyard. Next to the reception is a shared 即席 Bath and on the upper floor, while the ceilings and walls on the way up are used as exhibition space, you can rent small rooms which are fully equipped for short-term working and sleeping. In the morning, the receptionist makes you Japanese breakfast and you have a nice chat about the weather.

BOOK & BED

The Book & Bed was an interesting experience. It is located in a tower in Shinjuku, one of the most frequented stations in the world. You leave the buss and craziness behind when you enter the elevator, which gets you to the reception of a 即席 Space, which functions as a bedroom but also as a living room and bathroom. You can get different plans depending on how long you want to use the 即席 Space. After the reception area, there is a coffeeshop with a view which can also be used by humans who just want to enjoy a good cup of Scandinavian coffee and the view. You enter the library area with your phone and can enjoy a curated environment of nice art, design and architecture books as well as philosophical books and magazines of all kinds, which would cost a fortune to collect. The main material of the architectural space is wood. It provides a cozy feeling in the middle of Shinjuku. Quiet music is playing in the background, while you grab a book and read it next to unknown humans. When you read a lot and get tired you are invited to sleep in one of the wooden boxes, where you get a fully equipped sleeping package. The main function of this kind of architecture is not sleeping, it is reading and enjoying silence with others you don't know. You don't feel lonely, you are supposed to keep as quiet as in a public library. But the interior is different. New styles of sitting objects invite you to not just sit, but linger in them until your eyes are getting tired of reading exceptionally rare books. The thought of spending 1.5 hours on a train to your private apartment is awful and you are thankful to stay where you are. In the morning there is a option to sleep 1–3 hours longer, like a snooze button on your iPhone. The library contains the sleeping pods which are mixed gender. No gender difference is made in this 即席 Place.

THE TRAIN

The train is the most important transportation tool in a megacity like Tokyo. But it hides a lot of different functions and thus humans have adapted to the train as an architectural space. It starts with the stations, which function as small cities and make consumption necessary before you enter a train. Shopping malls, where you can buy anything you could possibly need, create a bubble between the outside world and entering the train, which gets you from one 即席 Room to another. Between 即席 Rooms, there are no clear boundaries at any time. In a conventional apartment, the door or hallway functions as a barrier or boundary. In the concept of 即席 Places, this boundary can be found in the time you spend on transportation and using the architectural space of transport as your living room or bedroom. The facilities for personal hygiene at transportation hubs like Shinjuku Station or any other train station meet the need for using a toilet before entering the train and are free of charge. You must pay for the train ride of course. The fee depends on the distance between the station you entered and the station you exit. You could drive in circles for hours and use the train as private space, if you wish.
I would fall asleep leaning on my neighbor. Humans sitting next to me leaning on myself, feeling comfortable and safe enough to fall asleep. Falling asleep on a train does not always come from being tired, in my opinion it is the feeling of comfort and that of a safe environment enabling passengers to fall asleep. There are exceptions of course.

Especially when women suffer from men who touch them inappropriately on trains. You can read about it in my diary, where I mention some incidents which happened to me. Of course, the more time you spend in the city, the more likely it is to happen to you, statistically speaking. It is not appropriate to eat odorous food or drink, since the train can be crowded at times thus offending the passengers. Sleeping and reading are the functions nurtured by the train.
If you should fall asleep in the train, you can wake up and get off the station of your choice. In my scenario it functions as a bedroom as well as a living room or library.
The quietness in trains even when crowded is fascinating. Nobody speaks. The silence is interrupted only by the noise of the train and, in certain intervals, by the songs of each station. Every single train station has a different jingle played upon arrival at the platform. It is a certain melody, which adds a personal touch and makes the platform feel like a living room.

Of course there are exceptions to the silence in the interior of the train. The last train has an almost mythological meaning. It is mostly inconvenient to take the last train and if you miss it you have to sleep in a love hotel or manga-kissa, at the station or in the streets waiting for the first train. It is very crowded and it smells like sake. There is a cloud of alcohol odor in the compressed air of the train wagon. A lot of salary men and others are drunk. They went to an *Izakaya* after work—drinking, laughing, forgetting about their day at work, enjoying being with their colleagues after work. They are heading home and drinking Pocari Sweat to help them recover when their day starts late and hungover. The last train is loud, a lot of laughing and screaming. Sleepy drunk people nearly missing their stations. The last train has another meaning as well. If you go on a date with a human and you don't really like the other person, you can call it a night and say that you have to catch the last train.
It has a deeper meaning and indirectly conveys that you don't have feelings for the other person.
On the other hand you could miss that train on purpose and stay up all night with that person...

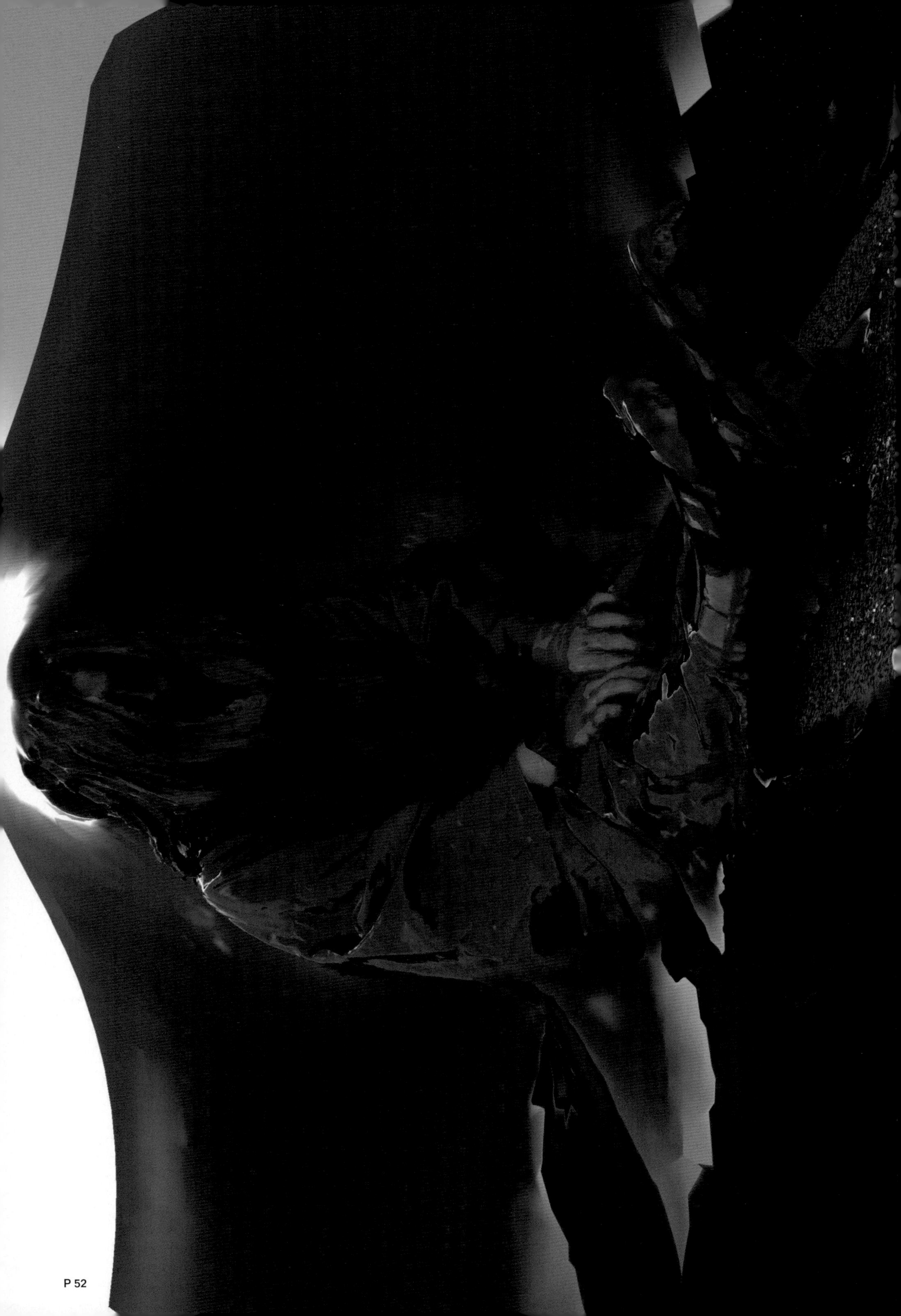

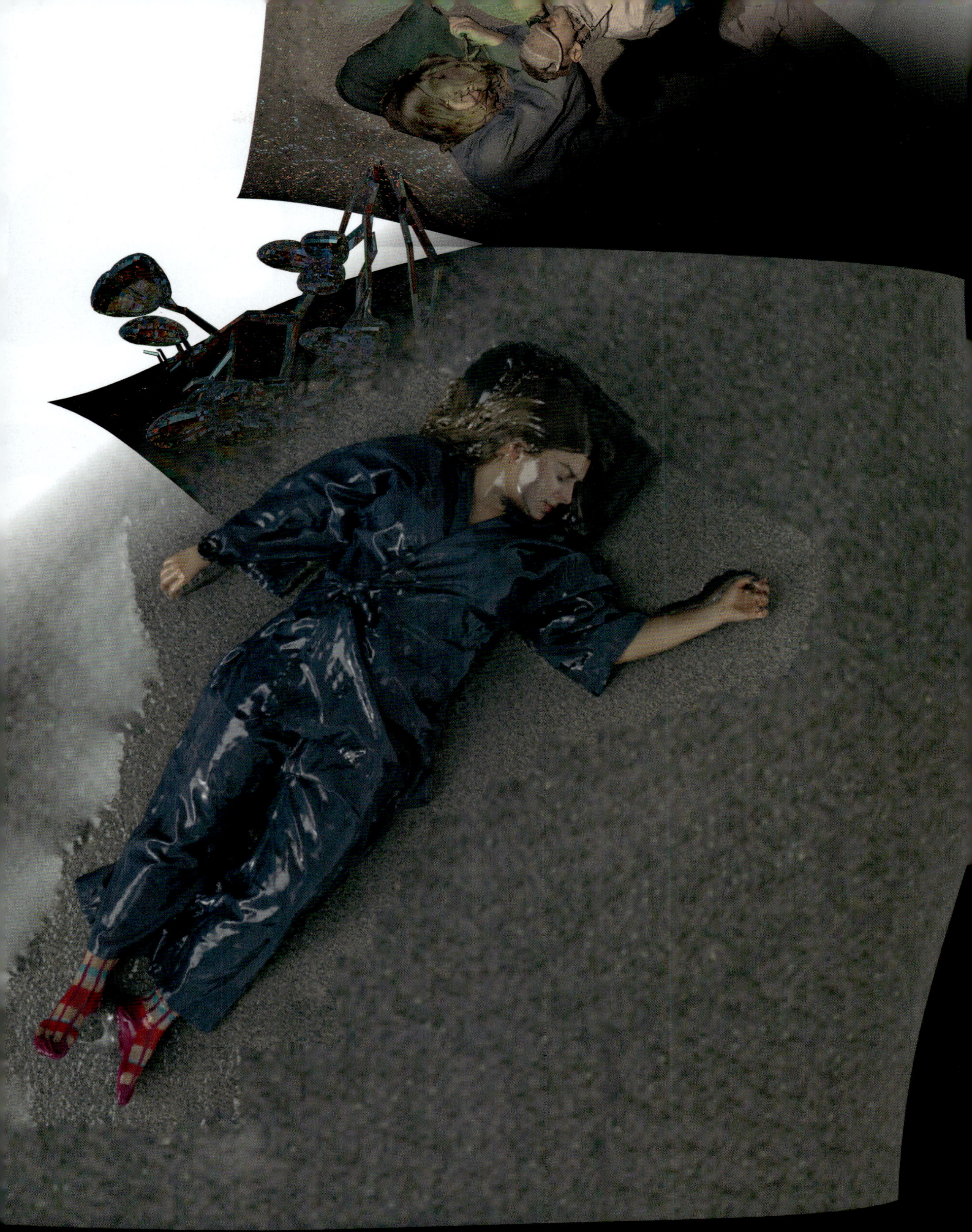

(i) Me, myself and I sleeping in a 即席 Bed.
Harald Stojans Head visible.

Ga

TheC

Ho

Part I

me

ityAs

use

The goal of using the game engine Unity is to help construct experiences made by a caucasian, European thirty-year-old human in a certain amount of time while not inhabiting a private apartment and let's the user relive the abstract experiences of 即席 Places at their own pace. It is based on Sou Fujimoto's primitive future theory in that it does not focus on the functional construction of architecture, but rather sees the 即席 Places as caves that one searches for and adapts to. 即席 Places clearly understand themselves as spaces that can have background functions, but are misused and reused by the individual. The 即席 Places attempt a reinterpretation of the functions and the search for private living spaces. This manifests itself in digital space by not reproducing reality in order to make it understandable, but by reducing it to essential elements. Namely, that of the subjective experiences of an individual. The scenes are reduced to their essentials and have a further level through interaction with objects. The protagonist tells the user anecdotes from this concept of life. The project is based on an alternative concept of life, which arises and grows through different parameters depending on the situation and time. The five scenes 即 Kitchen, 即席 Sleeping, 即席 Bathroom, 即席 Kitchen and 即席 Leisure concentrate on 24 hours of a day and represent the multitude of decisions that have to be made, opening up digital spaces constructed by life without an apartment. TheCityAsAHouse project sees itself in its subjective, individual radicalism as a continuation of Archizoom's no-stop-city concept, which is based on the level of perception and endless consumption or non-consumption. TheCityAsAHouse is based on the examination of the everyday life without the creation of new architecture. The architect has built enough. There is a feeling of loss of control and panic, which is satisfied with the repeated adaptation of urban space.

The hedonistic human deciding and evaluating and taking spatial decisions 24 hours a day.

MENU

The base for the menu is a map created from the 即席 Places I revisited in my memories. The map is created by photogeometry of the places I revisited online after the experiences, mapped and then unfolded. The floor of the menu, which is the map, represents the feeling of being lost and small in a huge neverending cityscape in Tokyo. The user searches in darkness for 即席 Kitchen, 即席 Bath, 即席 Sleep and 即席 Leisure. By choosing one need to be fulfilled, the user is transported into a scene. While living through the scene you can return to the menu to choose another scene. The menu invites the user to wander through the digitalized city, which displays five interactive buttons. By walking to the button of your choice based on your preferred need, which has to be fulfilled, you enter five different scenes containing experiences once lived by me. Bringing you into the scene, you can wander around and consume different content based on fragments of memories—scenes building up experiences for the user as well as growing into digital rooms where one can gather and occupy for a period of time. Extended rooms of the conservative private space that open up worlds of data, pleasure and loneliness.

The City vs. Unity

席 KITCHEN

The *konbini* scene shows a generic *konbini* facade. The user can interact with a can, an umbrella stand and the main protagonist to see hidden information. The forest of choices offers the protagonist an archive of consumed food and drink during the time of the experiment. The sound focuses on the accurate representation of experiences in the *konbini* and interactions with humans working for the store.

即席 BATHROOM

The bathroom scene takes the user to the world of *sento* baths throughout Tokyo. Interacting with the bathing and sitting body toggles the narration of the *sento* story in English and Japanese language. The foggy space soaks you into the bathtub, enjoying the cleansing of your body and soul. The entrance area consists of several curtains containing video material, different kinds of private, semi-private and public spaces before entering and exiting the bathing area.

即席 KITCHEN

One part of the 即席 Kitchen space shows a range of different kitchen spaces and choices. The video displays recorded and lived experiences by the human to be voyeuristically observed and relived by the user. The opening to a world of kitchens. Emotions are transmitted through texts read by the author, which can be triggered through interaction with different objects, such as the 3D scan of the author, the rotating ramen bowl or the highlighted udon sign. You can get lost afterwards in the fragments of food and interaction with others. The facades of the shops are building up to walls as in an actual apartment. You exit the scene after fulfilling your need for nutrition, giving you enough energy to return and walk through the menu/cityscape again to find the next room you want to enter.

TheCityAsAHouse is a subjective and experience-based piece of frozen moments

Harvey writes, in "The Right to the City," about the city as a phenomenon of class society, which consciously shares decision-making power among few individuals in control and focuses on productive urbanism. Controlled and financed by few individuals, a city should emerge that everyone is involved in and which promotes the community. A distinctly utopian view of urbanism.

I want you to recall your imagined Tokyo based on my experiences and create a home of your own. The experiences of TheCityAsAHouse relate to Christiaan Fruneaux, who sees cities as "places of reinvention—technologically, socially, but most of all personally." Driven by turbo capitalism, cities are emerging rapidly today, while the economic factor is a top priority. This does not happen immediately, but slowly and under the surface. Translating data gathered in Tokyo while not having a private apartment, the subject, I, experienced different still-life motifs which were captured through gathered data and translated with a game engine. The five scenes are a still life of contemporary city life reflecting our time now. The user can experience the moments by navigating and finding different scenes. The main focus lies not on replicating the real world, but creating a parallel world from memories of the subject, myself. It is a collection of frozen moments that are pleasant, awkward, scary, powerful, dull, interesting, intriguing. The user has the ability to see scenes of everyday life from different perspectives. Entering the human body to see its inner wishes or walking around objects interacting with them to get more information. Guided by a voice-, my voice. TheCityAsAHouse has a million choices to offer, but the subject, I, just chooses some. While living the experiment, a lot of choices were based on particular situations. Never the same, but always similar, needs had to be fulfilled. It is a journey through a real life where the user can be swept away to a different world. It is a subjective view which does not adhere to scientific research. The user becomes the voyeur of an individual approach to living in a city. According to Henri Lefebvre, humans as social beings need space with a view and openness as well as space that conveys security and offers protection. The city he sees is understood as a consumer-oriented tourism stronghold and devoid of any social aspect. The fear of privatizing a city is constantly felt, but not always comprehensible. In the Japanese metropolis of Tokyo, access to sanitary facilities is made possible and not dependent on compulsory consumption. The network of 即席 Places makes it possible for a human to survive and enjoy the city as well as suffer from the idea. It is a lived proposition of claiming space in the public by transforming and reprogramming places of different functions to satisfy your personal needs at anytime, anywhere. The architect has built enough. There is a feeling of loss of control and panic, which is satisfied with the repeated adaptation of urban space. By taking your time with the game engine, you sacrifice it and get glimpses of the experience. The five scenes represent an example of leaving the house. Countless doors open if you invert the image of the city becoming the private apartment. We have to think of a city as a complicated construction of various networks. The 即席 Kitchen connects with all the other 即席 Kitchens and creates a network that provides a more sustainable, ecological, and economical situation for the humans living in the city after the point of no return. The instant or 即席 Places are pearls on a chain, chains which multiply and autogenerate themselves. No complete overview can be given. The device we carry with us every day provides glimpses based on pure hedonistic preferences and previous encounters with the 即席 Rooms we have chosen to visit. We have to create experiences and situations, moments through which the monotony of the capitalist everyday routine may be disrupted by using already build spaces instead of relying on the need for new ones. The 即席 Places are places where a reinterpretation of the functions and the search for private living spaces are attempted. This manifests itself in digital space by not reproducing reality in order to make it understandable, but by reducing it to essential elements. The experiment, in terms of architecture, is the endless source of feeling and experiencing. For future projects, the outcome is impossible to deliver in one specific—let's say "building." Also, TheCityAsAHouse is to see the generic automation of these sorts of 即席 Places without one single entity to decide. I am not only dissolving built spaces, like apartments, I am compressing them to bits and bytes to take anywhere. The future of life within a cityscape is getting rid of housing architecture and implementing it in places where a different function is intended.

The End

Playing Time
07:18 Min

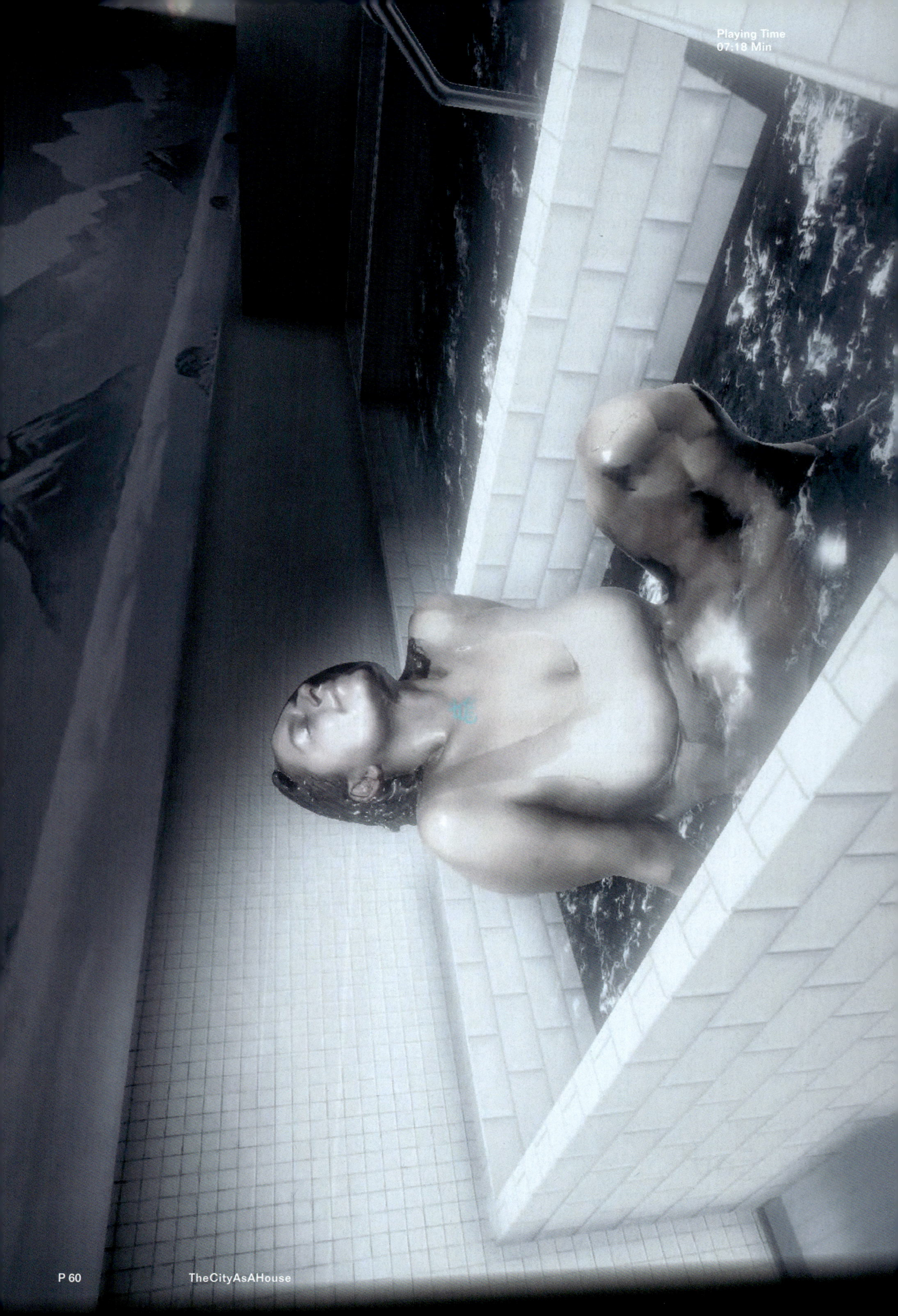

Play

Playing Time
00:00 Min

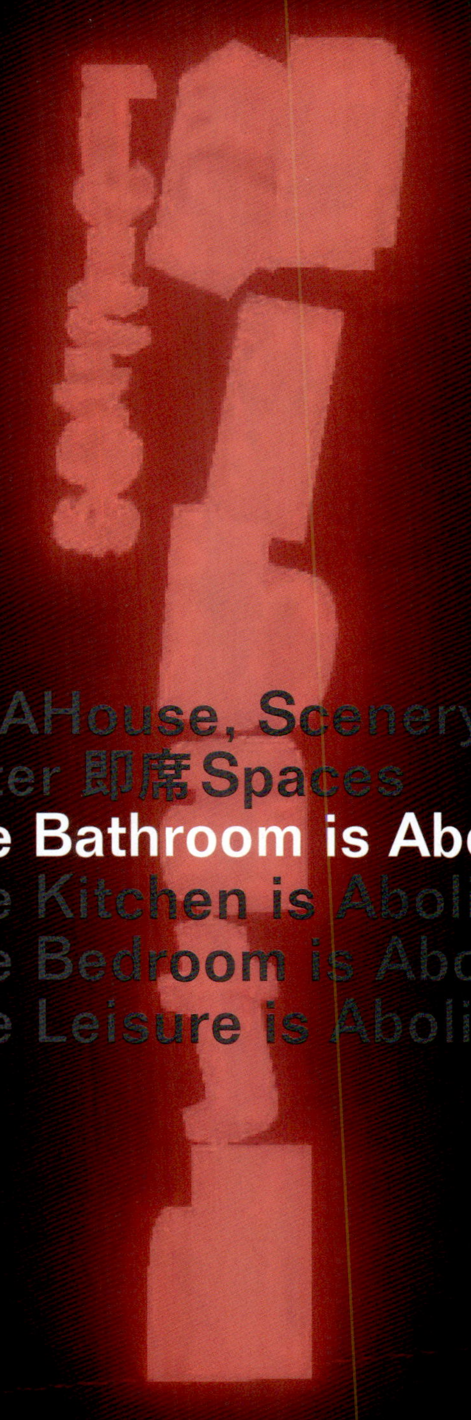

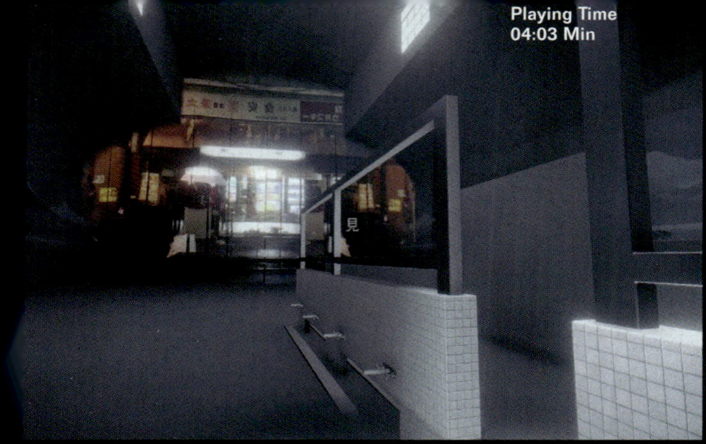
Playing Time
04:03 Min

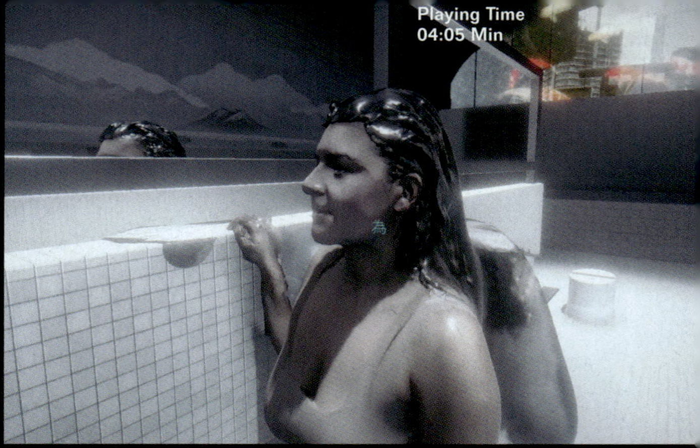
Playing Time
04:05 Min

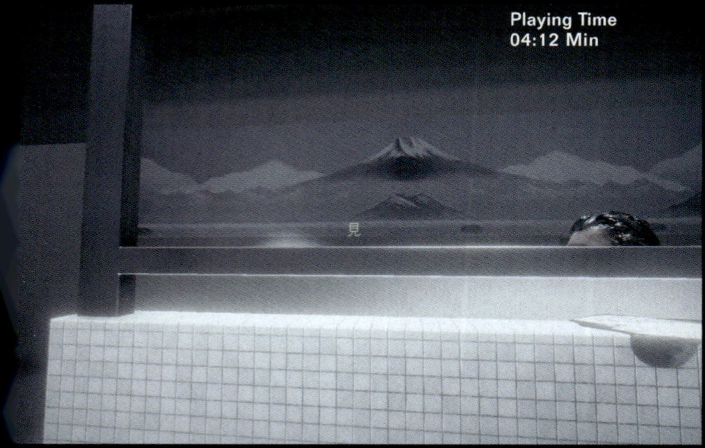
Playing Time
04:12 Min

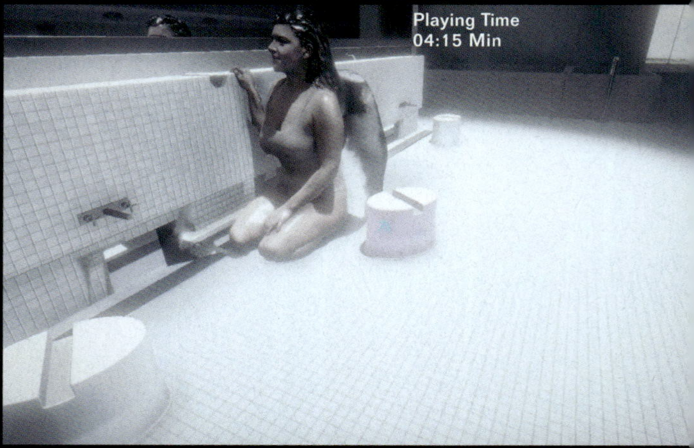
Playing Time
04:15 Min

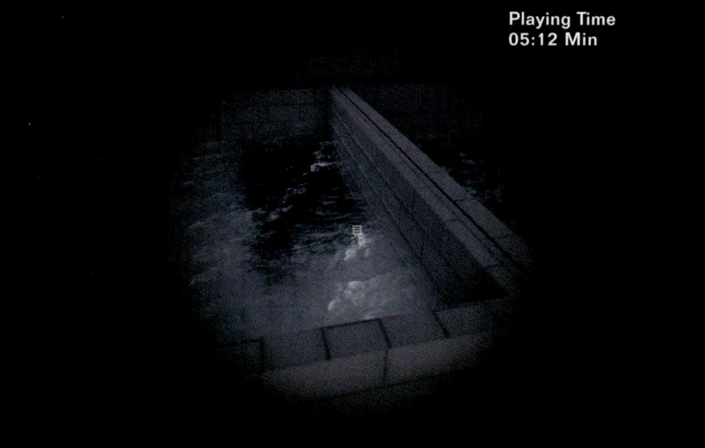
Playing Time
05:12 Min

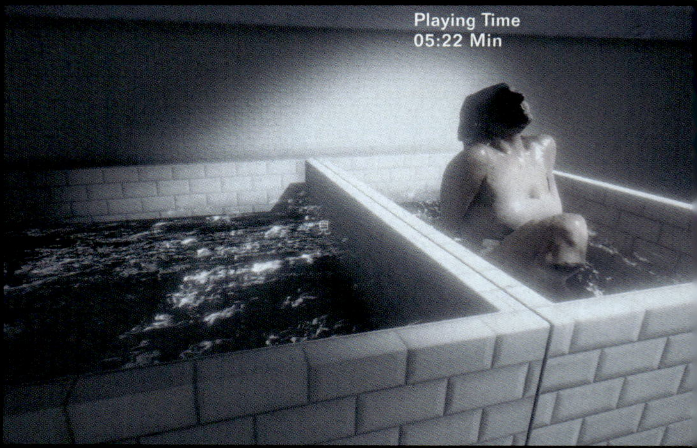
Playing Time
05:22 Min

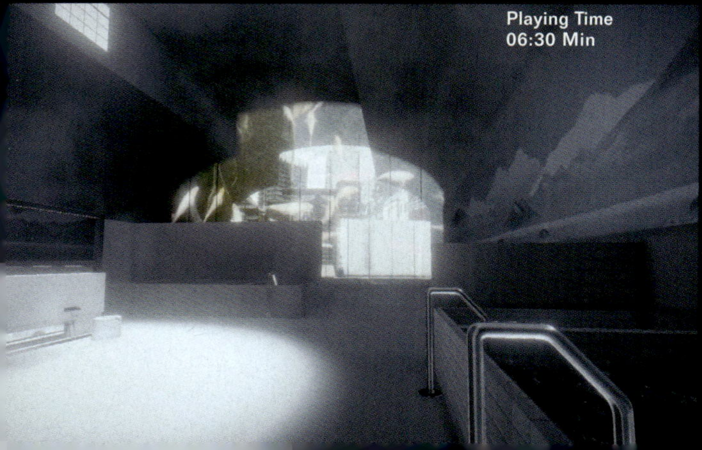
Playing Time
06:30 Min

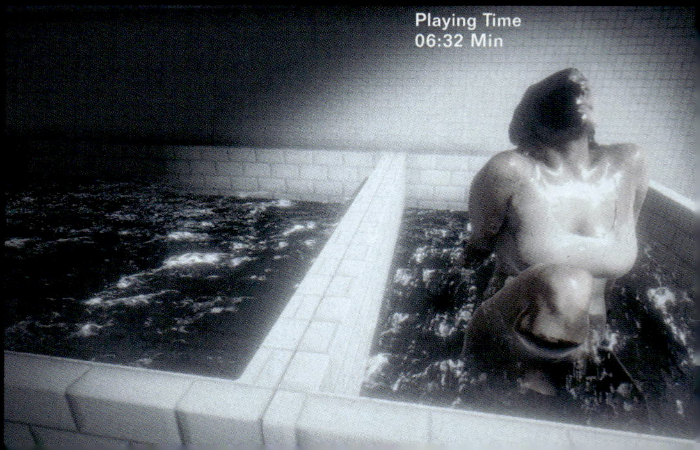
Playing Time
06:32 Min

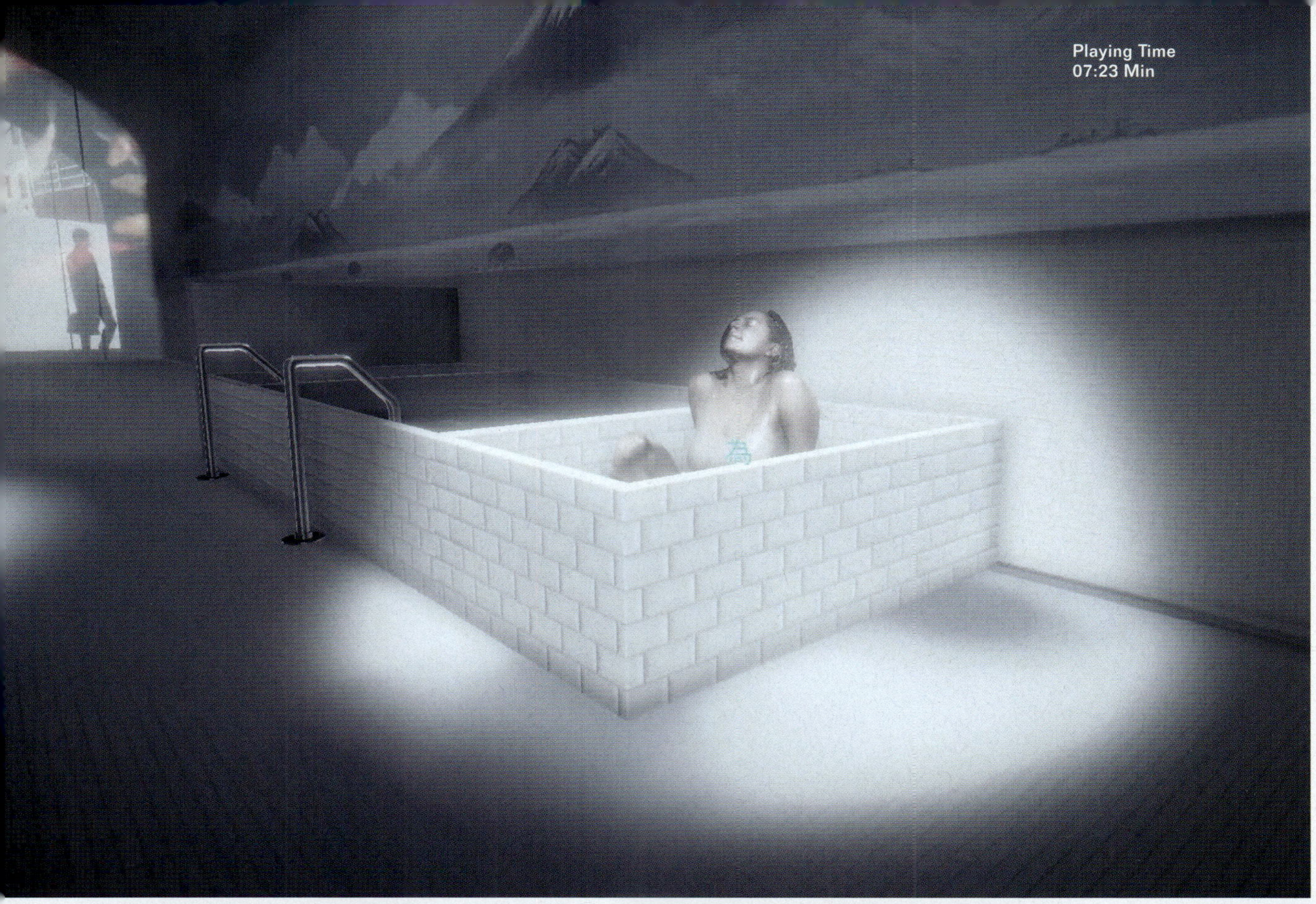
Playing Time
07:23 Min
為

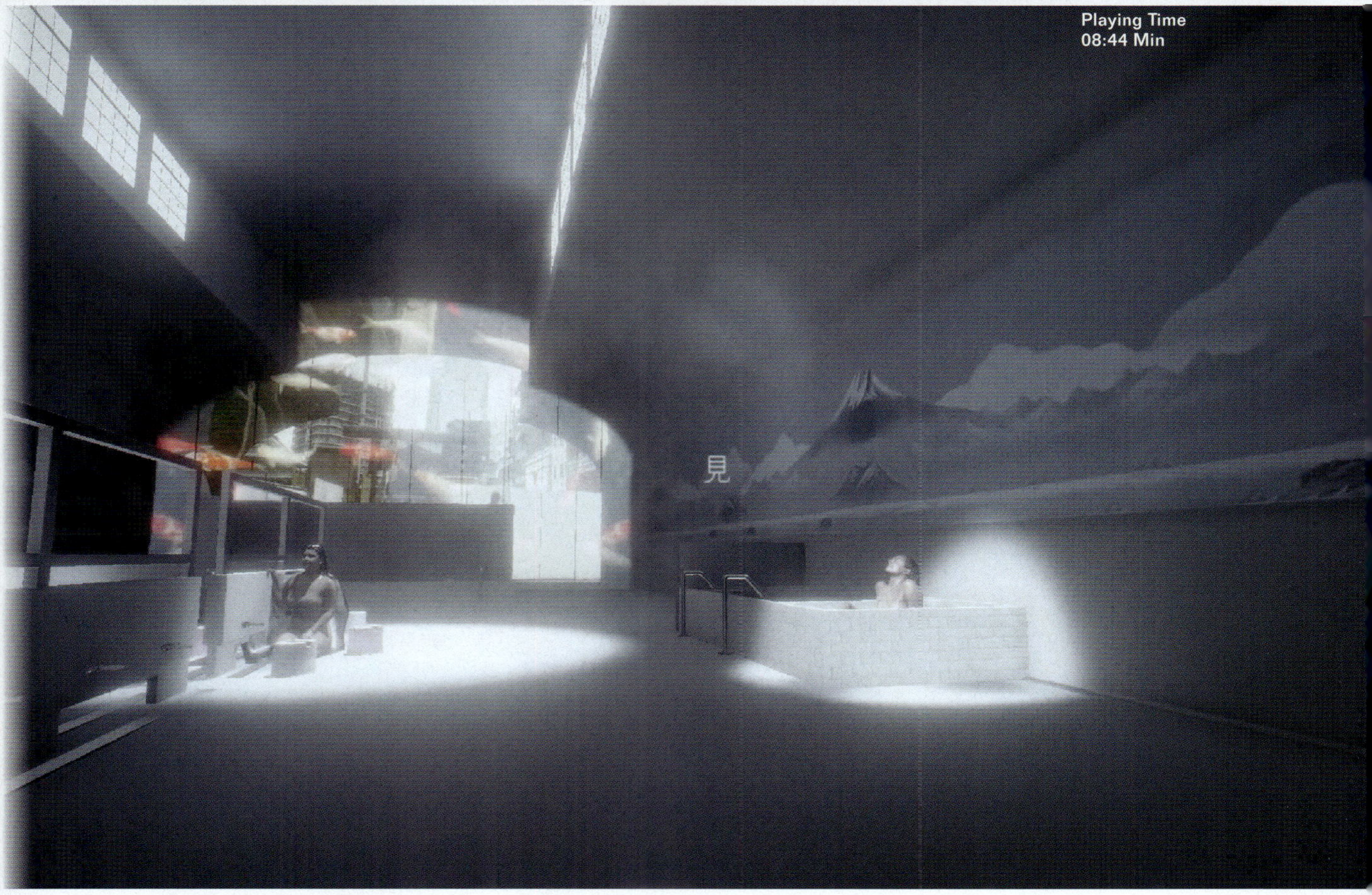
Playing Time
08:44 Min
見

Pause
08:49 Min

Pause
08:55 Min

Pause
09:12 Min

Playing Time
10:12 Min

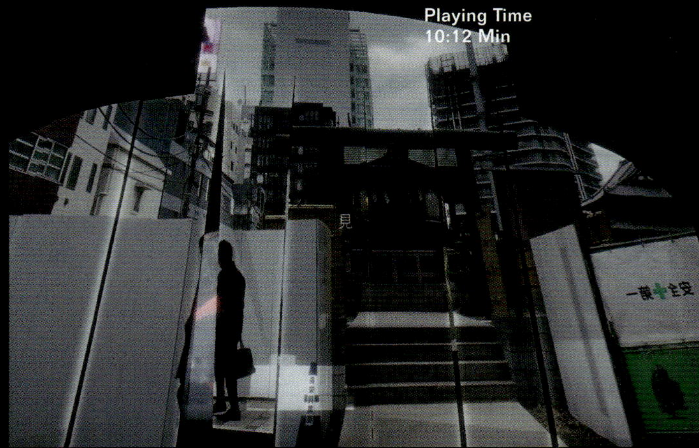

Playing Time
10:18 Min

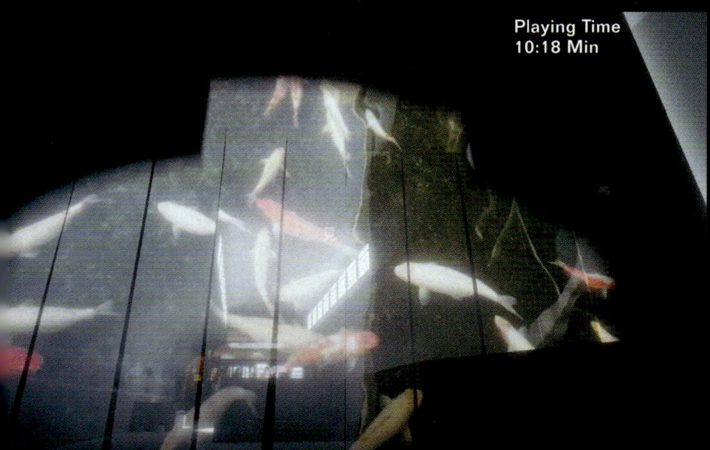

Playing Time:
10:36 Min

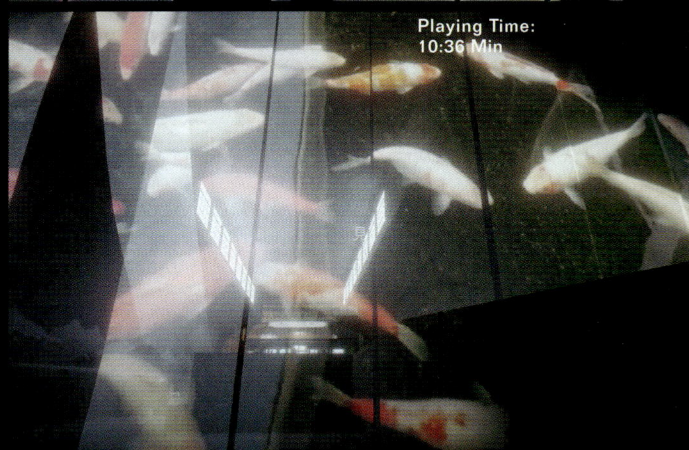

Playing Time
11:03 Min

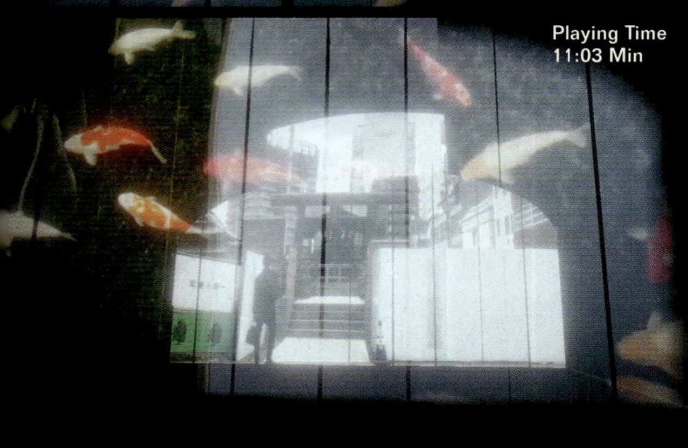

Playing Time
11:27 Min

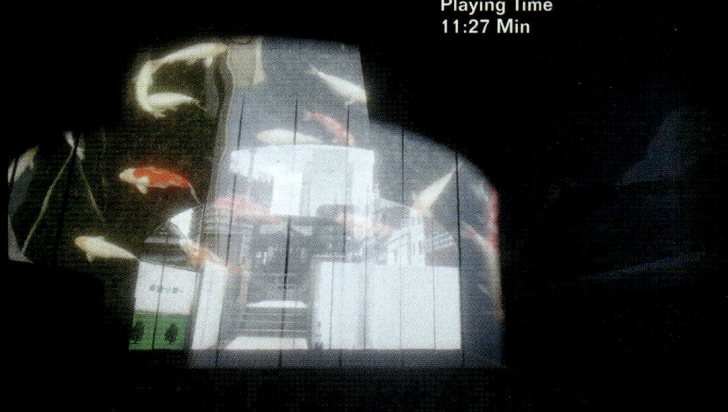

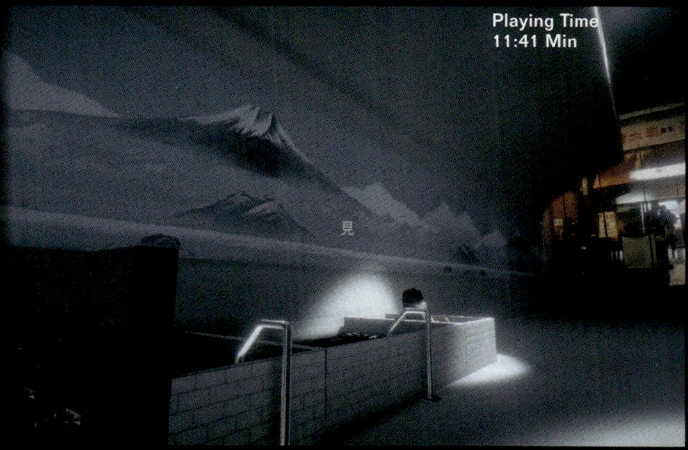
Playing Time
11:41 Min

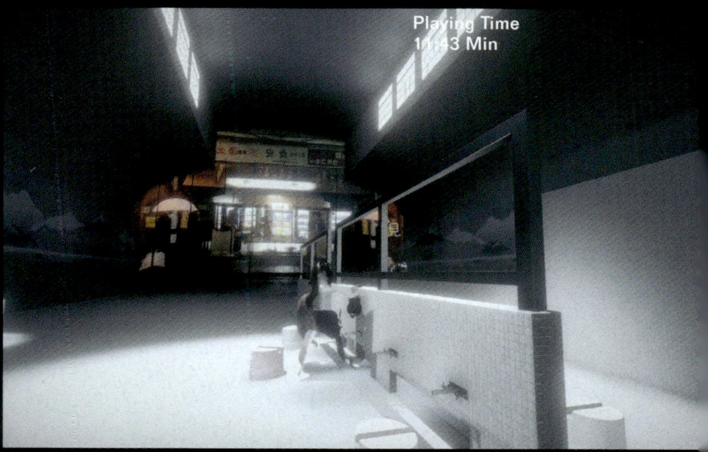
Playing Time
11:43 Min

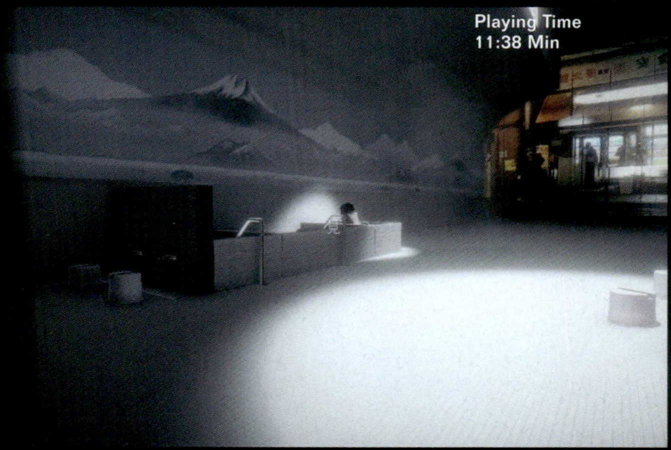
Playing Time
11:38 Min

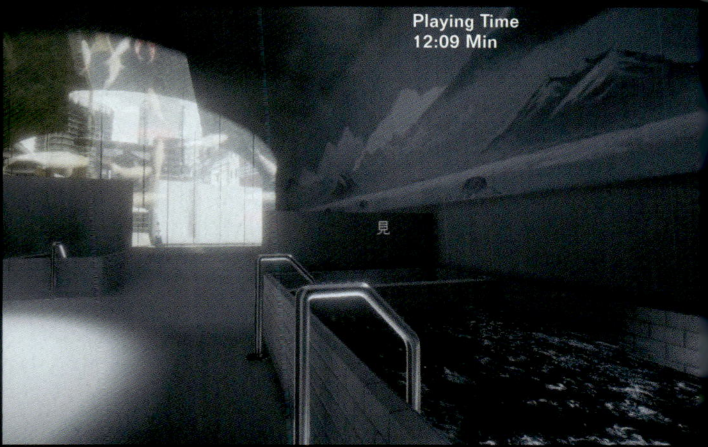
Playing Time
12:09 Min

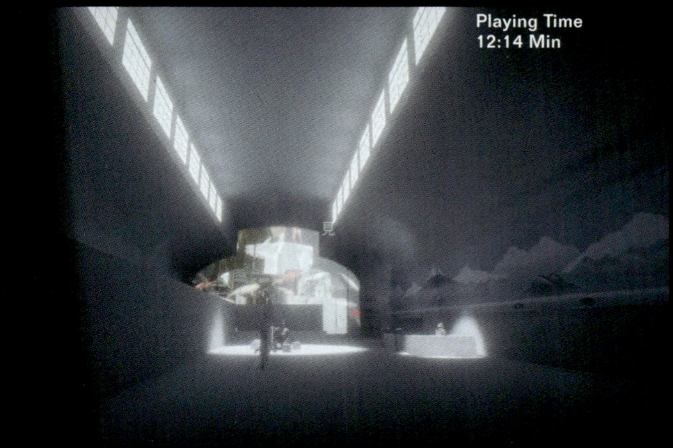
Playing Time
12:14 Min

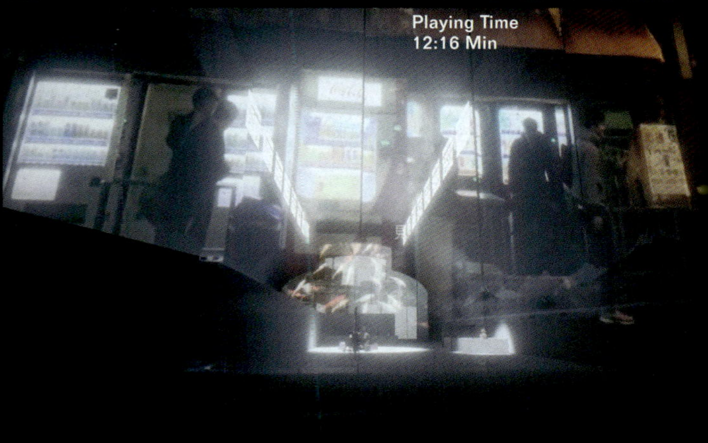
Playing Time
12:16 Min

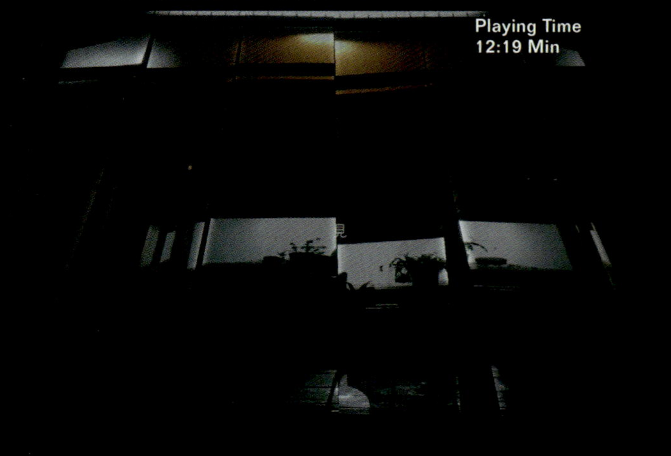
Playing Time
12:19 Min

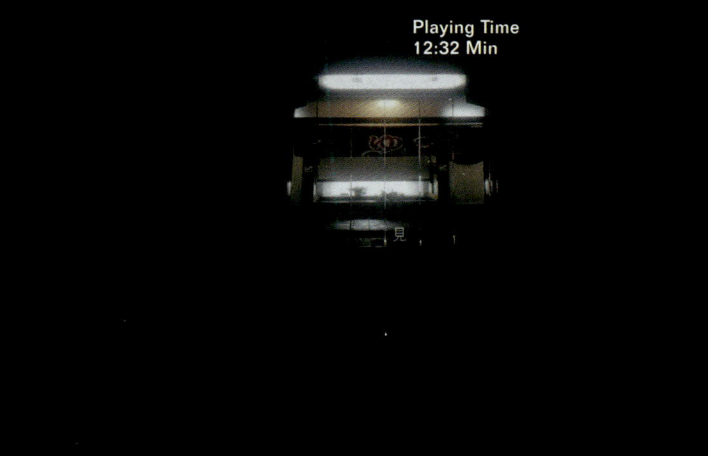
Playing Time
12:32 Min

Total Playing Time
IRL 10:42 Min

Playing Time
00:24 Min

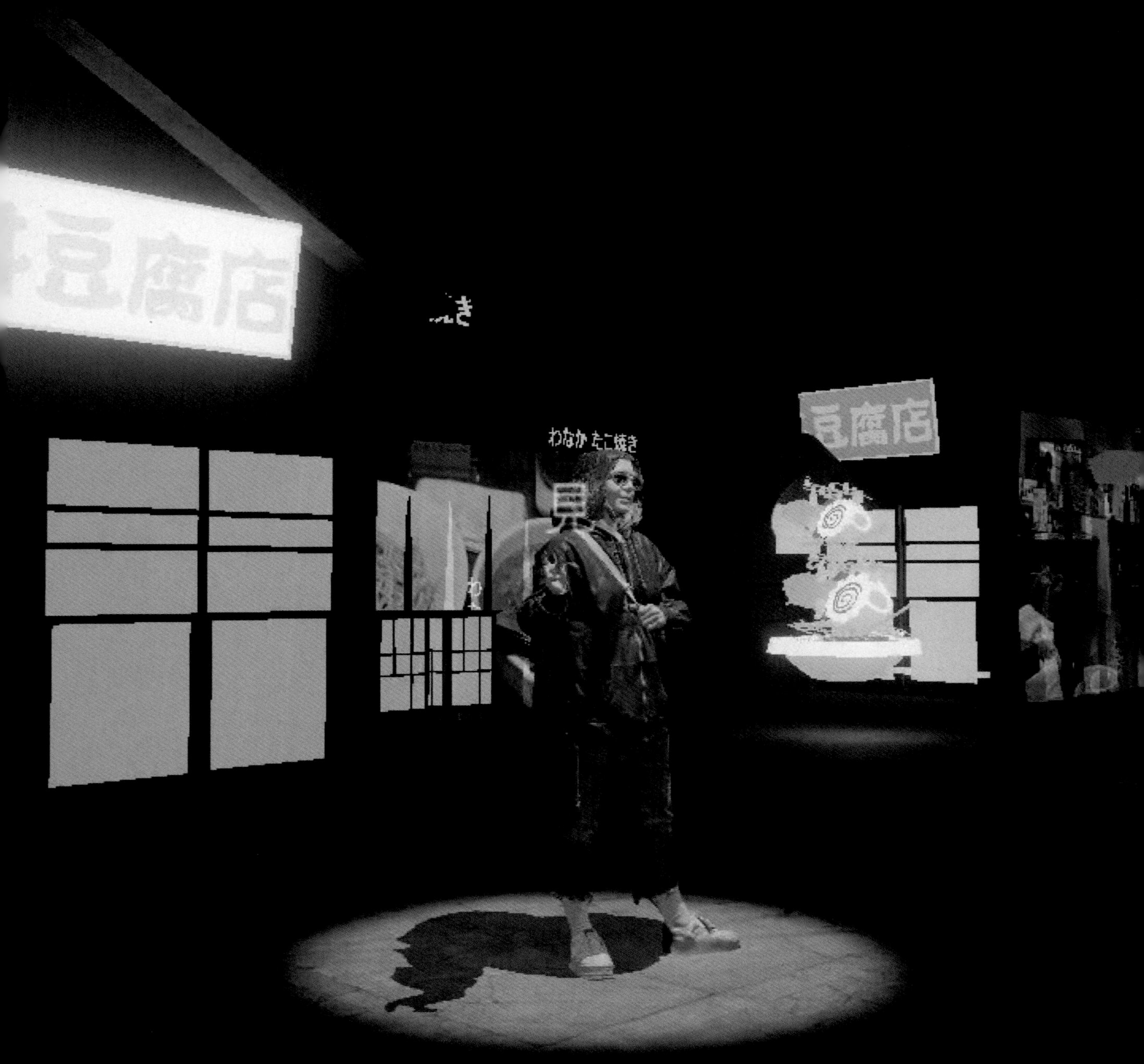

Play

Playing Time
00:36 Min

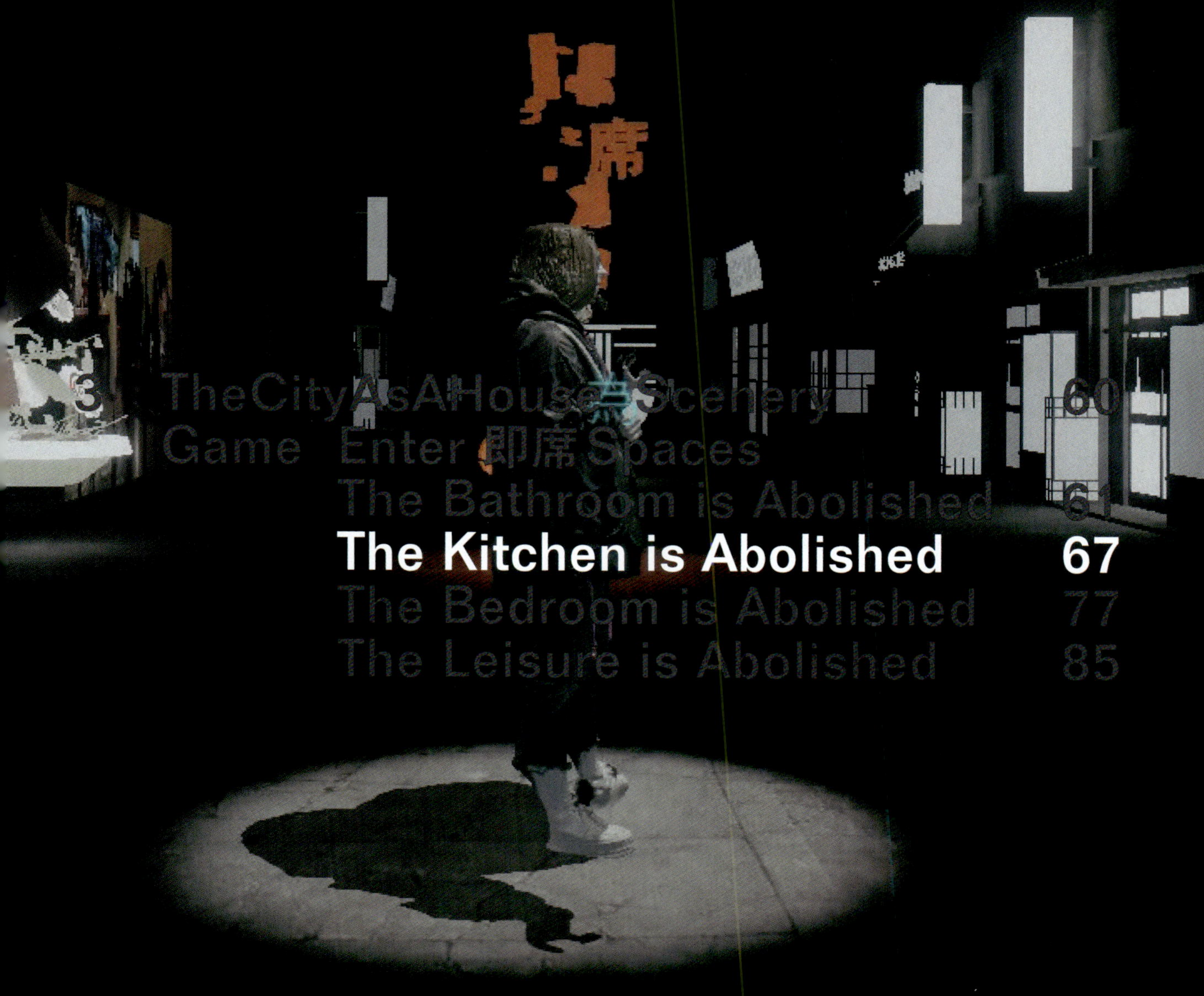

Pause
01:12 Min

Pause
01:13 Min

Playing Time
01:32 Min

Playing Time
01:43 Min

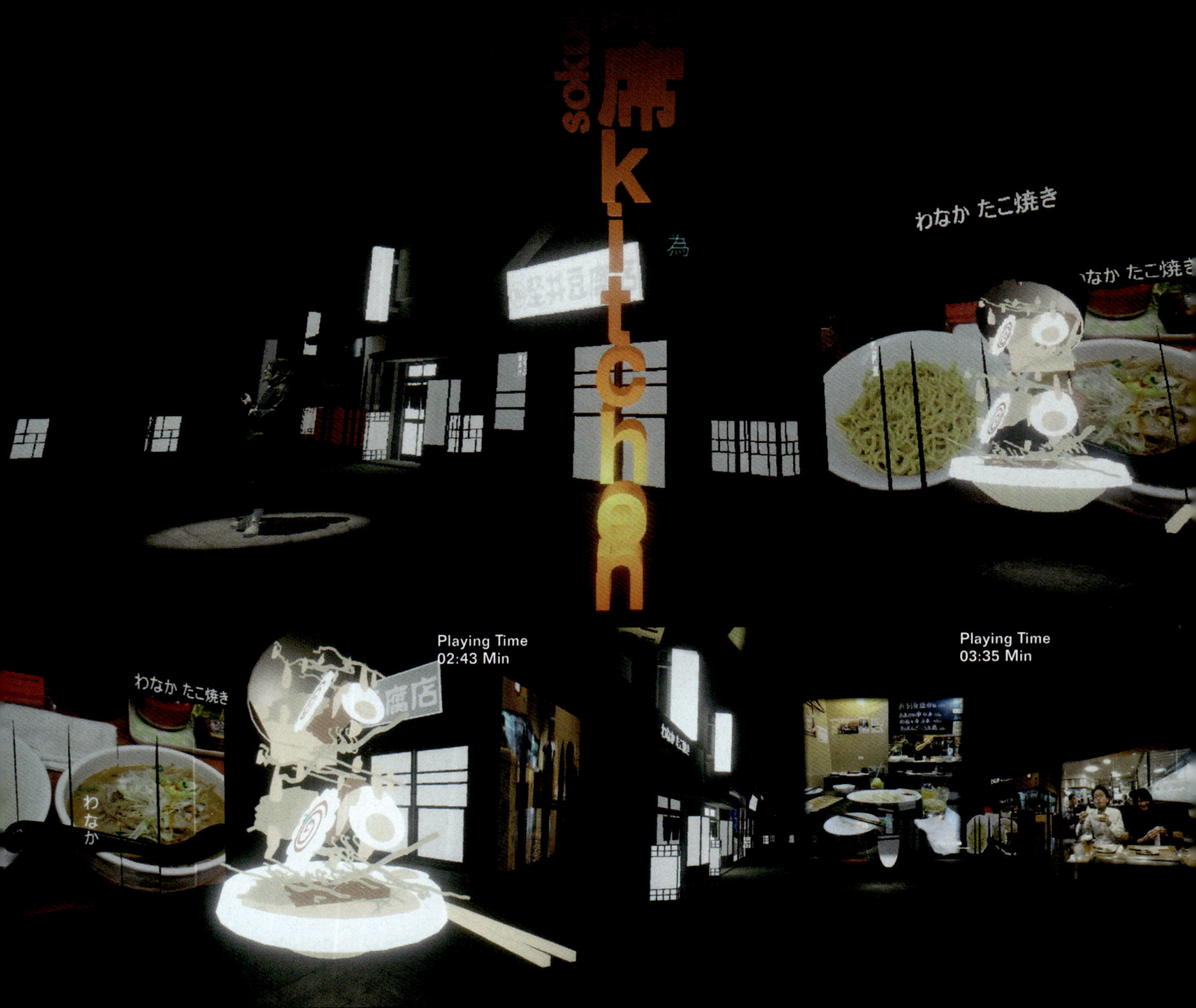

Playing Time
02:43 Min

Playing Time
03:35 Min

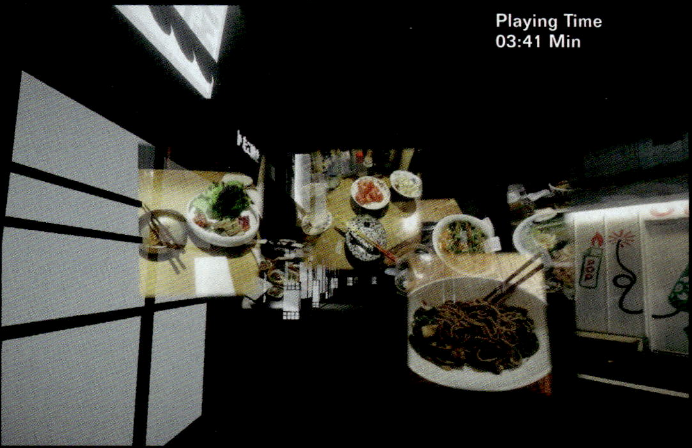
Playing Time
03:41 Min

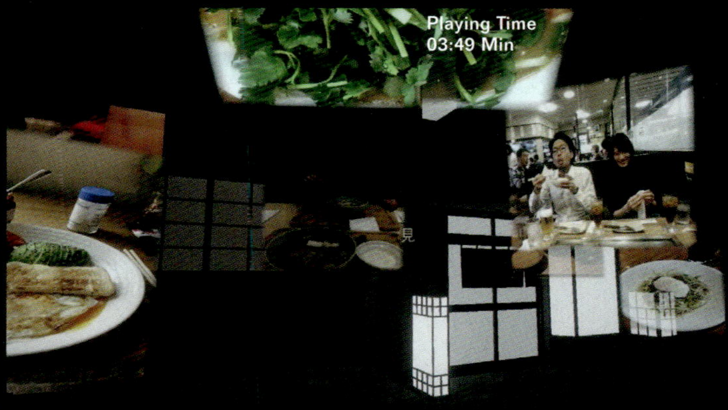
Playing Time
03:49 Min

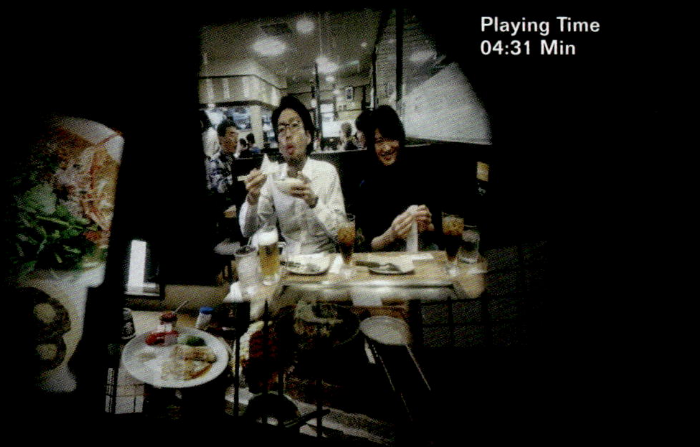
Playing Time
04:31 Min

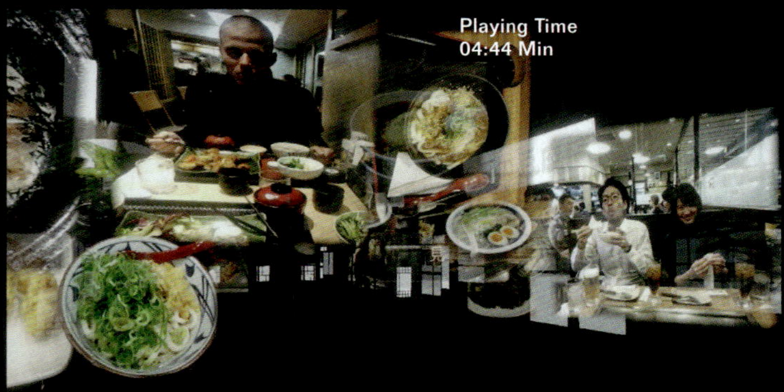
Playing Time
04:44 Min

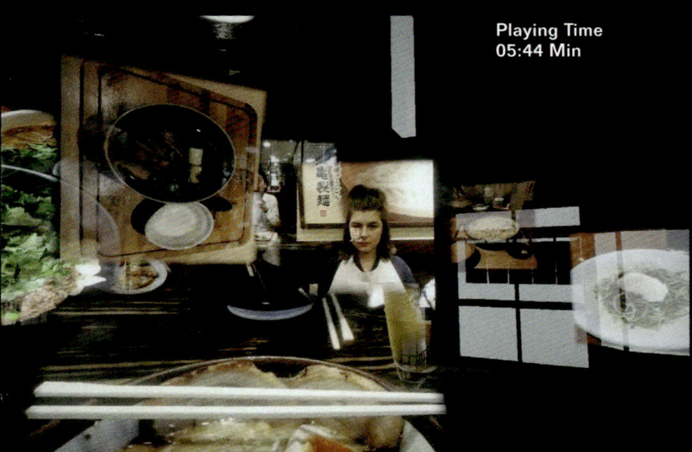
Playing Time
05:44 Min

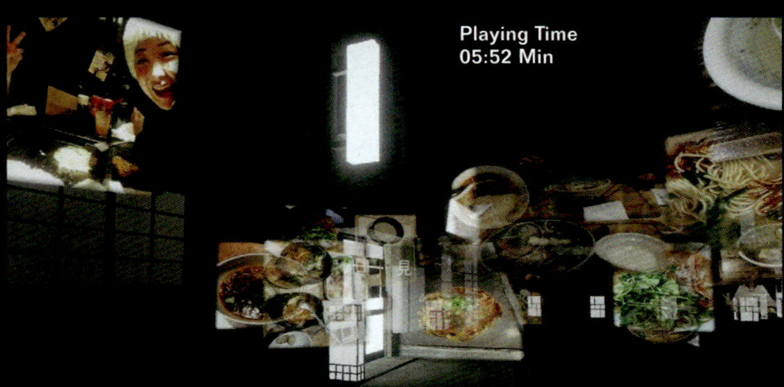
Playing Time
05:52 Min

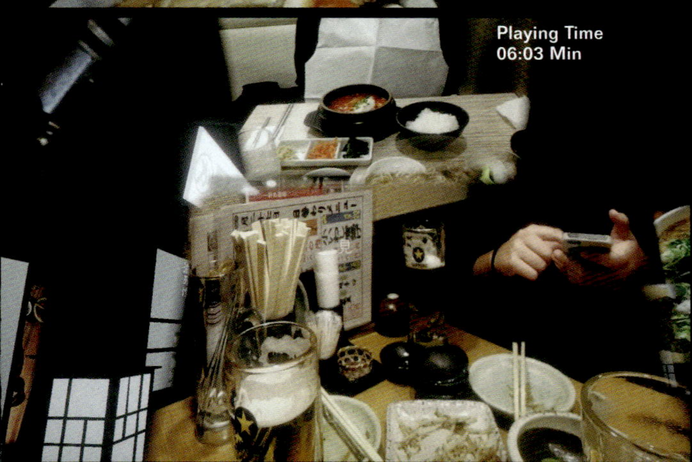
Playing Time
06:03 Min

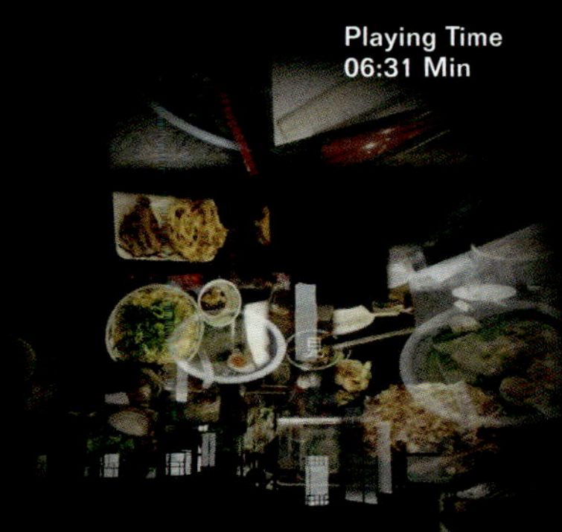
Playing Time
06:31 Min

Pause
07:00 Min

Pause
07:10 Min

Playing Time
07:11 Min

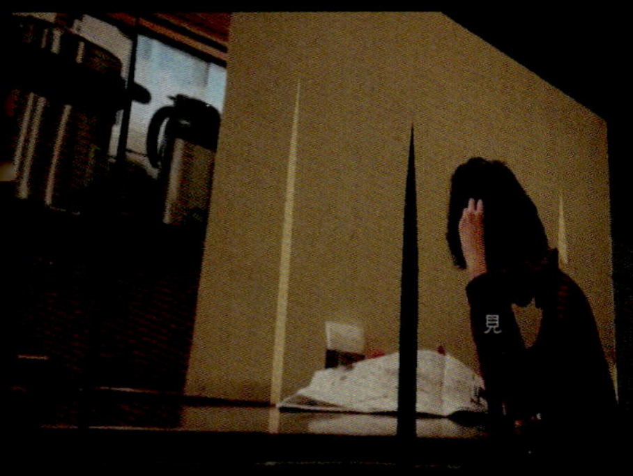

Playing Time
07:23 Min

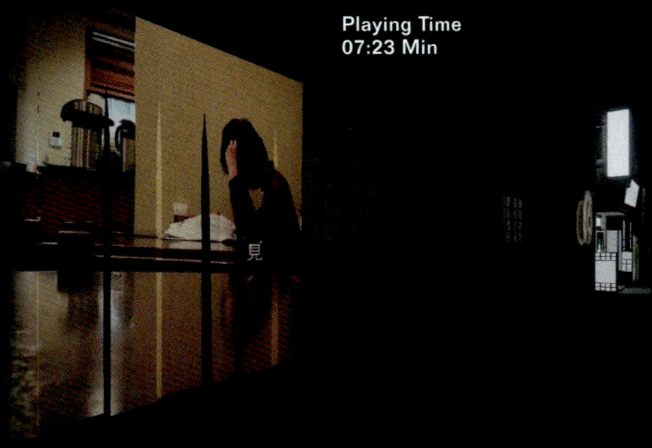

Pause
08:18 Min

Pause
08:19 Min

Playing Time
09:03 Min

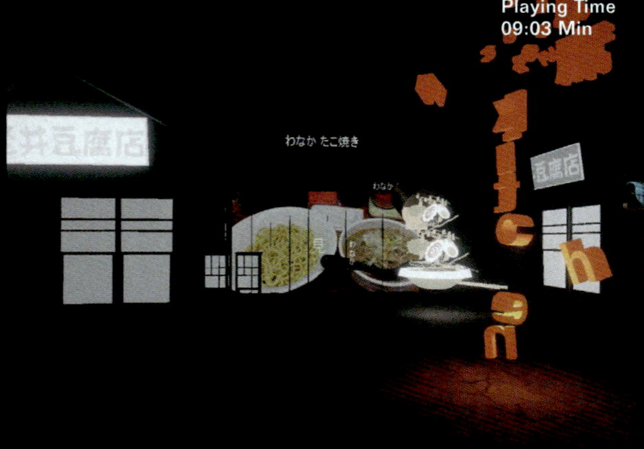

Playing Time
09:05 Min

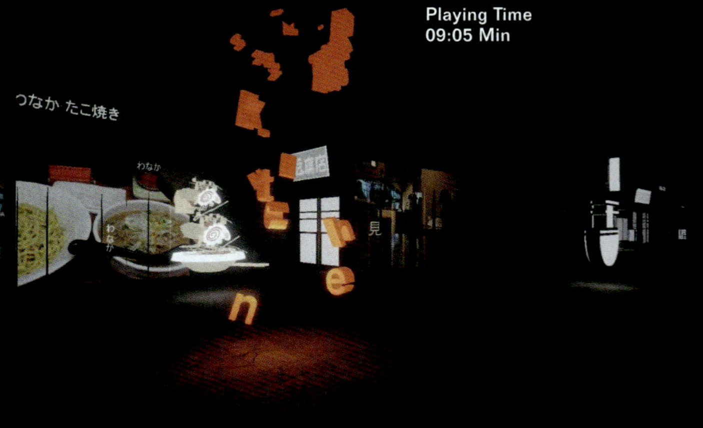

Playing Time
09:11 Min

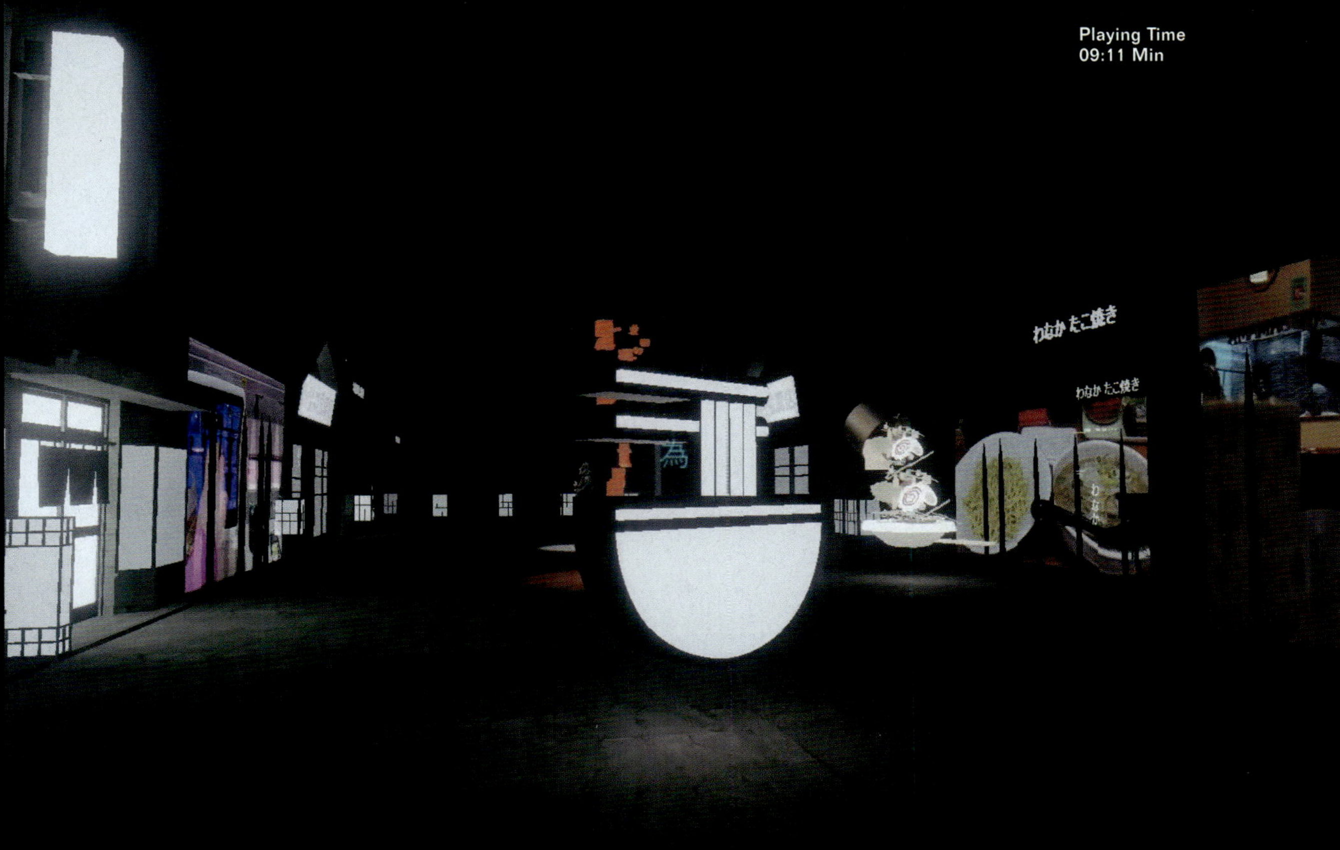

Playing Time
09:22 Min

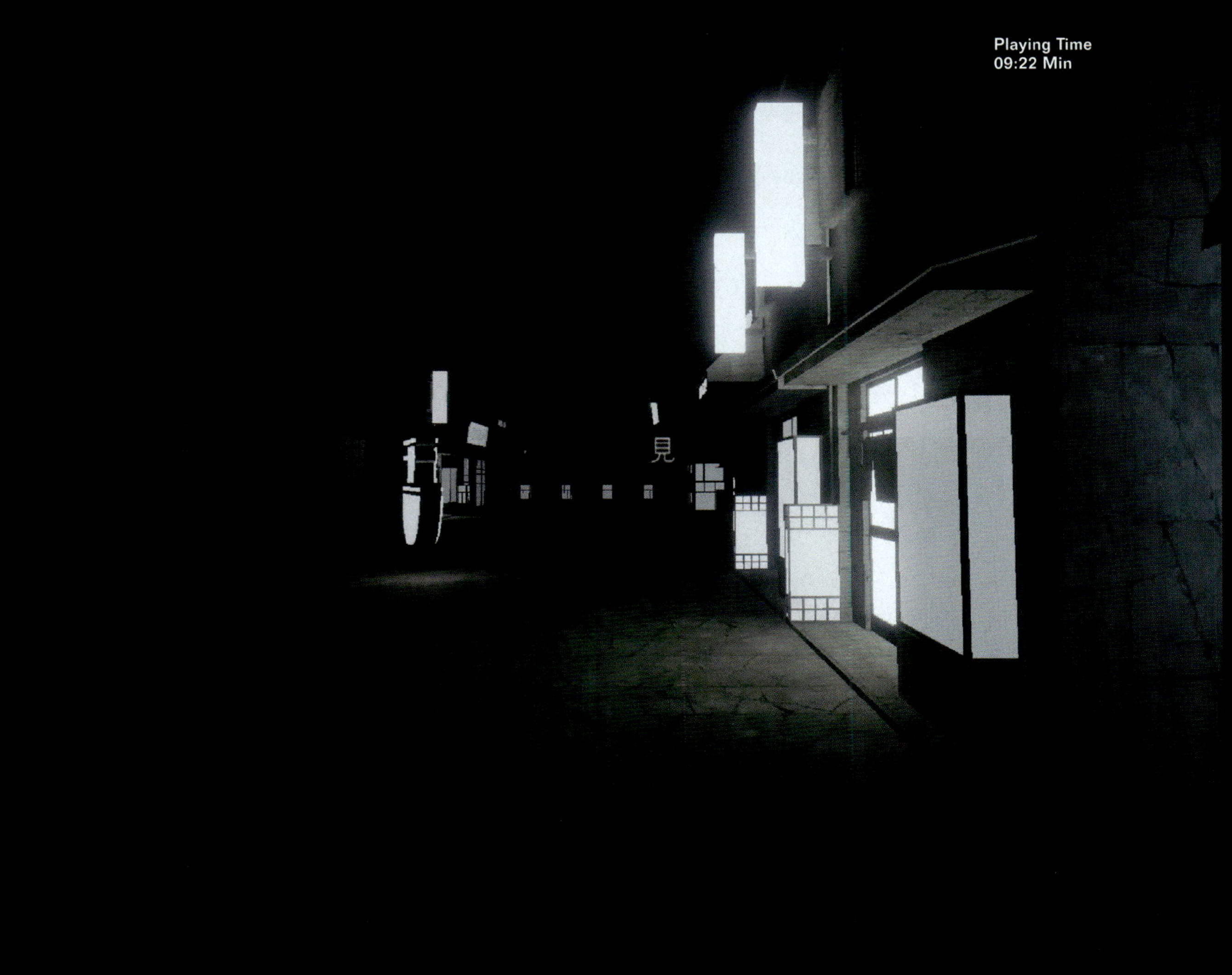

Playing Time
09:36 Min

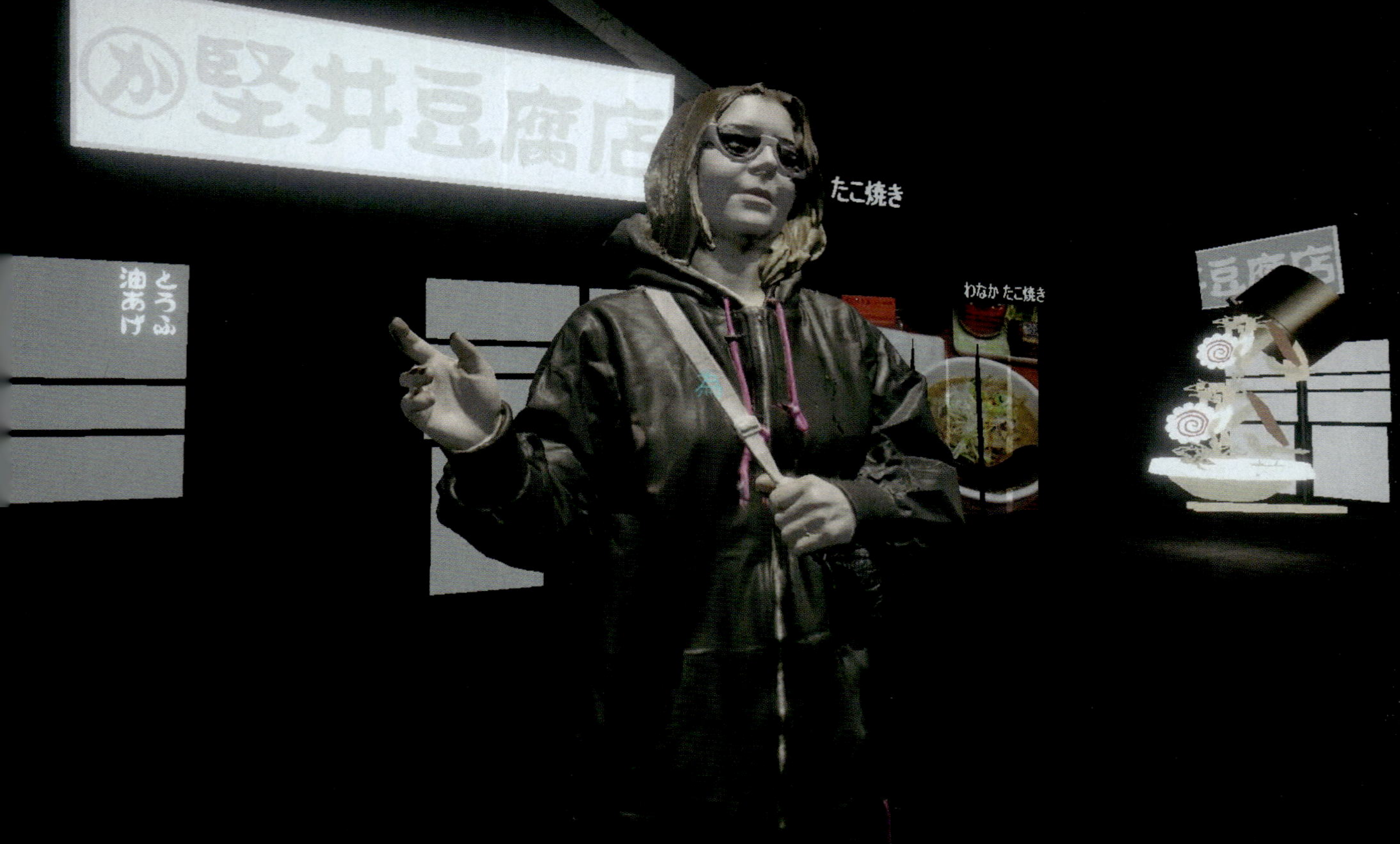

Playing Time
10:09 Min

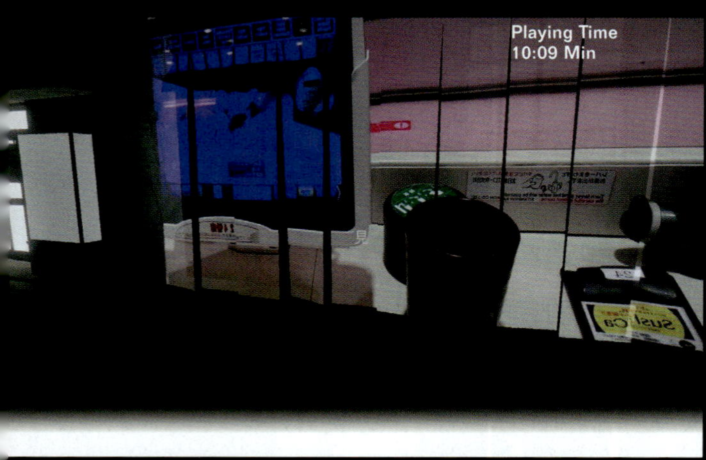

Playing Time
10:21 Min

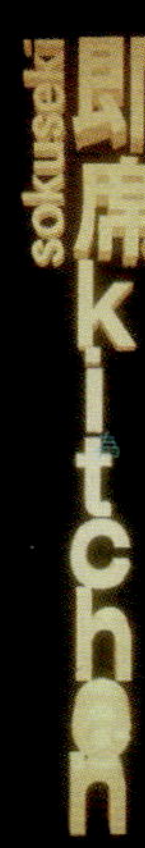

Playing Time
10:30 Min

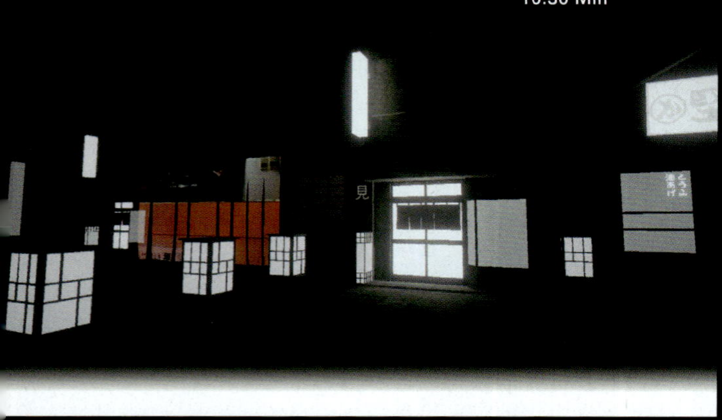

Pause
10:42 Min

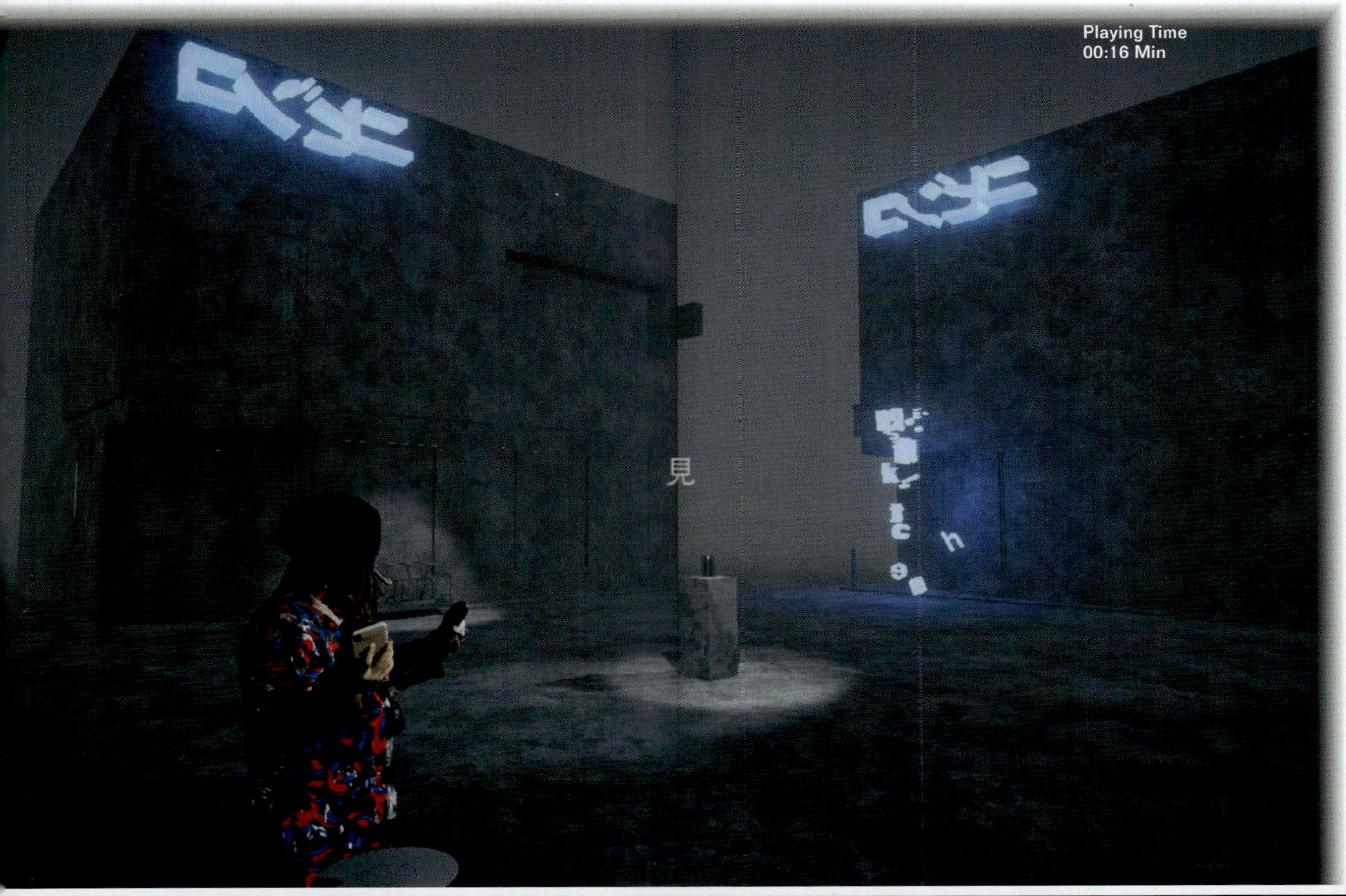
Playing Time
00:16 Min
見

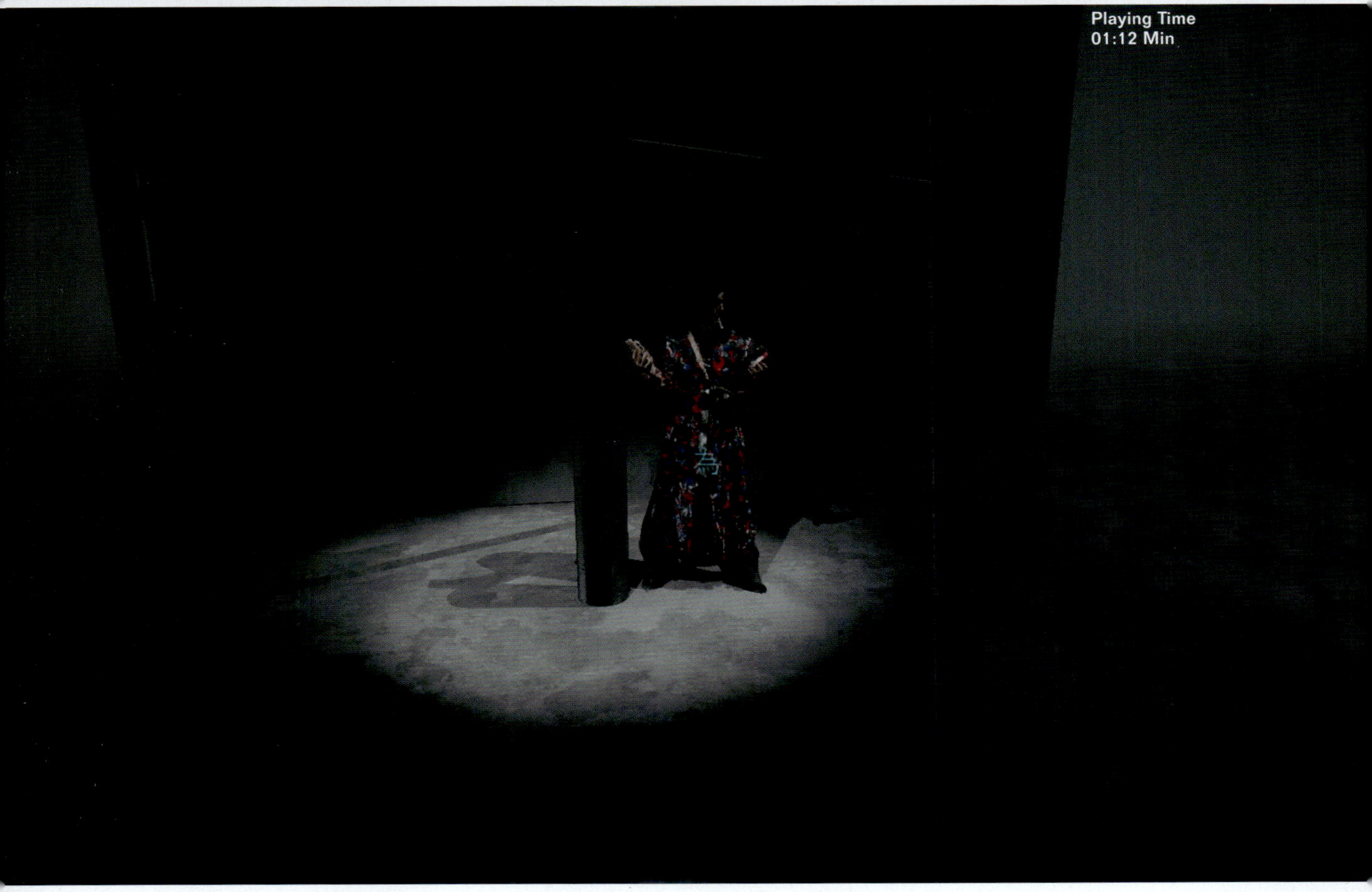
Playing Time
01:12 Min
為

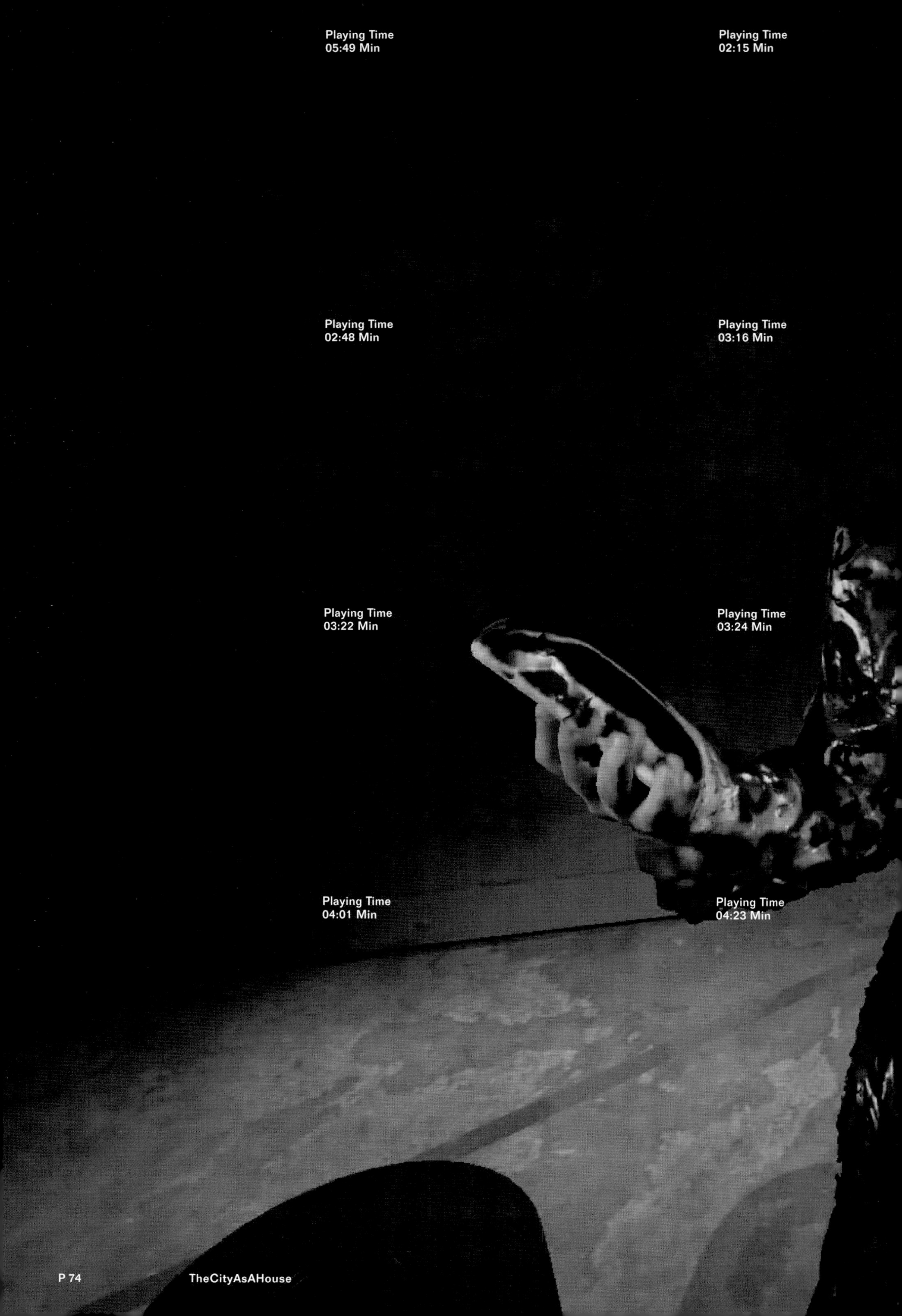

Playing Time
05:49 Min

Playing Time
02:15 Min

Playing Time
02:48 Min

Playing Time
03:16 Min

Playing Time
03:22 Min

Playing Time
03:24 Min

Playing Time
04:01 Min

Playing Time
04:23 Min

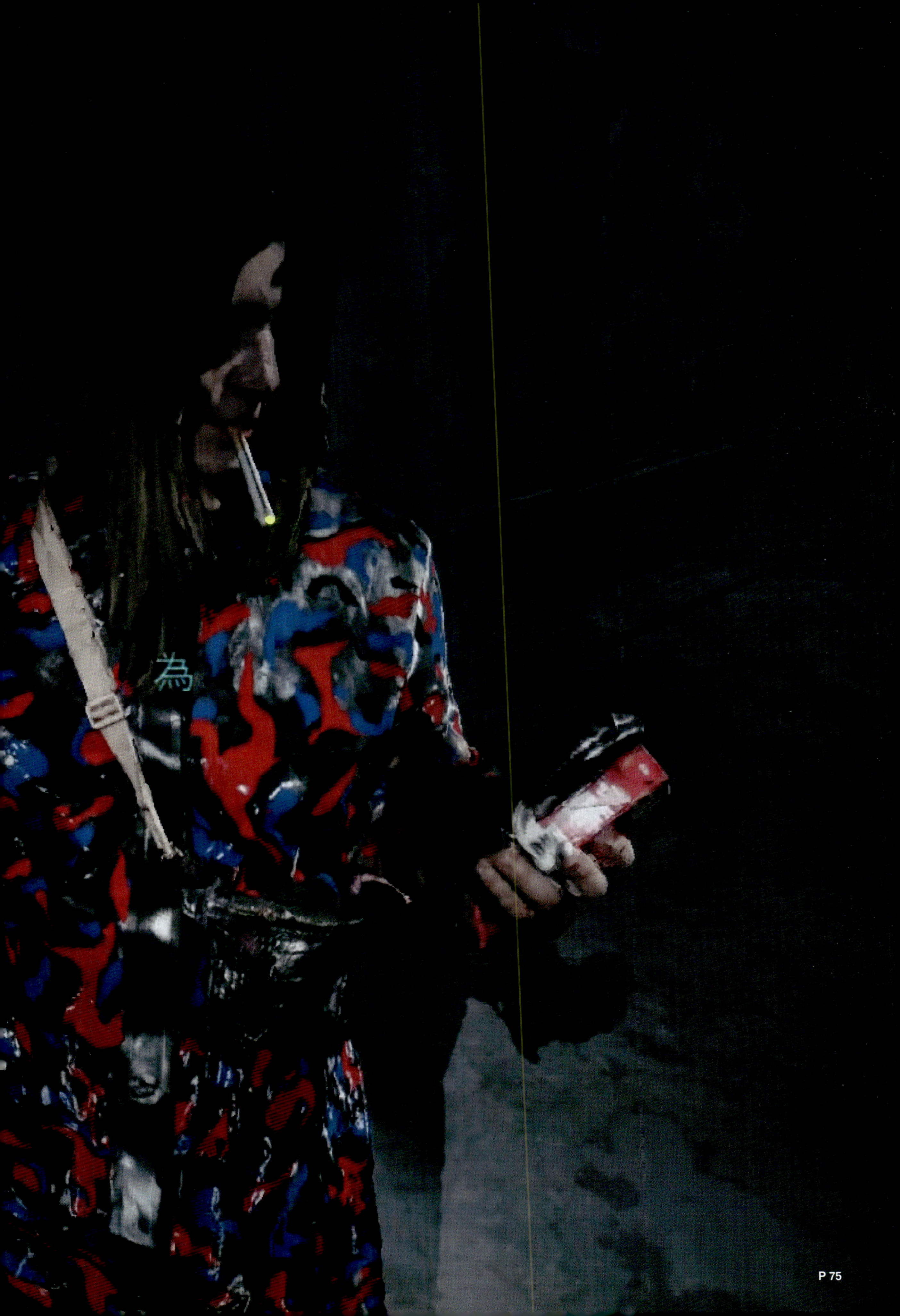
為

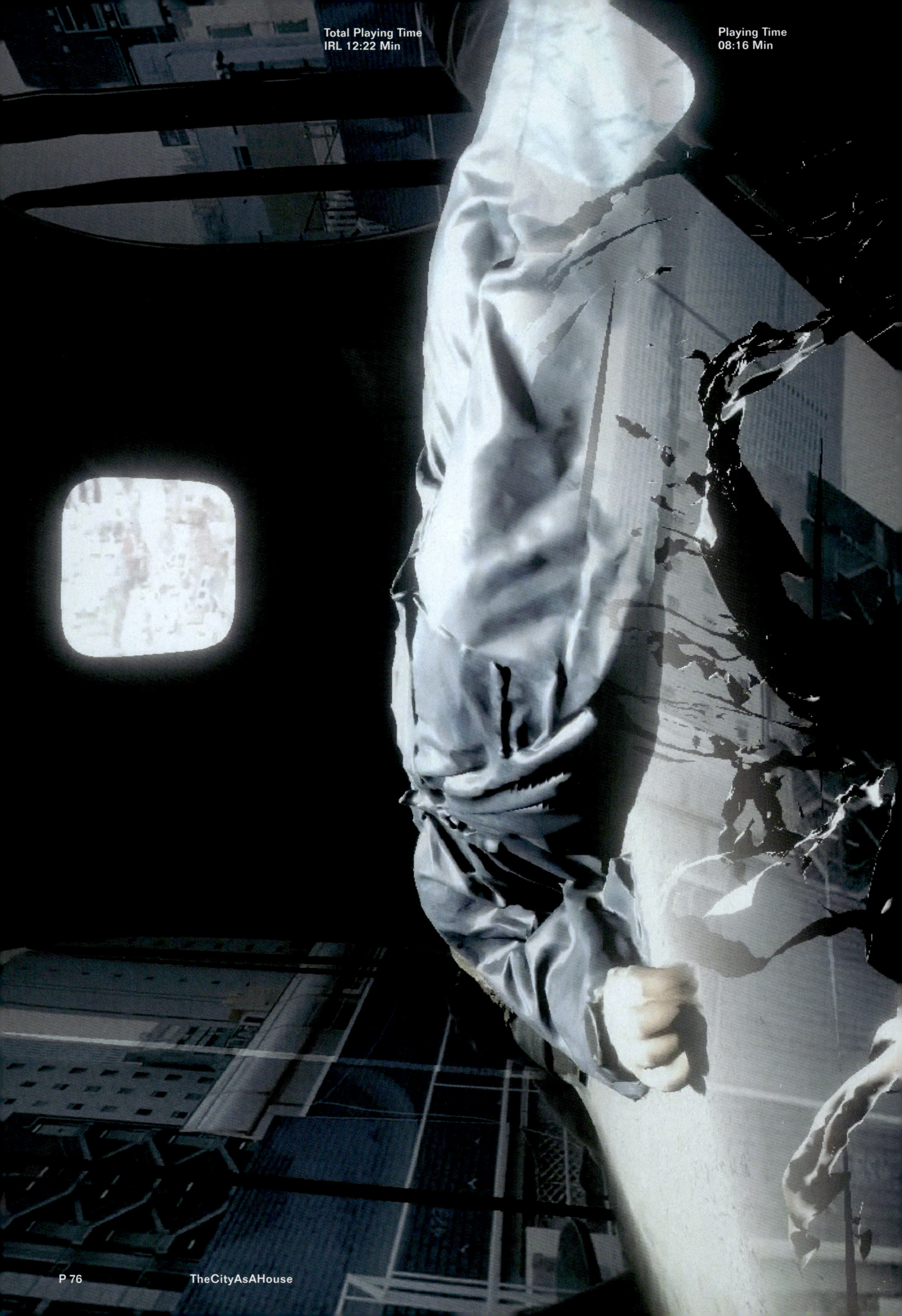

Play

Playing Time
08:25 Min

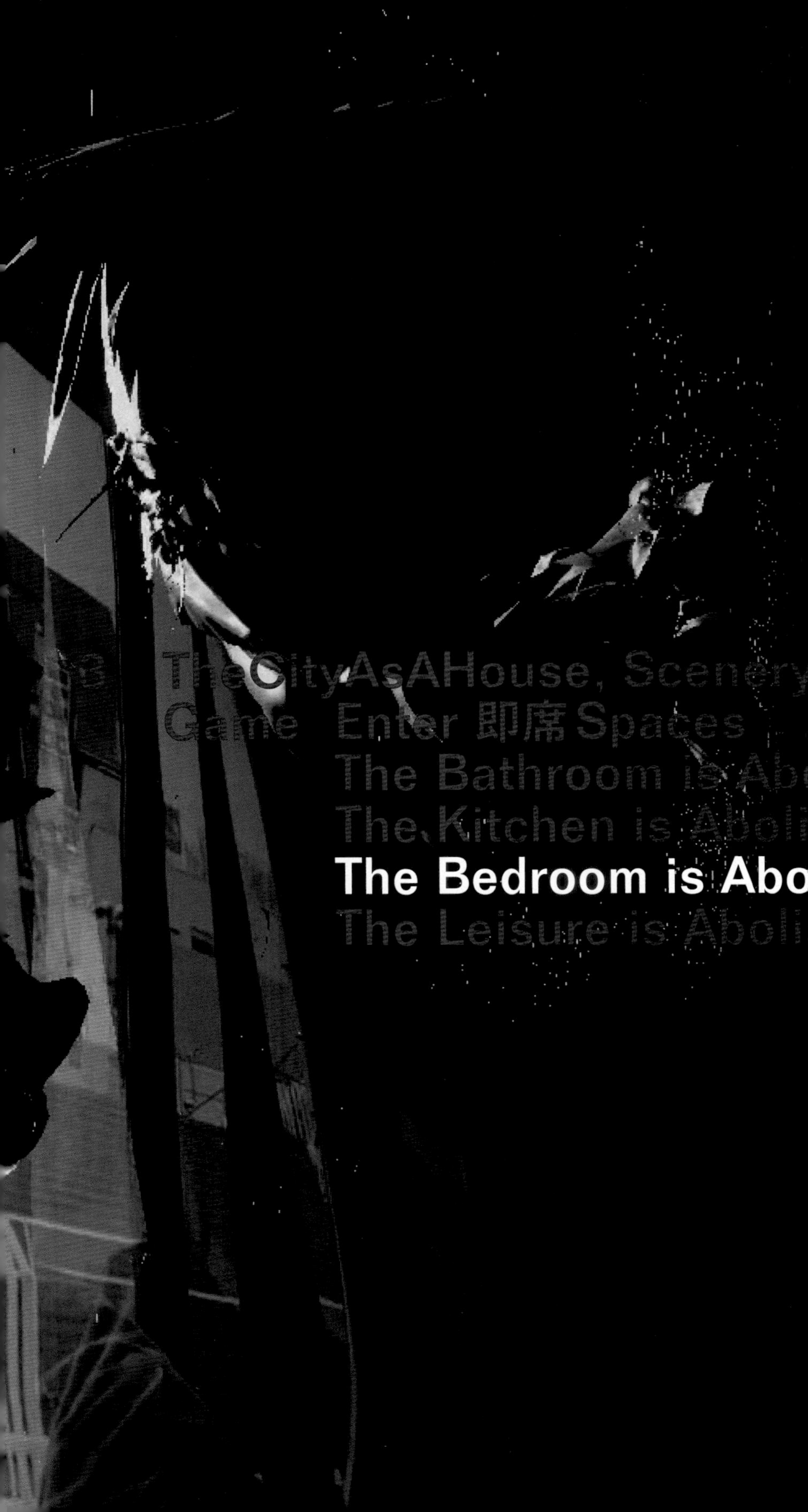

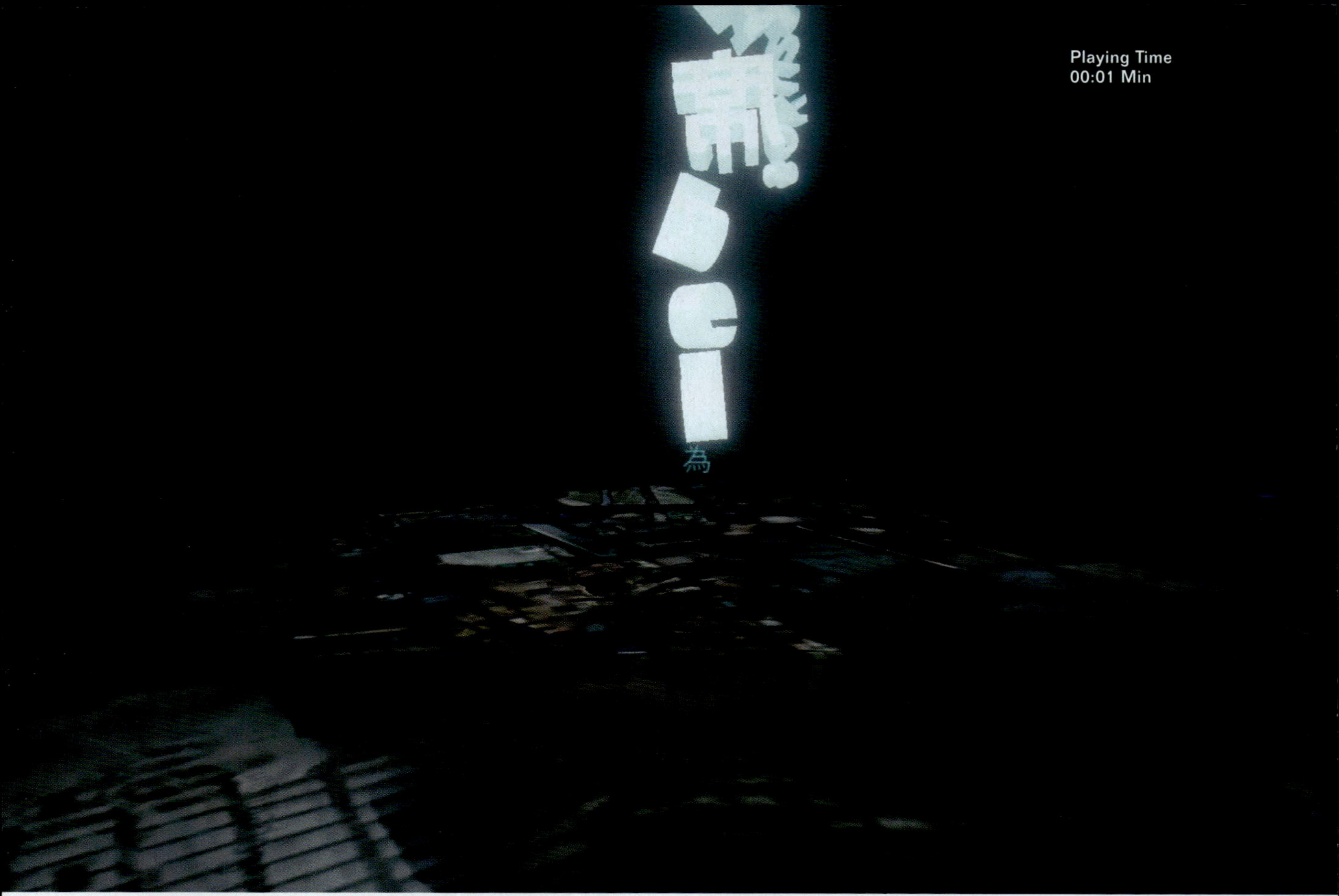
Playing Time
00:01 Min
為

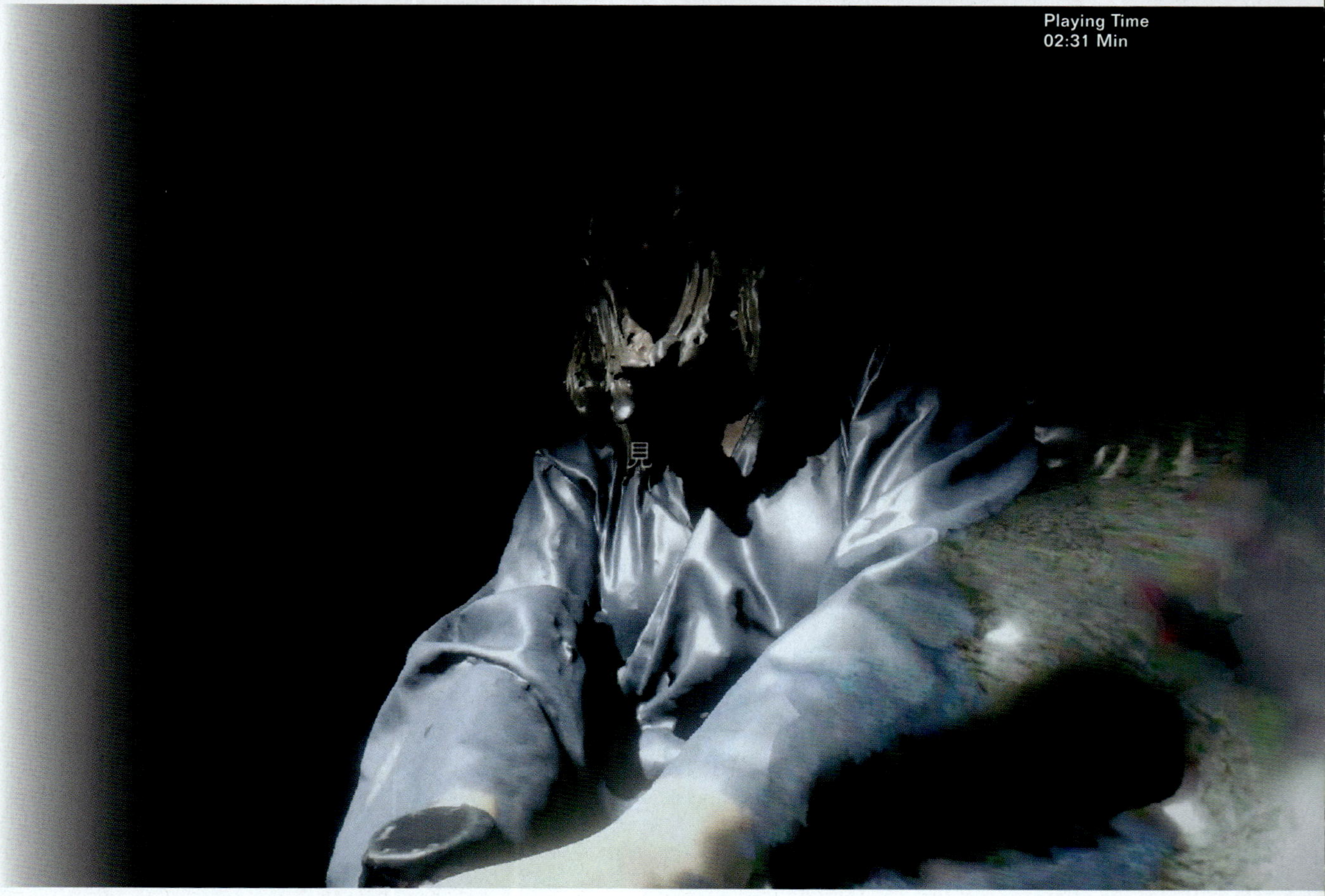
Playing Time
02:31 Min
見

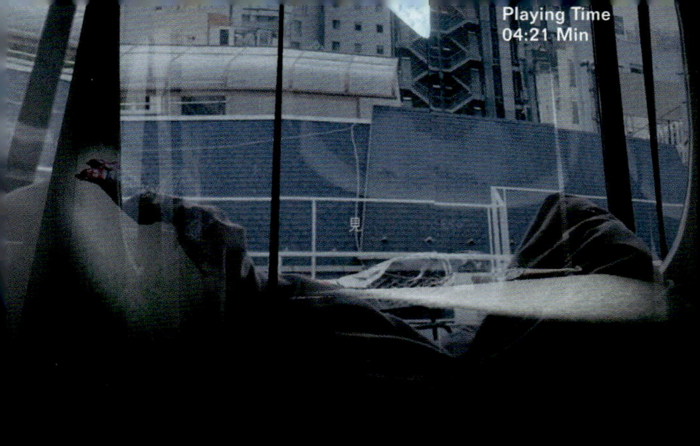

Playing Time
04:21 Min

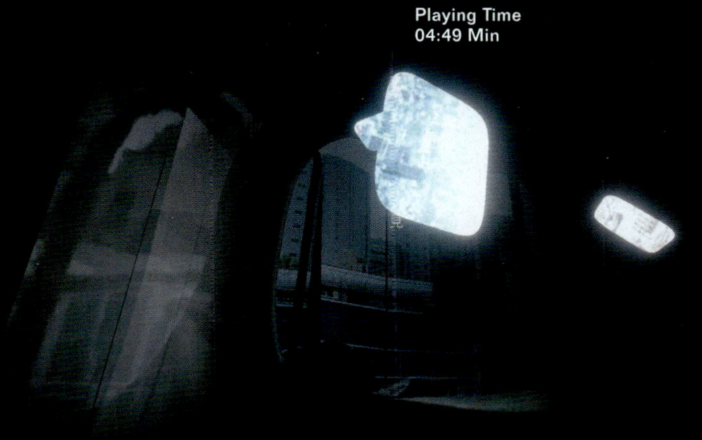

Playing Time
04:49 Min

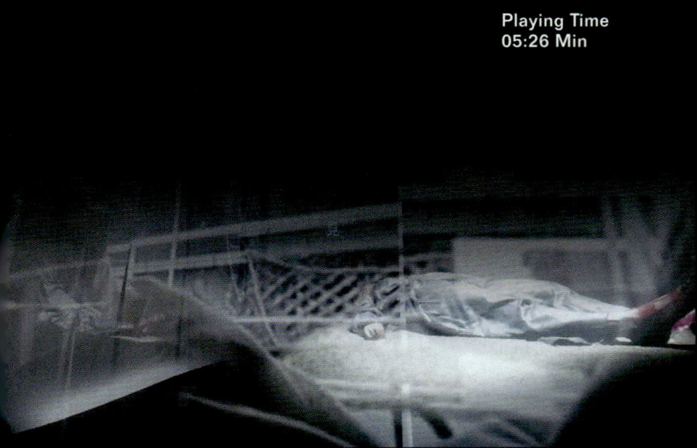

Playing Time
05:26 Min

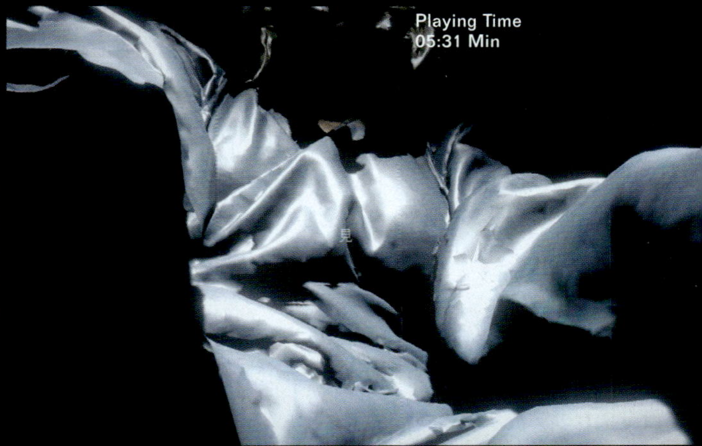

Playing Time
05:31 Min

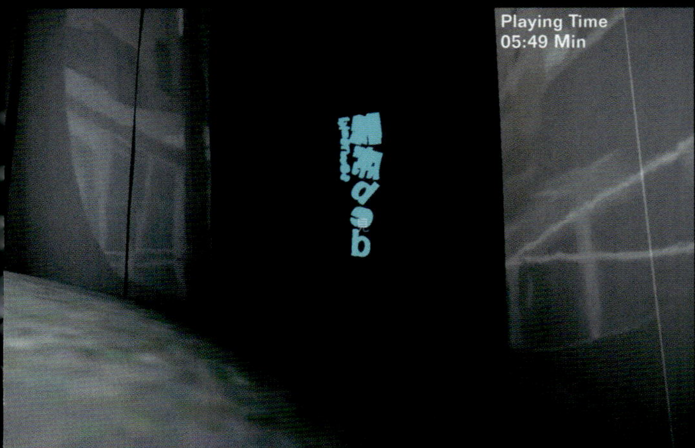

Playing Time
05:49 Min

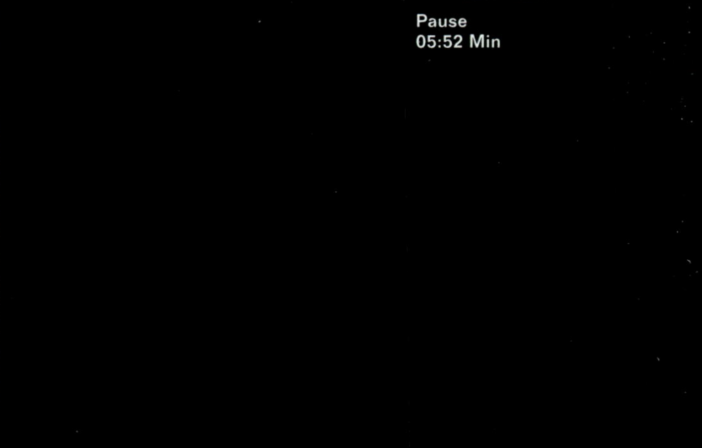

Pause
05:52 Min

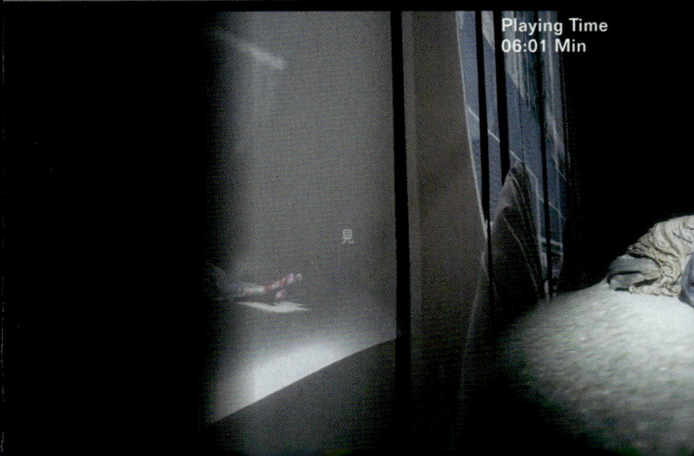

Playing Time
06:01 Min

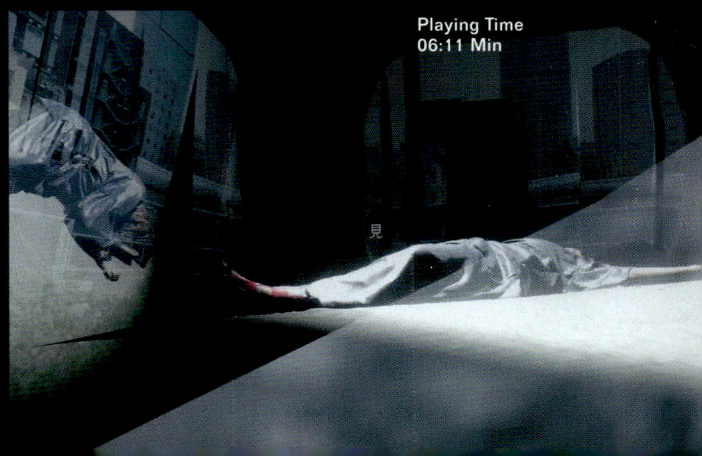

Playing Time
06:11 Min

Pause
06:45 Min

Playing Time
06:47 Min

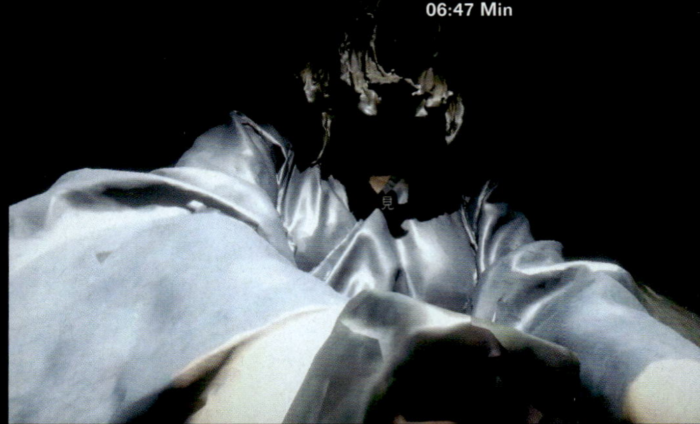

Playing Time
06:50 Min

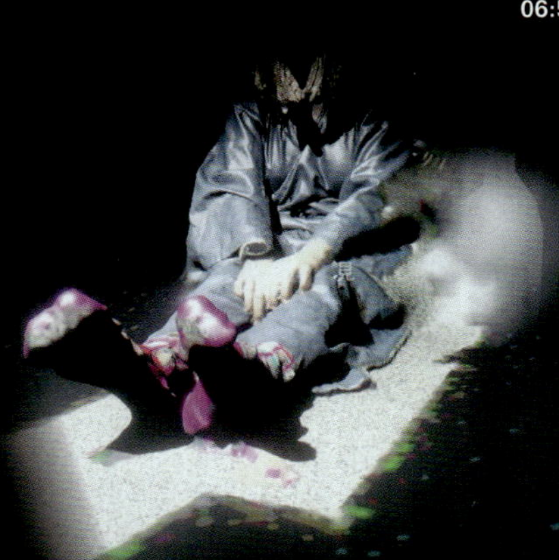

Playing Time
07:00 Min

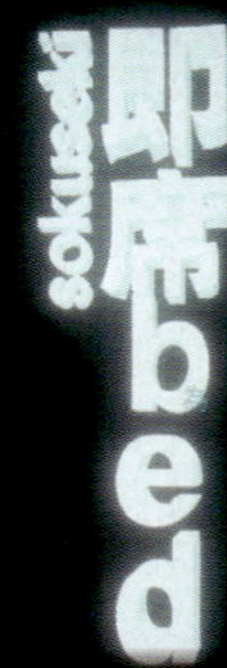

Playing Time
07:06 Min

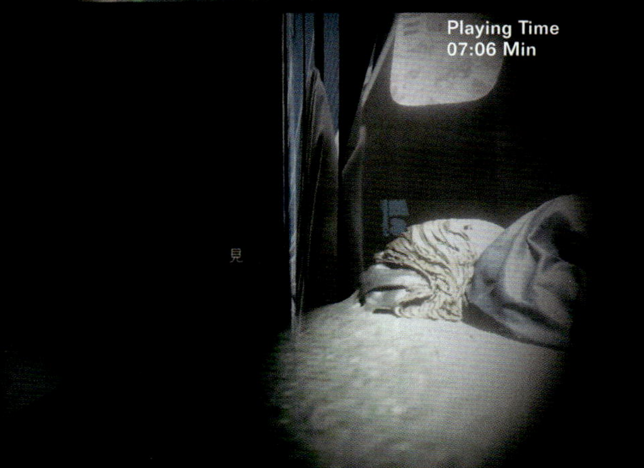

Playing Time
07:06 Min

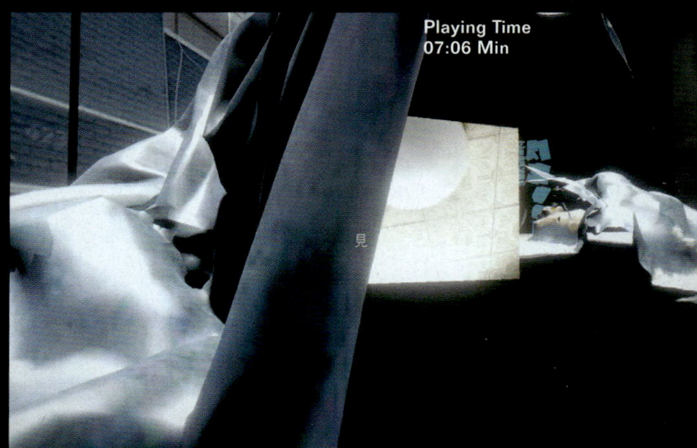

Playing Time
07:15 Min

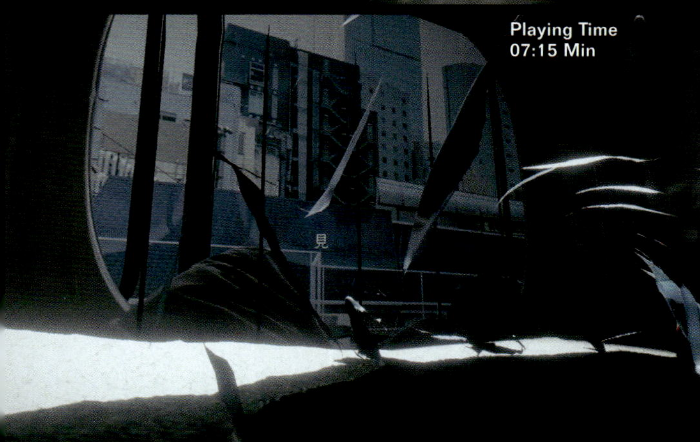

Playing Time
07:58 Min

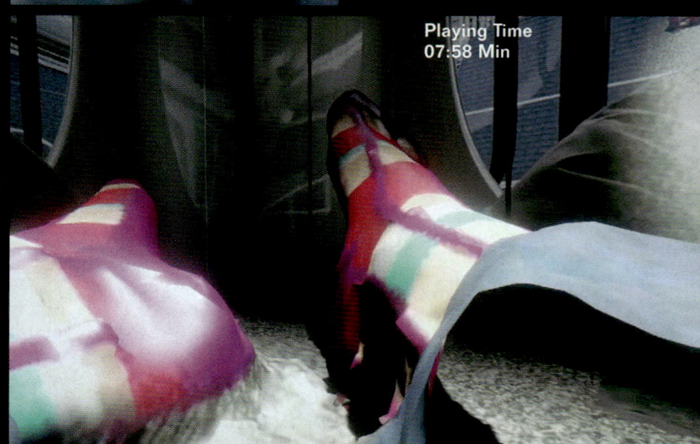

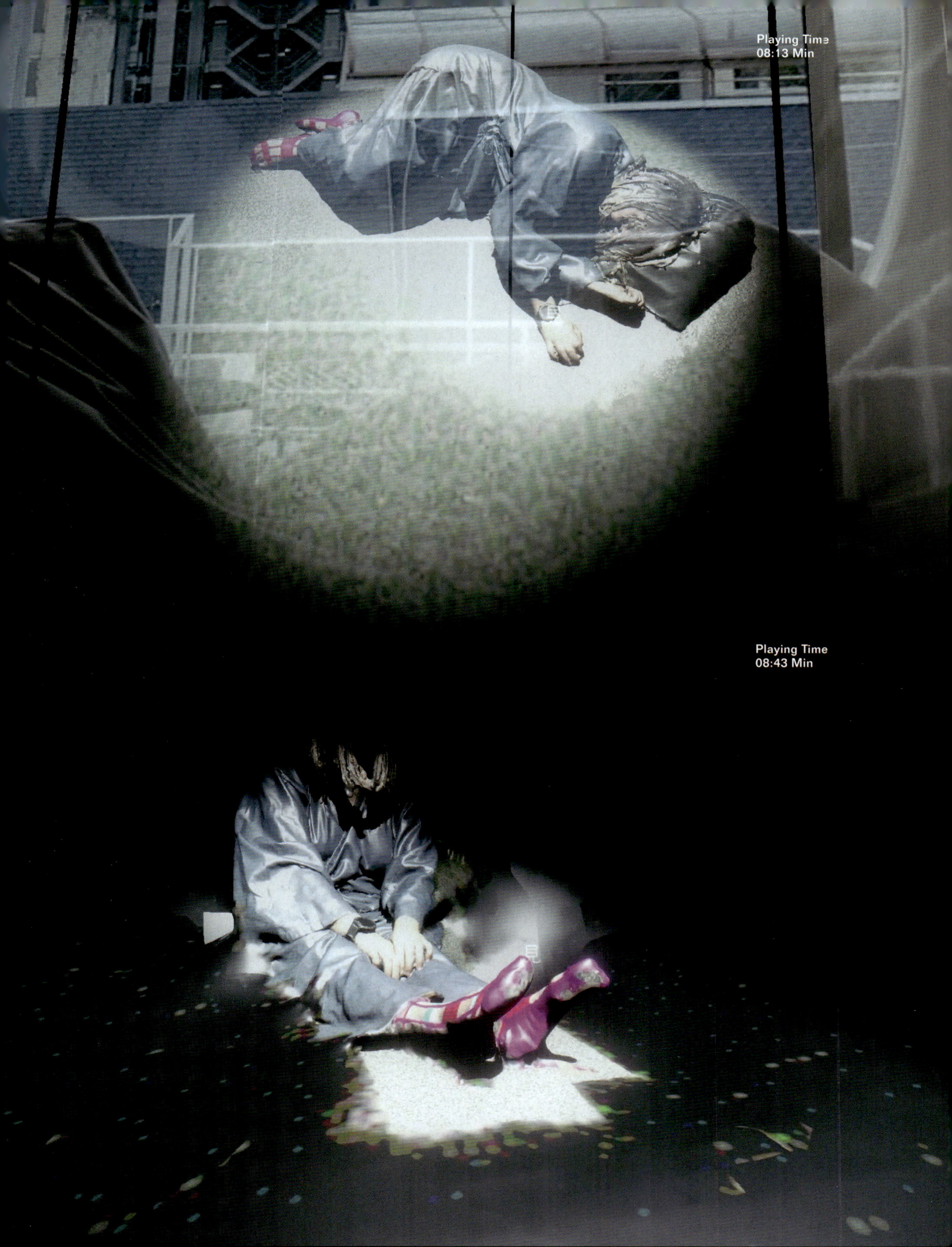

Playing Time
08:13 Min

Playing Time
08:43 Min

Playing Time
08:01 Min

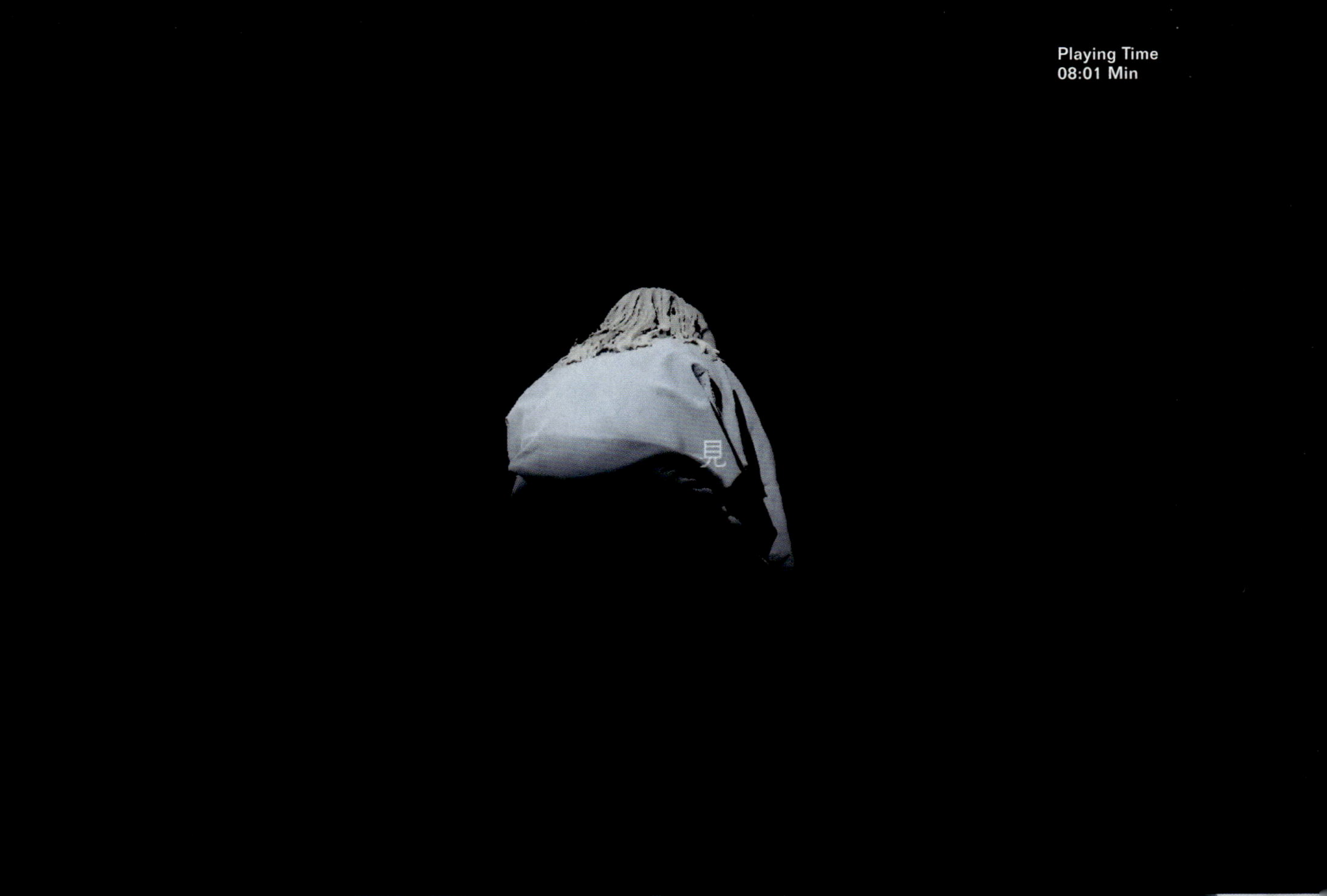

Playing Time
09:17 Min

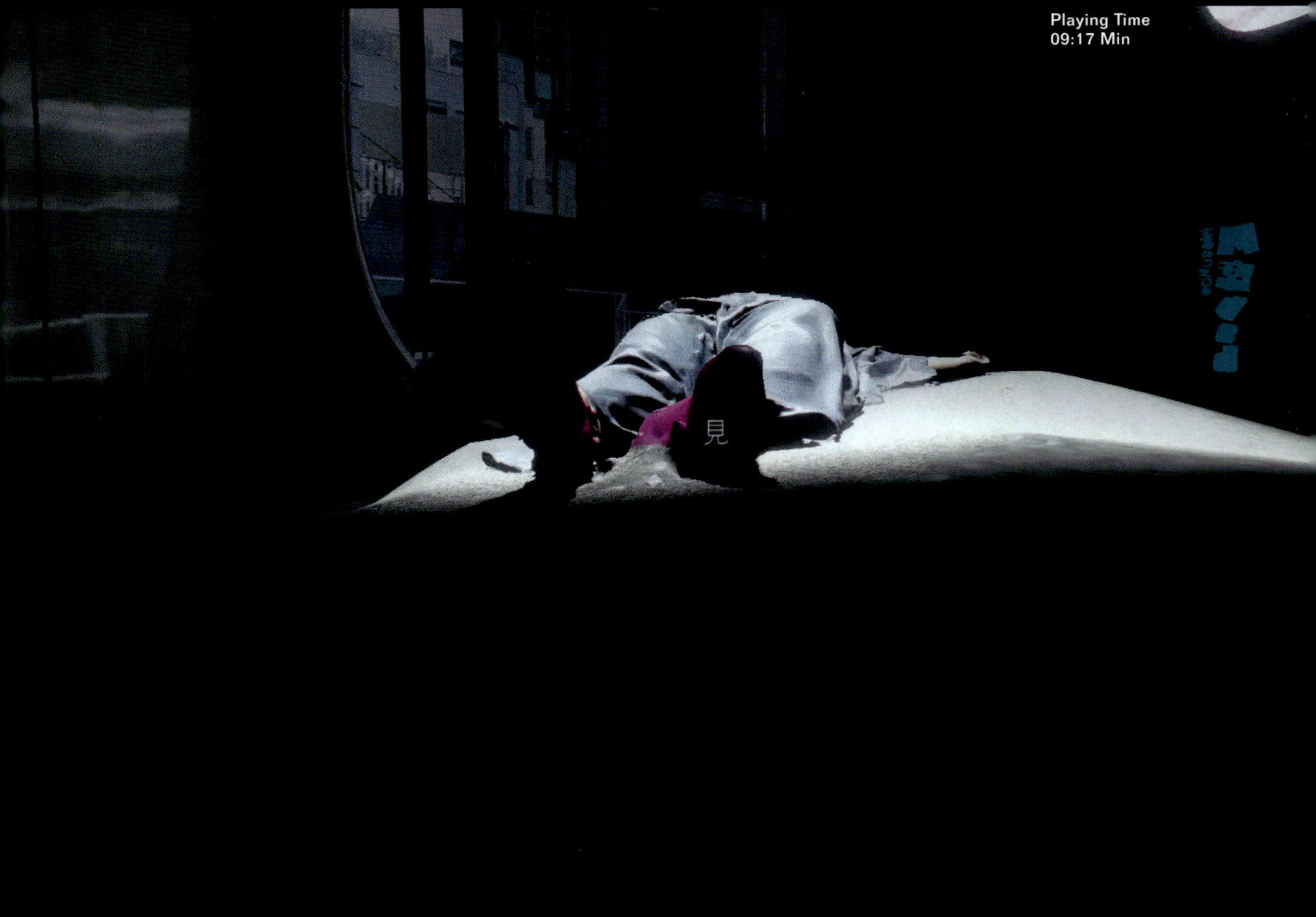

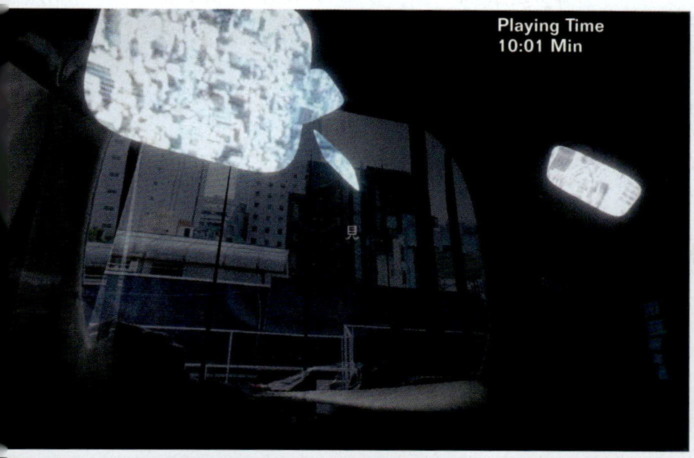
Playing Time
10:01 Min

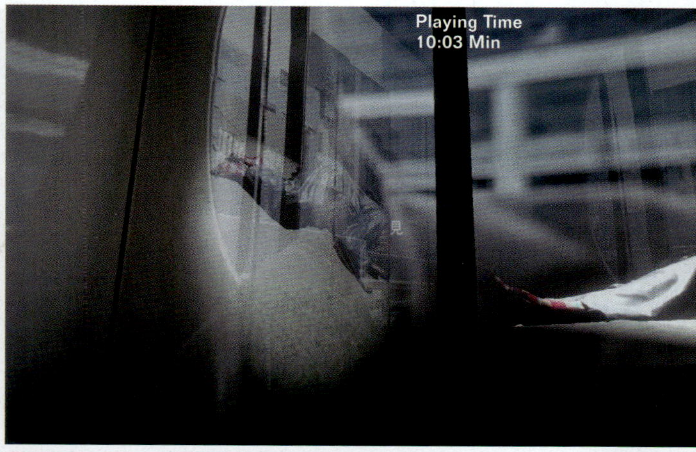
Playing Time
10:03 Min

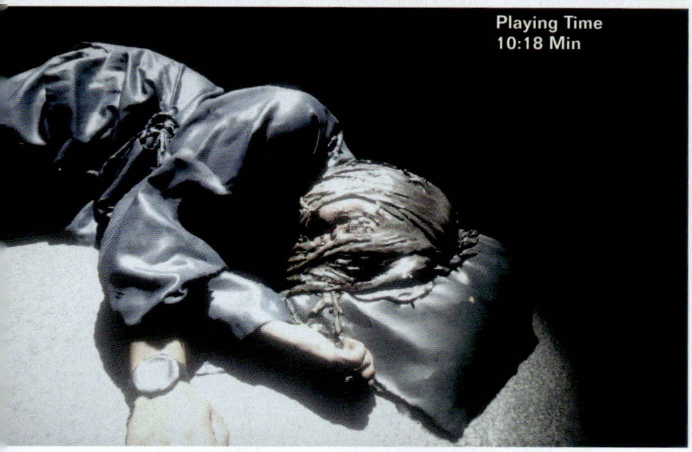
Playing Time
10:18 Min

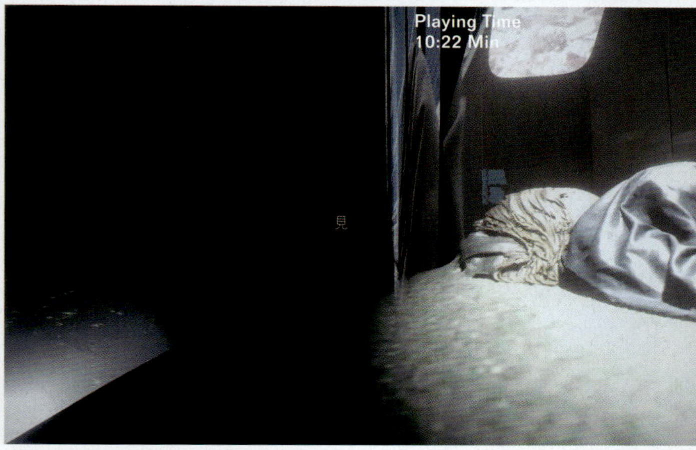
Playing Time
10:22 Min

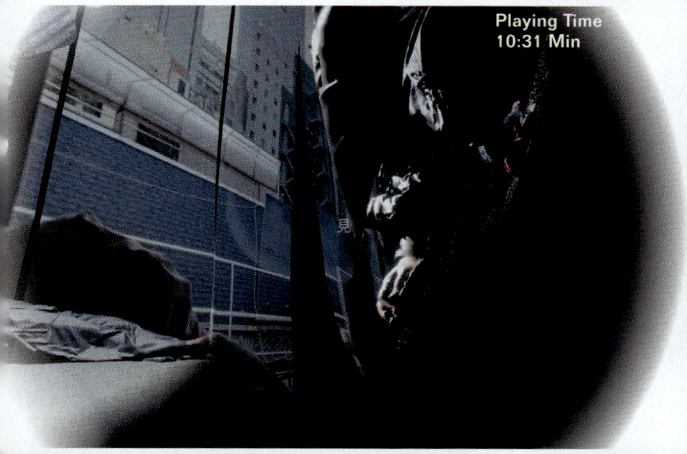
Playing Time
10:31 Min

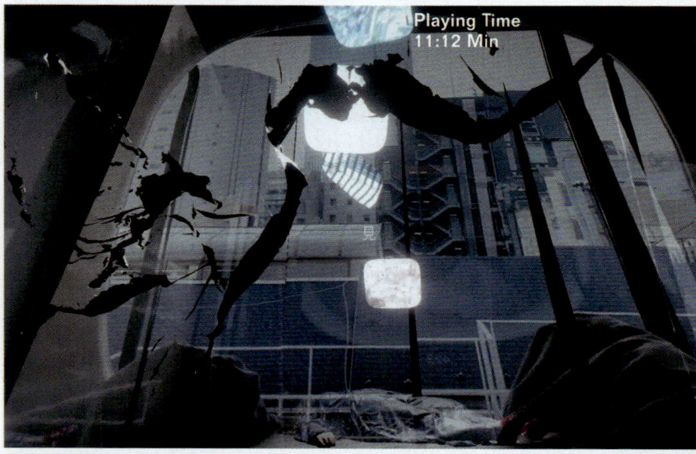
Playing Time
11:12 Min

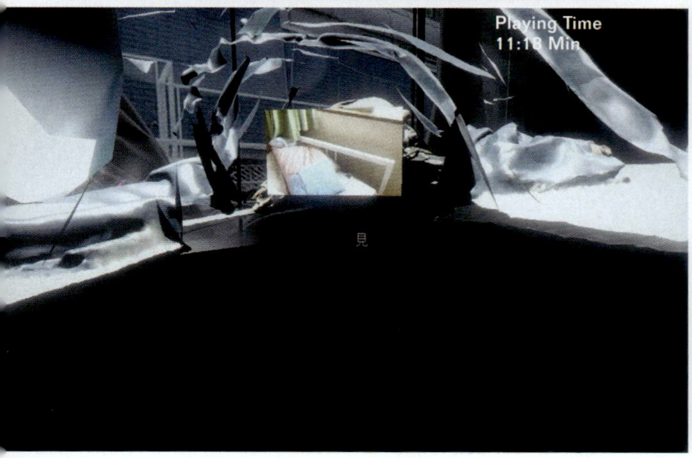
Playing Time

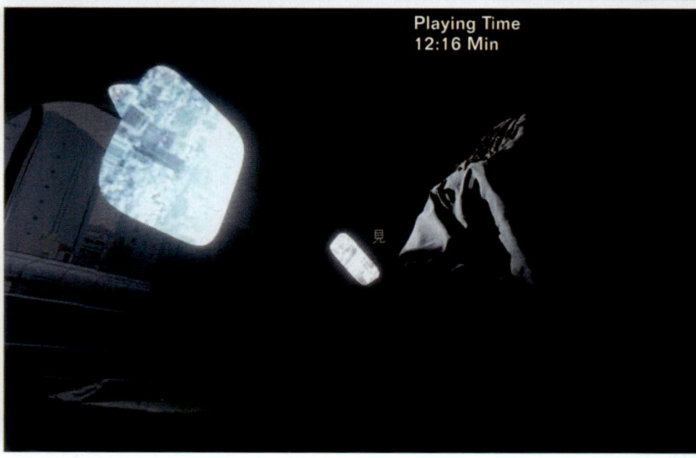
Playing Time
12:16 Min

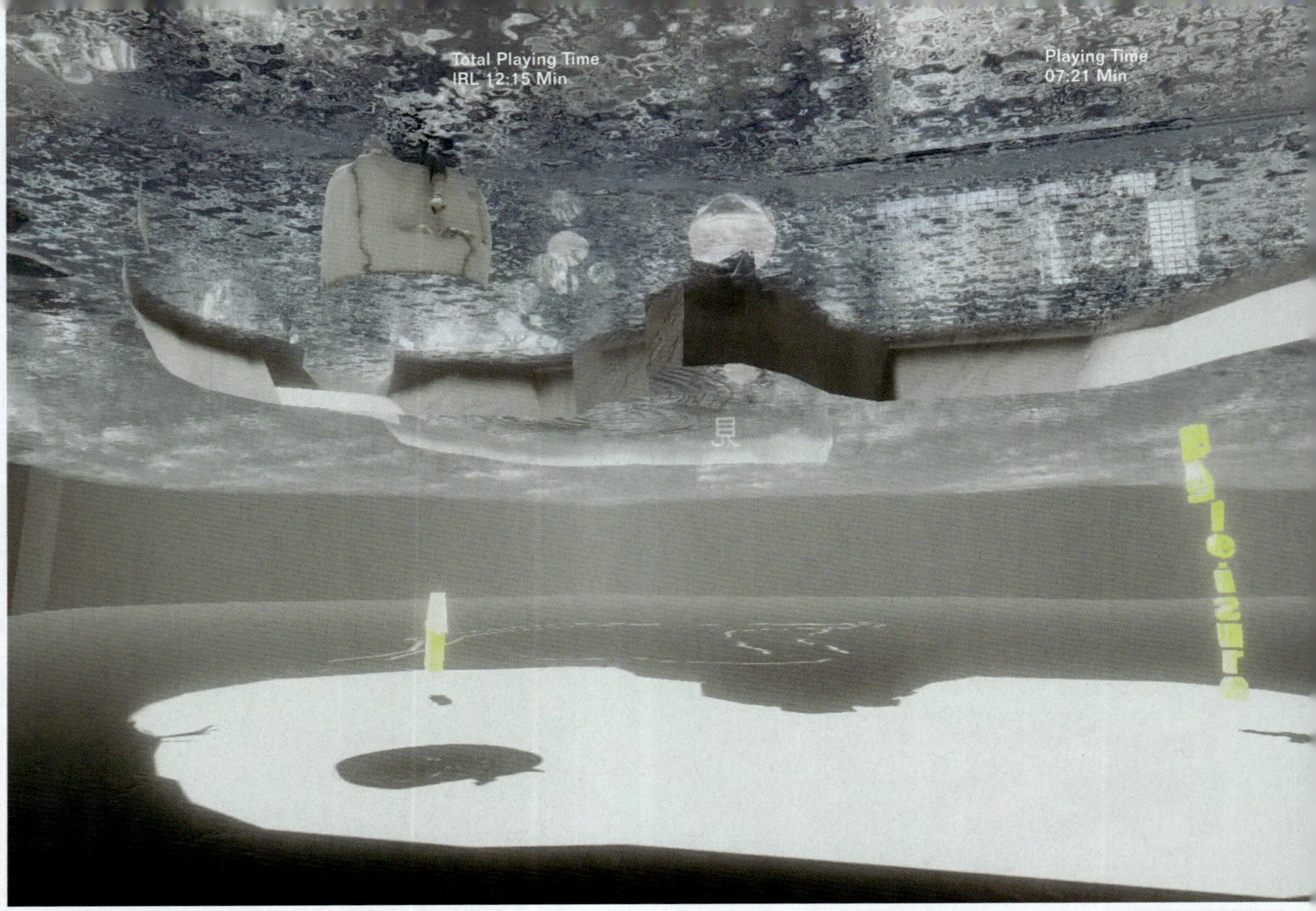

Total Playing Time
IRL 12:15 Min
Playing Time
07:21 Min

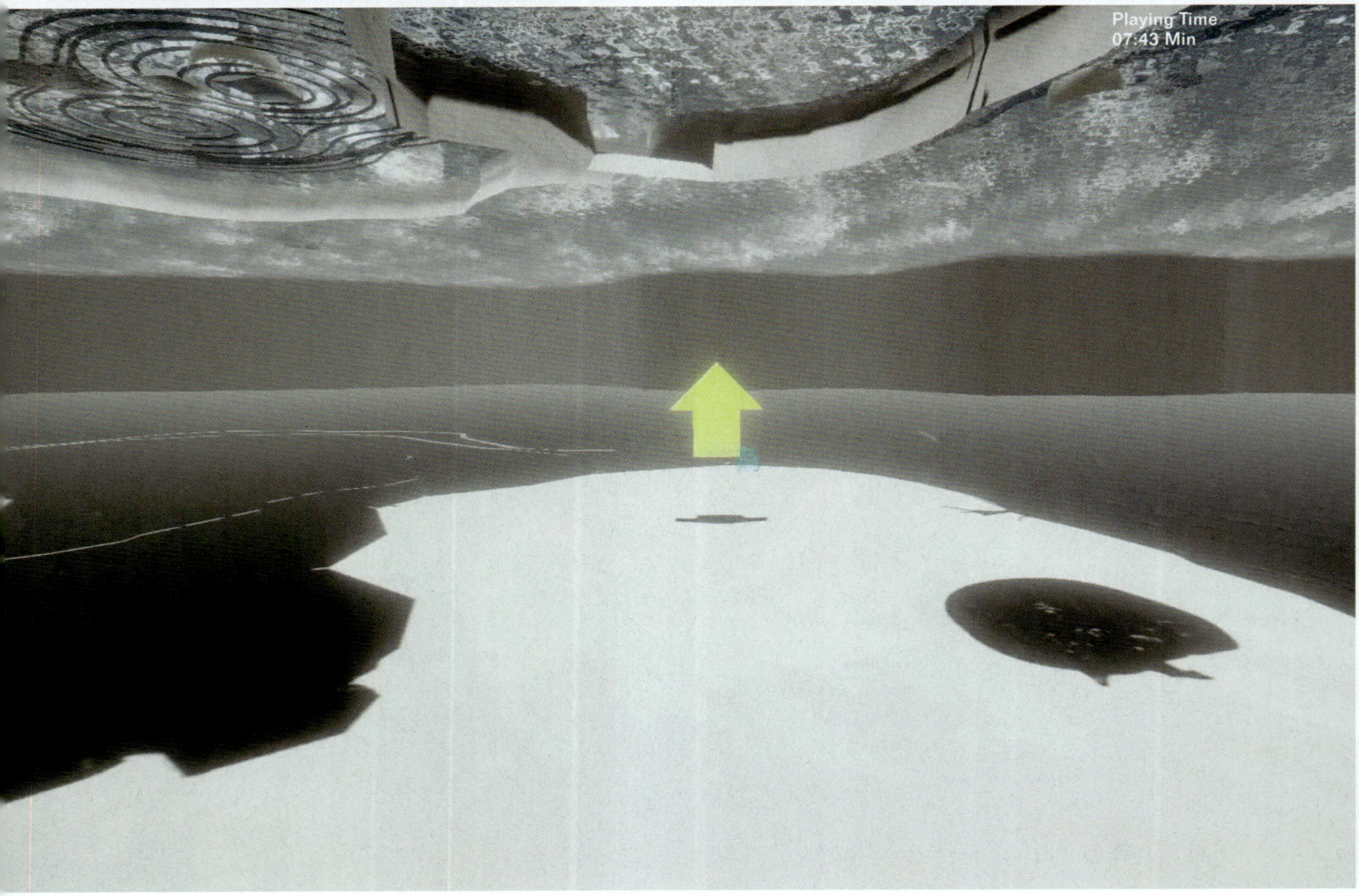

Playing Time
07:43 Min

Play

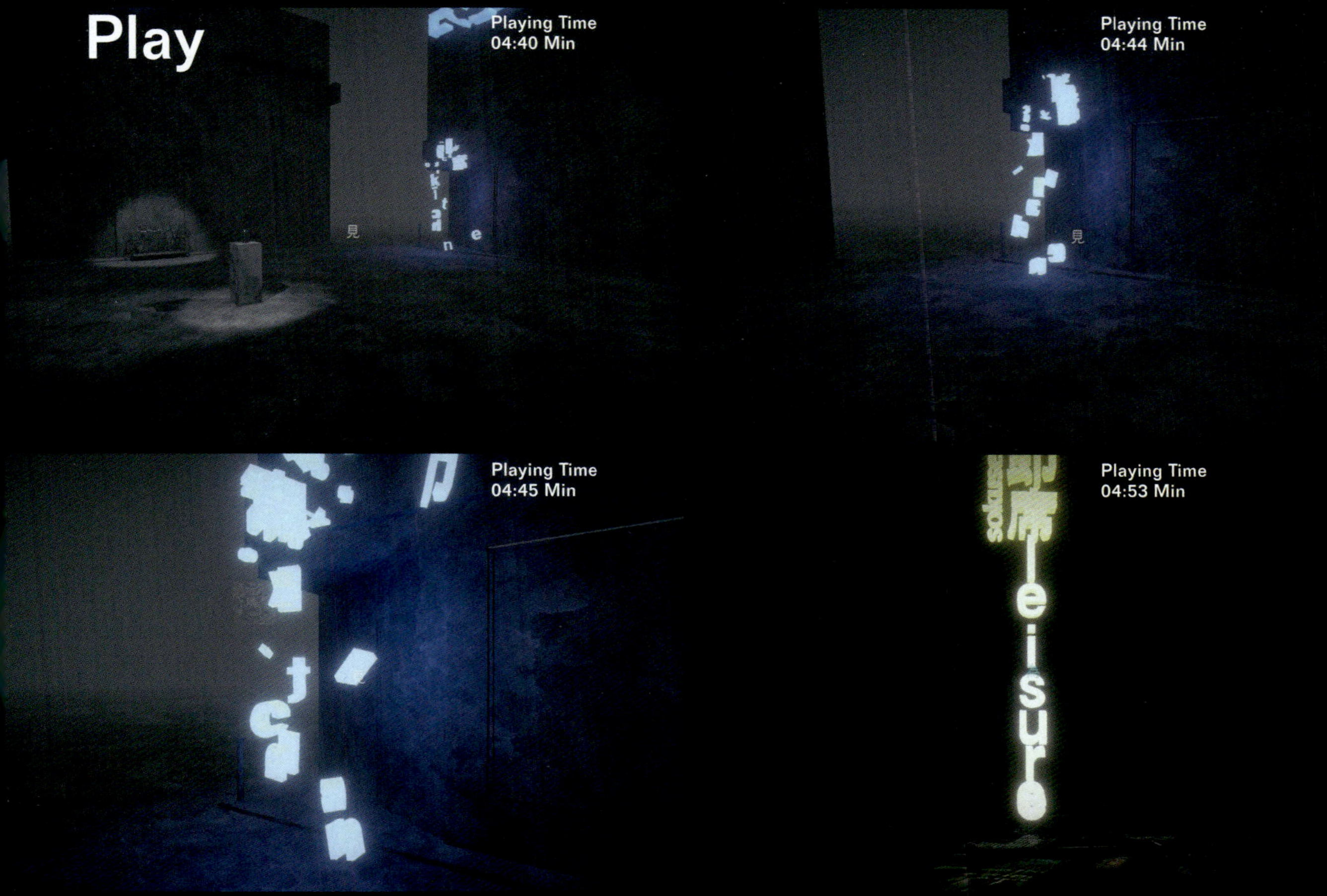
Playing Time
04:40 Min
Playing Time
04:44 Min
Playing Time
04:45 Min
Playing Time
04:53 Min
leisure

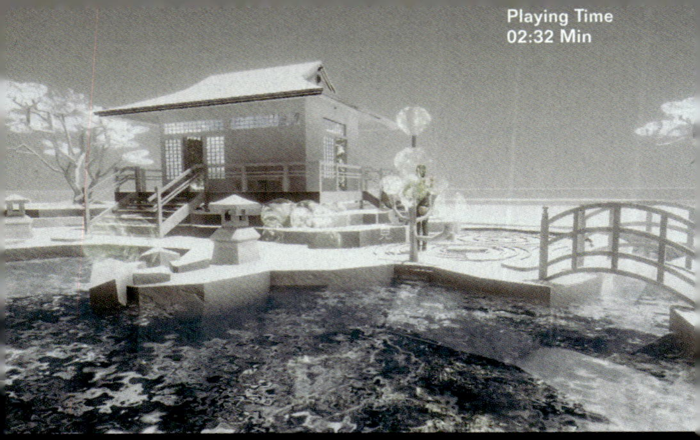
Playing Time
02:32 Min

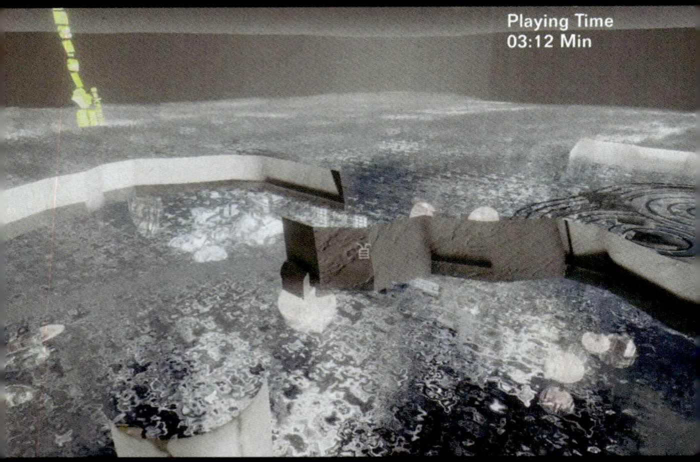
Playing Time
03:12 Min

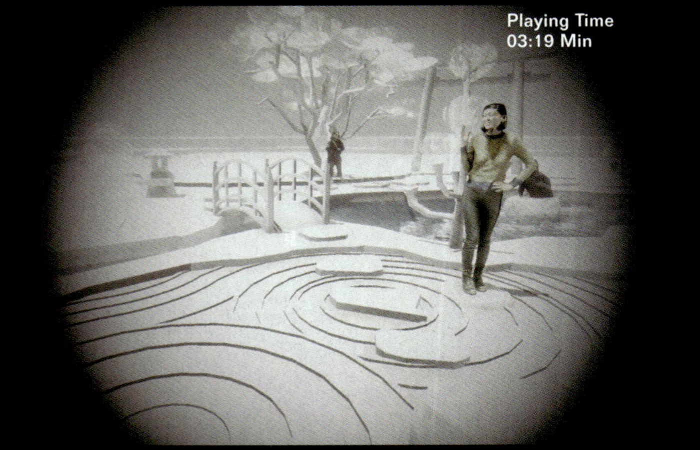
Playing Time
03:19 Min

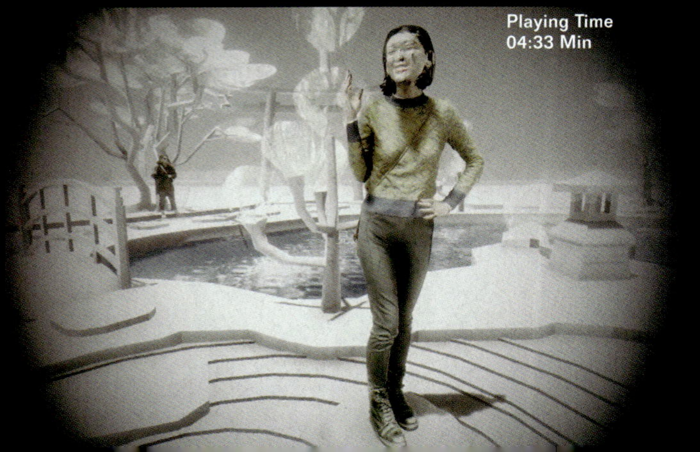
Playing Time
04:33 Min

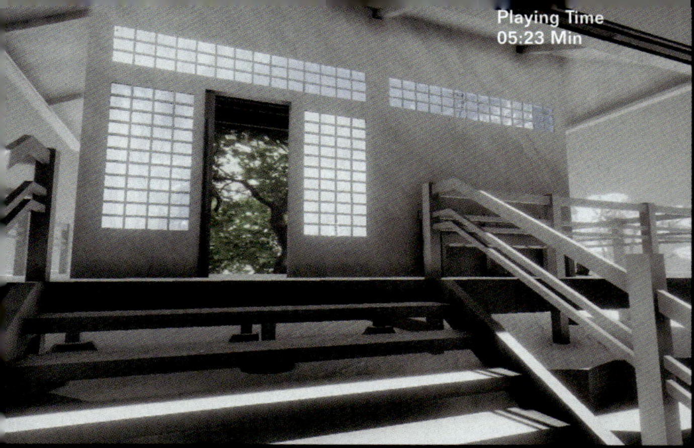
Playing Time
05:23 Min

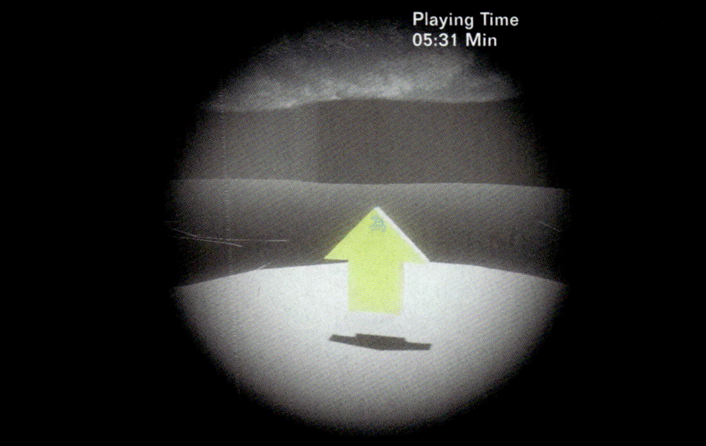
Playing Time
05:31 Min

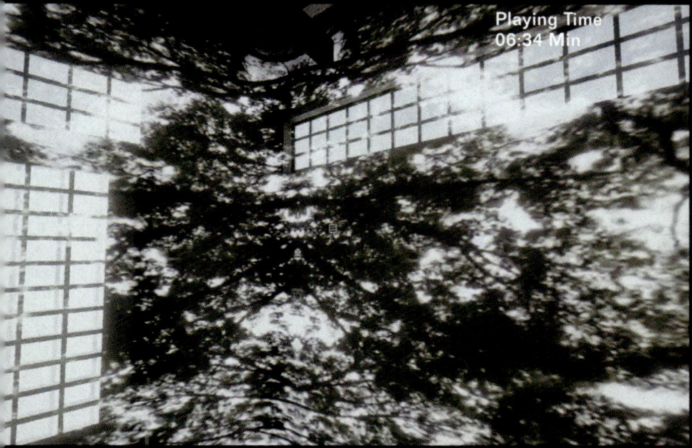
Playing Time
06:34 Min

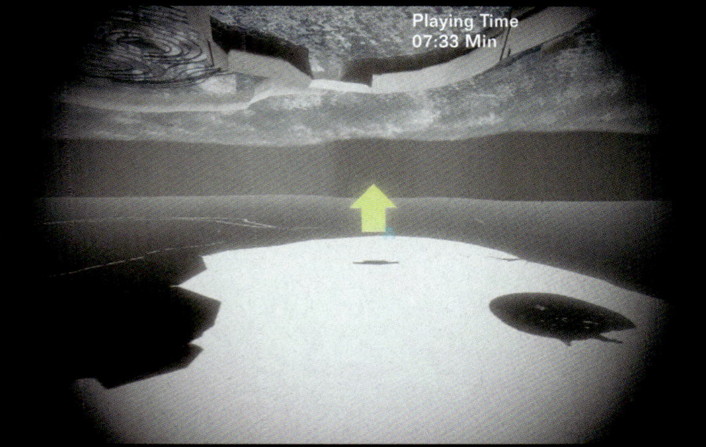
Playing Time
07:33 Min

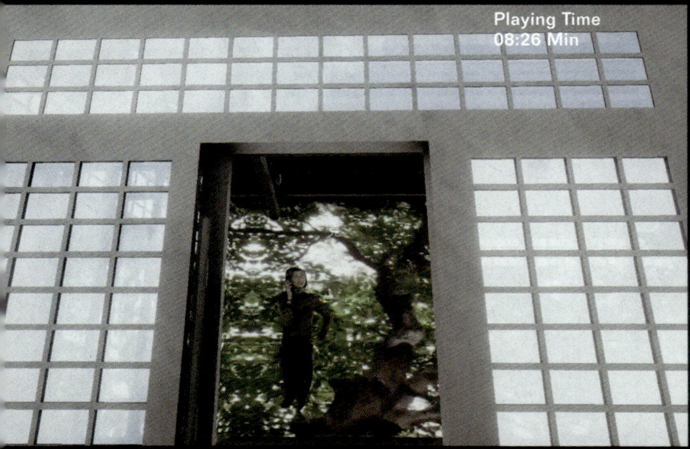
Playing Time
08:26 Min

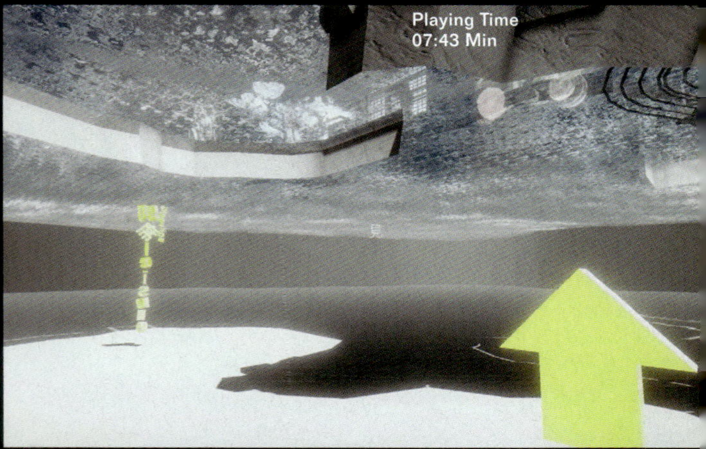
Playing Time
07:43 Min

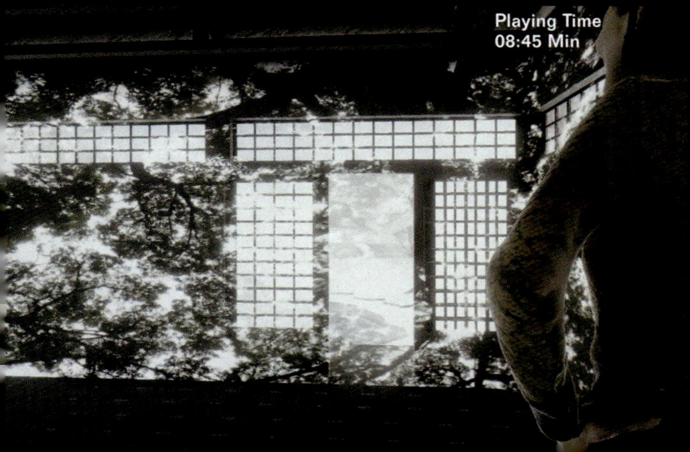
Playing Time
08:45 Min

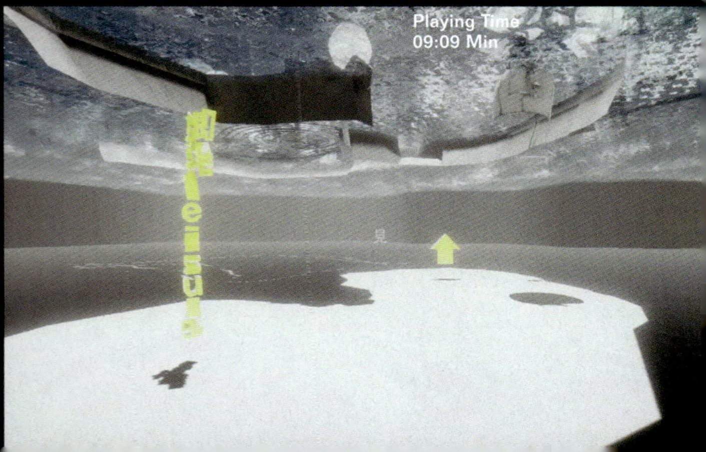
Playing Time
09:09 Min

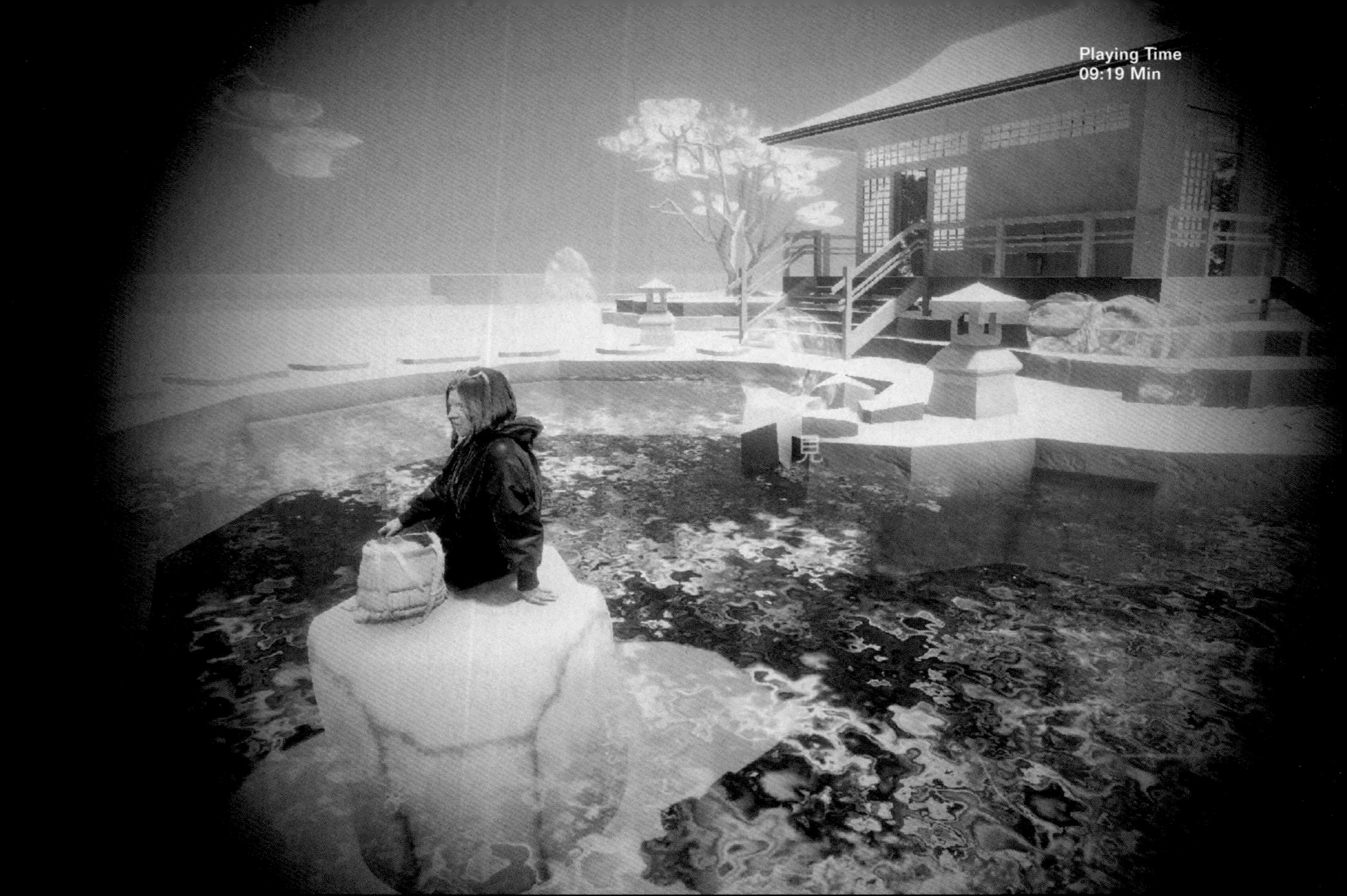
Playing Time
09:19 Min
見

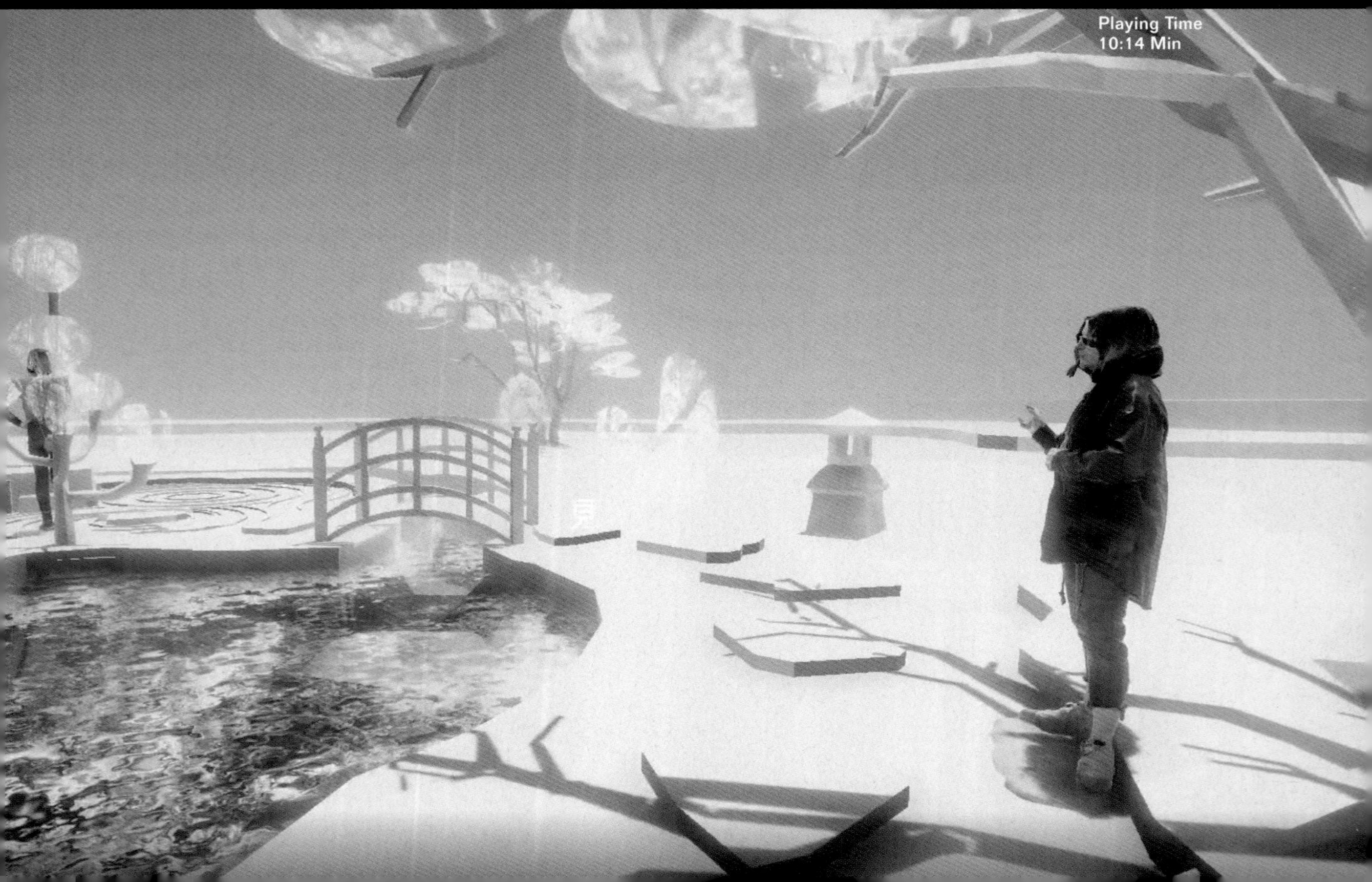
Playing Time
10:14 Min

Pause
10:15 Min

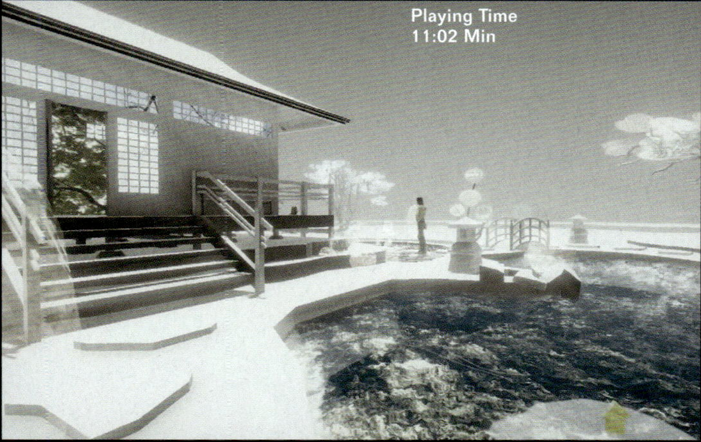

Pause
11:49 Min

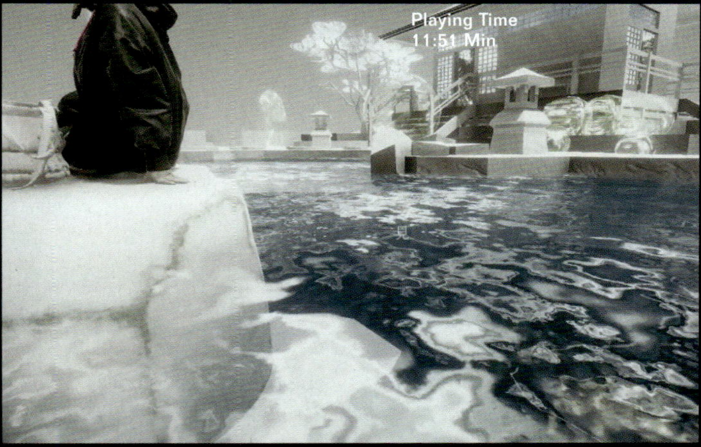

Pause
11:52 Min

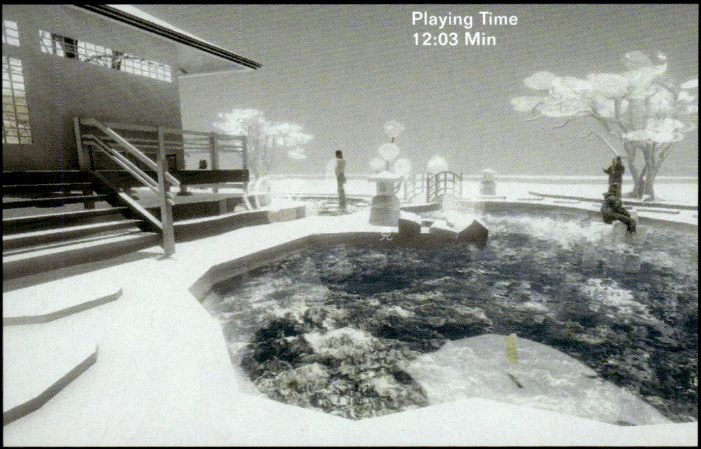

Pause
12:04 Min

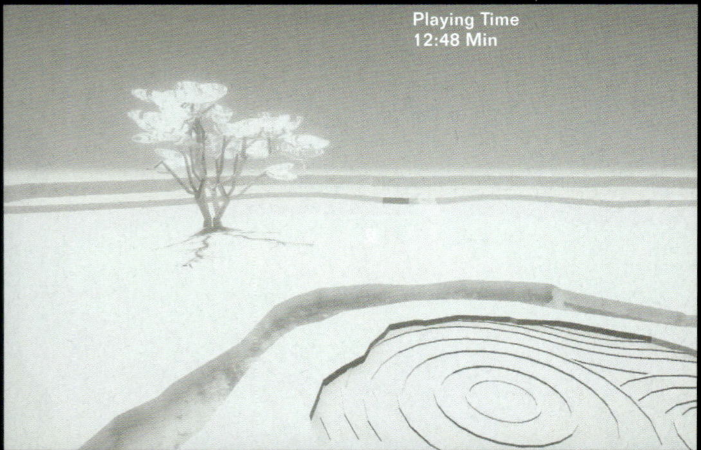

Ab
DOM
To
Itos

Part II

out

UM

yo

ima

DOMUM, TOKYO—ITOSHIMA

DOMUM—The Future of Home after Turbo-Capitalism Crashes is a research project taking place with a three-month fieldwork in Tokyo and the rural area of Itoshima on the island of Kyushu. The project is questioning the new term "digital home," fusing reality with digitality into a new version of "home"—living with Big Data in a protected way to produce a collaborate, collective and inclusive digital living. The project is created at Studio Kura, Itoshima in the framework of a strong collaboration with the Austrian Cultural Forum Tokyo and opens a virtual world that is not a reproduction of reality, but a parallel world fed by memories and data, using new technologies. During a period in rural Japan, Itoshima, Kyushu, personal data will be gathered with an OURA ring device worn by the subject—which is me as an artist, a 33-year-old European woman, Rebecca Merlic living as a digital nomad—to produce a game experience work which can be relived by players in the exhibition. The game scene consists of collected hybrid digital trees and nature from Itoshima combined it with the cityscene of Tokyo. It is a realtime data project creating the game scene based on the data the Oura ring device gathered. The artwork consists of reimagined digital nature, fog and rising sea levels depending on body data from the subject—me. Melting the body with the device and accessing its data use it to produce statements, visual novels, and experiences translated into the immaterial and networked forms of art production and translating the data findings and gathering 3d scans, made by a handheld scanner, to artistically answer the questions of our time about smart power, dataism, biopolitics in a female perspective, emotional capitalism and gamification—exploring new imagery and storytelling in the form of a visual novel about the future of home, focusing on the main narratives. My work is about being at home without being bounded, translating the feeling of home into digital space as a speculative exploration of the possibilities of abolishing known forms of habitation understood as an attempt to possess a certain amount of private space and create a digital space called "home."

It is a collection of frozen moments that are pleasant, unpleasant, scary, powerful, boring, interesting, or fascinating. These unique metaworlds, find their own paths where new improvised narratives keep emerging, linking definitions of home and new experimental digital spaces to enable collaborative, collective and inclusive digital living together.

Subjects of a digital nature, spaces of pleasure, spaces for the exchange of emotions and thoughts, orchestrated by data. In Domum, these phenomena are taken up and new dreamlike images, promises and conditions of home are created.

Learning from TheCityAsAHouse, *the project questions the new term of "digital home," fusing reality with digitality into a new version of "home." living with AI in a protected way to produce a collaborate, collective and inclusive digital living. The project is created in the framework of a strong collaboration with Austrian Cultural Forum Tokyo and opens a virtual world that is not a reproduction of reality, but a parallel world fed by memories and data using new technologies. "I will share, confide, and actively participate in activating, motivating and optimizing me, myself and I to critically reflect on the uses of data in creating a master and a slave in my body and mind."*

Project in collaboration with Austrian Cultural Forum Tokyo

Eng
DOM
To
Itos

Part II

gine

IUM

yo

ima

Playing Time
01:20 Min

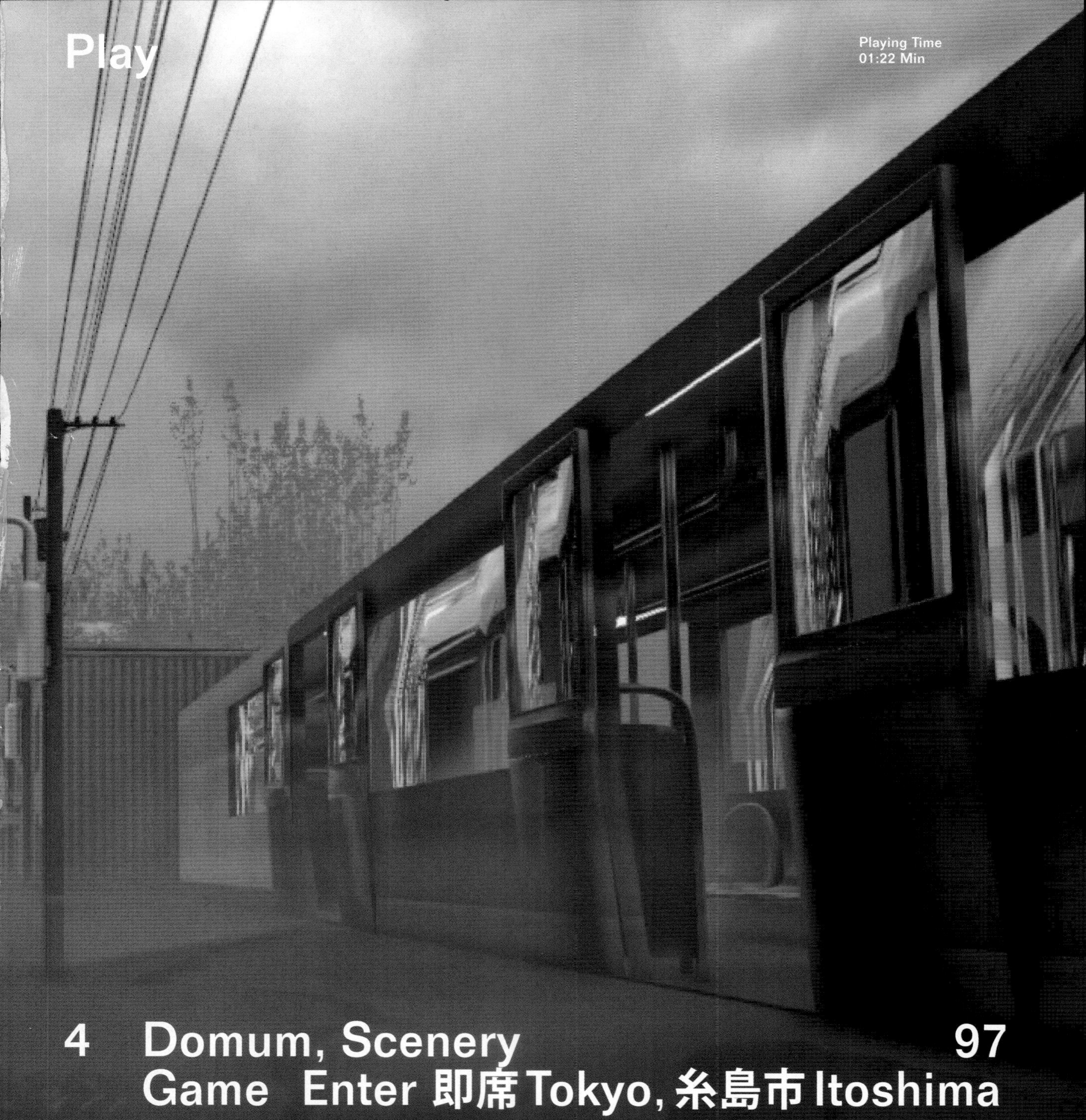

Play

Playing Time
01:22 Min

4 Domum, Scenery
Game Enter 即席 Tokyo, 糸島市 Itoshima

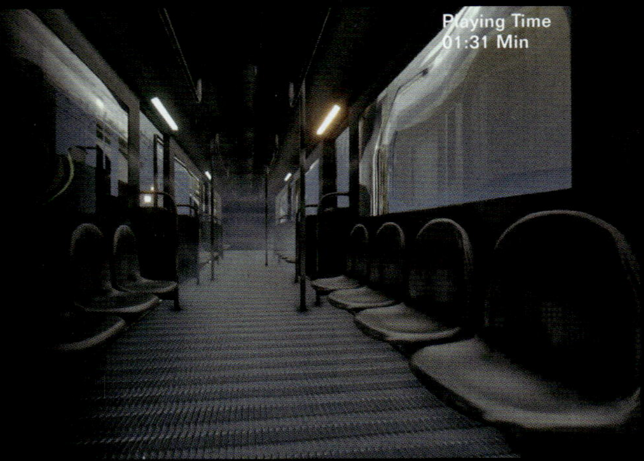
Playing Time
01:31 Min

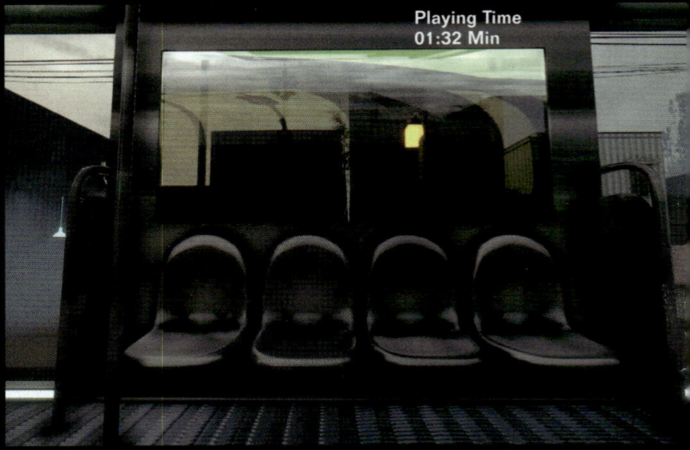
Playing Time
01:32 Min

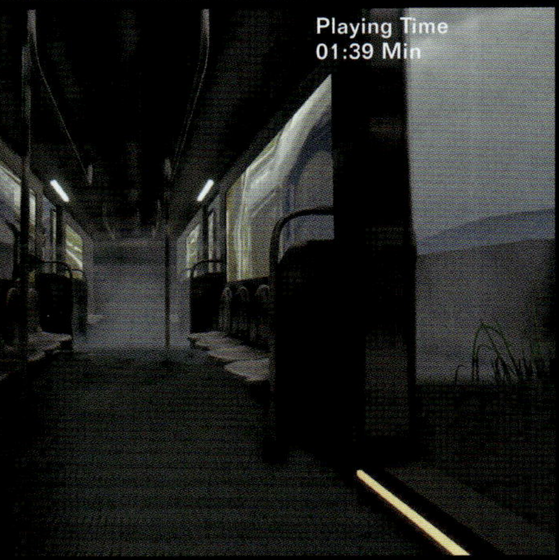
Playing Time
01:39 Min

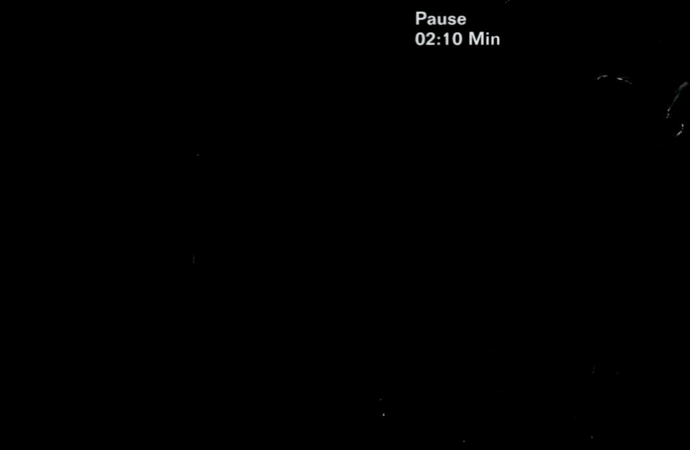
Pause
02:10 Min

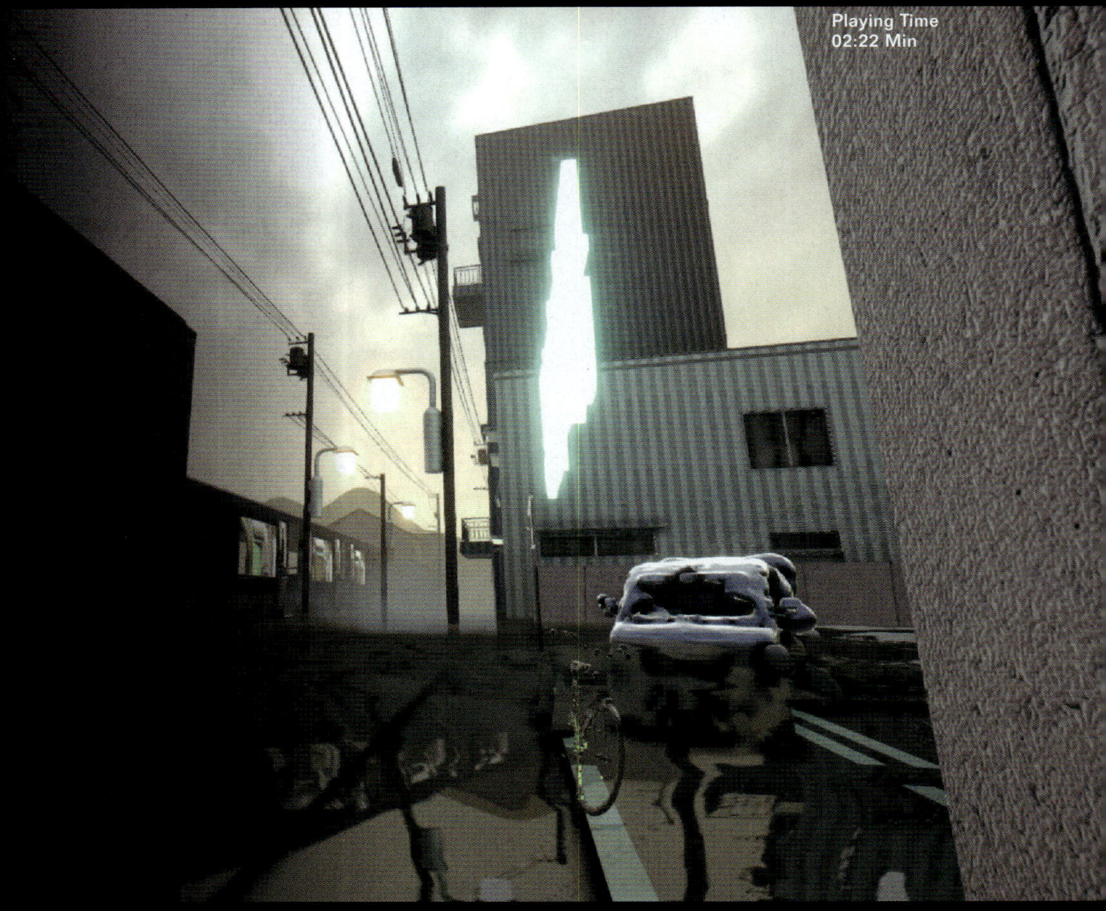
Playing Time
02:22 Min

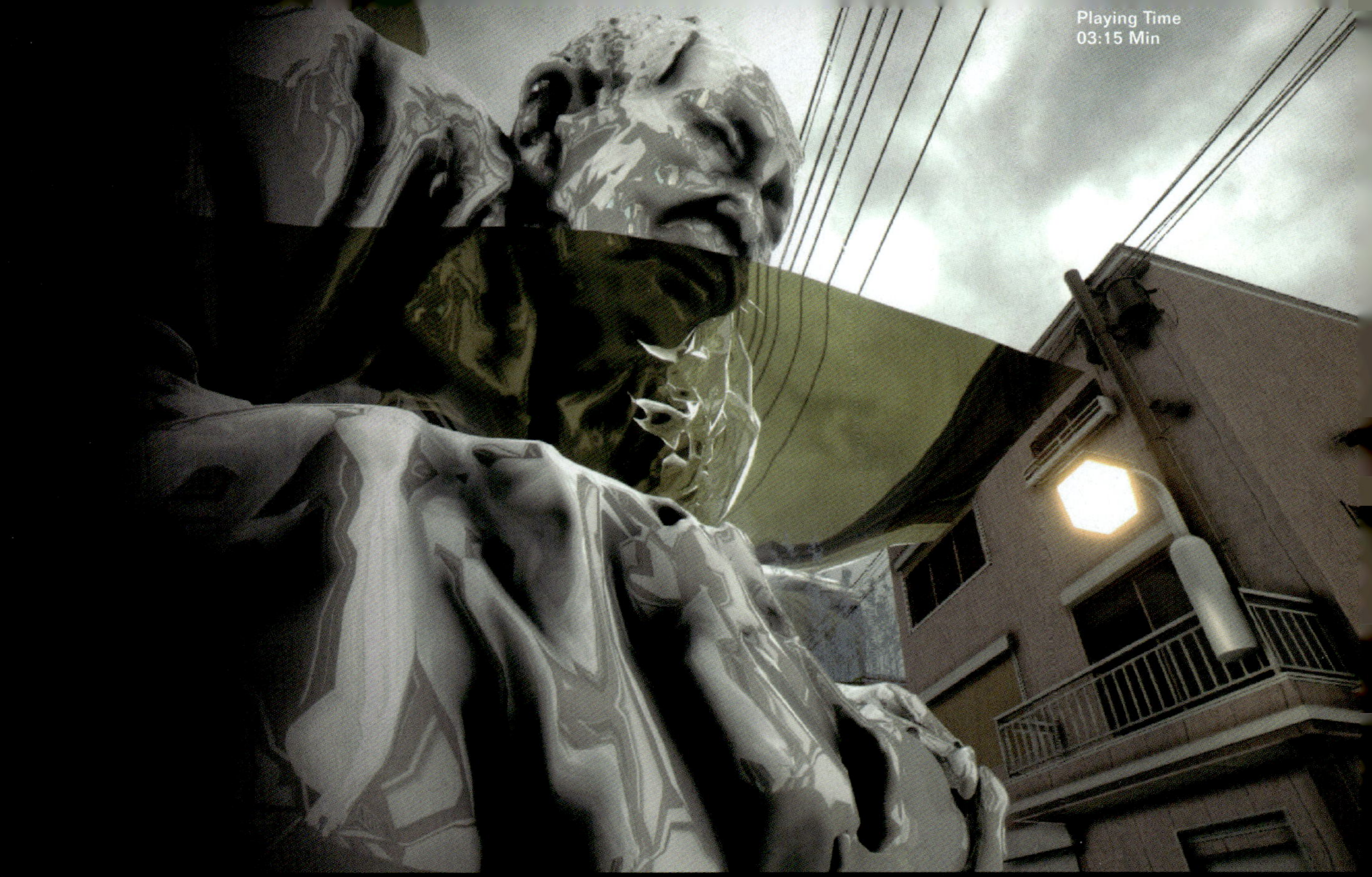
Playing Time
03:15 Min

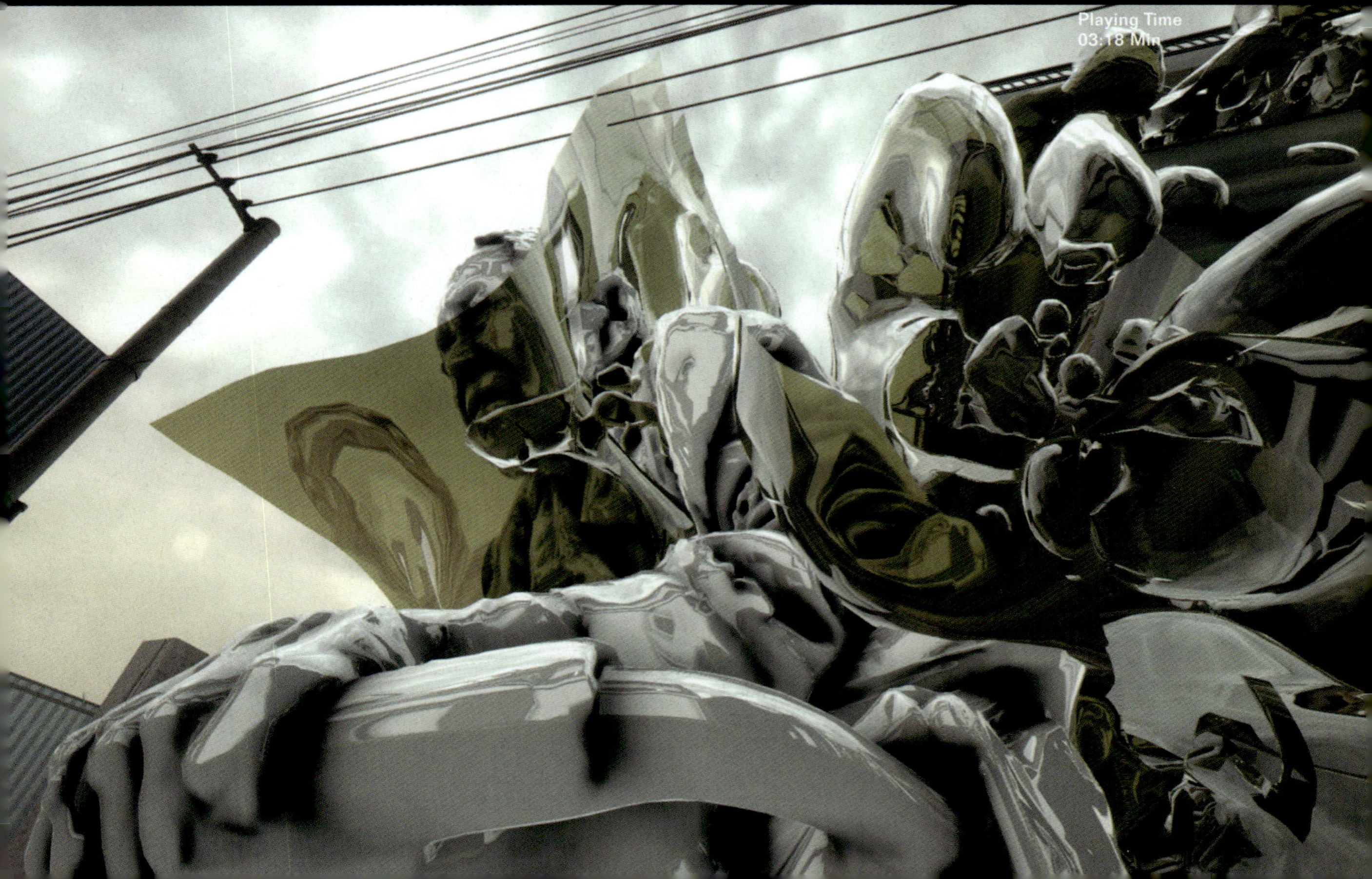
Playing Time
03:18 Min

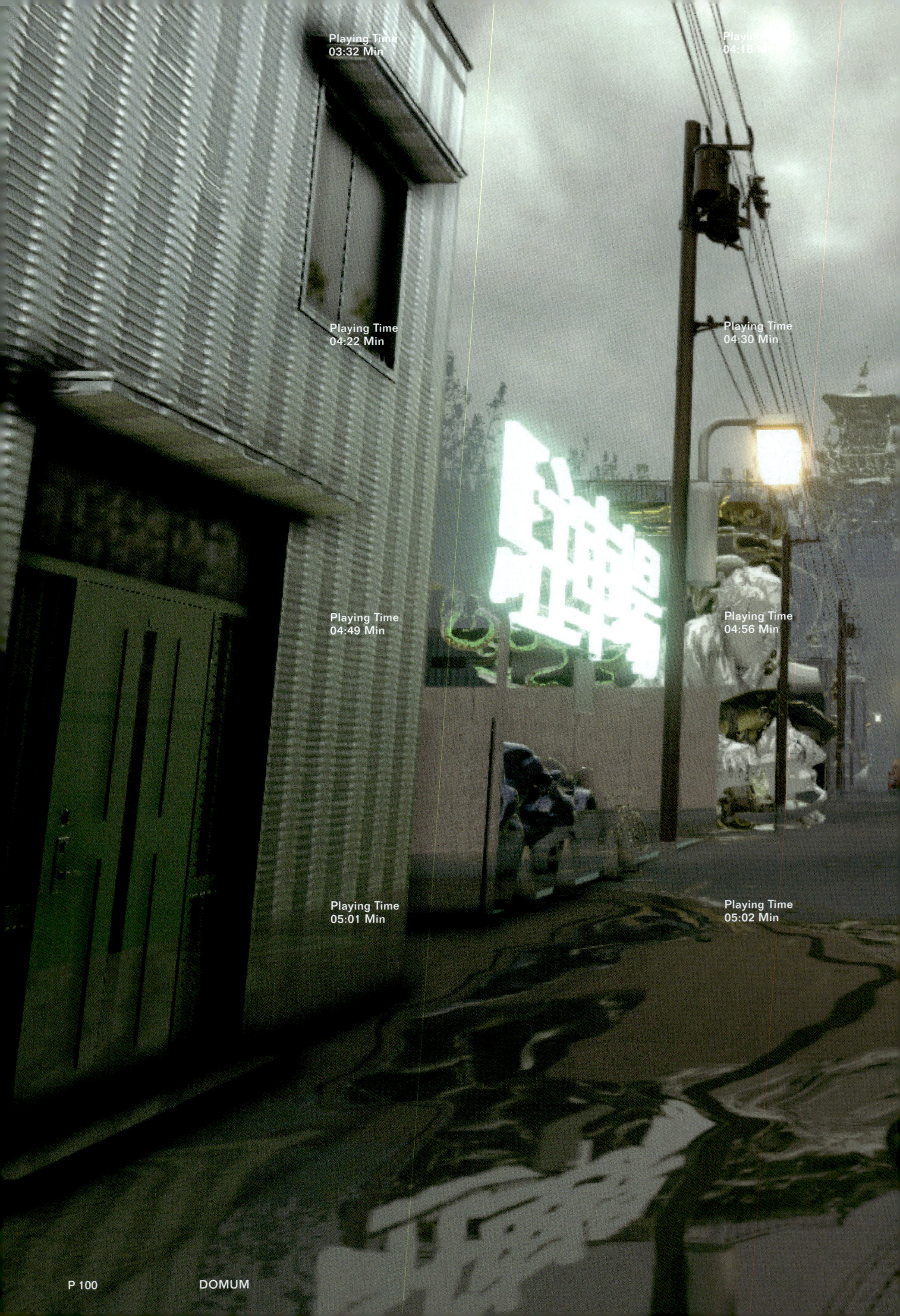
Playing Time
03:32 Min
04:18
Playing Time
04:22 Min
Playing Time
04:30 Min
Playing Time
04:49 Min
Playing Time
04:56 Min
Playing Time
05:01 Min
Playing Time
05:02 Min

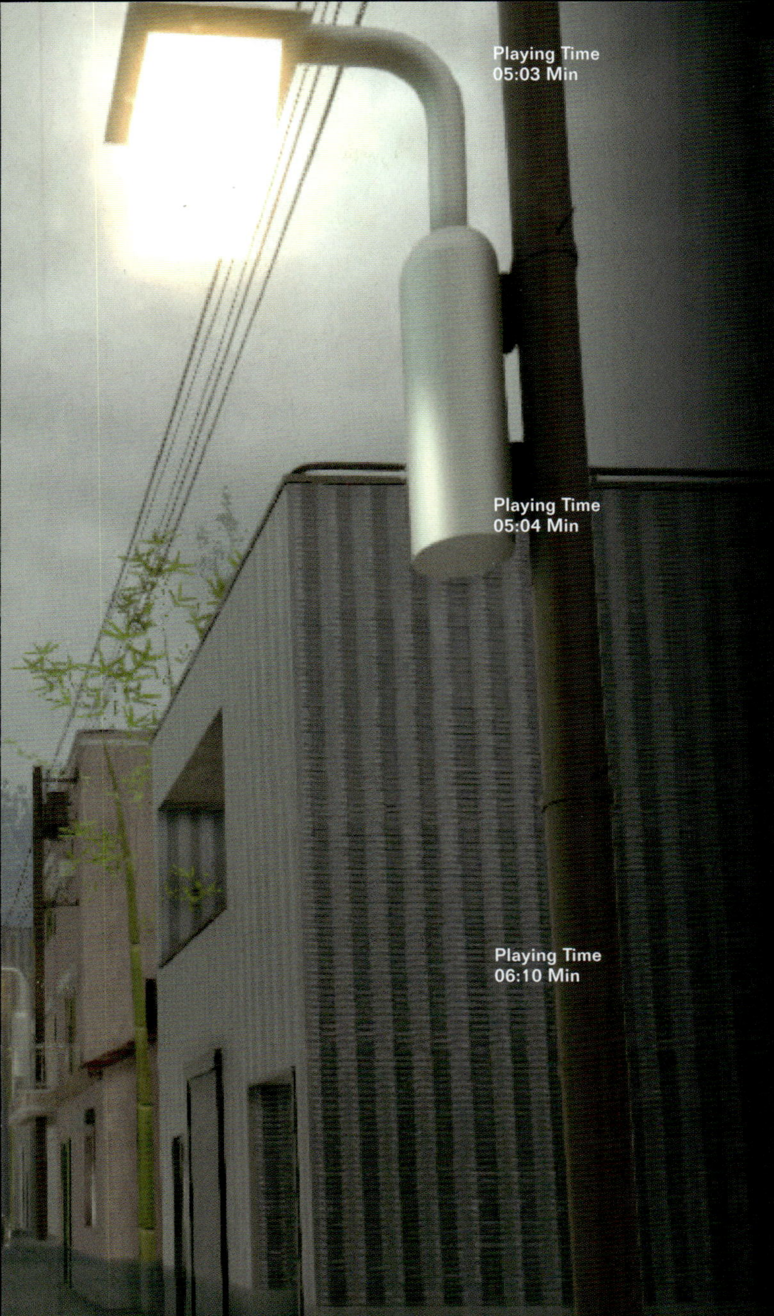

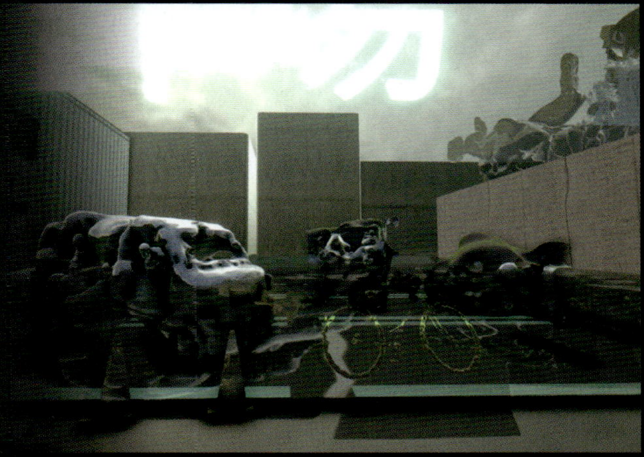

Playing Time
05:03 Min

Playing Time
05:04 Min

Playing Time
05:32 Min

Playing Time
06:10 Min

Pause
06:16 Min

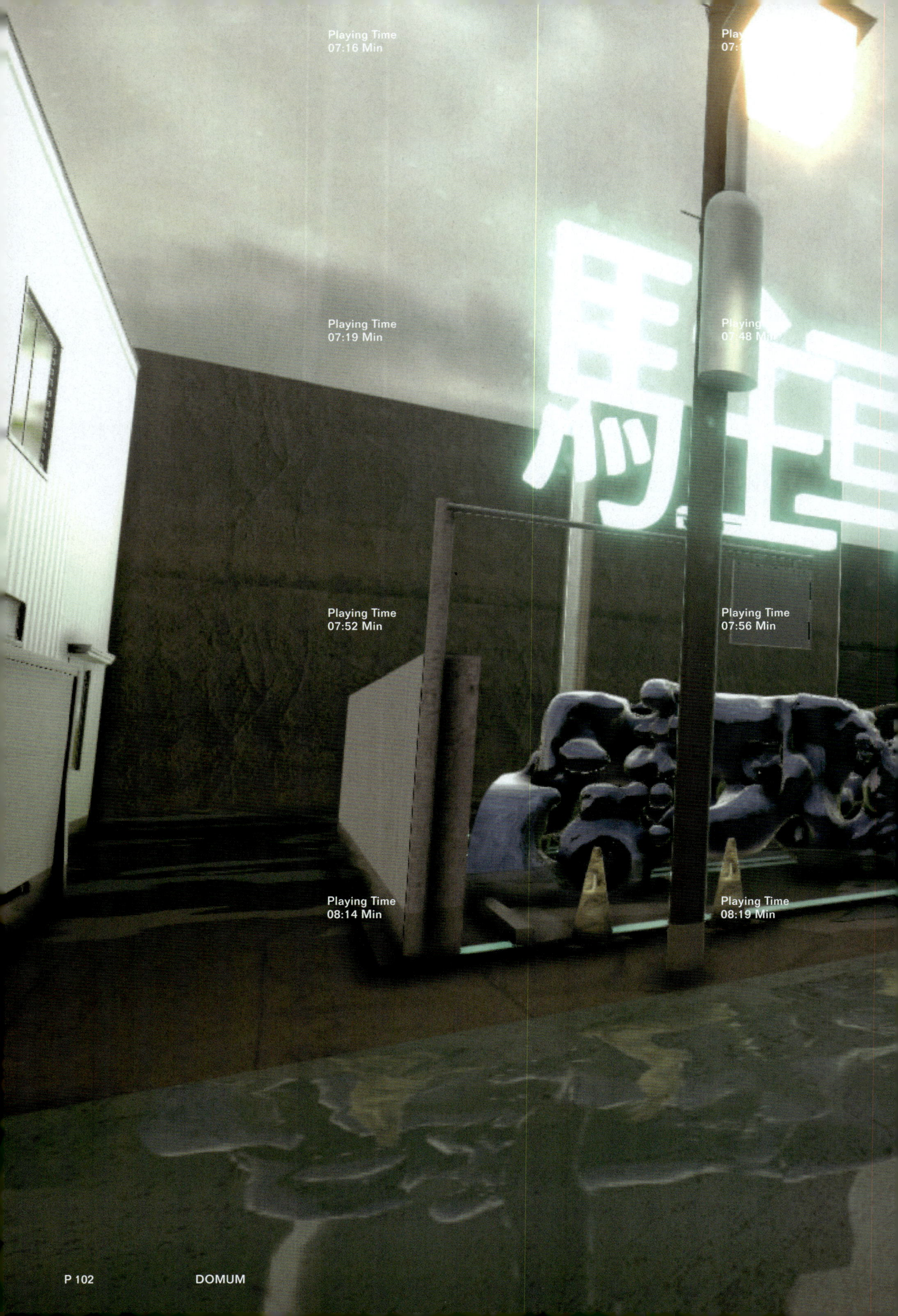
Playing Time
07:16 Min
Playing Time
07:19 Min
Playing Time
07:52 Min
Playing Time
07:56 Min
Playing Time
08:14 Min
Playing Time
08:19 Min

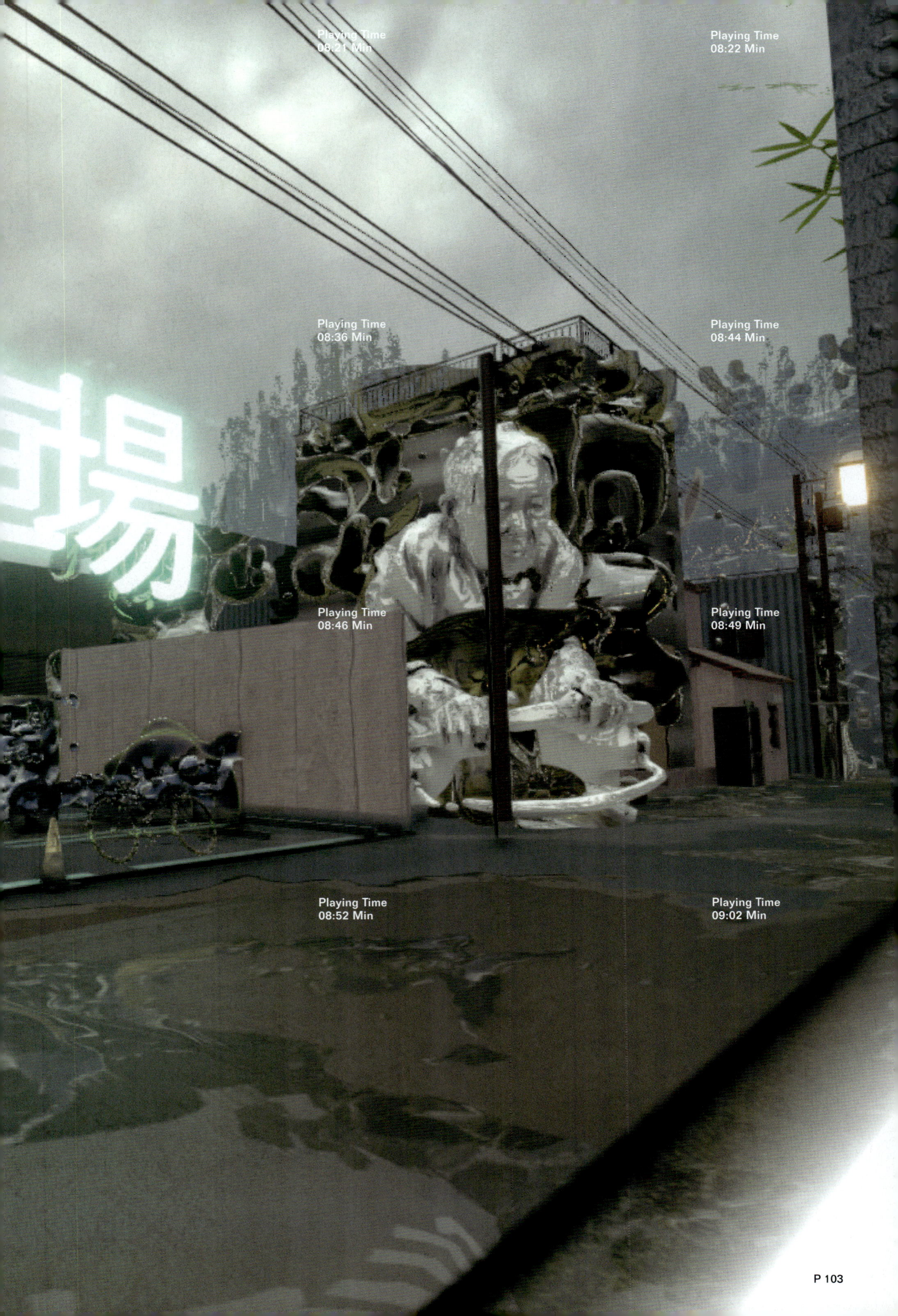
Playing Time
08:21 Min
Playing Time
08:22 Min
Playing Time
08:36 Min
Playing Time
08:44 Min
Playing Time
08:46 Min
Playing Time
08:49 Min
Playing Time
08:52 Min
Playing Time
09:02 Min

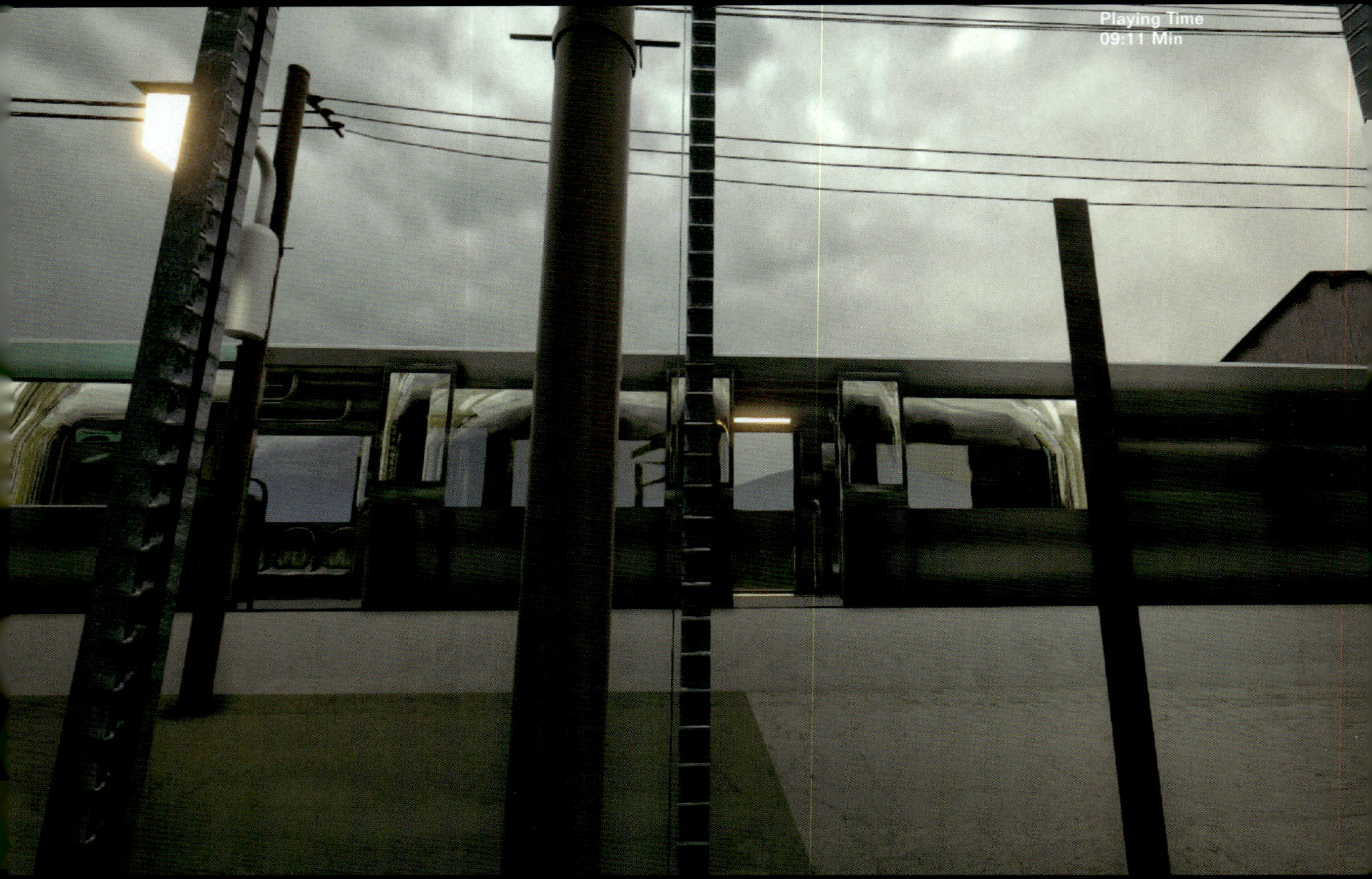
Playing Time
09:11 Min

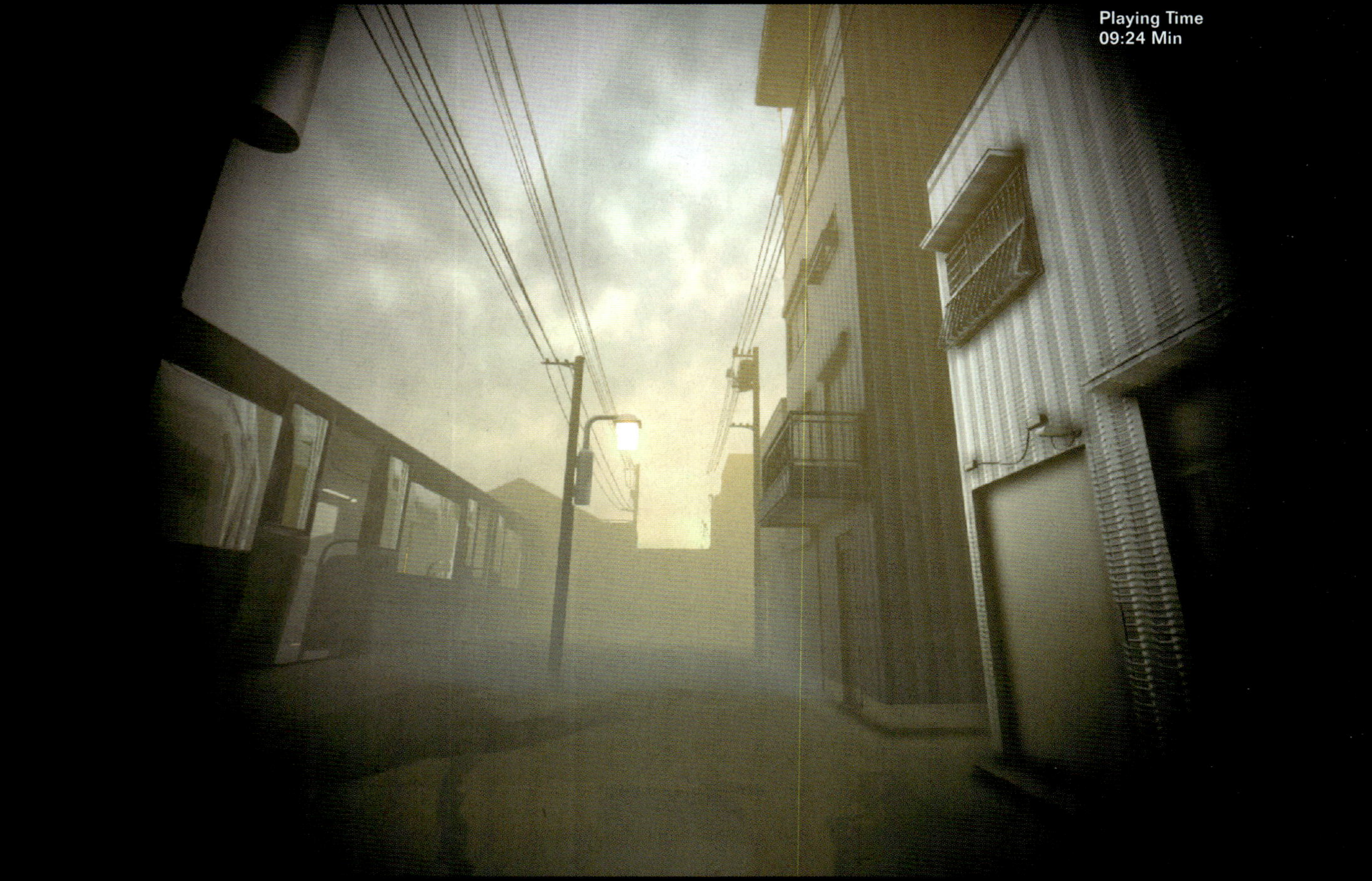
Playing Time
09:24 Min

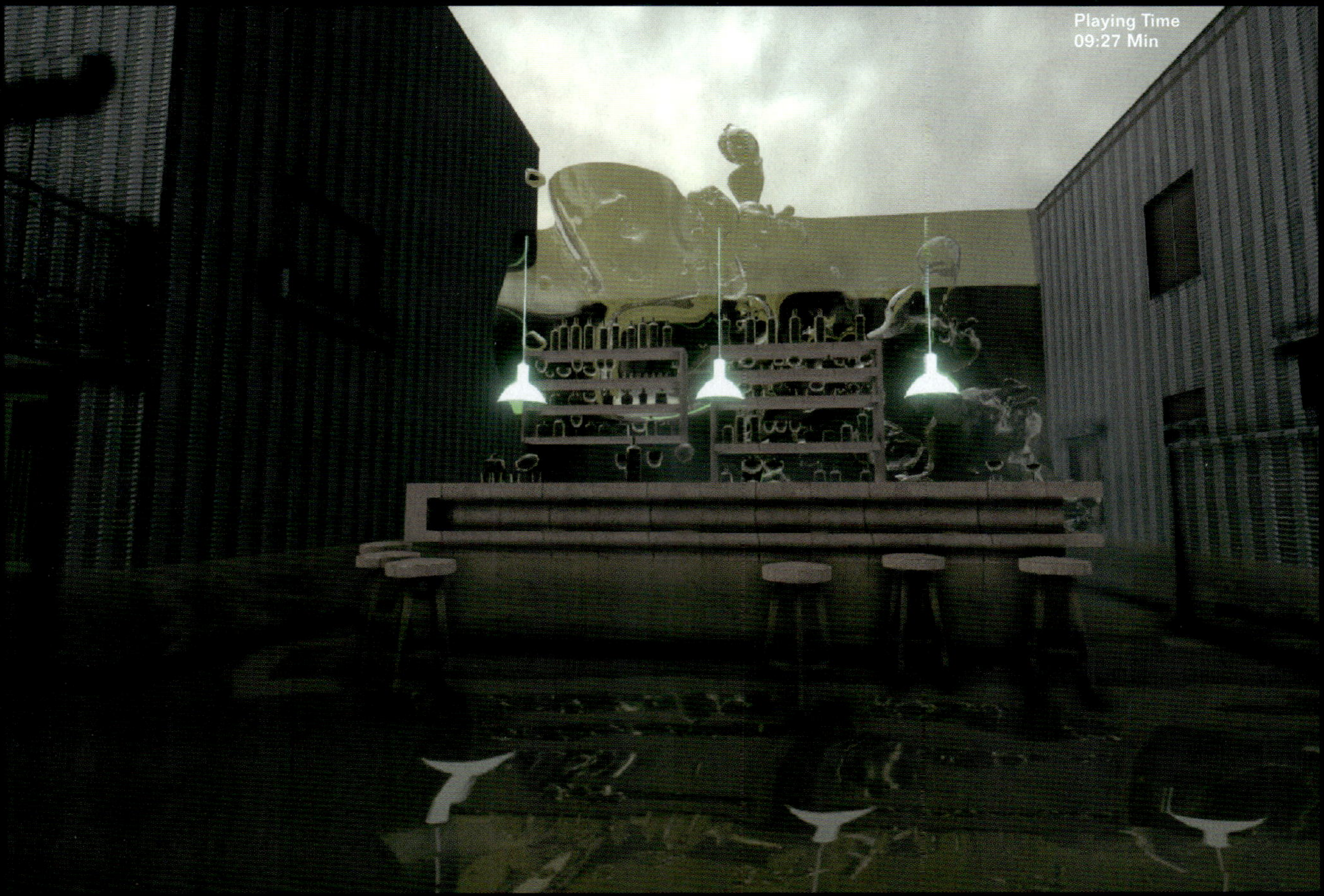

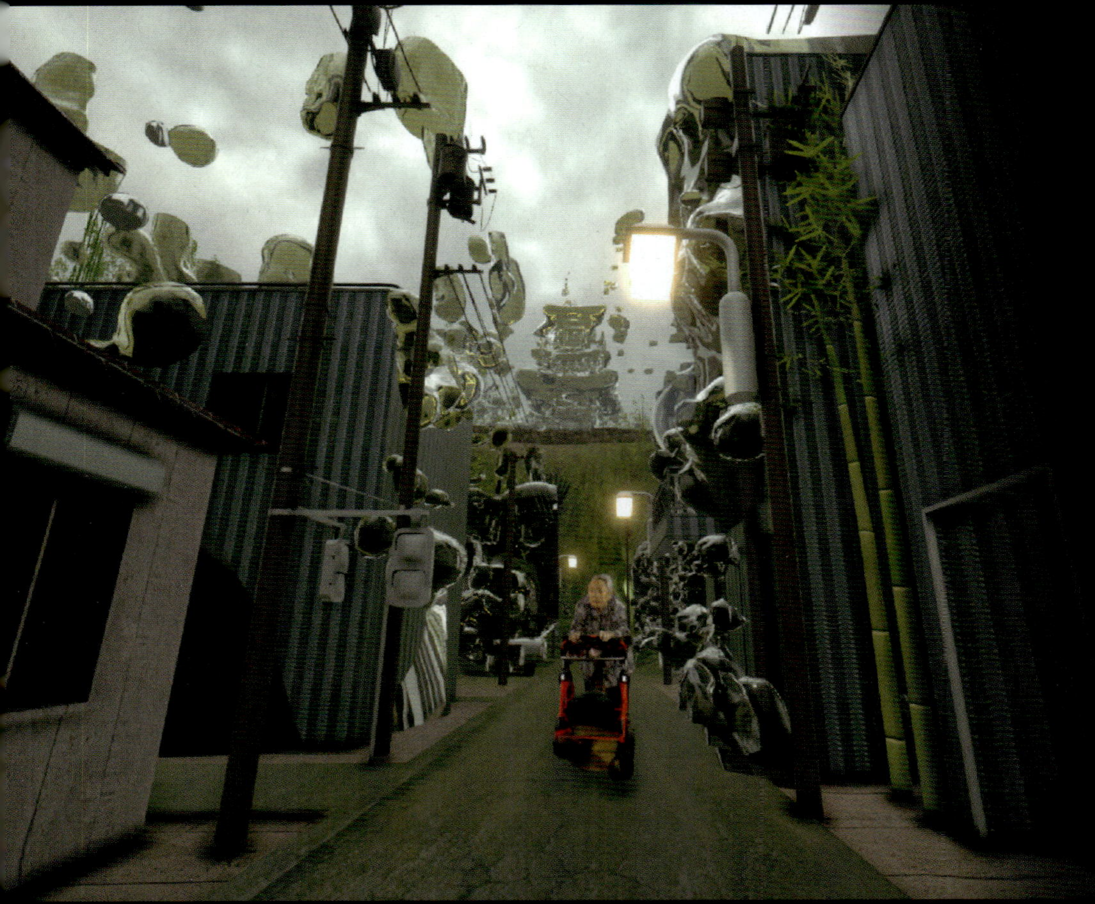

Playing Time
09:29 Min

Pause
09:34 Min

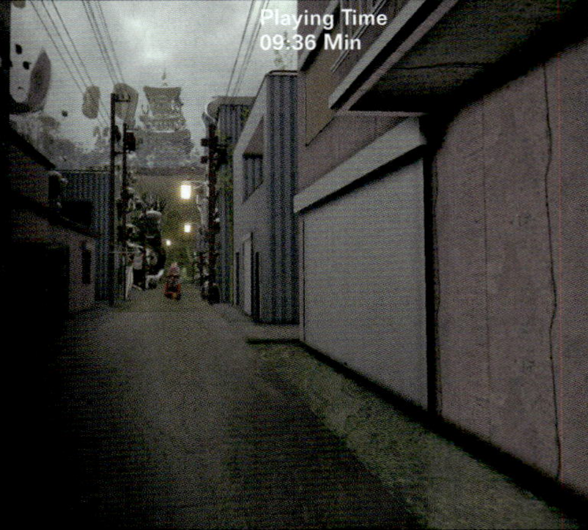

Playing Time
09:36 Min

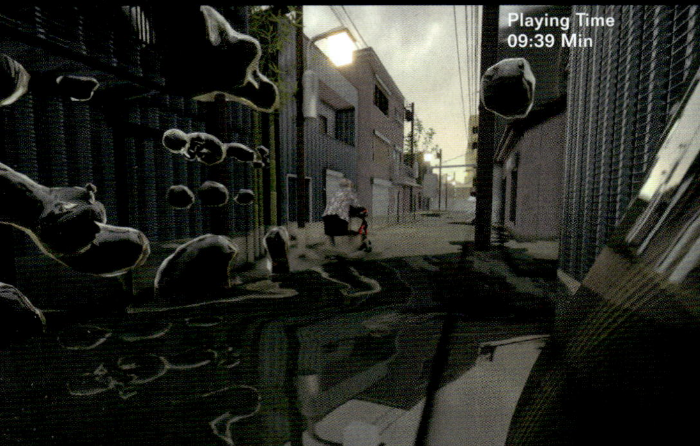

Playing Time
09:39 Min

Pause
09:40 Min

Pause
09:42 Min

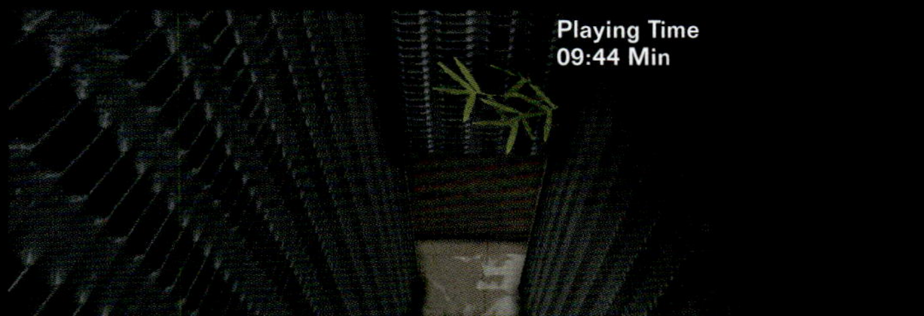

Playing Time
09:44 Min

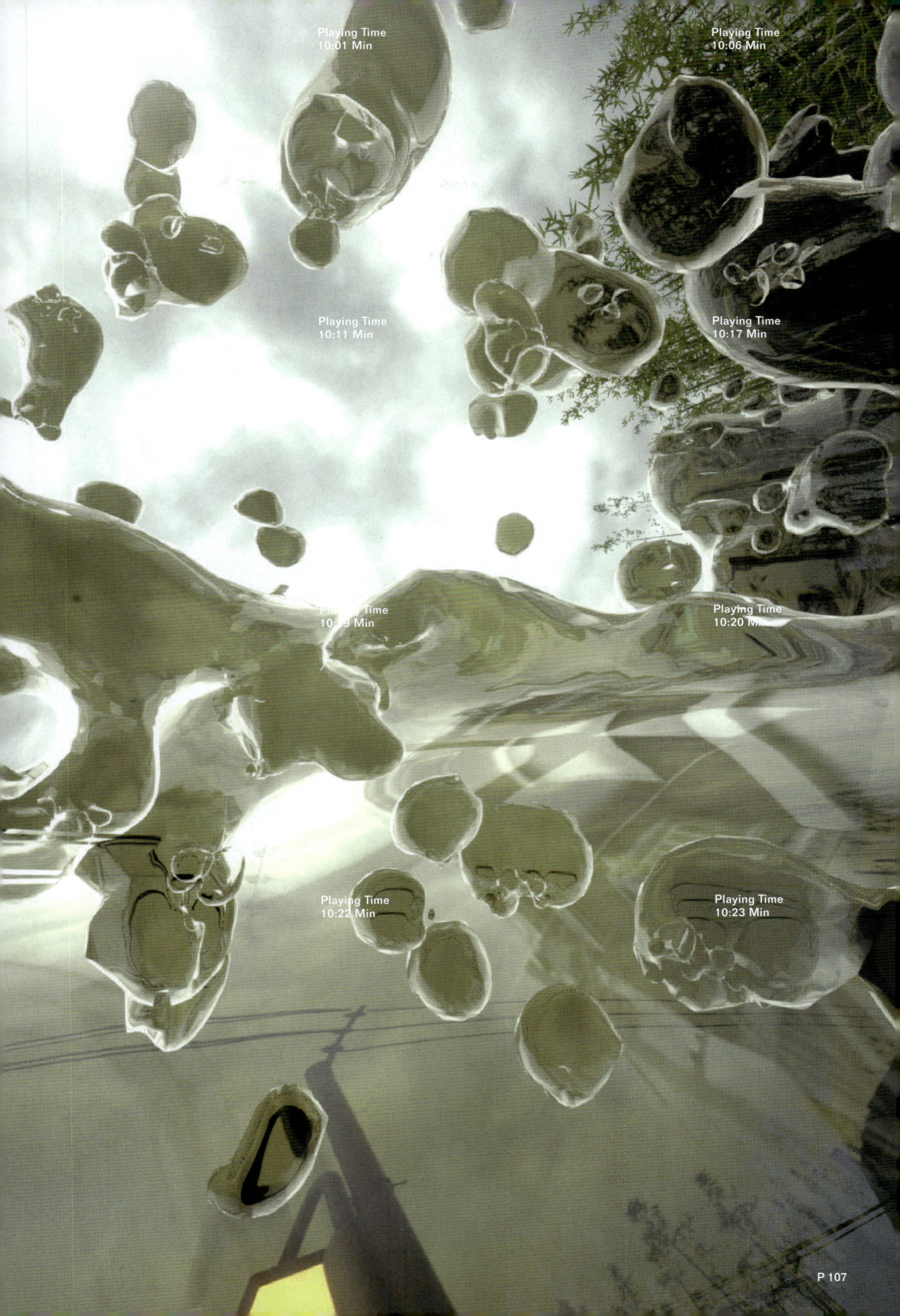
Playing Time
10:01 Min
Playing Time
10:06 Min
Playing Time
10:11 Min
Playing Time
10:17 Min
Playing Time
10:20 Min
Playing Time
10:22 Min
Playing Time
10:23 Min

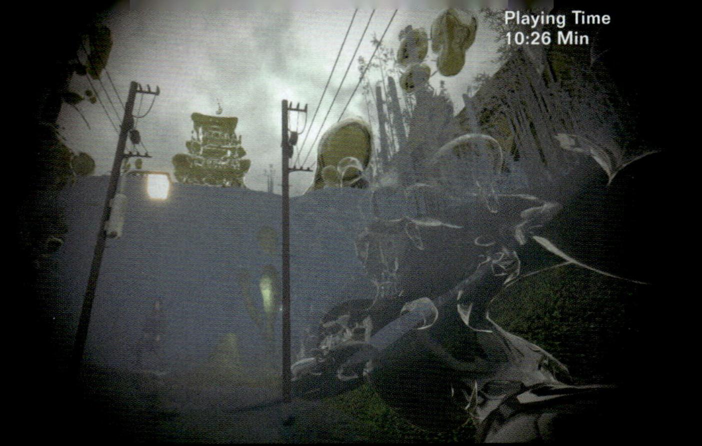
Playing Time
10:26 Min

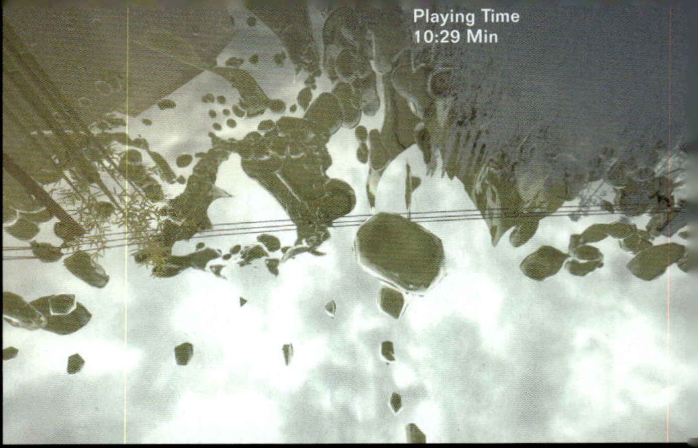
Playing Time
10:29 Min

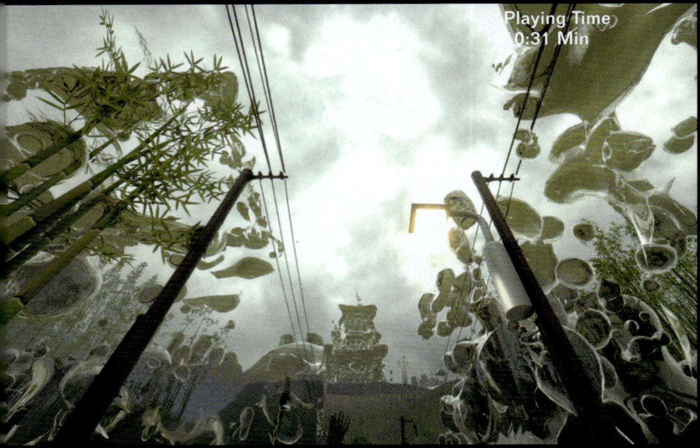
Playing Time
10:31 Min

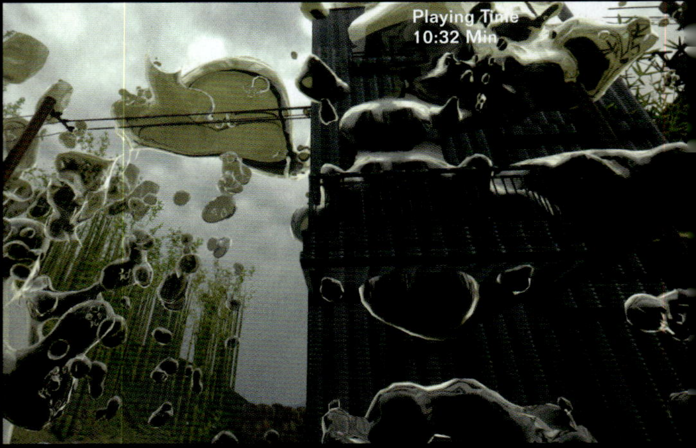
Playing Time
10:32 Min

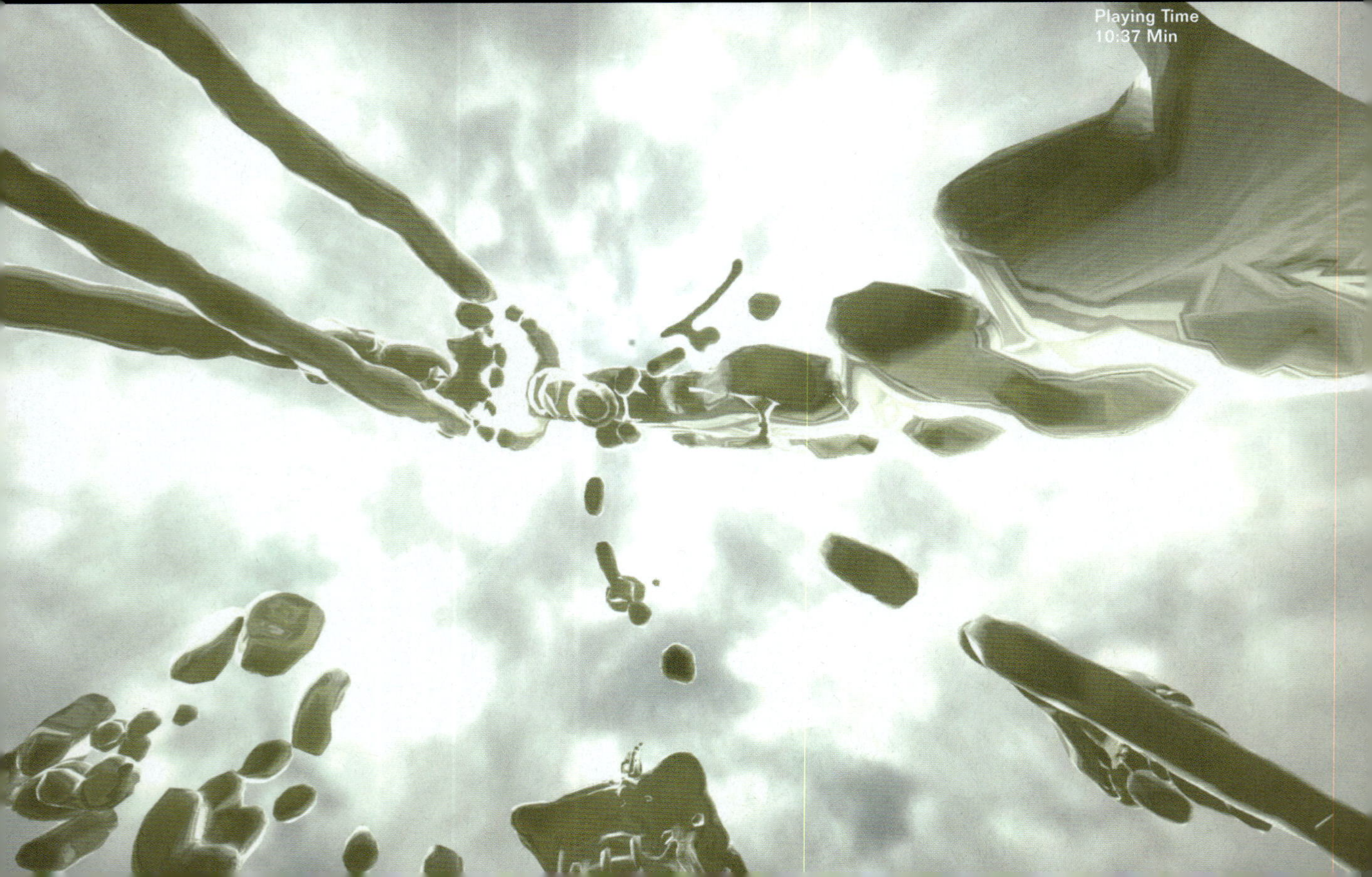
Playing Time
10:37 Min

Pause
10:38 Min

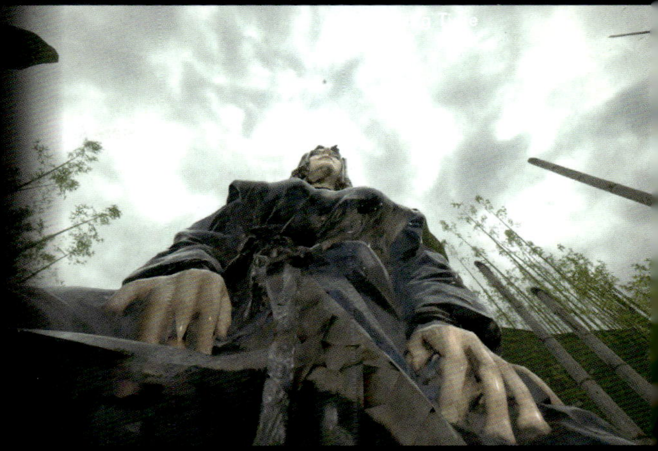

Pause
11:03 Min

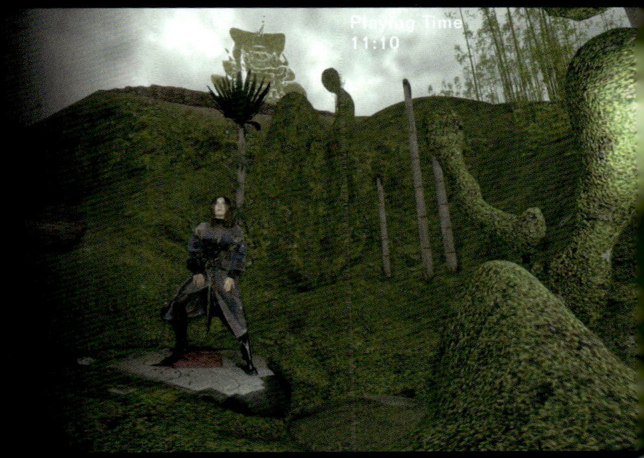

Pause
11:11 Min

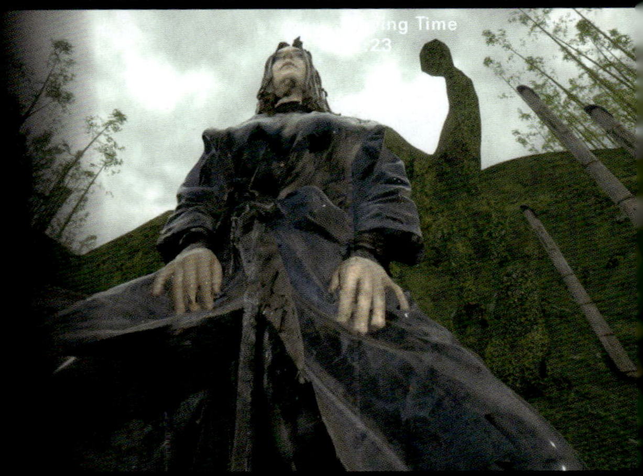

Pause
11:35 Min

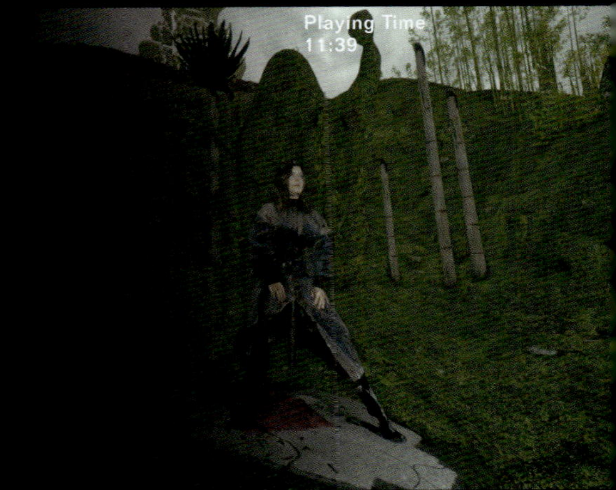

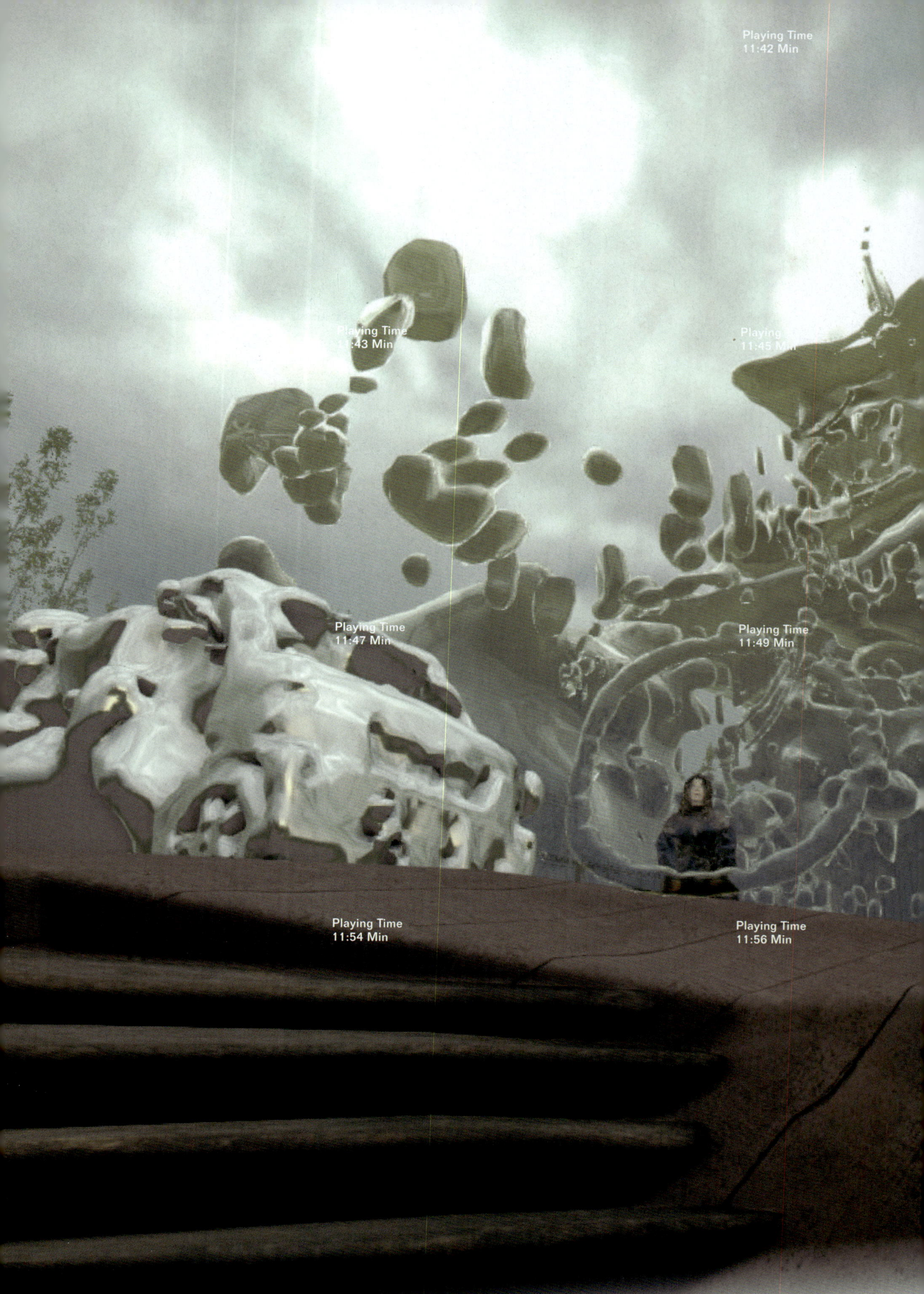
Playing Time
11:42 Min
Playing Time
11:43 Min
Playing
11:47 Min
Playing Time
11:47 Min
Playing Time
11:49 Min
Playing Time
11:54 Min
Playing Time
11:56 Min

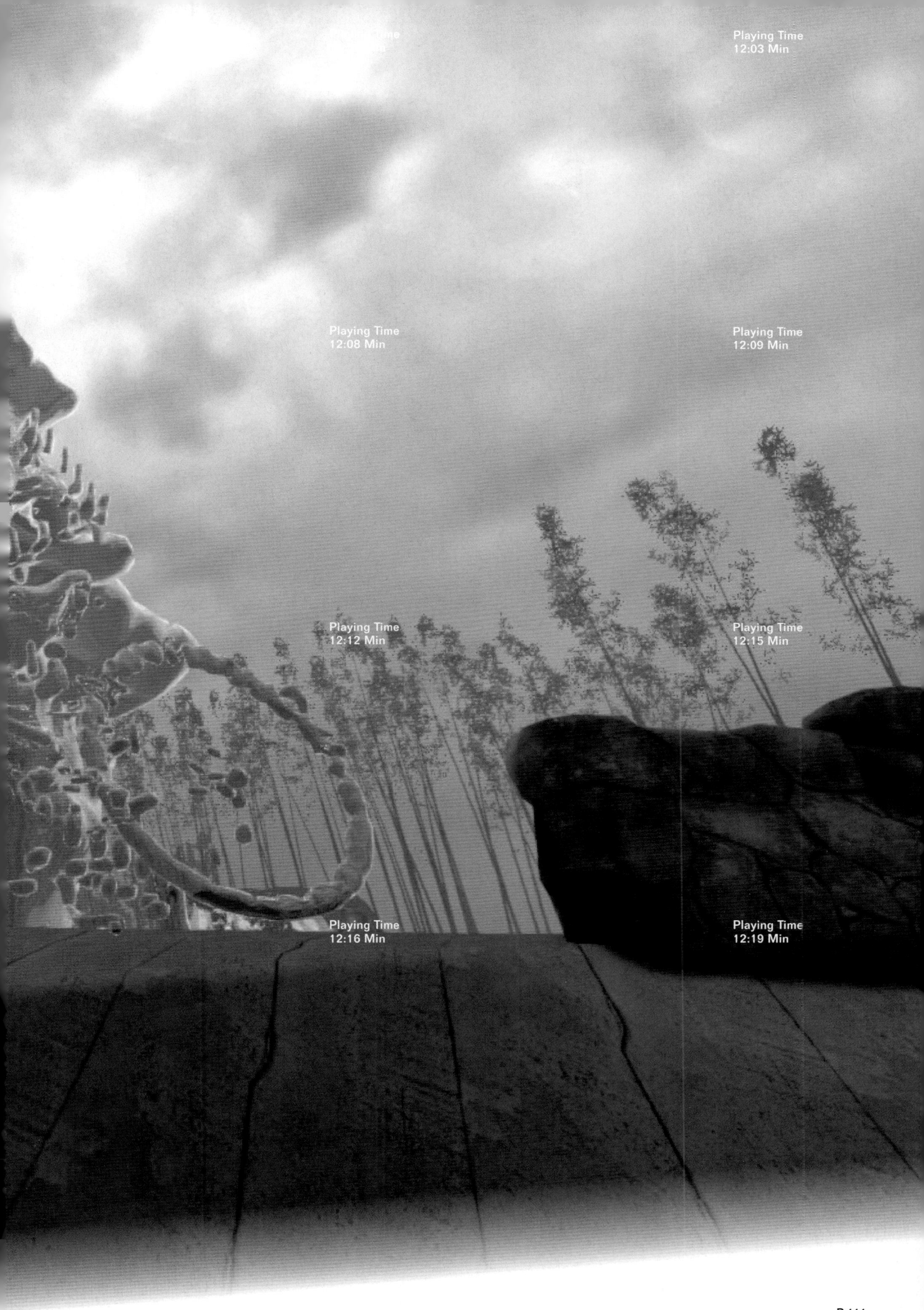
Playing Time
12:03 Min
Playing Time
12:08 Min
Playing Time
12:09 Min
Playing Time
12:12 Min
Playing Time
12:15 Min
Playing Time
12:16 Min
Playing Time
12:19 Min

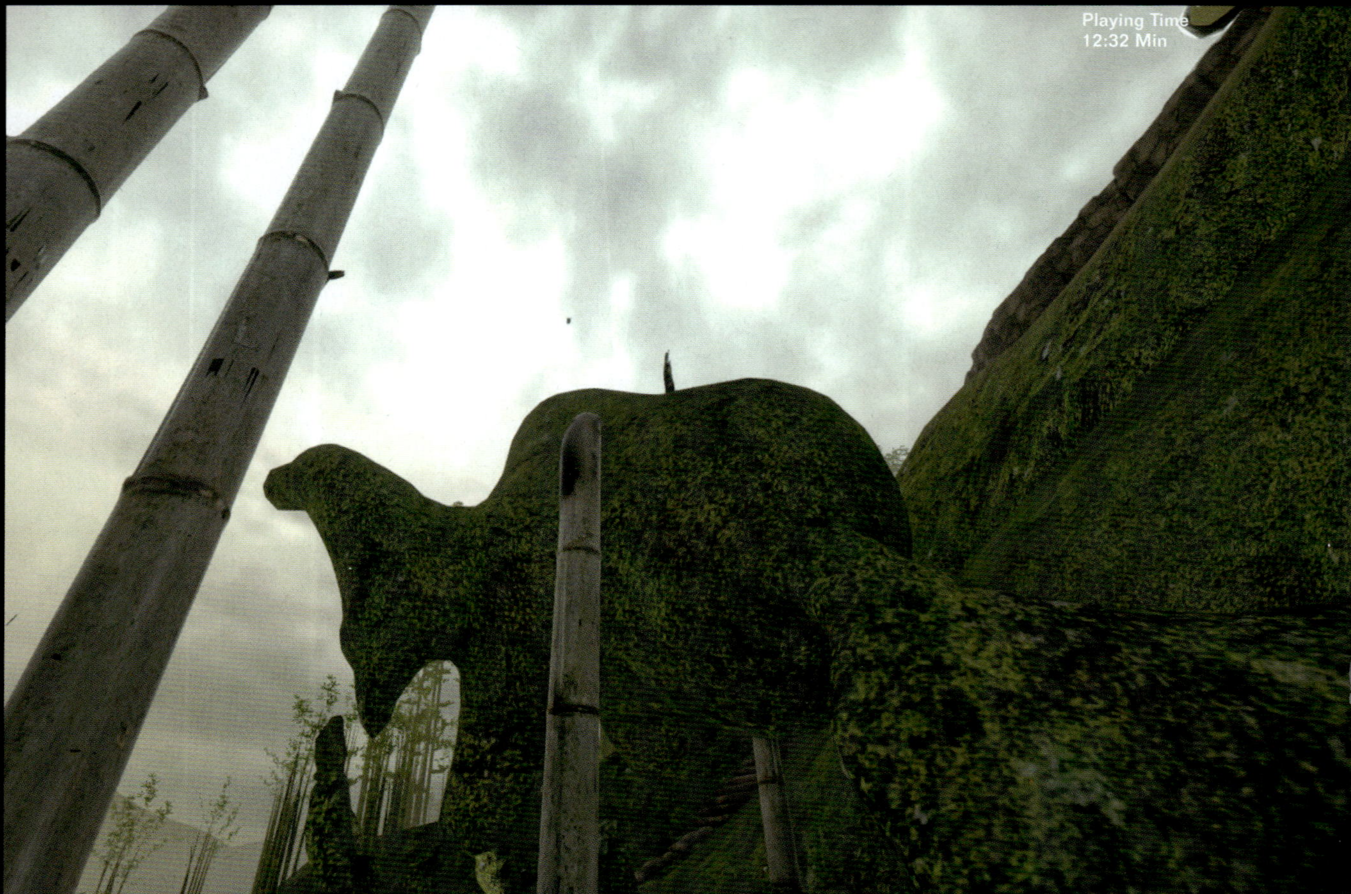

Pause
12:33 Min

Pause
12:34 Min

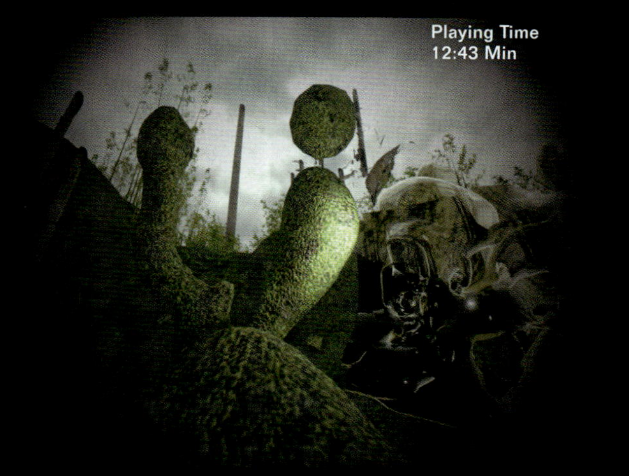

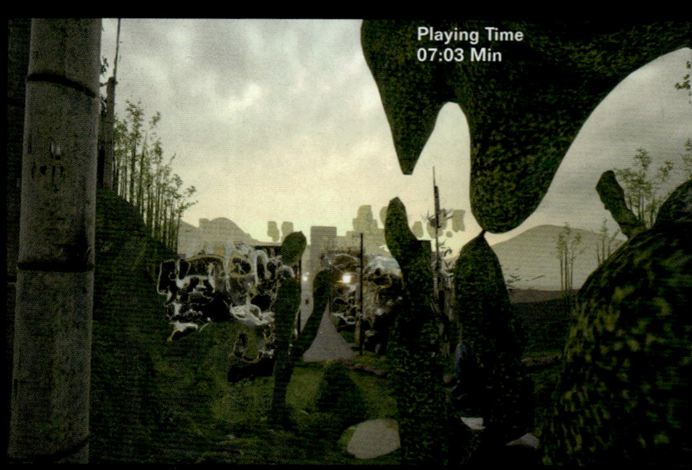

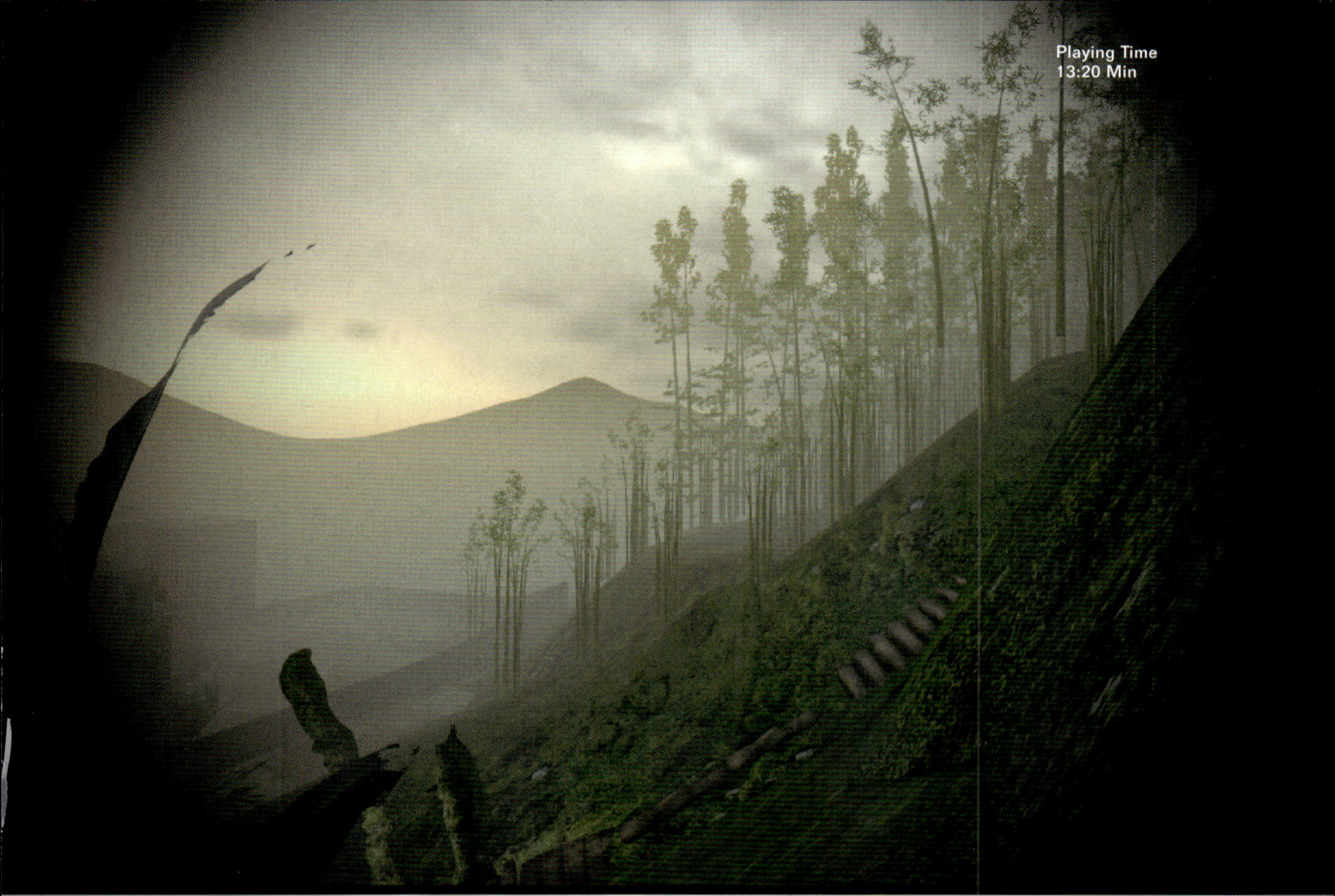
Playing Time
13:20 Min

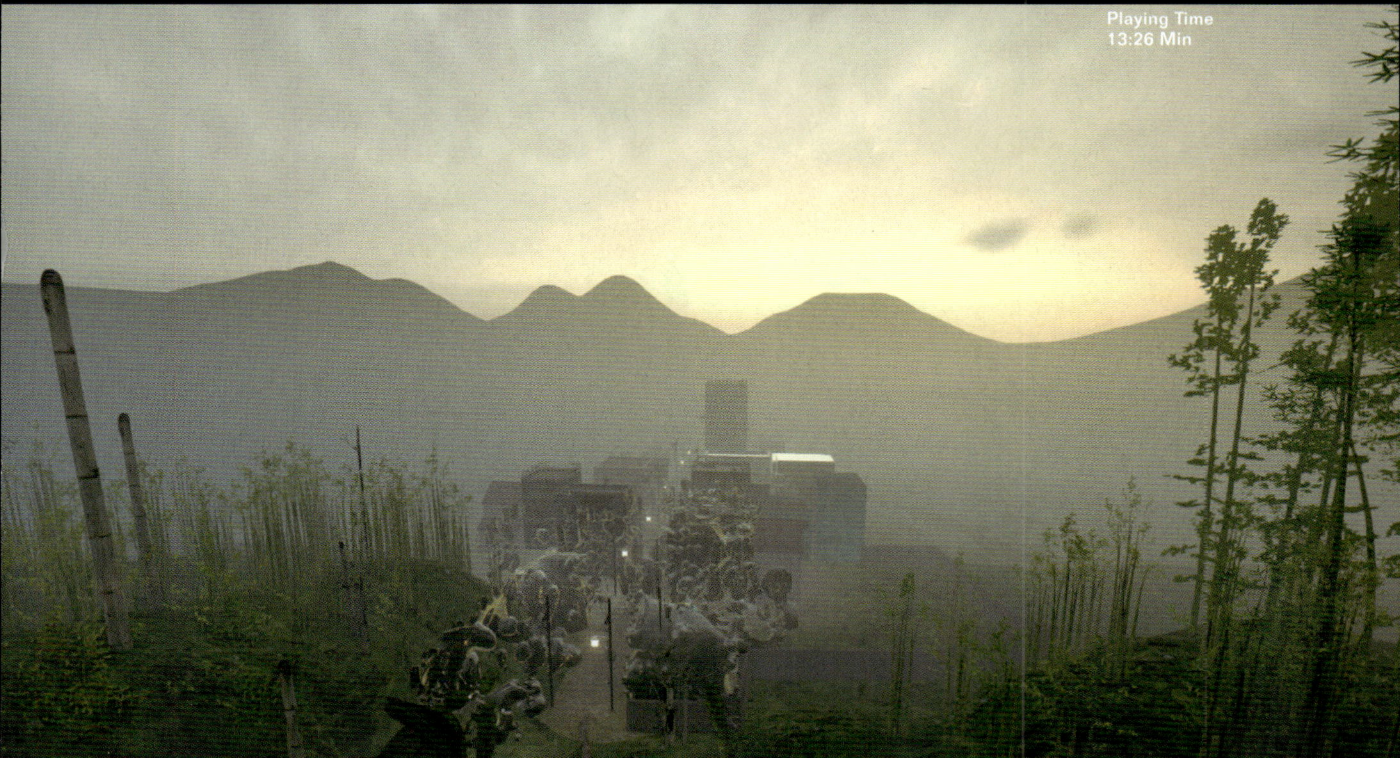
Playing Time
13:26 Min

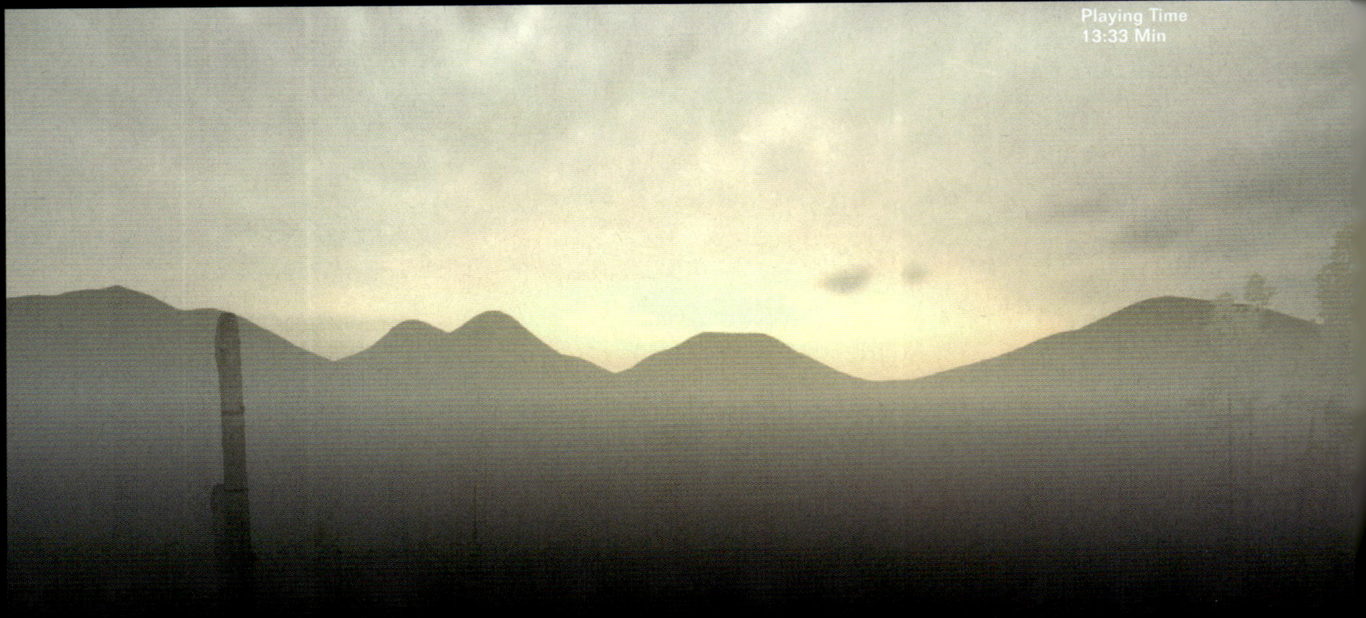
Playing Time
13:33 Min

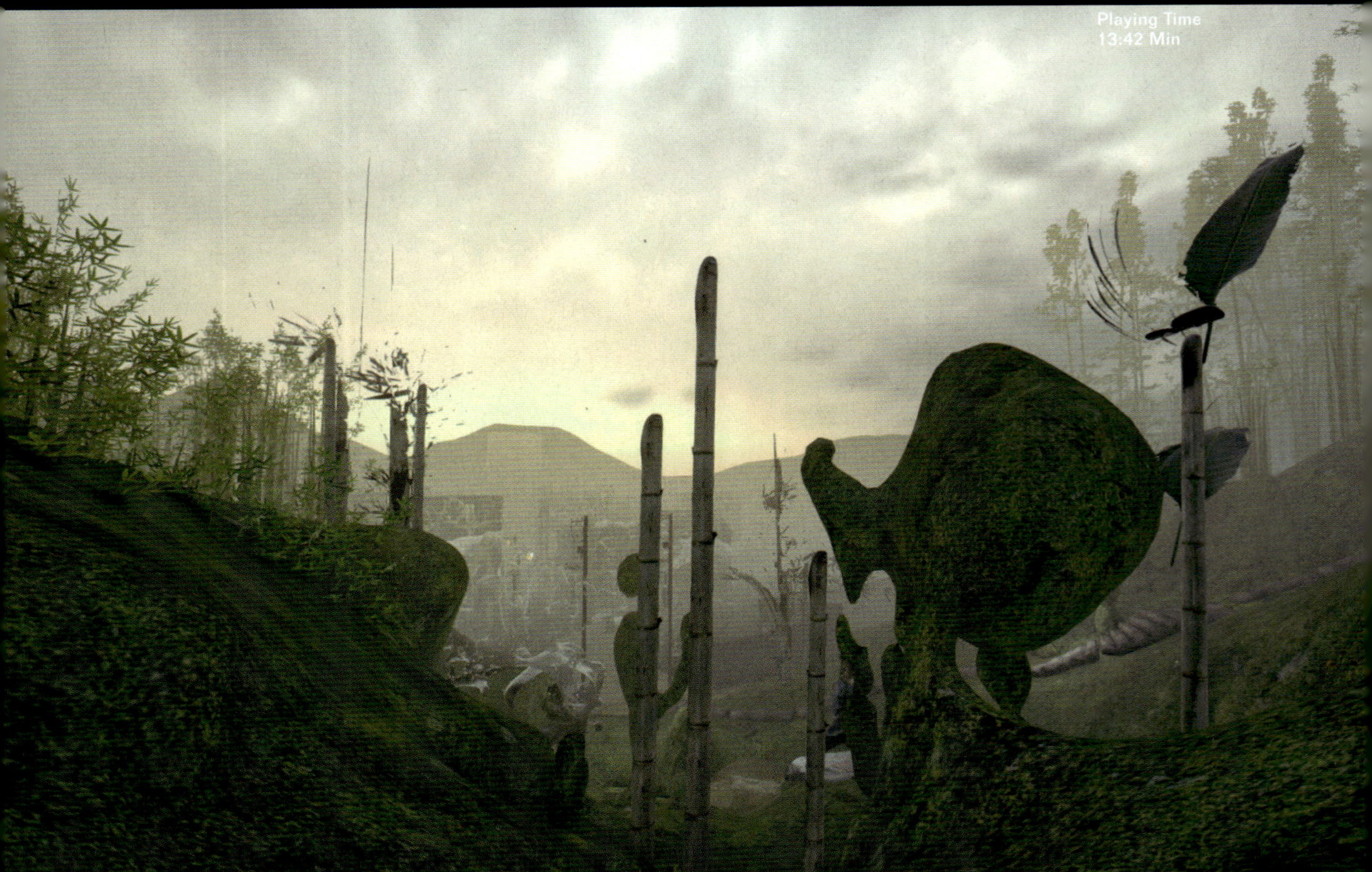
Playing Time
13:42 Min

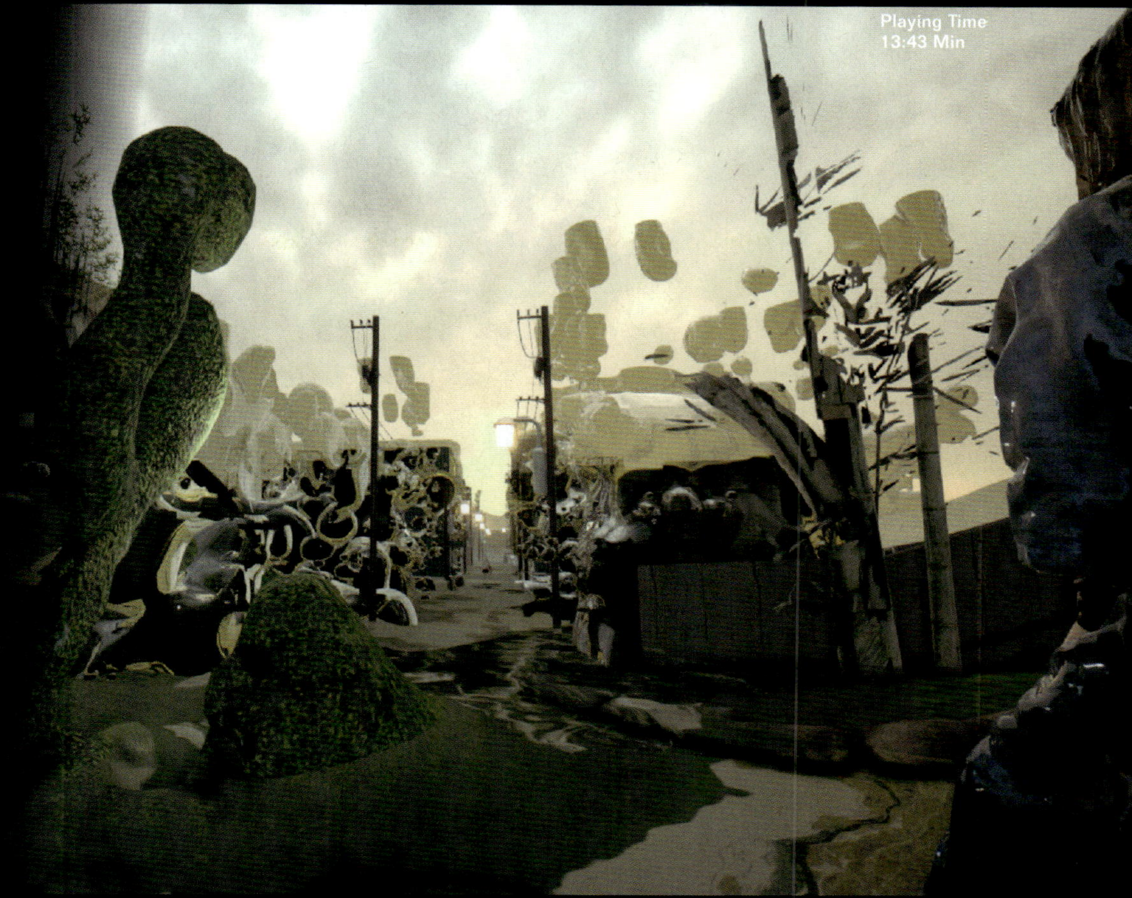
Playing Time
13:43 Min

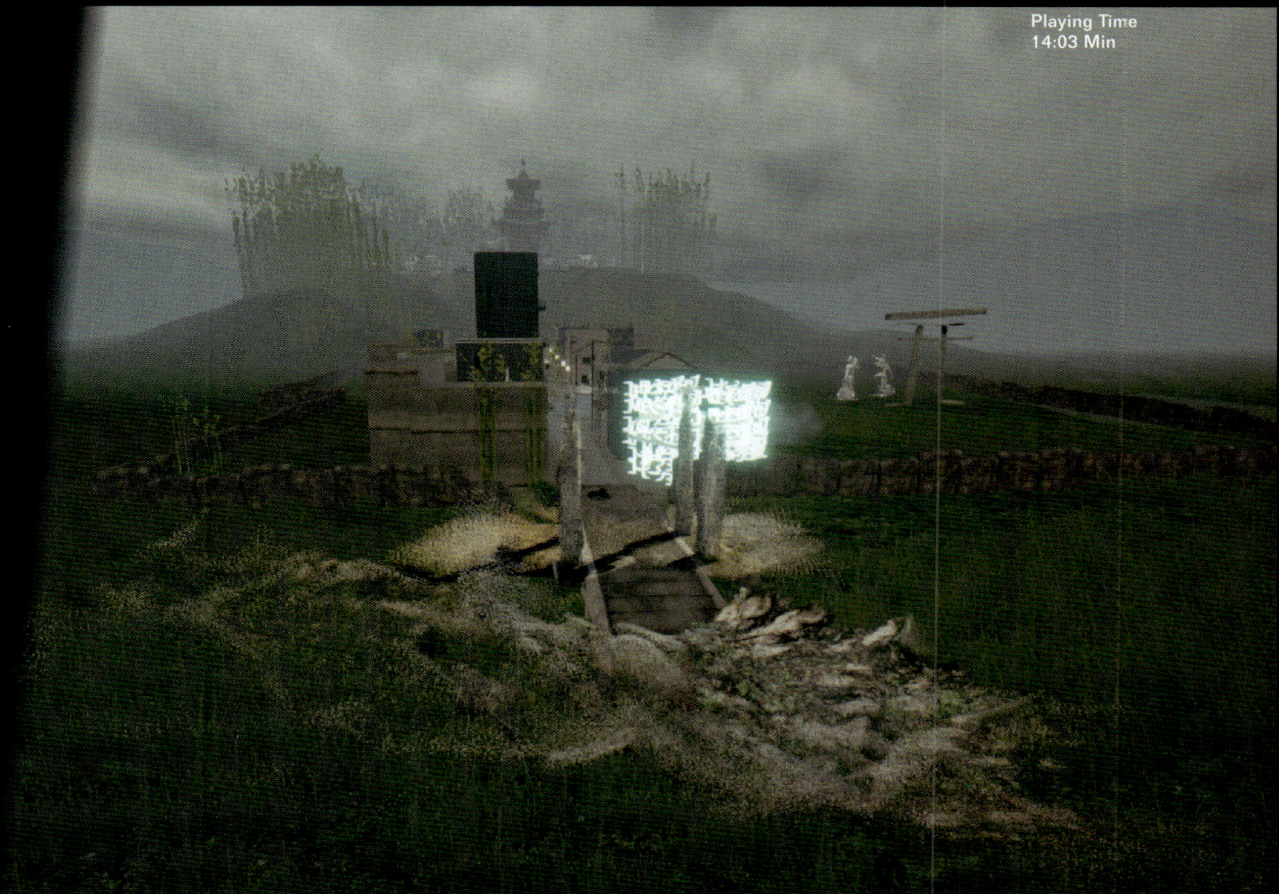
Playing Time
14:03 Min

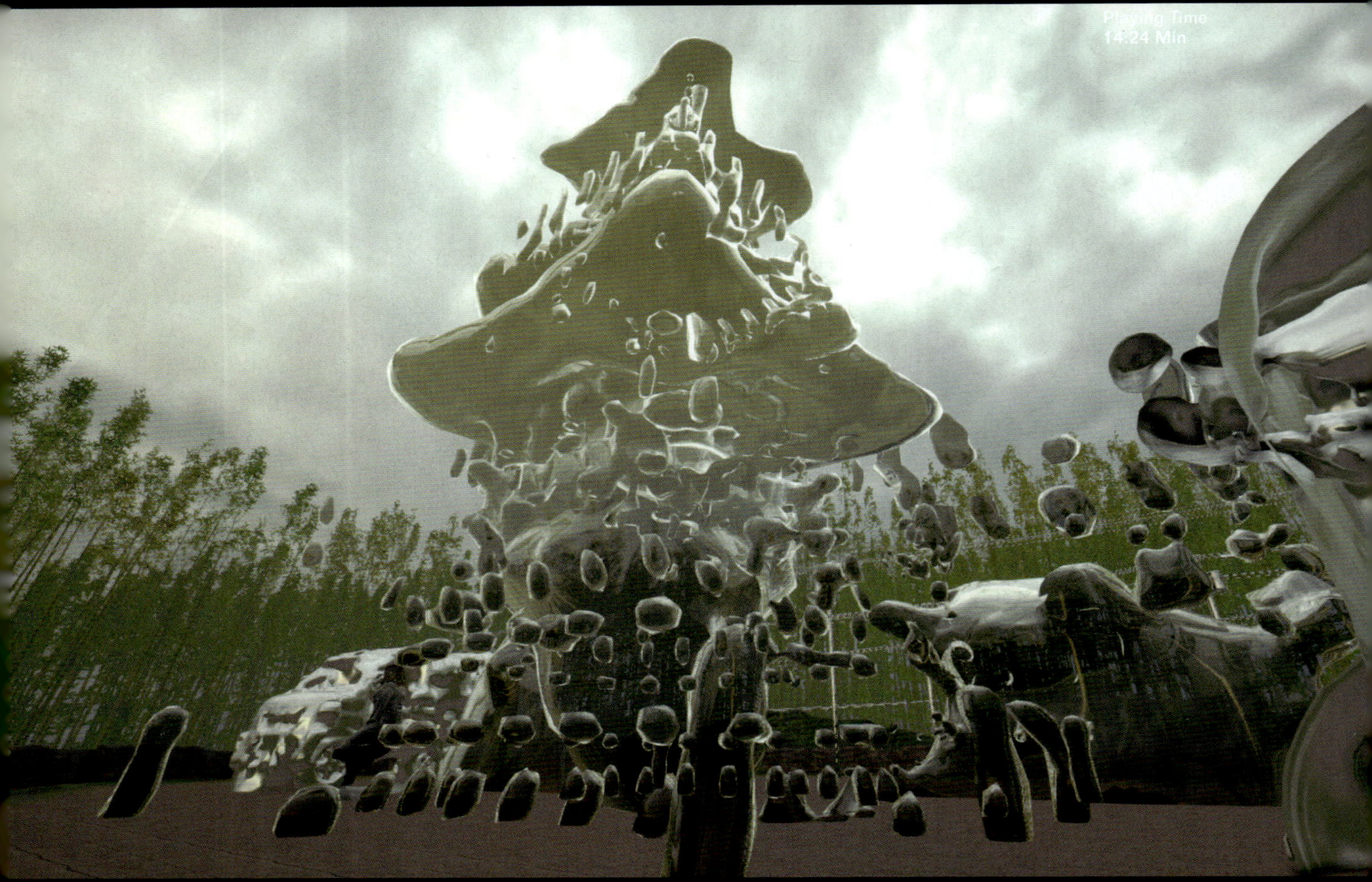

Pause
14:26 Min

Pause
14:28 Min

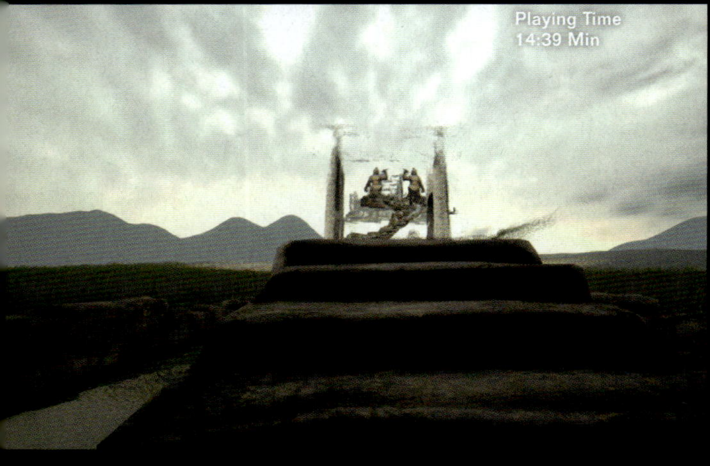

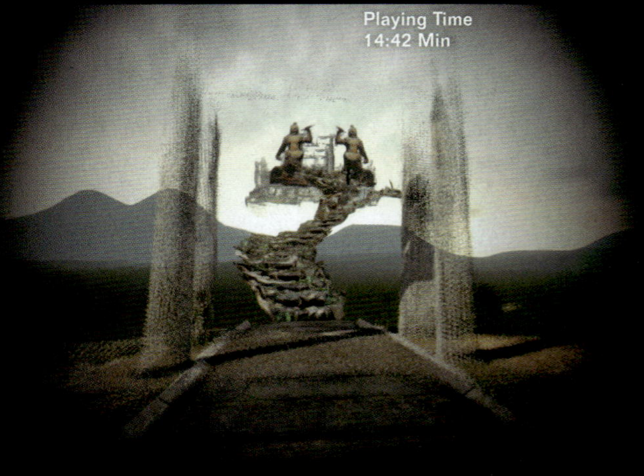

Pause
14:56 Min

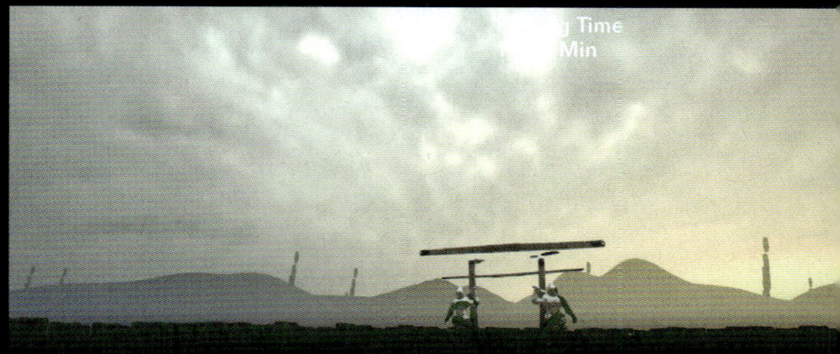

Pause
14:59 Min

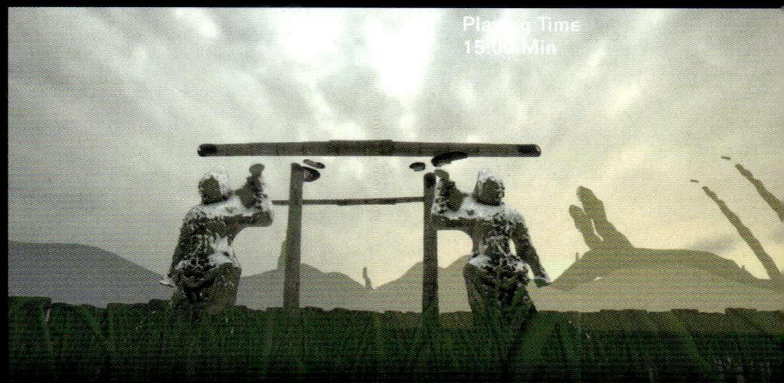

Playing Time
15:02 Min

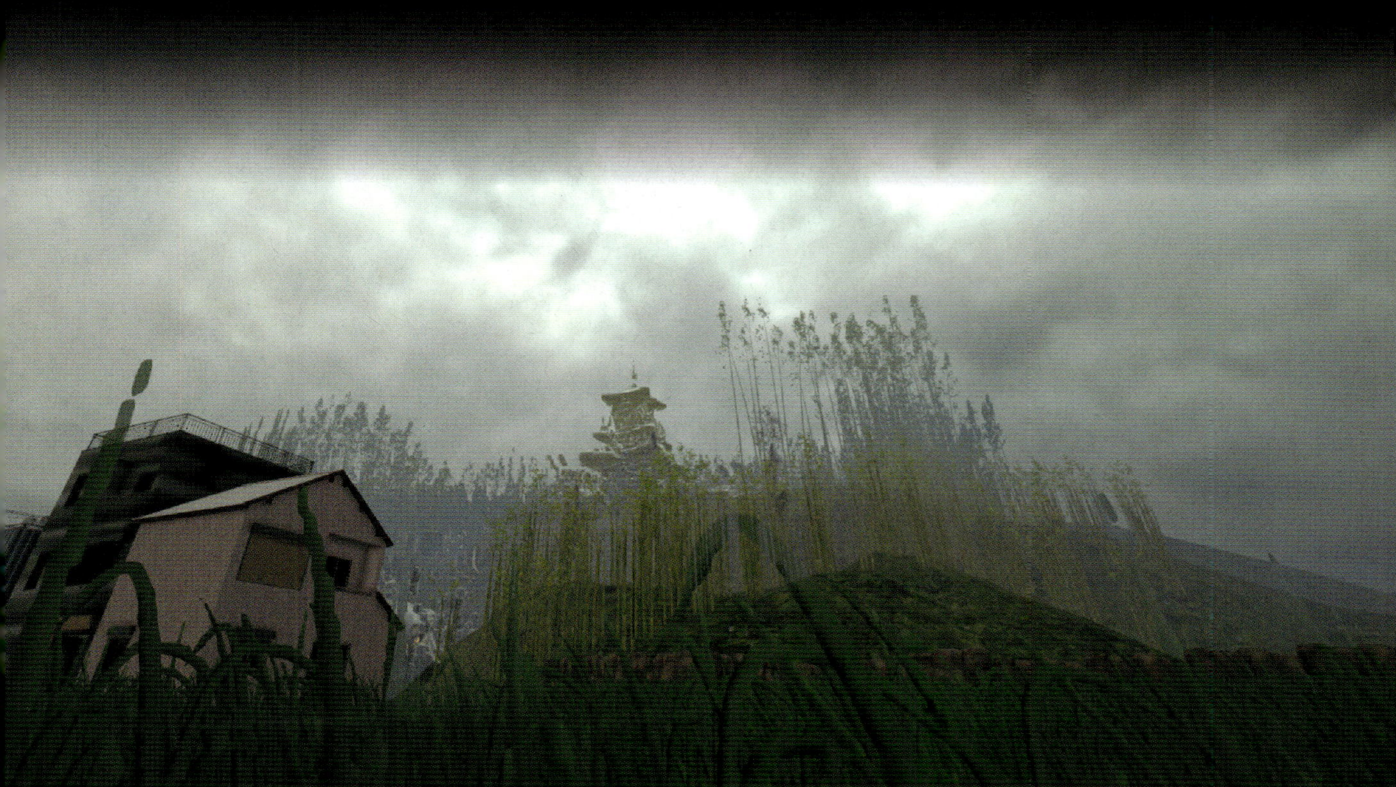

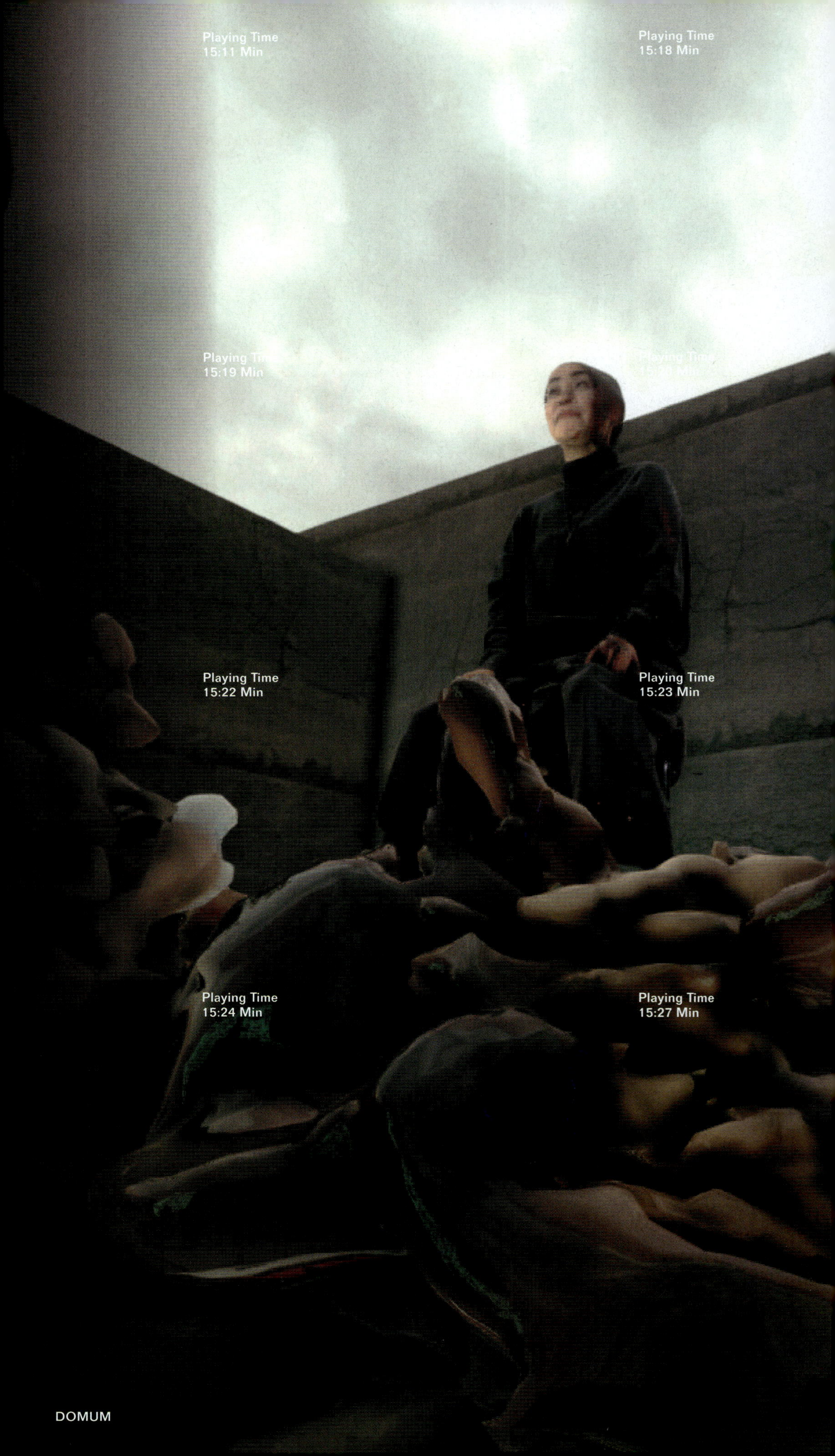
Playing Time
15:11 Min
Playing Time
15:18 Min
15:19 Min
Playing Time
15:22 Min
Playing Time
15:23 Min
Playing Time
15:24 Min
Playing Time
15:27 Min

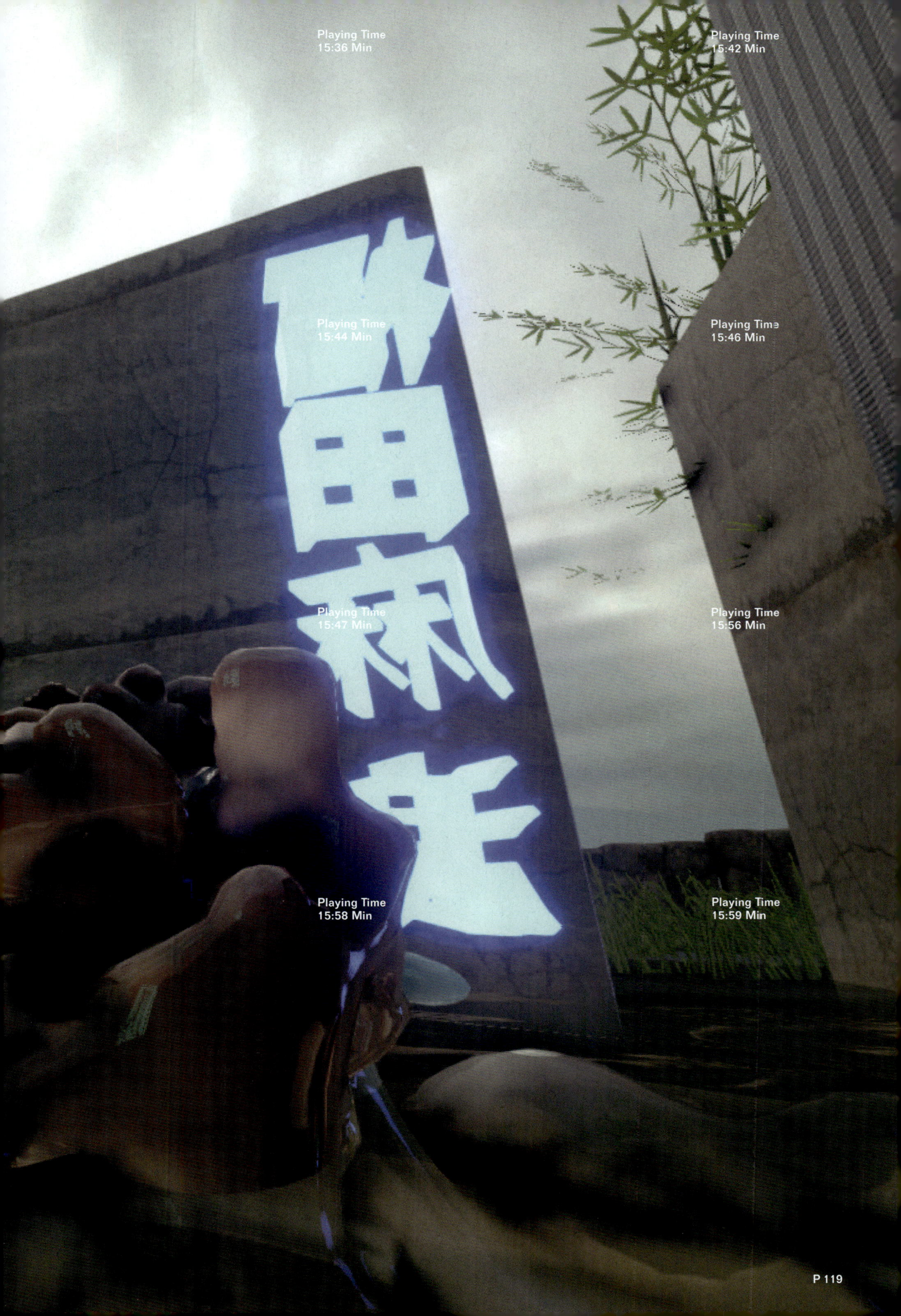

Playing Time
15:36 Min

Playing Time
15:42 Min

Playing Time
15:44 Min

Playing Time
15:46 Min

Playing Time
15:47 Min

Playing Time
15:56 Min

Playing Time
15:58 Min

Playing Time
15:59 Min

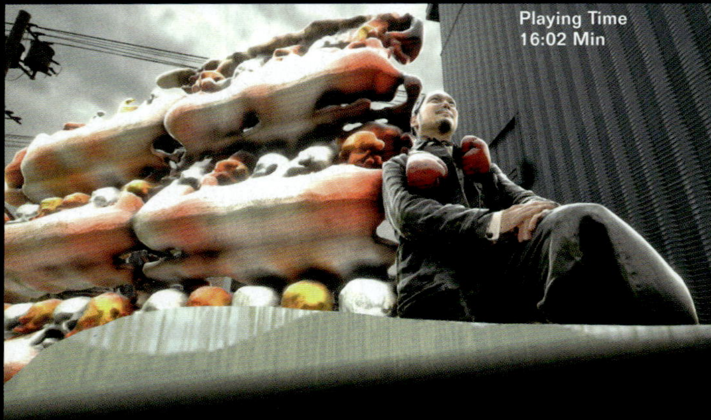

Pause
16:03 Min

Pause
16:04 Min

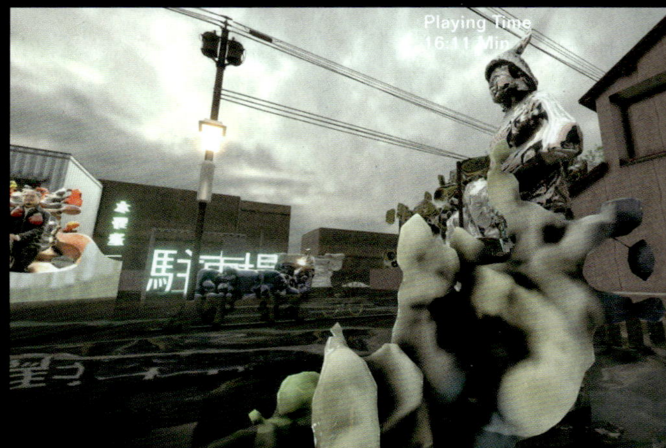

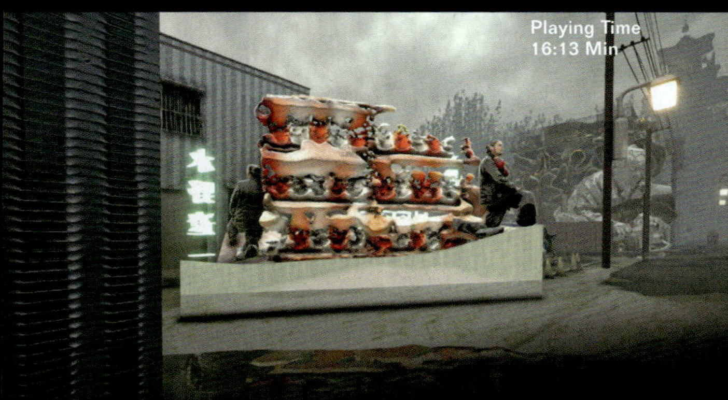

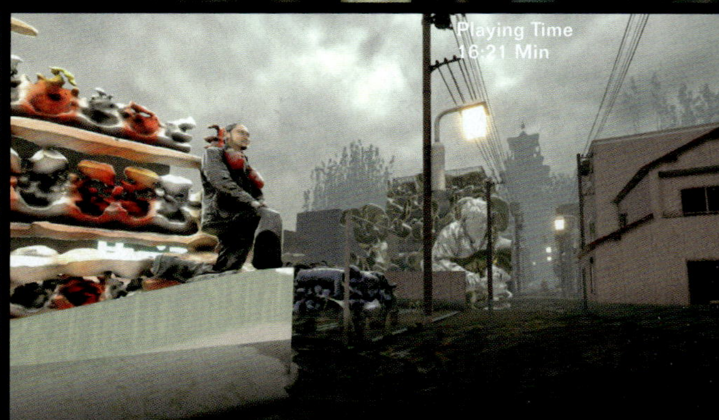

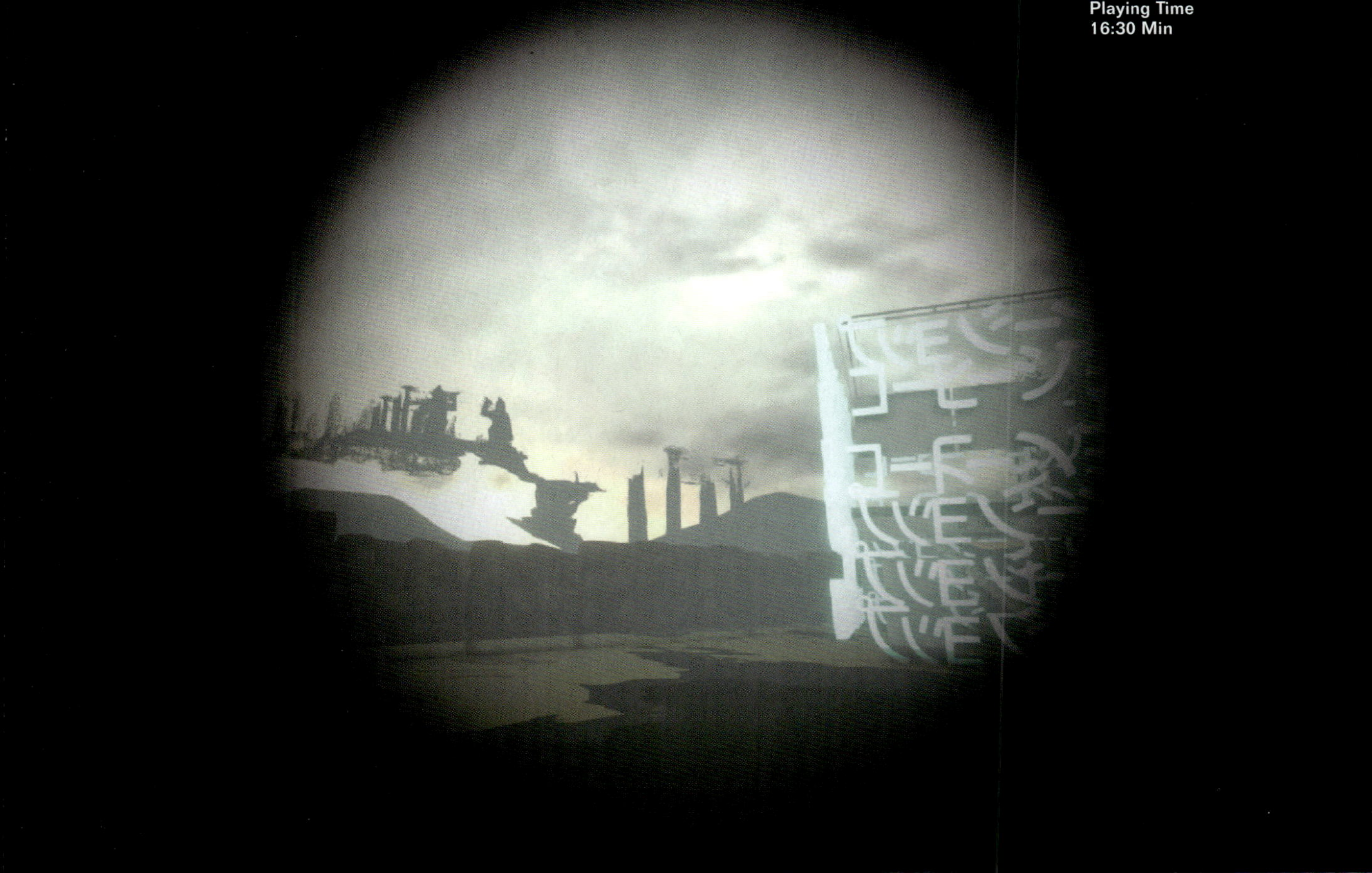
Playing Time
16:30 Min

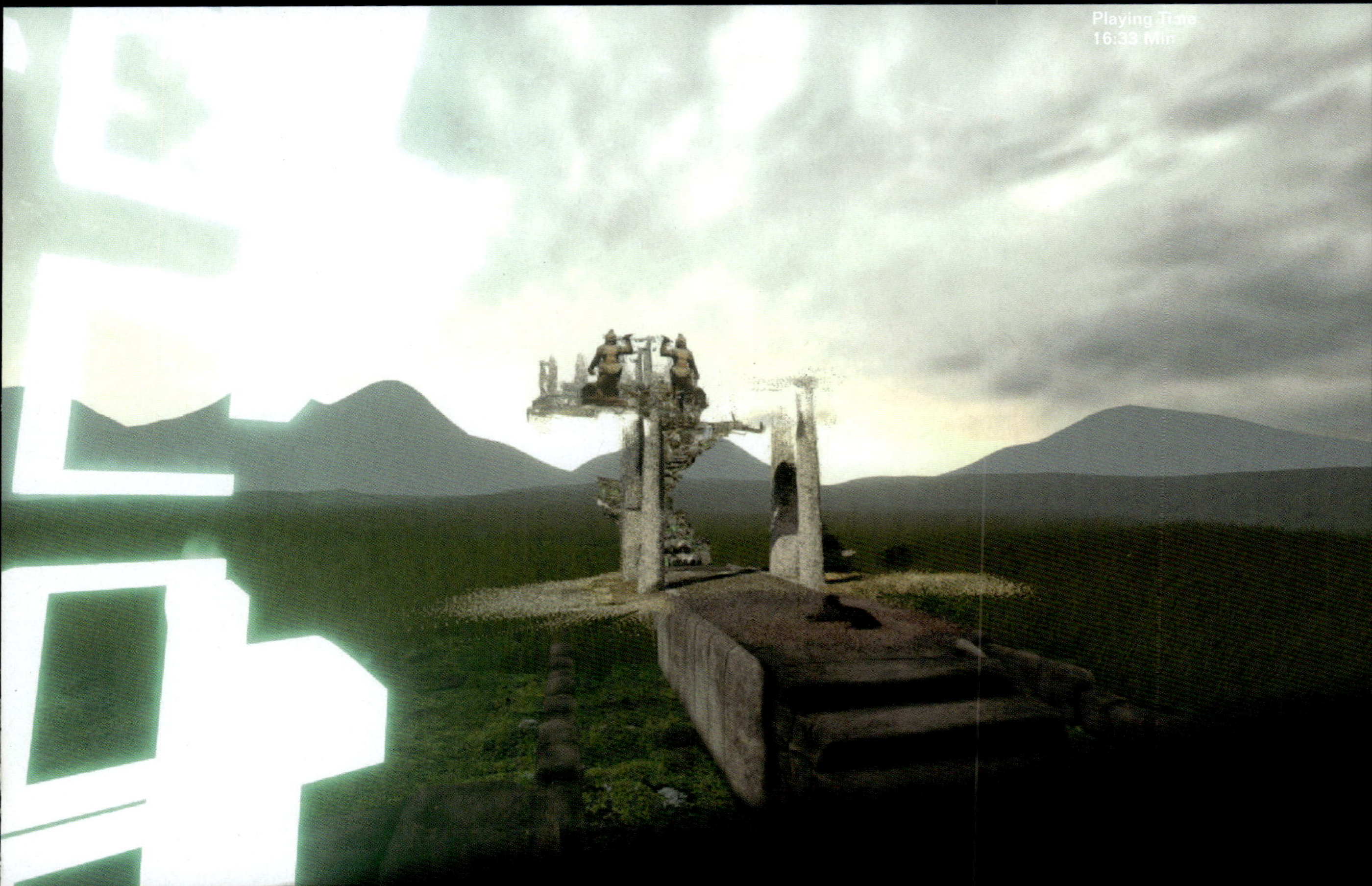
Playing Time
16:33 Min

14h awake. 7h ahead.

TAKAKO
KAZUKI
NAOKI

And Rebecca

The future is now.
I listen to disco in Aoyama tunnel. This is what invisible feels like.

The train goes so fast that the landscape blurs like in a Richter painting.

Train bound from Tokyo to Hakata. When I'm in Japan.

I think about death and my body all the time. Truth is a Forgotten memory.

How to use exploitative technology like a tracking ring that has retrieved my location 38 times in the last 24 hours and measured my body data excessively.

Compulsive.
Obsessive, like a stalker.

I want to resist this and use the data to create an incredible experience that shows the pain and pleasure of my actual everyday life in Japan.

To take back my data which is so easily given away everyday—all the time.

Imagine giving up everything:

Your bed,
your kitchen,
your bathroom,
your apartment.

From now on you live, eat and sleep in public spaces. Vast amounts of pictures, sounds, videos and 3D scans are organized as environments in Rebecca Merlic's TheCityAsAHouse, in the form of an interactive visual novel. A work about the experiment of a caucasian, European 30-year-old human living in Tokyo without inhabiting a private apartment over a period.

A speculative exploration of the possibilities of abolishing known forms of habitation.

In 1903, Hermann Muthesius said:
"Japan is in many respects the country that comes closest to one's dream of paradise." The current situation in Tokyo allows for the

emergence of a turbo-dense, capitalism-driven space generator for satisfying one's personal longings and needs.

TheCityAsAHouse depicts an illusion of private ownership of a place we call home.

A strategy of successfully surviving without being bound to physical space. It proposes a new form of society. The next self-improvement of humanity or going back to our roots.

A conservative private space consists of rooms to sleep, wash, eat, delight and store.

I sleep in public spaces.
In a train,
in the love hotel,
in a capsule,
in an anime cafe,
book and bed,
9h hotel,
or at a workplace.
The bedroom is abolished.
The infrastructure of the so-called konbini and affordable food in restaurants, fast-food restaurants and street food stalls are abundant and an integral part of Japanese everyday life and culture. The kitchen is abolished.

Words cannot express the
feelings I have about this city.
How much it
changed me,
gave me
the feeling of being lost,
letting me go and
letting me come back.
To feel
the pain
and pleasure
this city has to give,
the rush,
the pleasure,
the pain.

Again
and
again.

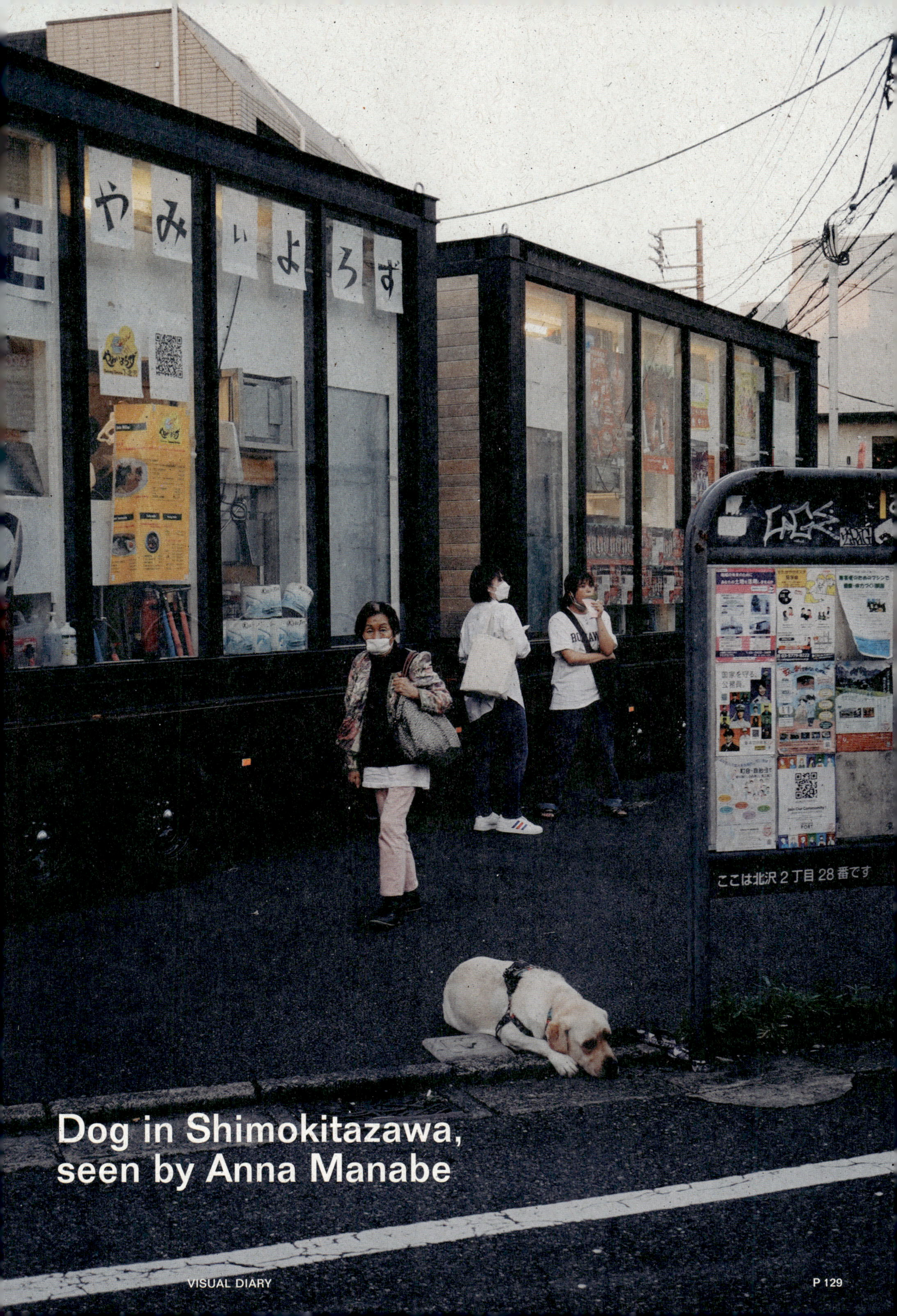

Dog in Shimokitazawa, seen by Anna Manabe

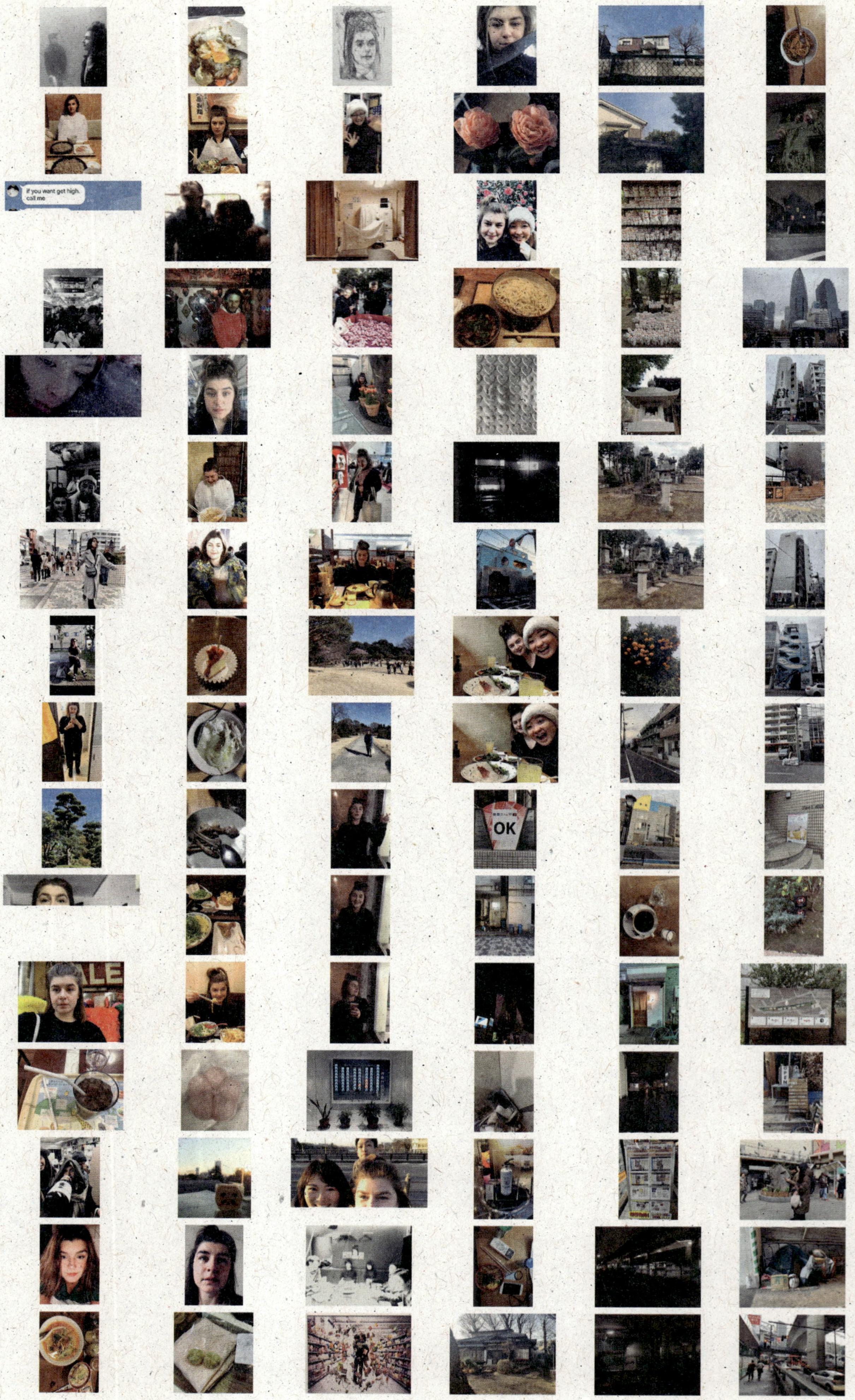
if you want get high.
call me
OK
ALE

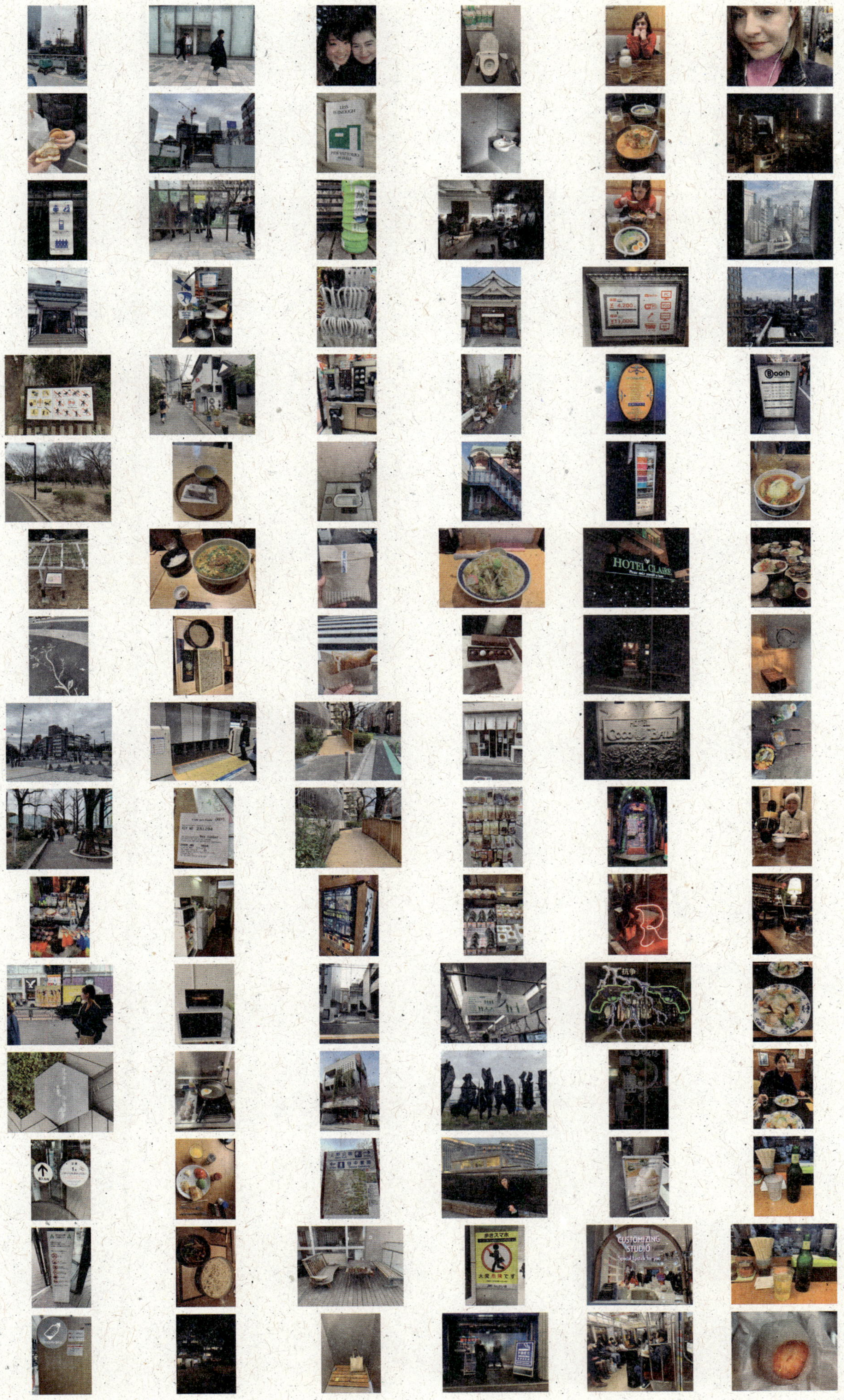
HOTEL CLAIRE
CUSTOMIZING STUDIO

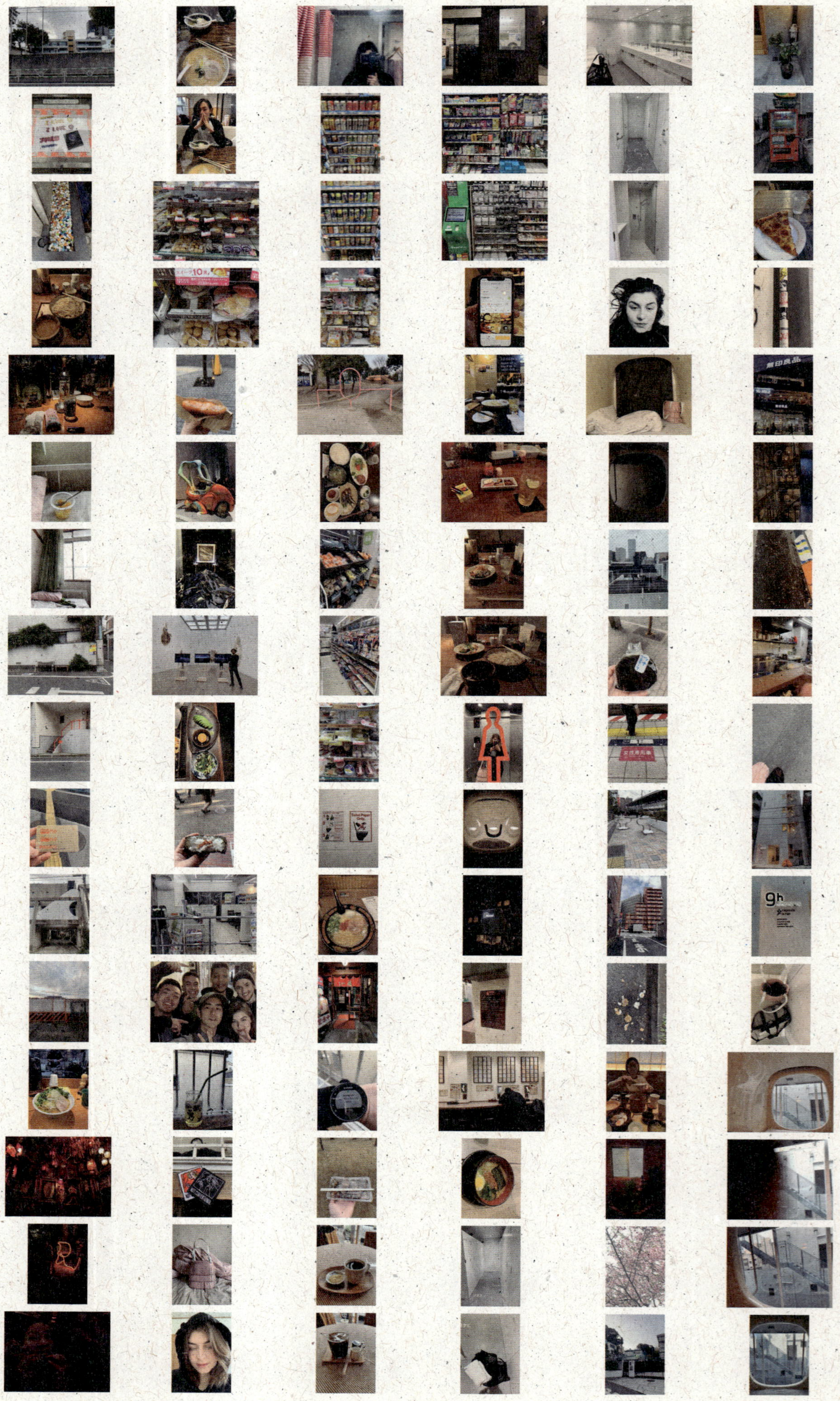

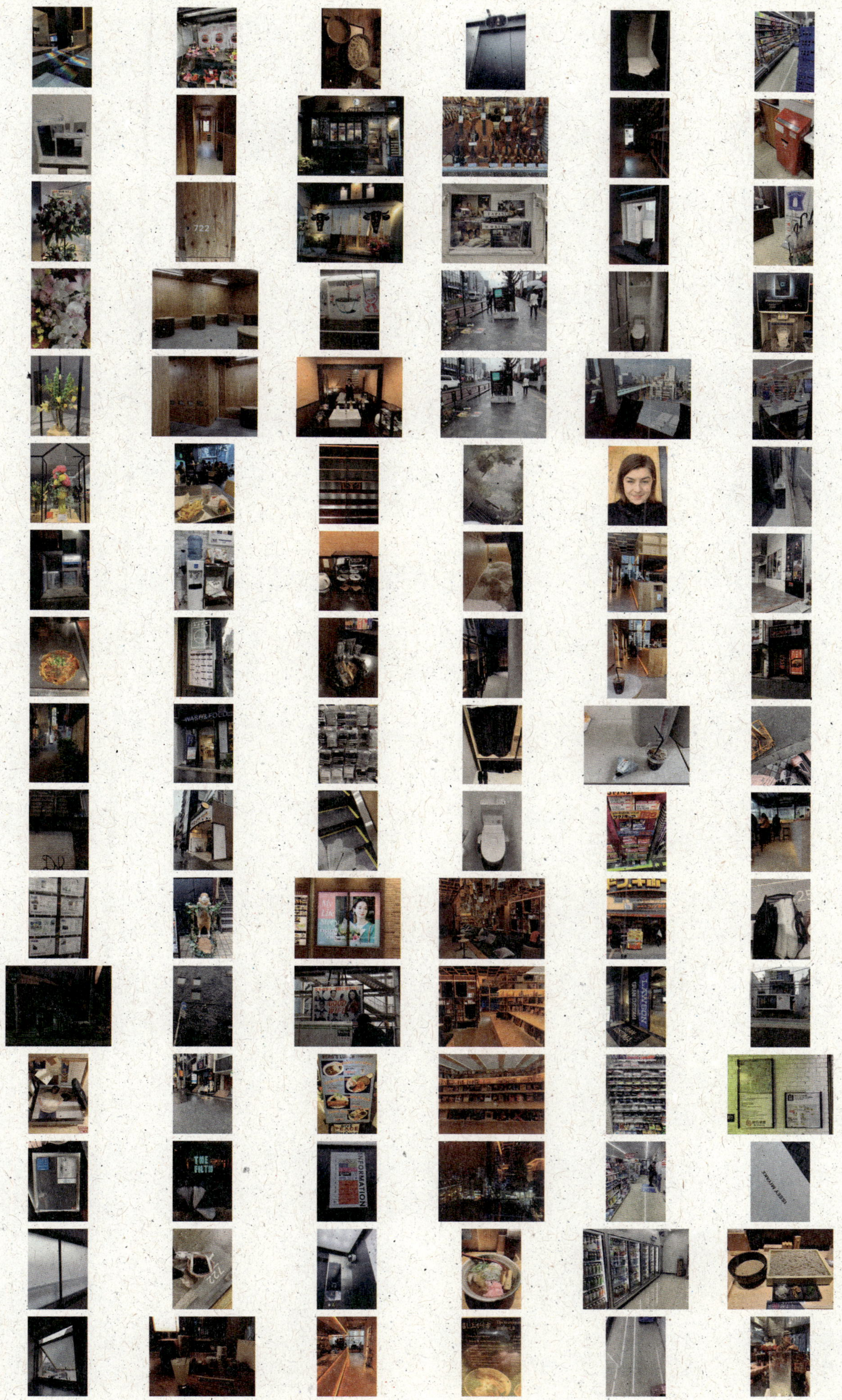

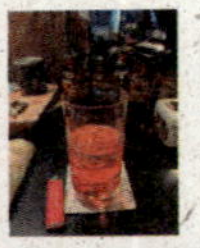
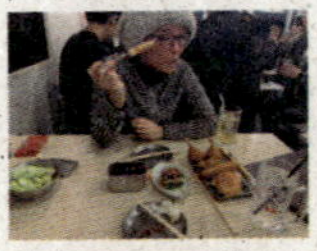
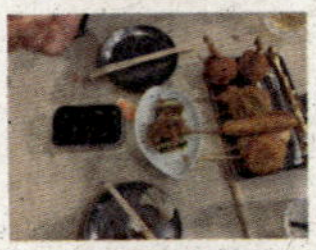
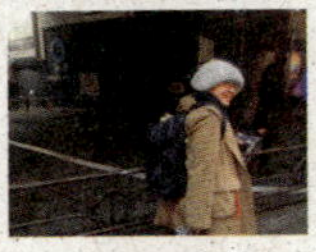
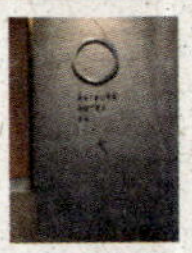
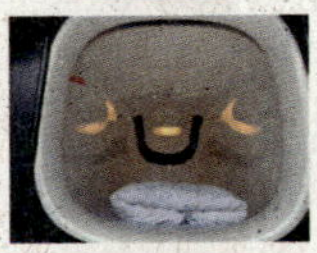
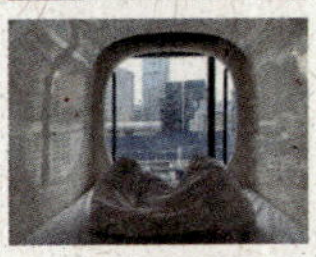
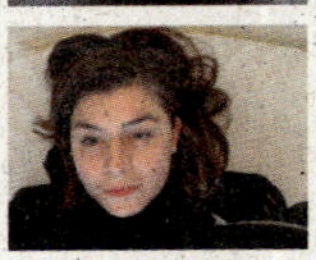
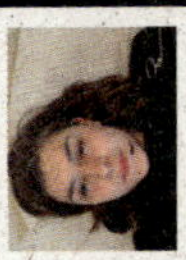
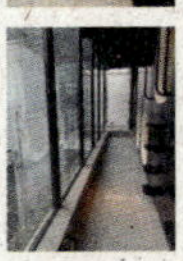
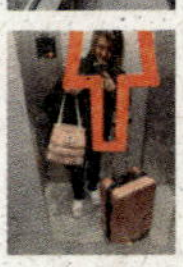
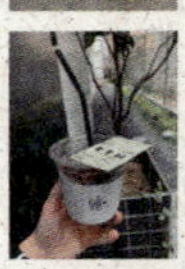
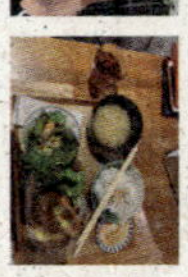
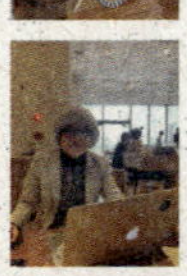
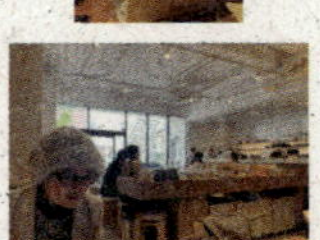

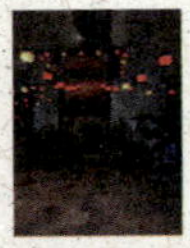
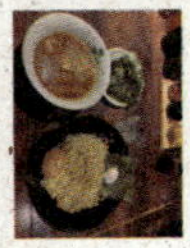

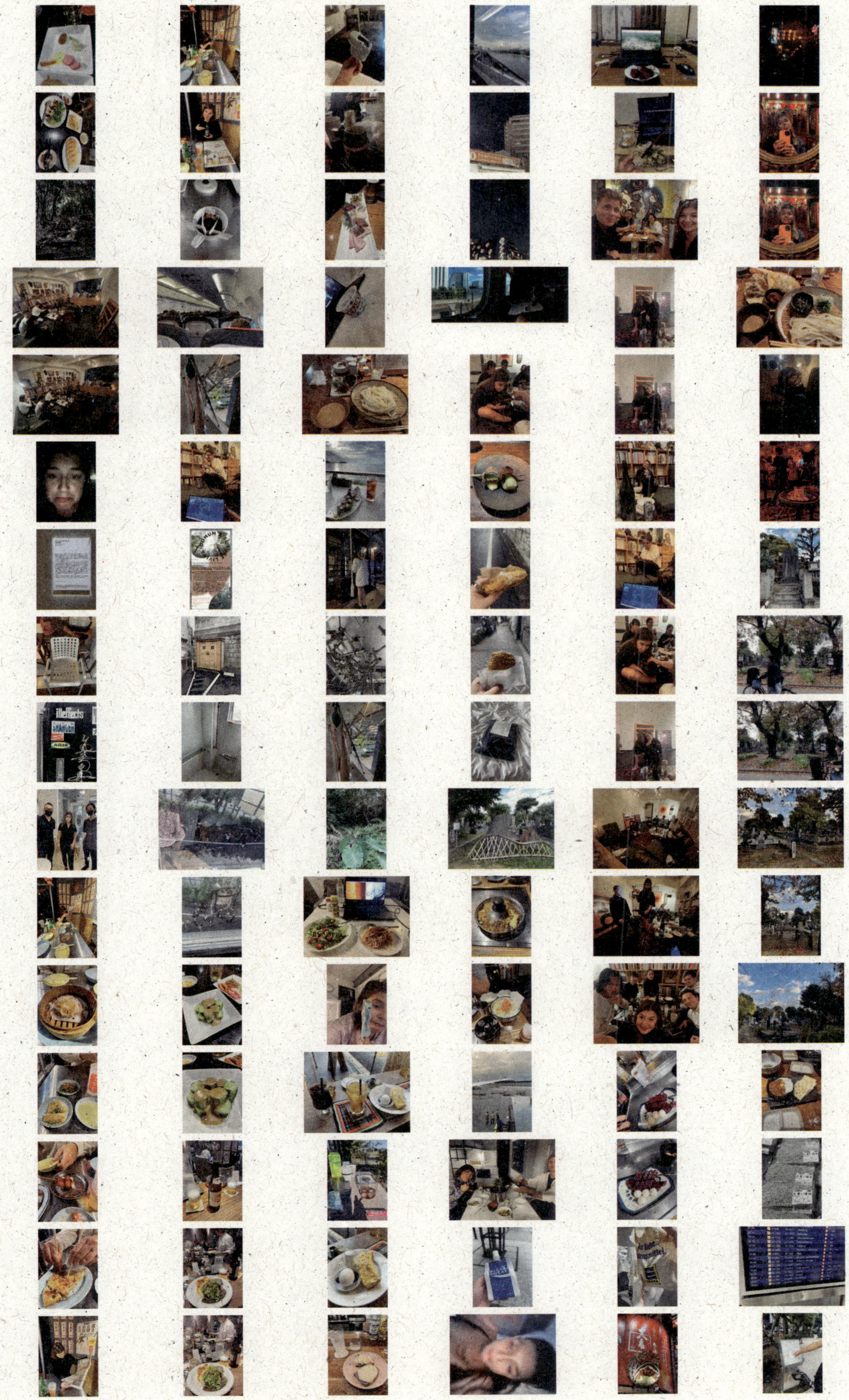

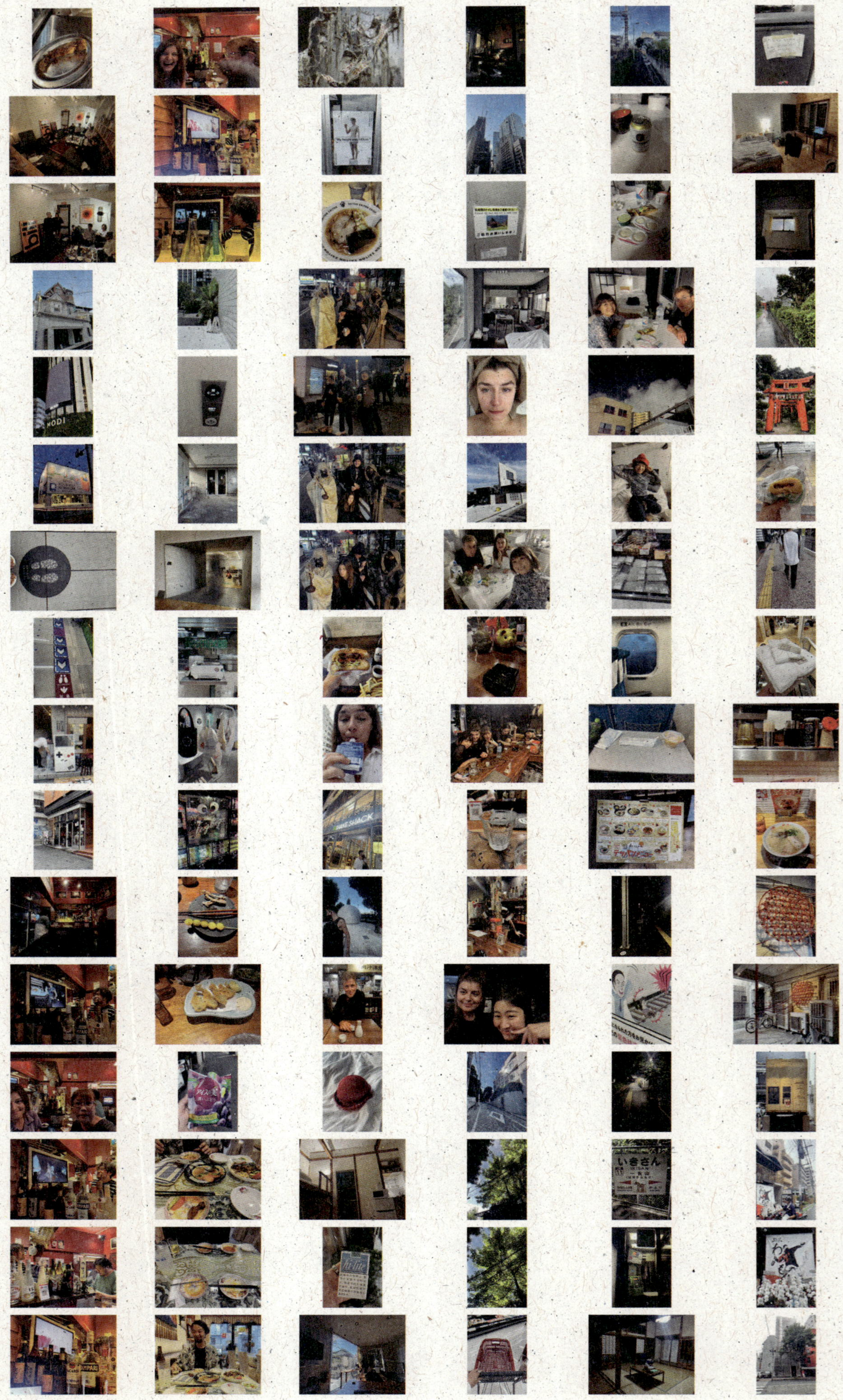

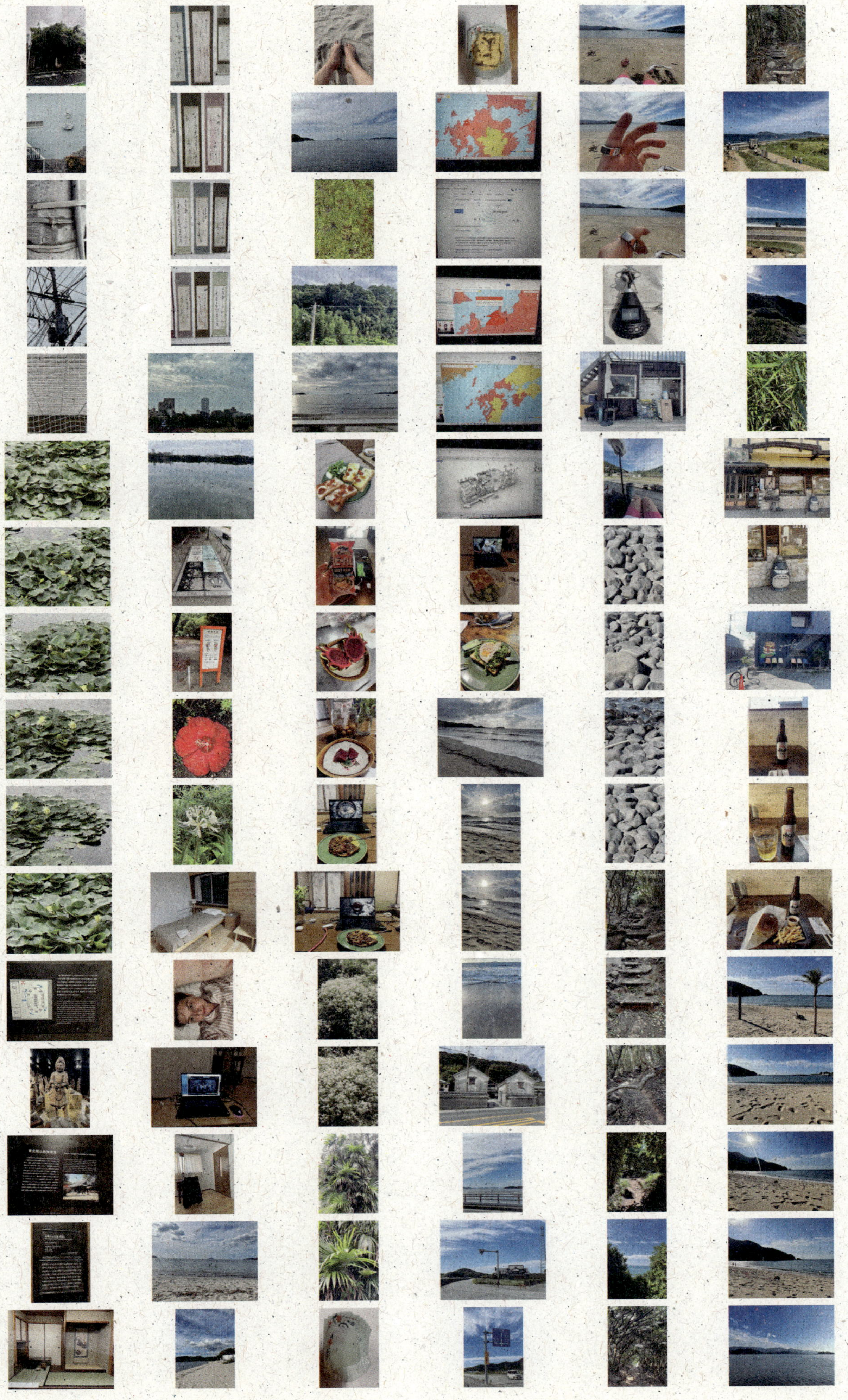

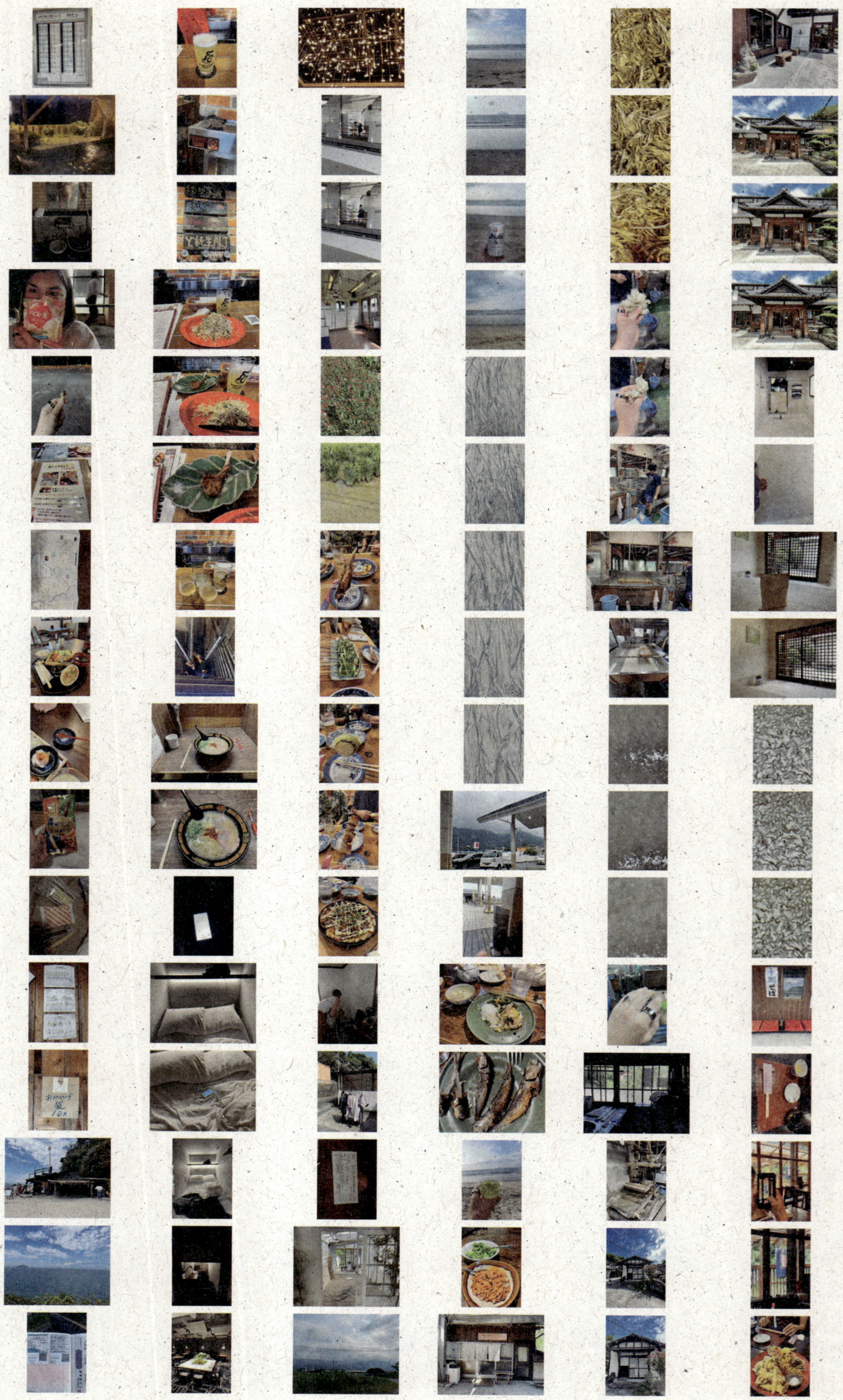

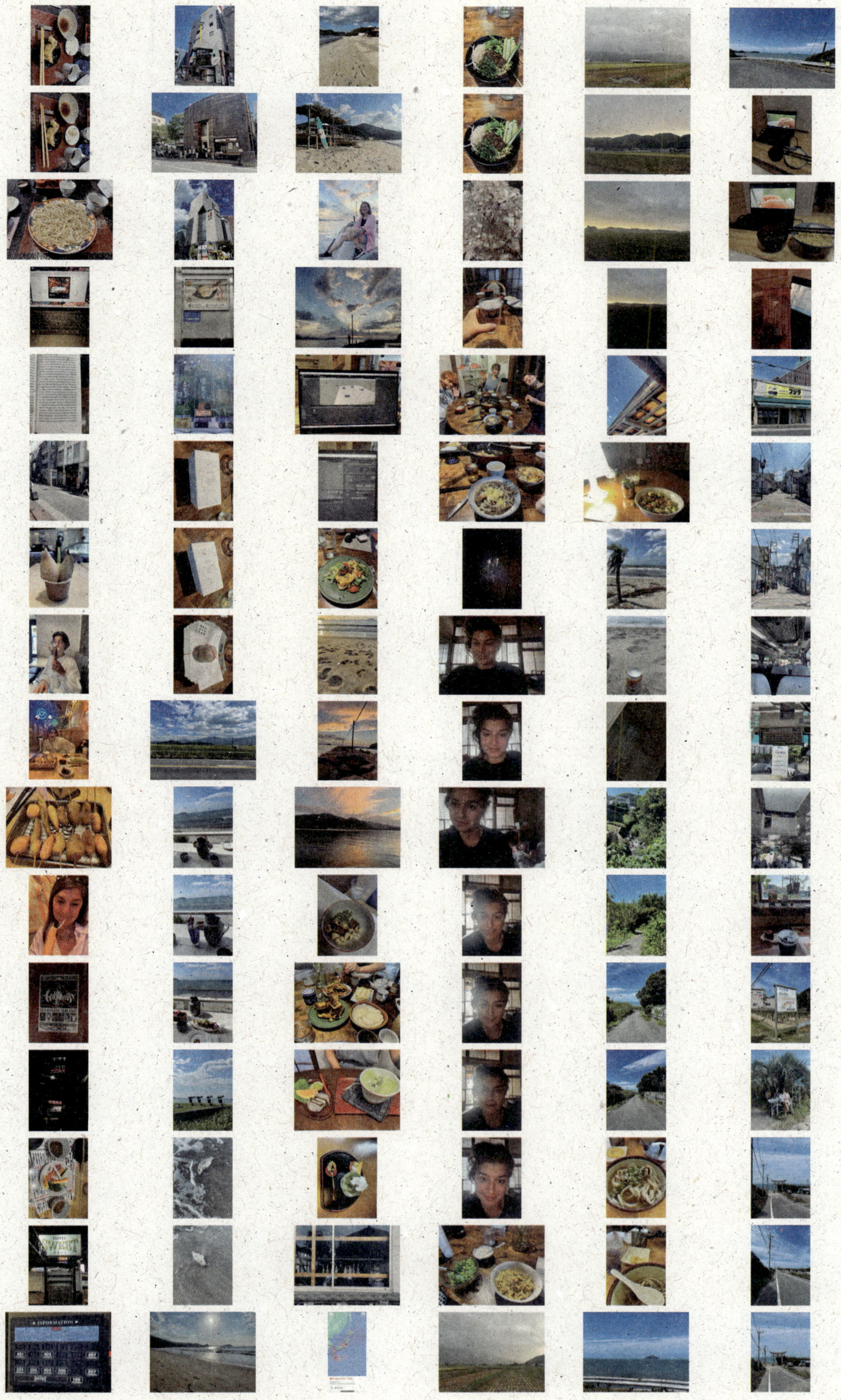

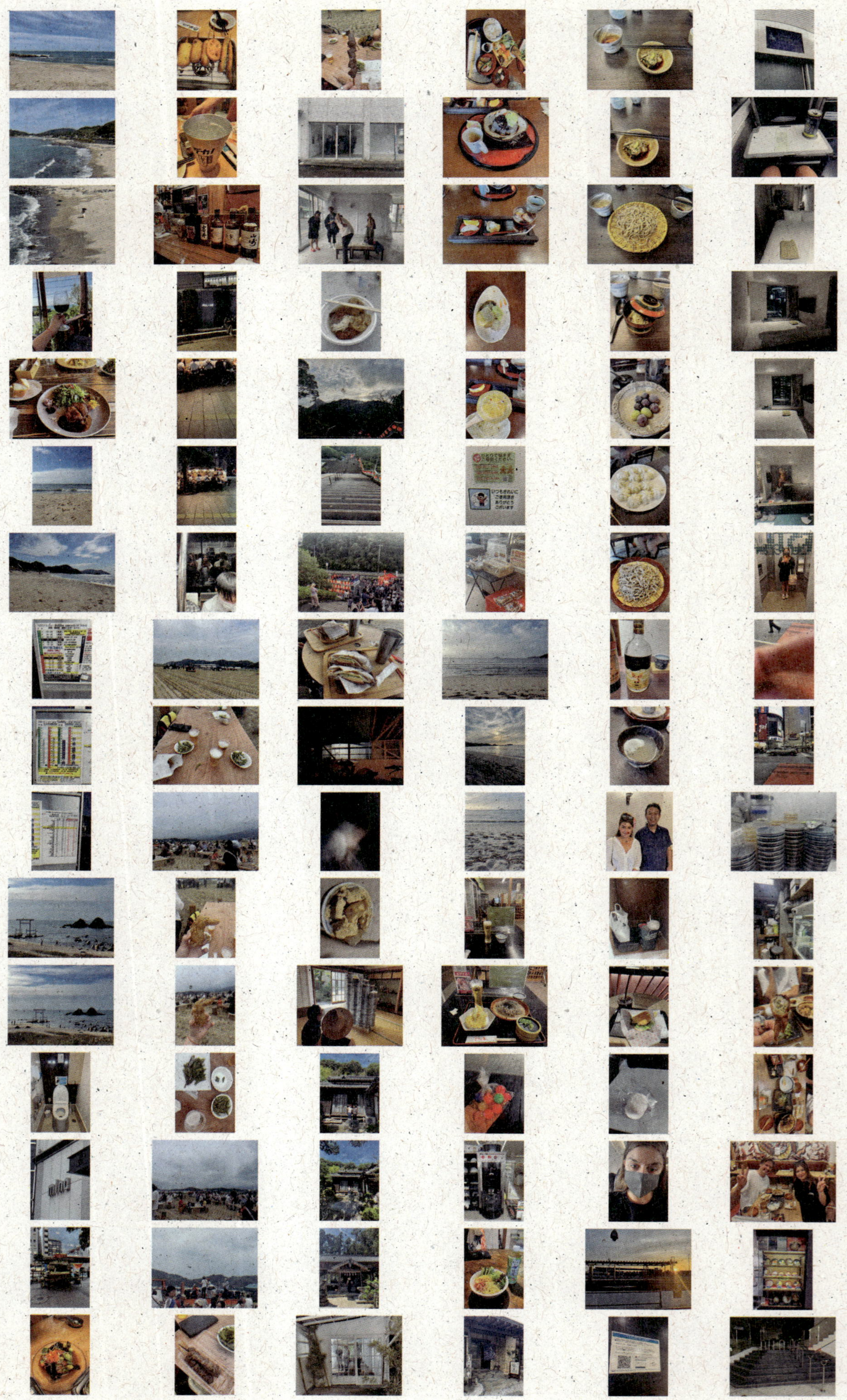

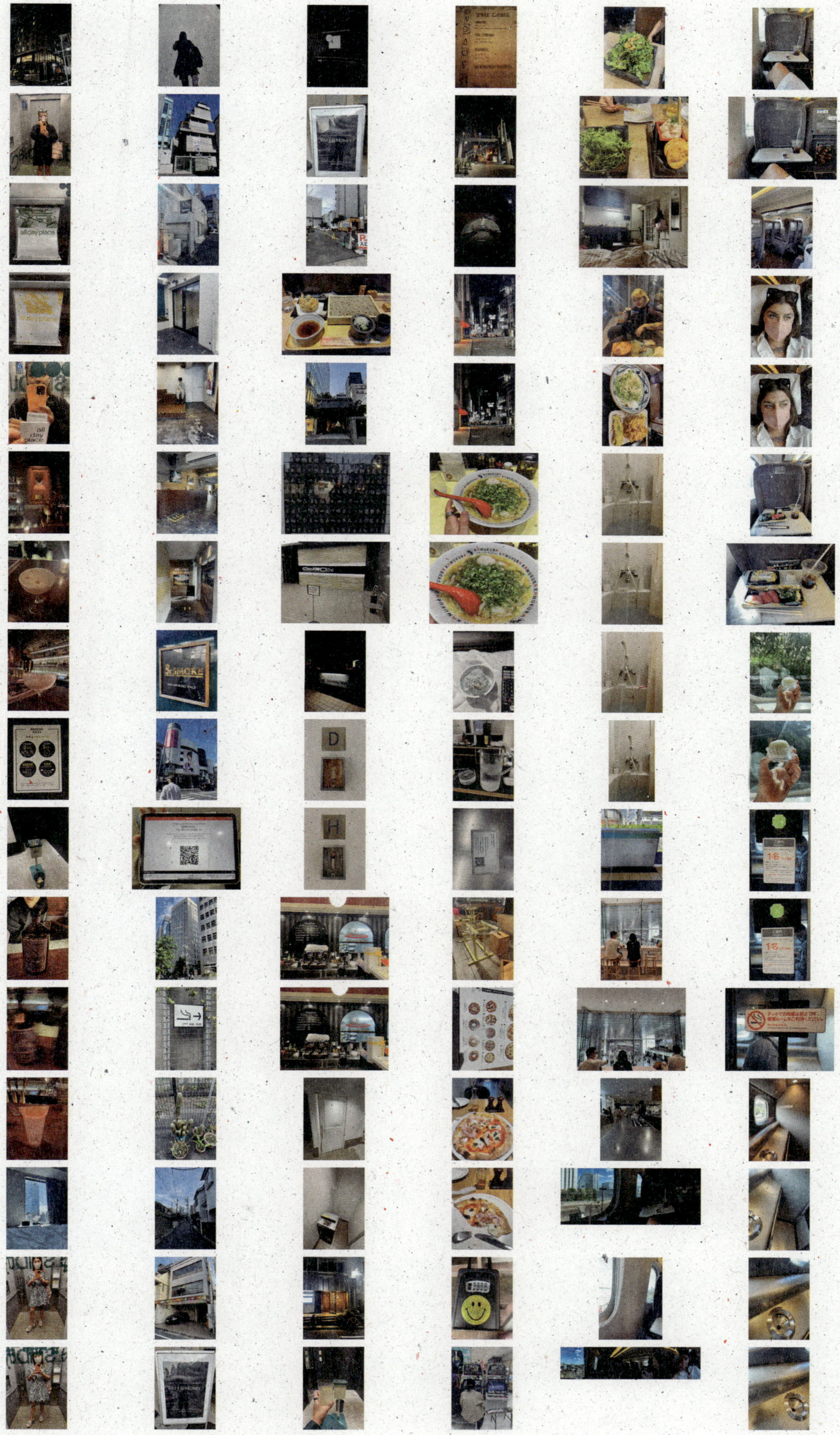

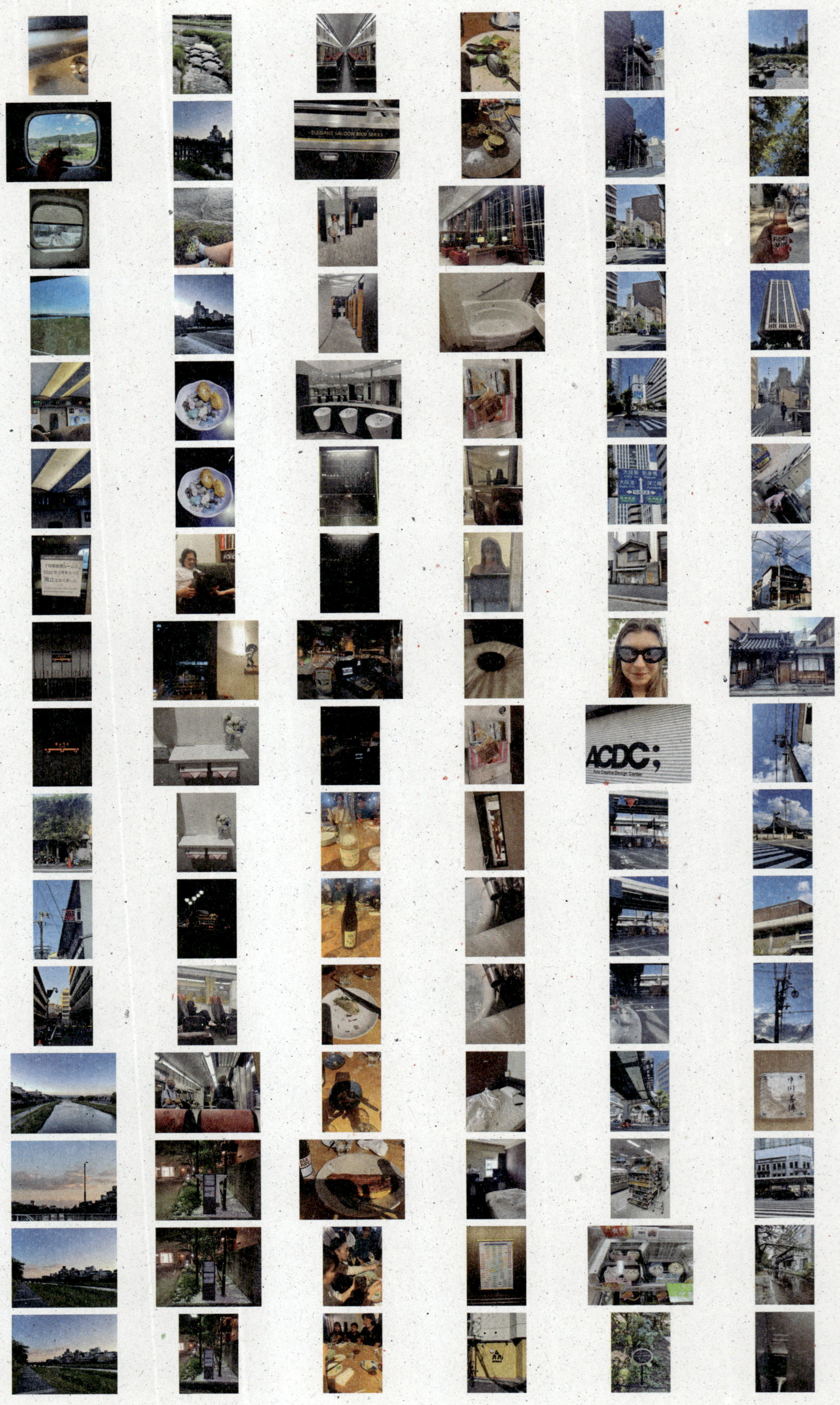
ELEGANT SALOON 8000 SERIES
ACDC;
Asia Creative Design Center

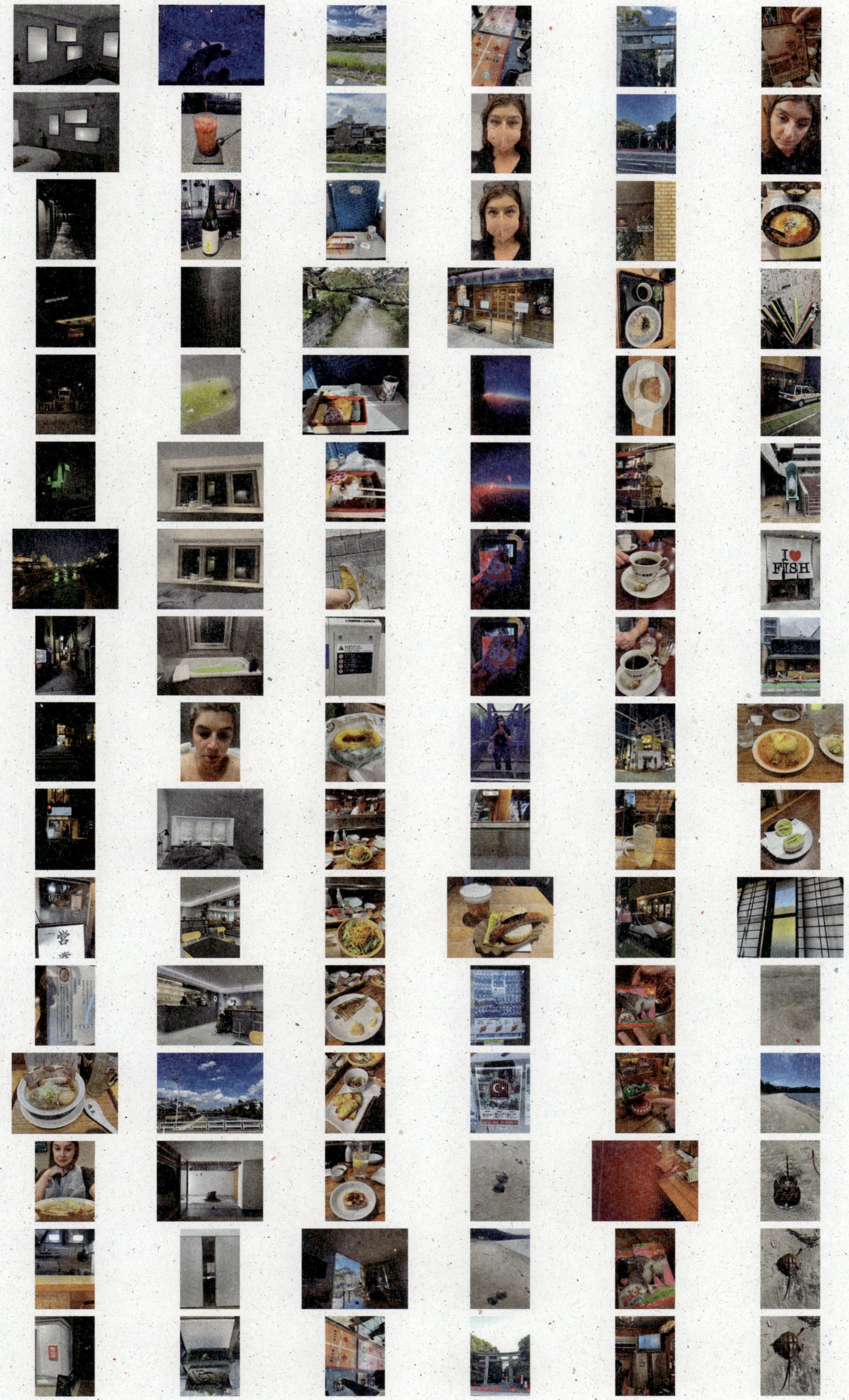
I ♥ FISH

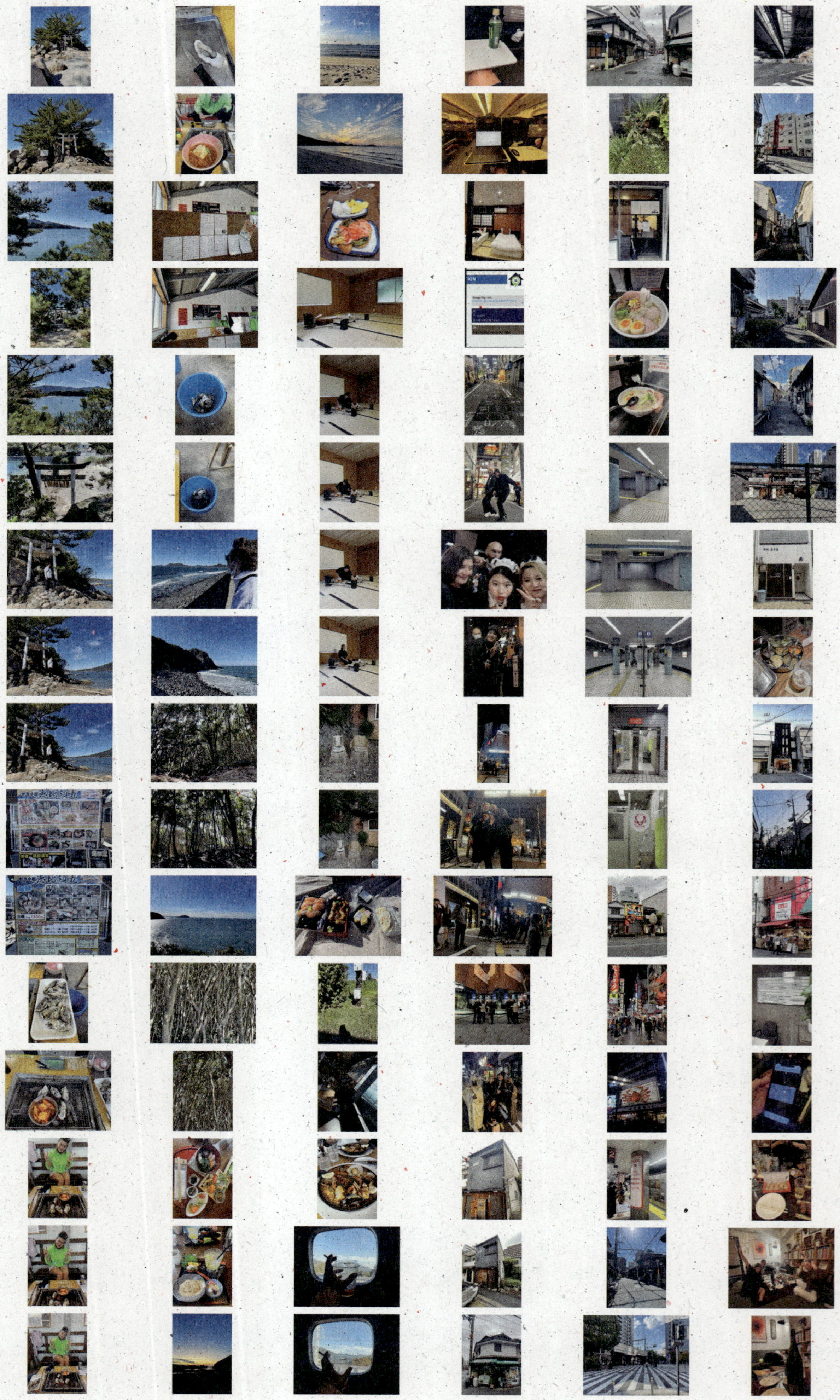

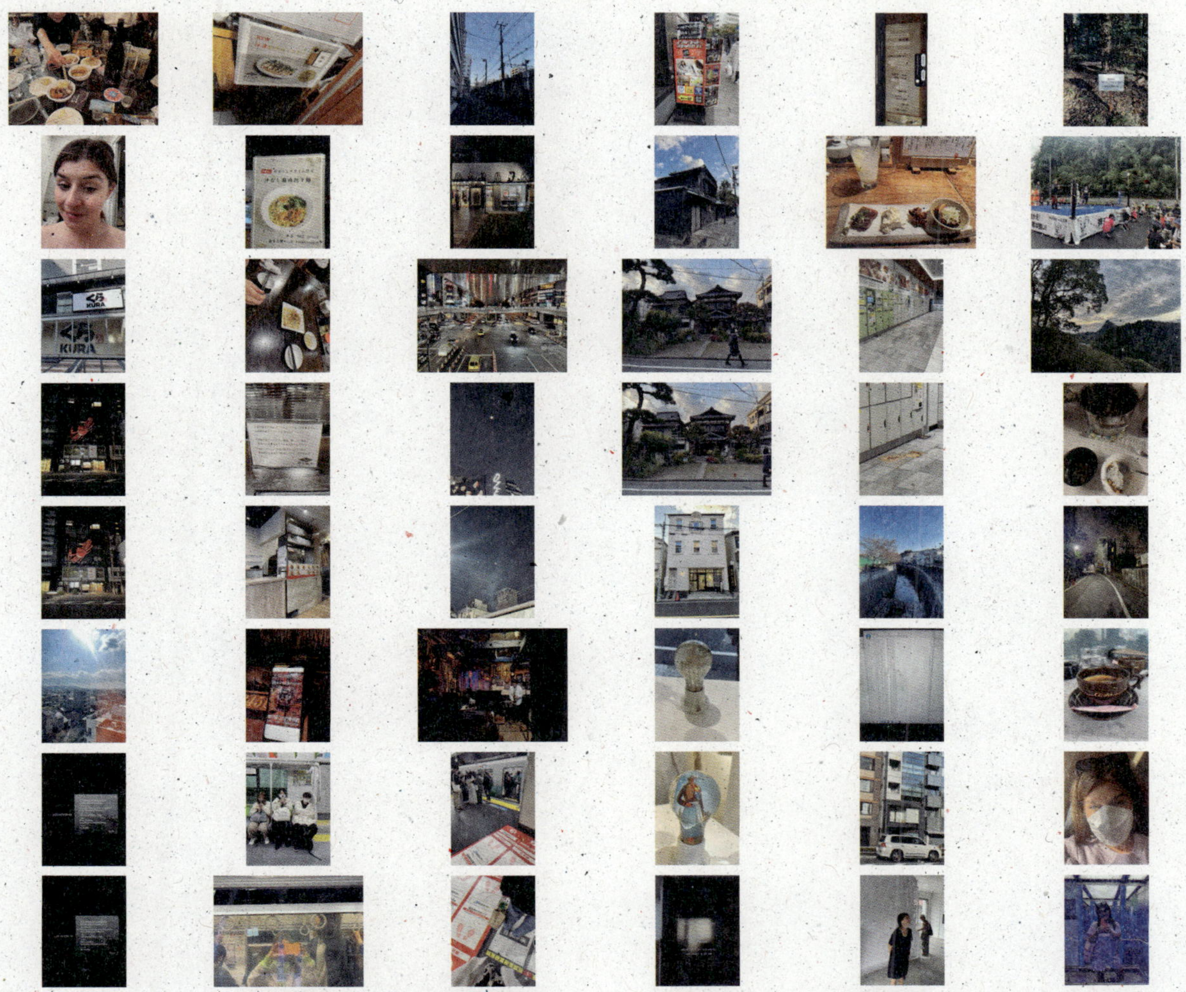

Verrechnet - Verbindungsentgelte Oktober 2022

Daten

0,01 MB Japan Mobil Roaming Daten

Preis inkl. USt

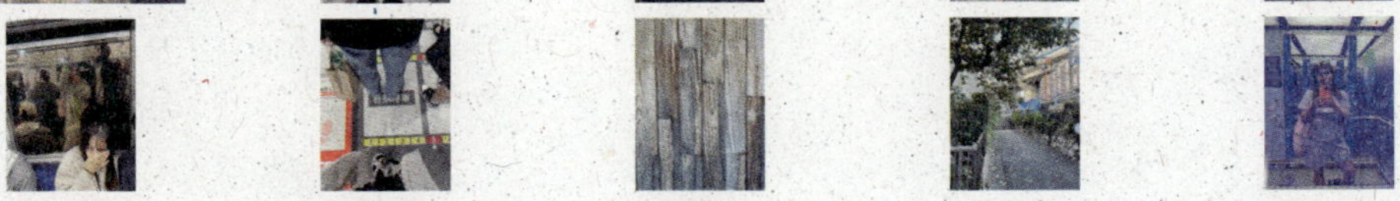

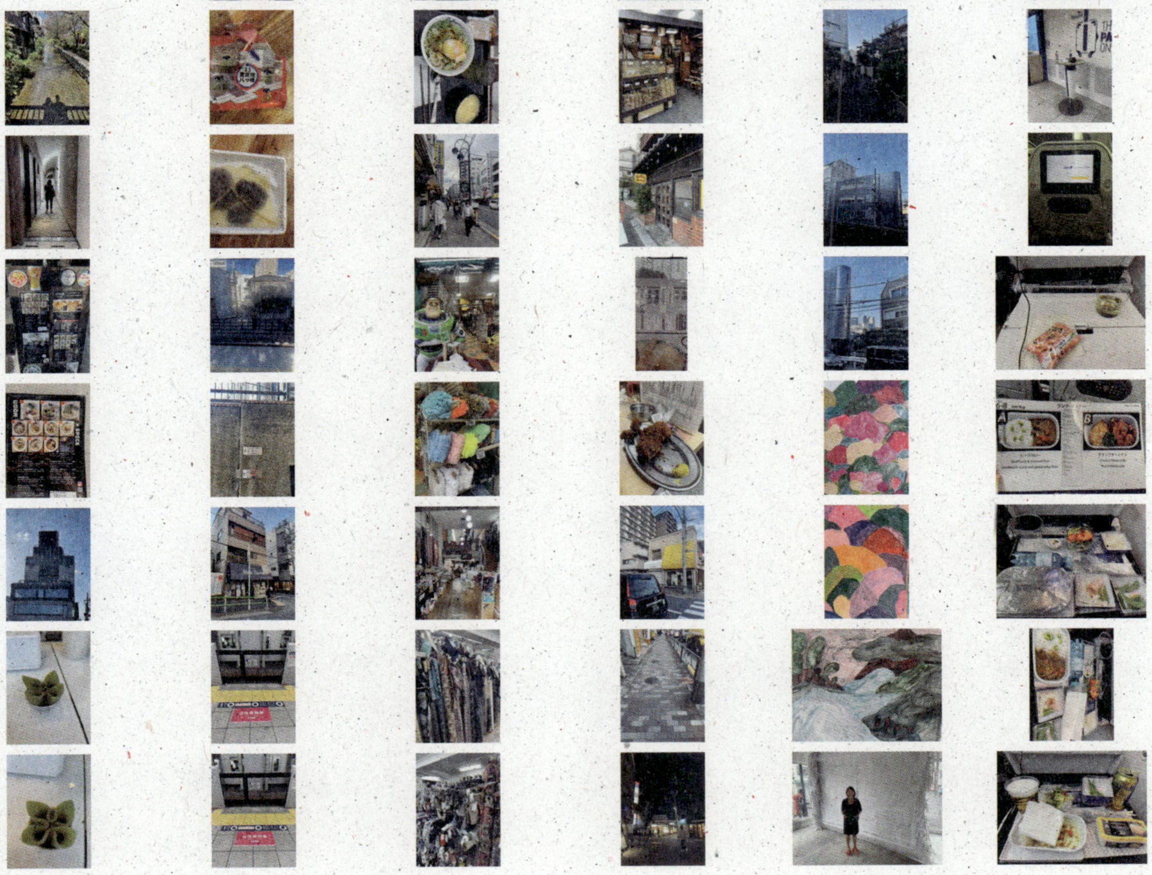

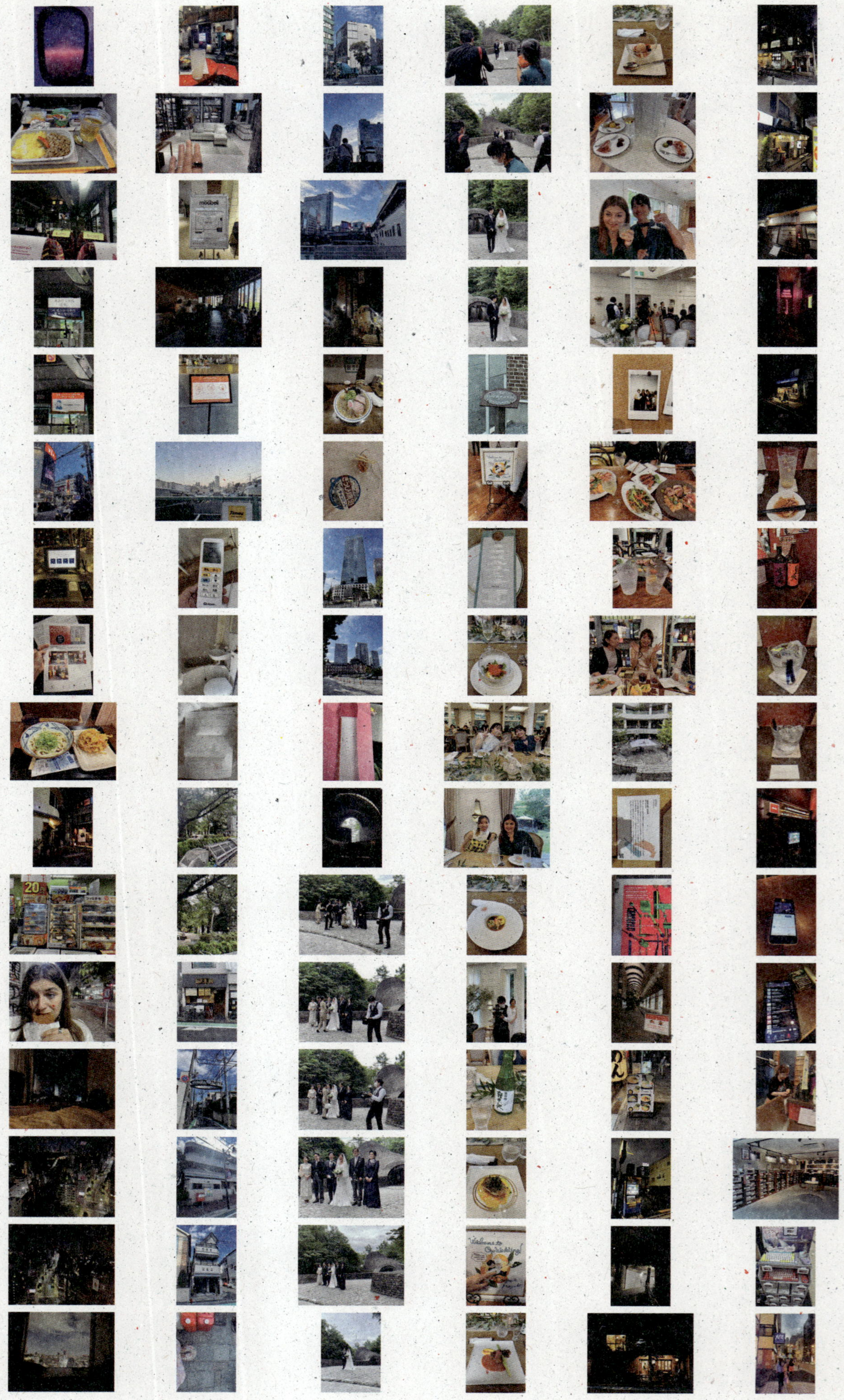

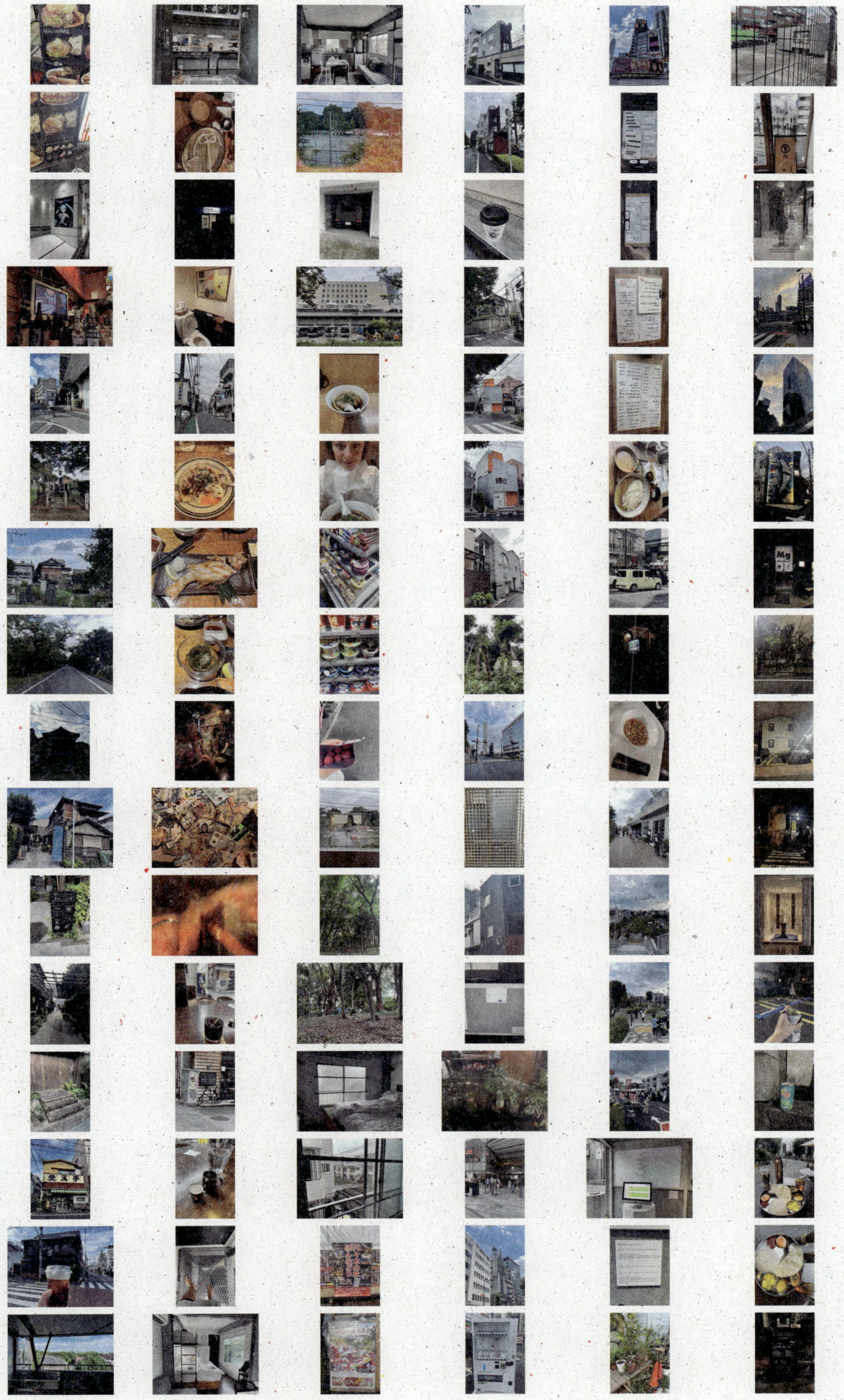

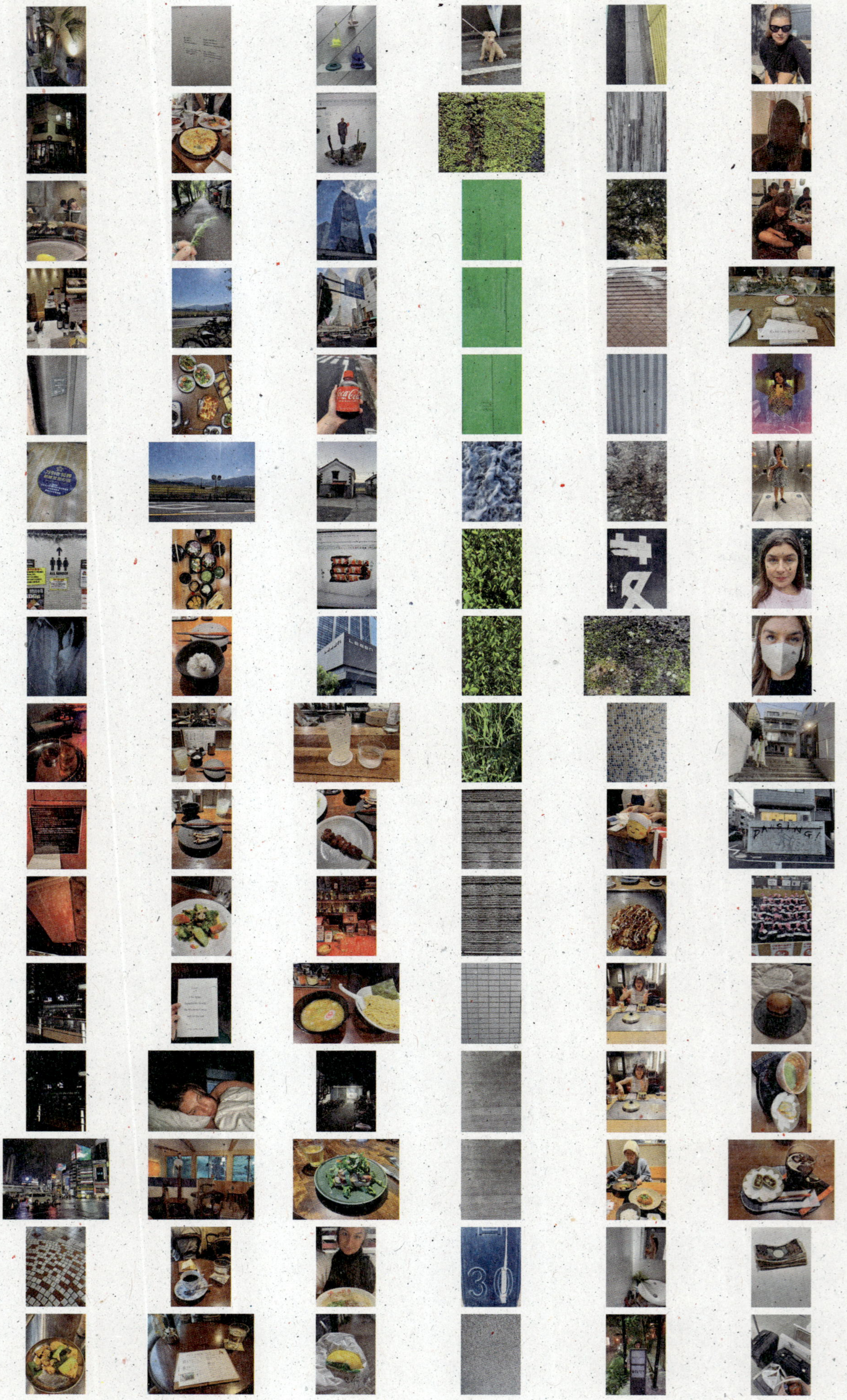

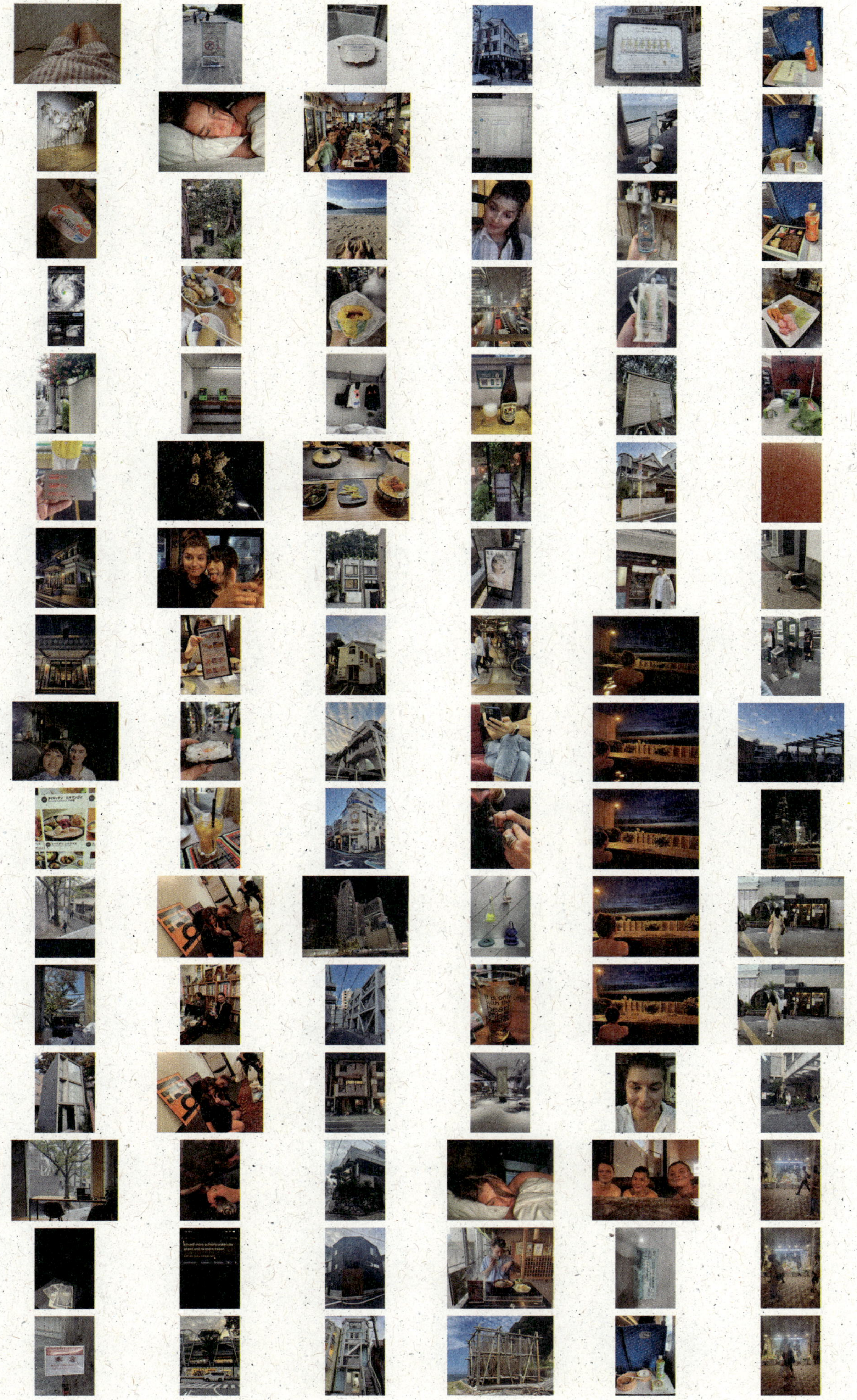

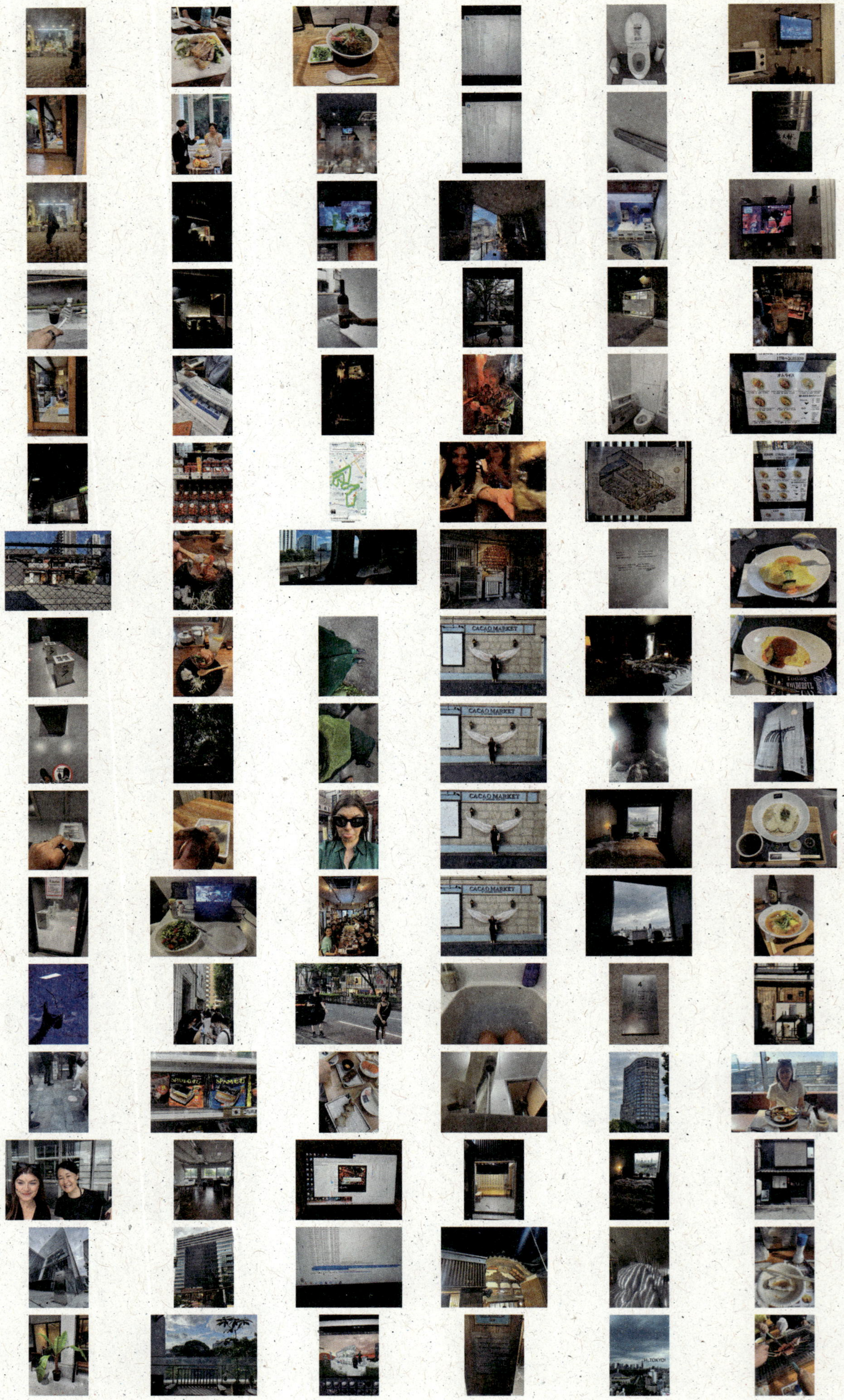
CACAO MARKET

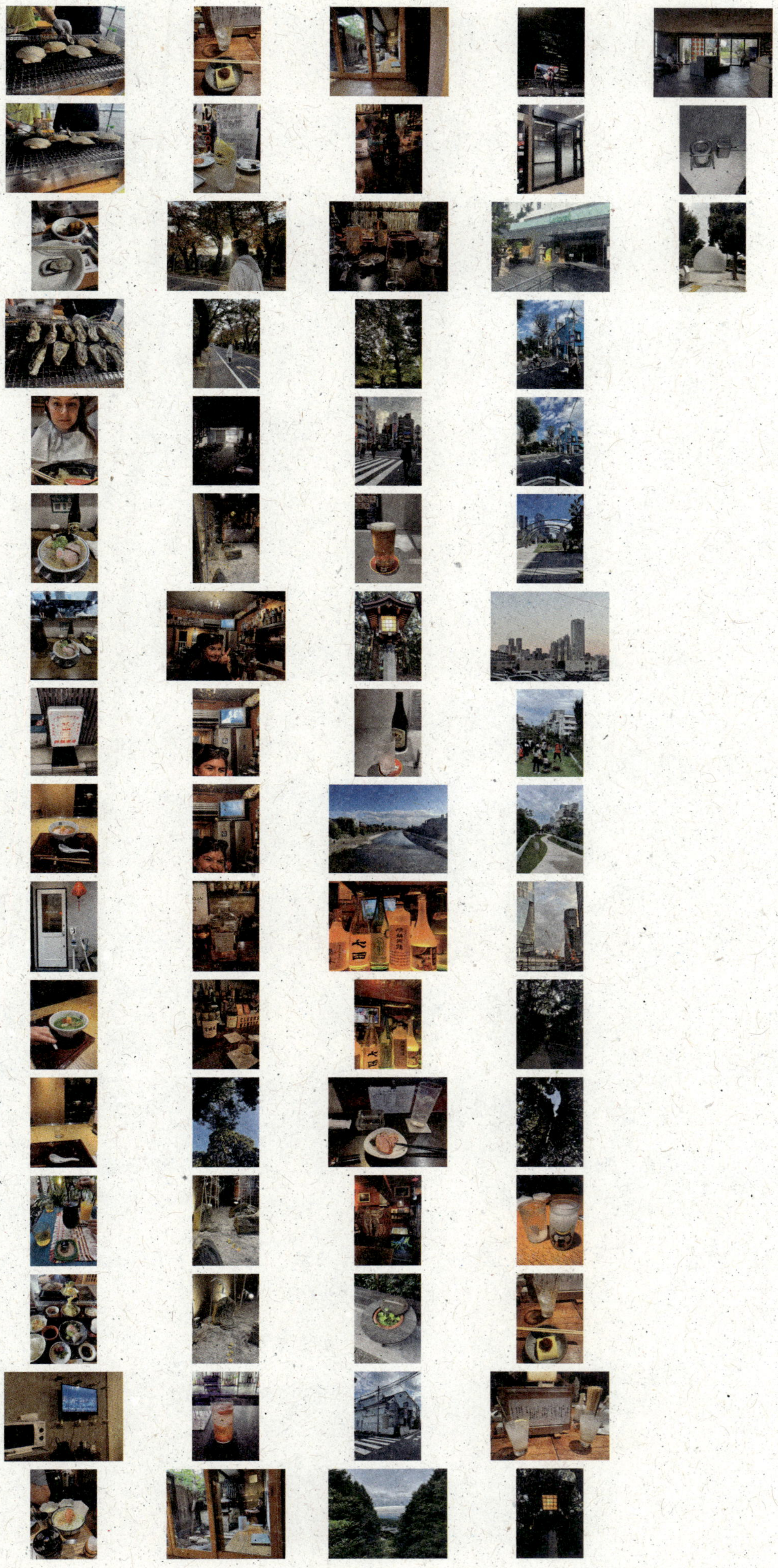

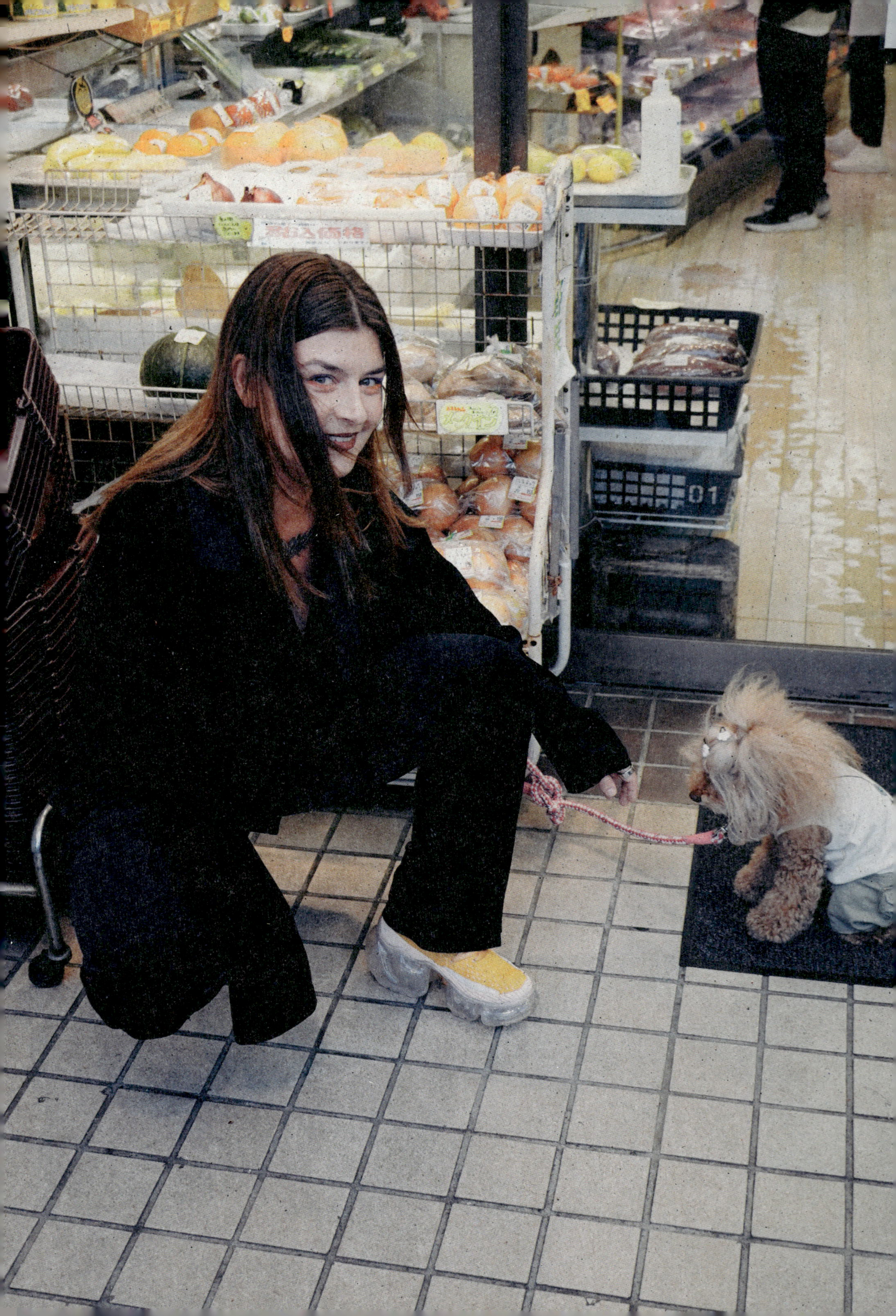

Fruit and vegetable store
Shimokitazawa
SEIJO ISHII Shimokitazawa West
03-5431-3833, Japan, 2022
Captured by Anna Manabe

Diary GMT Tokio, Japan
March 5, 2019 Time: 12:23

Q: What are the notable things which
happened to me today?
A: Yesterday I felt so sad and lost—
but today getting up and having a view over Shinjuku from the
eighth floor was amazing...
I could even extend my sleep for two hours—
A special treat from book and bed.
It seems if you have the luxury to extend the time of your stay
and you don't need to check out at a certain time
it makes you feel good and comfortable.
Like staying in bed all Sunday.
It gives you flexibility almost like in your own home.
The girl from the counter was pissed at me because you have to
say that you want to extend but then it was all forgotten.
I got an iced coffee at the cafe and enjoyed the view.
A room with a view.
They have all the expensive art magazines.
A lot of young girls and boys are staying over.
But more girls.
It's mixed-gender sleeping rooms with different kinds of size.
I love it.
The surrounding in Shinjuku—I hate
A lot of girl's bars and '80s vibe lights.
It's doing something with you're mind when you look at
lights all the time.
So they created a nice atmosphere in the middle of this district.
Like a library.
Or gallery space.
Or Viennese coffeeshop.
Q: What activities did I participate in today
and with whom did I share information?
A: I bought a suitcase at Don Quijote Shinjuku Kabukicho.
Awful place.
But cheap.
I'm heading to 9h now.
He reminds of a long-lost love of mine.

Q: Did I care about others or be concerned by others?
A: What's the feeling of the heart?
The girl and boy from the counter said goodbye.
And they shouted かわいい and laughed with me.

Diary GMT Tokio, Japan
March 5, 2019 Time: 21:19

Q: How many coughs?
A: There was an older man in the subway today starring
at me and not turning away.
There was a second one, too.
They behaved in an unusual way.
Then one seat was free, and I offered it to him.
Maybe he regrets now that he was looking at me this way.
He did not take the seat.
Offered it to me instead.
Now he's not looking anymore.

Diary GMT Tokio, Japan
March 4, 2019 Time: 14:19

Q: What are the notable things which happened to me today?
A: I went out until morning.
Harajuku, Vent and then I stayed in a love hotel.
Then I chilled in the lobby because the move out of capsule was at 10.00.
I took a train to Shinjuku.
A man was kind to me.
He let me out of the subway before him.
I had some thoughts that he wants to touch me because
it happened before.
But he was just nice.
I went to Don Quijote to buy a suitcase
Absolute horror.
I left my baggage at the book and bed.
You have to pay by card.
Everything.
All the time.
Printed money is gone.
I pay with my phone.
I choose my bedroom by phone.
I choose my fashion too.
Everyday.

Today I am wearing a naked coat.
Painted by a famous designer.
It has a nice atmosphere.
So, I took a walk until I could enter the booth.
I walked and walked Shibuya, Harajuku; Omotesando, everywhere.
Without a destination.
Q: Did I care about others or be concerned by others?
A: What's the feeling of the heart?
I was angry at humanity.
I did not know—what to do or where to go or what to feel.
I hate Shinjuku.
It's so loud too many lights—too much...
Prostitution and drinks.
Tourists love it—they can't see it clearly.
They like the lights.
They like the cliché too much to care.
I went to an exhibition about RGB in Laforet.
I sat there for hours.
On the floor.
Looking at the animations.
Listening to sound.
Q: What did I eat today?
A: Hikarie South Korean tofu and fish soup.
Ramen fish style around the corner of book and bed.

Q: How many coughs?
A: Six.

Q: Did I receive any surprise today?
A: Kodai does not want to hang out anymore.
I insulted him somehow.
I don't know what I did wrong.
Maybe he doesn't trust Europeans anymore.

Q: Where did I sleep tonight?
A: In a booth.
book and bed.

Diary GMT Tokio, Japan
March 3, 2019 Time: 01:16

Q: What are the notable things which happened to me today?
I did laundry at a special laundry service.
I had coffee in smoking areas.
I went to the sauna.
I taught some Japanese women how to use the sauna in our bedroom.
I met Omar.
I had an interesting time.
I did not go to his friend's gig but went to have a walk and bought
some new shoes.
Got really special ones from Nike.
They are already out of stock in japan.
After 24 hours.
They are so かわいい.
So then I picked my laundry from wash and fold.
My underwear was warm and folded perfectly.
It felt good.
My mother used to iron everything.
Even underwear.
It reminded me of home.
It felt good to have fresh clothes.
Then I went to Ebisu—to my favorite sake bar.
Where I used to meet Leander one year ago.
Before I went to udon Yamacho.
They know me already I don't need to order.
They bring a grapefruit sour and sesame udon.
I love being there—and the atmosphere.
This is the name of the sake place.
How I will miss this life.
Just partying all the time.
Later I went to a love hotel for my research.
Then ramen of course.
Then a different love hotel again.
It was 突拍子もない.
The ending was weird.
Q: Did I care about others or be concerned by others?
What's the feeling of the heart?
A: I was thinking about my family in Croatia and Germany.
Feeling guilty for living so far away.
I was discussing my identity.
So I was thinking about my heritage.
I think I have none.
So, I am very lost in this world.
I think this is the reason I want to stay in Tokyo.
To have no identity or create a fictional one.

Q: What kind of inspiration/information do I need today to improve my future?
A: Focus. Focus. Focus.
But somehow not focusing is part of the experiment.
Living the underground youth culture in Tokyo.
Focus. Focus. Focus.
But somehow not focusing is part of the experiment.
Living the underground young culture in Tokyo.
Focus. Focus. Focus.
But somehow not focusing is part of the experiment.
Living the underground culture in Tokyo.

Q: What did I eat today?
A: Udon at Yamacho.
Ramen with Chilean drunk guy.
Q: How many coughs?
A: 3–4
Q: How was my physical condition today?
Ok.
Excited.
Then again not.
Q: How many insults happen within sexism?
A: Not so many at least.
He's a mess.
Even more than me.

Q: Did I receive any surprise today?
Where did I sleep tonight?
A: Love hotel.

Diary
March 2, 2019
GMT Tokio, Japan
Time: 22:39

Q: What are the notable things which happened to me today?
A: I just slept three hours because of check out.
I sat in a konbini.
Thinking about where to go.
I don't really know where to go.
It is the weekend.
Every capsule takes five times the price.
I decided to write Kodai-chan
So, Kodai wanted to meet me so I went to Gokusai station
Waiting for him.
To pick me up.
We went to a park and talked a lot about Europe and Japan.
Days ago he said to me I can always use his private apartment.
If I miss having one.
Or I need one.
Then we went to his home.
I wanted to go to the countryside, but I felt so lost and weird.
I enjoyed the familiar atmosphere at his place.
It was cozy and personal—so many memories.
So many things in this tiny room.
He let me stay there.
We listened to old records of his mother.
We went to an okonomiyaki place—
He treated me Hiroshima style and some Okinawa sours.
He is from Hiroshima.
His brother lives in Texas and he has relatives all over the world.
He was still heartbroken because of a French girl he loved so much.
I slept good in his bed.
In the morning we met again for milktea and chatted, and I decided to go to my next accommodation—
the do c Ebisu.
Q: Did I care about others or be concerned by others?
What's the feeling of the heart?
A: I felt lost because I did not know where to go.
I'm tired and the experiment is exhausting
I thought it would be easier.
I can't think clearly.
I am lost.

Q: What did I eat today?
A: Onigiri.
Bento.
Okonomiyaki.
Q: How was my physical condition today?
A: Bad.
Hangover.

Q: What activities did I participate in today and with whom did I share information?
I am taking a train to Ginza.
To buy outfit and underpants for today and tomorrow.
Then I was heading to Nakameguro to meet my friend Kodai.
I saw a very interesting flower exhibition in a Ginza shopping mall.
My life with flowers.
Q: How many coughs?
A: Too many. It is weekend. People get 狂しい.
How many insults happen within sexism?
Kodai told me this story about boy meets girl in Japan.
It makes me very sad that this society still works like this.

Diary
March 2, 2019
GMT Tokio, Japan
Time: 15:06

Q: What are the notable things which happened to me today?
A: I woke up at the 9h in Asakasa.
It's so nice to sleep in a capsule.
It's like an 子宮 uterus.
Q: Did I care about others or be concerned by others?
What's the feeling of the heart?
What did I eat today?
A: Set menu.
Shitty, shitty tooo spicy ramen.
Q: How was my physical condition today?
A: Ok, ok… so so so…
Q: Did I receive any surprise today?
A: French guy attacked me in a konbini
And yelled that I am ugly.
He was on drugs big time.

Q: Did I receive any surprise today?
A: French guy attacked me in konbini
And yelled that I am ugly.
He was on drugs big time
Q: What activities did I participate in today and with whom did I share information?
A: I'm heading to Midori's office now.
To have lunch and work a little bit.
We had the best lunch.
It was some kind of pork stew and the best rice!!
We talked about our life and Midori's plan to move to Berlin
And my plan to move to Tokyo.
Then we went to the office.
I broke a bottle.
I tried to work but decided to go shopping instead.
In the evening I met Hans—we were discussing Japanese architecture and his diploma work.
Then we went to Aoyama tunnel
I stayed there and went to see Omar in Womb where he was DJ there.
It was quite nice.
Q: What kind of inspiration/information do I need today to improve my future?
A: I want to create something in Japan.
It seems everything is possible here.
Or maybe open an office with Hans.
Would be so great!
Q: How many coughs?
A: Too many.
Q: How many insults happen within sexism?
A: A lot.
One guy didn't want to let me go in the club.
Then he was really angry.
Because I left to talk to Omar and his friend who's having a bike shop.
Then there was this old guy in the club who didn't stop talking to me.
Then in the ramen shop everyone was drunk
I was so angry.
I called Philip and the connection was bad.
Q: Where did I sleep tonight?
A: I slept at 9 h Takebashi.

No Notes
March 1, 2019
GMT Tokio, Japan
Time: 00:00

Diary
February 28, 2019
GMT Tokio, Japan
Time: 02:34

Q: What are the notable things which happened to me today?
A: I had to move out of my apartment in Umegaoka this means it's my last week in Tokyo.
I brought my luggage to Midori in her office.
I went to sento in the evening
I think there was a red-light district.
Q: Did I care about others or be concerned by others?
What's the feeling of the heart?

I'm happy to have such good friends like Midori.
So, she lets me keep my belongings at her office.
And she even offered me to work there, too.

Q: What did I eat today?
A: Ramen in the night.
Ramen in the night.
Good salada and cold udon.
Q: How was my physical condition today?
A: I feel weird because I am leaving Tokyo soon.
Q: What activities did I participate in today and with whom did I share information?
How many coughs?
A! Two- I think I behaved myself.
Q: How many insults happen within sexism?
A: One man wanted to give me 30.000 ¥ in Shinjuku.
Ok I think I was in kind of prostitution district because two other men approached me, too.
But one guy touched my behind in rush hour.
Q: Where did I sleep tonight?
9h Asakasa.

Diary GMT Tokio, Japan
February 27, 2019 Time: 01:22

Q: What are the notable things which happened to me today?
A: I took a walk through the Hinagi park and ate Takoyaki.
I met myself in a kohi shop.
I tried to do 3D scans and I read.
I met Miyamoto in an izakaya near Umegaoka.
He walked me home.
We showed each other music and talked about careers.
His English improved.
But my Japanese did not.
Q: Did I care about others or be concerned by others?
What's the feeling of the heart?
A: I really like my friends in Tokyo.
But I sometimes I think I do not like anyone for real.
I love Philip.
What is happening to our society.
Or is it just growing up.
Q: What did I eat today?
A: Ramen dipping noodles.
Fried chicken.
Q: Did I receive any surprise today?
A: I said goodbye to my favorite kohi shop owner in Hibashi Matsubara.
One day I am going to live in Tokyo and come back here again.
Q: What activities did I participate in today and with whom did I share information?
A: I shared private stuff with Miyamoto.
Q: Where did i sleep tonight?
A: Umegaoka apartment.

Diary GMT Tokio, Japan
February 26, 2019 Time: 23:22

Q: What are the notable things which happened to me today?
A: I was drinking from my new straw I got from Mayuko-chan.
And did some teenage pictures for Instagram.
Then I took a walk to the kohi shop to read.
I stopped at the Hanegi park.
It's so nice.
Everybody uses it.
There is a big baseball field and a lot of furniture.
Q: Did I care about others or be concerned by others?
What's the feeling of the heart?
A: Somebody lost their budgie.
And is searching for it in the park.
I went to Arugamama to have dinner.
It was very nice.
But I think I have a fishbone in my throat.
I'll go to see a doctor when I'm back in Vienna.
Q: What kind of inspiration/information do I need today to improve my future?
I wrote the paper for Gabu Heindl seminar at the academy.
Q: "Wem gehört das Klo am Urban Loritz Platz?"
A: Finally, one thing of my list.
Q: Where did i sleep tonight?
A: Umegaoka.
But not really sleep.

Diary GMT Tokio, Japan
February 25, 2019 Time: 22:21

Q: What are the notable things which happened to me today?
A: Hashimura and Sawada-san showed me their New York City apartment project.
Amazing.
I met four German and one Japanese American in my fav. beer bar in Shibuya.
I took them to Oiran bar and to red bar.
They were a little boring.
Q: Did I care about others or be concerned by others?
A: What's the feeling of the heart?
I'm happy about my great family.
They are such a good backup all the time.
Since I'm not so often in Germany to see them.
I feel guilty.
Q: What activities did I participate in today and with whom did I share information?
A: I'm trying to meet Wataru Sawada-san.
But it's hard to find for me.
Somehow, it's problematic I am heading to Meguro now an hour late.
I don't have an address of his office yet.
I met him for an interview.
It was great.
Q: Did I care about others or be concerned by others?
What's the feeling of the heart?
A: I'm happy about my great family.
They are such a good backup all the time.
Since I'm not so often in Germany to see them.
I feel guilty
Q: What kind of inspiration/information do I need today to improve my future?
A: I need a finance plan how to return to Tokyo.
Q: How many coughs?
A: Three by women.
Q: How many insults happen within sexism?
A: One man changed his seat in the bus.
Q: Where did I sleep tonight?
A: Capsule.

Diary GMT Tokio, Japan
February 24, 2019 Time: 23:03

Q: What are the notable things which happened to me today?
A: I met Hiro for an interesting interview at a Hawaii beer bar.
Then Mayu and me got shoes at Boopers Harajuku.
She gave me a present from Hong Kong.
I was very happy.
We ended the day eating okonomiyaki in Harajuku.
Talking about our lives and boys.
Q: What kind of inspiration/information do I need today to improve my future?
A: I need to establish a routine to get up earlier.

Q: What did I eat today?
A: Fried chicken from a konbini.
Onigiri.
Okonomiyaki.
Some drinks...
Q: How was my physical condition today?
A: Ok, I felt sad because I need to leave soon...
Q: Did I receive any surprise today?
A: I got a sweet present from Mayu-chan.
She got me earings and a straw from Hong Kong.
Q: Where did I sleep tonight?
In Yotsuya-Sanchome.
Ruka came by to visit.

Diary GMT Tokio, Japan
February 23, 2019 Time: 21:46

Q: What are the notable things which happened to me today?
A: The westerners got on my nerves.
They don't play by the rules
It embarrassed me.
A lot of men are looking into my eyes.
Q: What activities did I participate in today and with whom did I share information?

A: I met Goro and he took me to Roppongi hills.
We went to Media Ambition in Mori.
It was a disappointing exhibition.
Everyone was there just for the view.
So bizarre.
But then he took me to his exhibition.
In National Art Centre Tokyo.
It was amazing.
His works are so inspiring.
Sacred.
We went to a cheap izakaya later.
Eat mussels and sashimi.
I saw him differently.
He told me about his divorce and new girlfriend.
Very interesting.
I'm happy to be his friend.
Q: Did I care about others or be concerned by others?
What's the feeling of the heart?
A: I fell in love with Goro's art.
And I'm glad that after all his loss in his young life he seems well.
Q: What kind of inspiration/information do I need today
to improve my future?
I want to be an artist, too.
I hope I get into an amazing PhD program here in December.
I feel so inspired and numb at the same time.
Q: What did I eat today?
A: Izakaya.
Later ramen with milkman.
Q: How was my physical condition today?
A: Hungover tired but good.
Q: How many insults happen within sexism?
A: None
With Goro I felt save.
Even the looks weren't bad.
Q: Where did I sleep tonight?
Umegaoka.

Diary GMT Tokio, Japan
February 22, 2019 Time: 22:12

Q: What are the notable things which happened to me today?
A: Today I woke up at noon and got a mail from Gabu.
I have to hand in my essay about Urban Loritz Platz.
I'm stressed.
Don't want to spend too much time on Vienna.

Q: Did I care about others or be concerned by others?
What's the feeling of the heart?
I had a nightmare about Deborah.
I called her in the morning.

Diary GMT Tokio, Japan
February 21, 2019 Time: 22:59

Q: What are the notable things which happened to me today?
I met a great artist Midori introduced me to machina from Korea.
I hope I can use her music for my film.

Q: What activities did I participate in today and with whom
did I share information?
A: I went to digital choc x mutek in WWW.
I love the building my sensei designed.
I got a lot of inspiration!!
The visual work was amazing and interesting.

Q: Did I care about others or be concerned by others?
What's the feeling of the heart?
A: I went to my new fav ramen place.
The owner knew me.
And was the kindest.
We had a good laugh.
Q: What kind of inspiration/information do I need today
A: to improve my future?
I took a walk to Shimo-Kita.
Everything was so perfect and nice.
Alles war so schön heute.
Q: What did I eat today?
A: Hanbaga at eight burgers.
Ramen before bed.
Q: How many coughs?
A: Five. Fünf.
Q: How was my physical condition today?
A: Tired but fine.
Q: Did I receive any surprise today?
I met machina.
A: And good networking evening with visual artists.
Q: Where did I sleep tonight?
A: On the train.

Diary GMT Tokio, Japan
February 20, 2019 Time: 00:16

Q: What are the notable things which happened to me today?
A: I was smoking in the smoking area at Ebisu station and met
one guy from New Zealand—he wanted to have sake with me.
We ended up in a club Harlem with hundreds of Japanese teenagers.
I showed him golden ball.
Q: What did I eat today?
A: Udon in Yamacho.
Q: How many coughs?
A: Two.
Q: How was my physical condition today?
Okok.

Diary GMT Tokio, Japan
February 19, 2019 Time: 02:29

Q: What are the notable things which happened to me today?
A: I didn't t sleep and went to Geidai.
Met Hiro by the koi.
Did an interview with Tom-san.
Felt great afterwards.
Q: What activities did I participate in today and with whom
did I share information?
A: I did my interview with Tom-san.
It was amazing feeling.
I was so nervous.
Q: Did I care about others or be concerned by others?
What's the feeling of the heart?
A: I still think about family a lot.
Q: What kind of inspiration/information do I need today to
improve my future?
A: I need to focus on filming more elevations.
And infrastructures.
Q: What did I eat today?
A: Toast with marmalade + coffee.
Onigiri.
Glibber Chinese vegetables with crisp noodles with Hiro.
Dipping Ramen noodles for dinner.
Best mochi ever—strawberry taste.
Beer and coffee
A lot of cigarettes.
Q: How was my physical condition today?
A: Tired.
Now sleepless.
Q: How many insults happen within sexism?
None.
Learned a lot about feminism in architecture in Japan from Tom-san.
Q: Did I receive any surprise today?
A: The man from my fav. kohi shop asked me if I need an
umbrella when I left the shop.
He gave me one.
So nice.
The ramen man was supernova to me and his cooking was delicious.
Q: Where did I sleep tonight?
A: Shinjuku in a fresh sheet.
Q: What are the notable things which happened to me today?
I was at a nice kohi shop preparing questions for
Tom-san's interview tomorrow.
They even have German beer and internet and you can smoke.
Then I met Mayuko-chan to discuss the questions in another coffee shop.
She agreed to do an interview too.
Q: What activities did I participate in today and with whom
did I share information?
A: I met Mayu in the evening.
And worked on the interview.
Q: Did I care about others or be concerned by others?
What's the feeling of the heart?
A: I had nightmares the whole night.
Dreaming about my sister.
I couldn't t sleep all.

night.
I called her at 6.00 am.
She is well.
Q: What kind of inspiration/information do I need today to improve my future?
A: I need to focus on my career in Japan and finish my studies soon.

Diary
February 18, 2019
GMT Tokio, Japan
Time: 23:36

Q: What did I eat today?
A: Onigiri + iced coffee
Toast with marmalade.
Lunch in the park rice with meat and egg, sour veggies.
Some pasta dish from supermarket for dinner.
A lot of green tea.
Q: How many coughs?
A: It was a nice day with no insults.
Q: How was my physical condition today?
A: During day good.
Fight with Philip in Vienna.
Nightmares during night.
Until the morning.

Q: Where did I sleep tonight?
A: Ikebukuro.
Q: What are the notable things which happened to me today?

Diary
February 17, 2019
GMT Tokio, Japan
Time: 23:48

Q: What are the notable things which happened to me today?
A: I woke up on the 13th floor of a hotel in Roppongi.
I felt weird.
But then good.
I had coffee.
Smoked a cigarette in the smoking area.
Then I walked in Shinjuku station all day.
I didn't t know where to go because the weather was so beautiful and I needed to think.
Q: What activities did I participate in today and with whom did I share information?
A: I met Juliana to say goodbye to her.
At Shinjuku station.
She took the wrong exit.
It took ages to find her.
Q: Did I care about others or be concerned by others? What's the feeling of the heart?
A: I am concerned about my sister.
She looks so tired and depressed on the picture my mum send me.
Q: What kind of inspiration/information do I need today to improve my future?
A: Hans showed me a little kohi shop where I can work.
I will go there tomorrow to work a little.
Q: What did I eat today?
A: Tomato ramen.
In the evening a set with Hans.
We make this Sunday's Sonntagsbraten eating out thing.
Q: How was my physical condition today?
A: Depressed and lonely.

Diary
February 16, 2019
GMT Tokio, Japan
Time: 22:06

Q: What are the notable things which happened to me today?
A: We went to an experimental music concert in the evening.
It was amazing but very deep.
I got sad so I left for a drink in Oiran bar.
There I met navy soldiers.
Their chief was female.
Later sang karaoke.

Q: What activities did I participate in today and with whom did I share information?
A: I met a lot of different people
Had interesting conversations.
Q: Did I care about others or be concerned by others?
What's the feeling of the heart?
A: I didn't t care about others.
Just about me.
Q: What kind of inspiration/information do I need today to improve my future?
A: This question is so hard.
I need to develop a strategy how to proceed and visualize my feeling towards the dissolving space.
Q: What did I eat today?
A: Sushi at a kentai restaurant.
No breakfast.
Q: How was my physical condition today?
A: Hangover.
Q: Where did I sleep tonight?
A: Hotel in Roppongi.

Diary
February 15, 2019
GMT Tokio, Japan
Time: 05:25

Q: What are the notable things which happened to me today?
A: I had a nice day with Juliana.
We went to Omotesando and catstreet.
I showed her architecture in Tokyo.
In the evening we went to Aoyama tunnel, a small small club in Shibuya.
We danced all night.
We met some DJ from Tokyo and talked.
Q: What did I eat today?
A: Ramen in Shibuya at my fav. place.
Mine was too spicy. Again.
Q: How was my physical condition today?
Tired but happy.

Diary
February 14, 2019
GMT Tokio, Japan
Time: 23:47

Q: What are the notable things which happened to me today?
A: I wish I was seventeen again.
First I went to red bar and then took a cab to Shimo-Kita to listen to a jazz concert in a little bar called Apollo.
Midori showed me once.
Q: What activities did I participate in today and with whom did I share information?
I'm going to study at the Geidai library.
And shoot some scenes at Ueno area.
In Shibuya and Shimokitazawa.
Did I care about others or be concerned by others?
What's the feeling of the heart?
I had a dream about my sister.
Q: What did I eat today?
A: Toast with strawberry jam and avocado coffee
Iced coffee for the train ride to Ueno.
Vegan tanmen in Ueno.
Q: How many coughs?
A: None.
A view weird looks.
Q: How was my physical condition today?
A: Super tired.
Q: Did I receive any surprise today?
Maybe I'm meeting a monk later evening.
I got chocolate in a Maybach limousine.
Q: Where did I sleep tonight?
A: ?

Diary
February 13, 2019
GMT Tokio, Japan
Time: 00:29

Q: What are the notable things which happened to me today?
A: I thought I lost all my project data from last two years.
Stressed out.
Juliana broke the aircon.
We were freezing.
I fixed it and don't know how.

Then I tidied up to work.
I tried to do maps but helped Laurie with the hotel in Bali.
Q: What activities did I participate in today and with whom did I share information?
A: I shared with Mayuko.
With Juliana I didn't.
She's ignoring me because of the aircon.
I think.
I don't care.
I have a lot on my plate now.
Tomorrow I'll have another meeting.
Q: Did I care about others or be concerned by others? What's the feeling of the heart?
A: I'm concerned about Mayuko.
I'm meeting her for dinner.
I went home.
It was a nice evening with her.
I am very happy to have her in my life.
Q: What did I eat today?
A: I made eggs and avocado breakfast.
Yamacho udon.
Q: How many coughs?
A: None.
I listen to music all day.
On my way home the train smelled like sake and sweet vomit.
I escaped one old drunk to press himself on me while exiting the train.
Q: How many insults happen within sexism?
One guy touched my face at Uniqlo.
Q: Did I receive any surprise today?
A: I sold a painting and earned 750 euro.
So I'm glad to not have to worry about money.
Q: Where did i sleep tonight?
Umegaoka station.
Train
Q: What are the notable things which happened to me today?
A: I refused.
I refused.
A store in Harajuku.
I didn't t go.
Q: What activities did I participate in today and with whom did I share information?
A: I showed Juliana Omotesando and Shibuya.
My favorite spots.
Also, by night.
Q: Did I care about others or be concerned by others? What's the feeling of the heart?
A: It's difficult to keep up relationships.
I'm glad that the barkeeper from
Oiran bar was so happy to see me
...and we dissolved the discussion.
Q: What kind of inspiration/information do I need today to improve my future?
A: I was filming a lot of street life.
What did I eat today?
Onigiri and hanbaga
Best soba with walnut sauce in Omotesando.
Q: How many coughs?
A: One.
Q: How was my physical condition today?
A: Ok.
Some pain in my stomach.
Q: Did I receive any surprise today?
A: I met interesting persona on the streets.
He abolished his family to become an entrepreneur.
He invited me for a drink and told me about his life
without a private apartment.
I will invite him to do an interview
Q: Where did I sleep tonight?
A: Umegaoka apartment.

No Notes
February 12, 2019
GMT Tokio, Japan
Time: 23:02

Diary
February 11, 2019
GMT Tokio, Japan
Time: 19:23

Q: What are the notable things which happened to me today?
A: Today Michi left.
I miss her already.
She woke me up at six.
Juliana and I slept long.

Diary
February 10, 2019
GMT Tokio, Japan
Time: 06:22

Q: Did I care about others or be concerned by others? What's the feeling of the heart?
A: I really got even closer to Michi and Laurie on this trip.
I am very happy that they took the long journey to Tokyo so I could show them my Tokyo.
Q: How was my physical condition today?
A: Ok.
Q: How many insults happen within sexism?
A: None.

Q: What are the notable things which happened to me today?
A: It was Michi's s last day in Tokyo.
We went to a temple in Gotokuji.
The cat temple.
Later we took a tram to Setagaya.
Juliana and her went to Akihabara.
I didn't t want to confront myself with manga today.
So I walked home.
Watched a movie and cooked for the first time since I arrived.

Q: What activities did I participate in today and with whom did I share information?
A: I met with the Tokyo Tech. people.
We went to a cheap izakaya.
Michi wanted to go out because it was her last night.
We went to a concert to life freak.
We got drunk and waited for the first train in a ramen shop with Noemi.
Q: Did I care about others or be concerned by others? What's the feeling of the heart?
A: I went to the concert to please Michi's last wish.
Q: What kind of inspiration/information do I need today to im prove my future?
A: I should be braver and should focus on my art.
Q: What did I eat today?
A: Onigiri + iced coffee.
Rice bowl small with egg and meat.
Izakaya with the girls.
And Ichiran ramen in the early hours.
Q: How was my physical condition today?
I am very awake and feel sleepless.

https://maps.app.goo.gl/hicmB8mPHKyMdjm27?g_st=ic ...Type text here

Check Downs

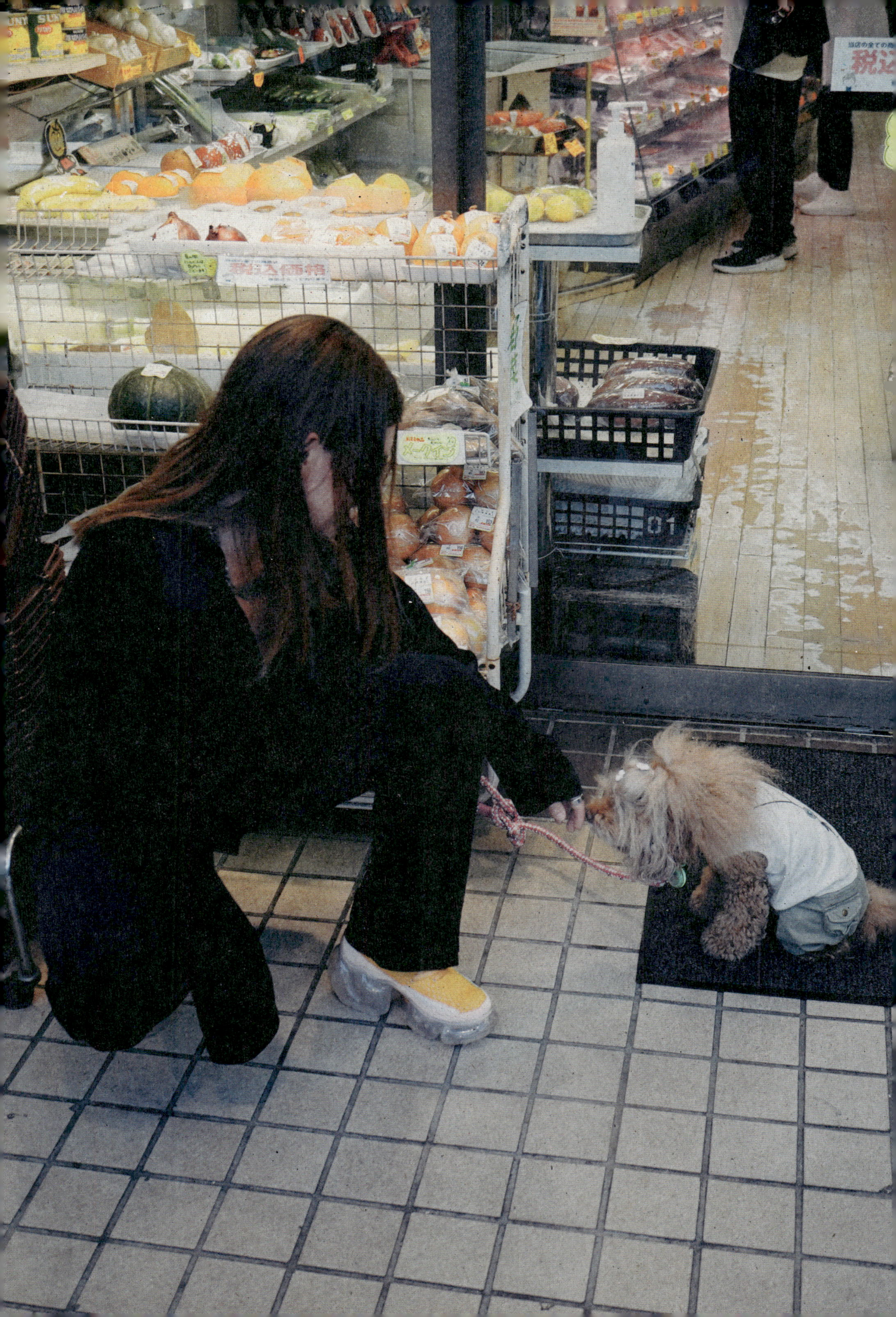
01

PHOTO INDEX (Title)	GPS LATITUDE (Numbers)	LONGITUDE (Numbers)	ALTITUDE (Numbers)	CREATE DATE (Date, Time)	DAILY STEPS (Human)
HERMES.jpeg	-	-	-	-	-
IMG_0904.jpeg	-	-	-	-	-
IMG_1001.jpeg	-	-	-	-	-
IMG_4150.jpeg	-	-	-	-	-
LOVE.jpeg	-	-	-	-	-
PHARELL.jpeg	-	-	-	-	-
THE GIRLS OF OMOTESANDO.jpeg	-	-	-	-	-
UNOPORT.jpeg	-	-	-	-	-
IMG_0526.jpeg	35,72152222	139,7323611	31,21252372	2017-10-29, 22:01:52	-
TREE.jpeg	-	-	-	2017-11-01, 10:56:40	-
IMG_1015.jpeg	35,72149167	139,7323	30,72653061	2017-11-09, 14:52:22	-
HANGOVER.jpeg	35,66205278	139,7003167	33,24023438	2017-11-19, 12:13:07	-
IMG_1412.jpeg	35,71696111	139,7380056	28,99092971	2017-11-23, 23:29:02	-
UNI.jpeg	35,71832222	139,7723222	16,0713073	2017-11-25, 01:45:33	-
IMG_1549.jpeg	35,72146944	139,7324361	40,30425963	2017-12-01, 04:31:33	-
IMG_1629.jpeg	35,73014167	139,7291417	35,41547278	2017-12-02, 17:14:51	-
IMG_1660.jpeg	35,71832222	139,7723528	15,23245214	2017-12-03, 18:44:18	-
IMG_1982.jpeg	35,65894444	139,6977222	44,26342711	2017-12-16, 21:33:29	-
IMG_1985.jpeg	35,66486389	139,7130139	46,30049261	2017-12-17, 04:09:48	-
IMG_1994.jpeg	35,65773056	139,6992806	38	2017-12-17, 08:41:47	-
IMG_2031.jpeg	35,70303333	139,7003944	20,92938209	2017-12-17, 10:47:31	-
CHRISTMAS.jpeg	-	-	-	2017-12-23, 21:06:30	17.791
CHRISTMASEVE.jpeg	-	-	-	2017-12-24, 19:15:51	-
IMG_2480.jpeg	-	-	-	2017-12-27, 20:00:50	-
2CHRISTMASCELEBRATION.jpeg	35,73576111	139,7245639	27,00054555	2018-01-02, 20:22:45	10.904
2CHRISTMASCELEBRATION (2).jpeg	35,73574444	139,7245028	26,94183865	2018-01-02, 20:35:47	-
IMG_2547.jpeg	-	-	-	2018-01-03, 11:22:01	-
IMG_2549.jpeg	-	-	-	2018-01-03, 11:27:26	-
EMPEROR.jpeg	35,71825	139,7723083	14,03281853	2018-01-05, 18:51:22	-
PANDABABY.jpeg	35,71815833	139,7722167	13,00274725	2018-01-13, 16:20:55	-
SAD.jpeg	35,735875	139,7243806	30,13598673	2018-01-16, 12:32:38	-
IMG_2940.jpeg	34,85814722	135,700225	65,40832396	2018-01-20, 16:45:43	-
ROBOTPOTRAIT.jpeg	35,01393611	135,78125	61,97637795	2018-01-22, 15:41:47	-
IMG_3143.jpeg	35,71827778	139,7722944	15,0528169	2018-01-25, 19:59:28	-
HOME2.jpeg	35,68927778	139,7229	42,00612245	2018-01-30, 01:05:42	-
GONEFISHING.jpeg	35,92736111	139,4884806	12,08318584	2018-02-12, 16:23:26	-
WHITEDAY.jpeg	-	-	-	2018-02-17, 15:59:16	-
CROATIA.jpeg	-	-	-	2018-02-17, 16:35:25	-
IMG_6560.jpeg	-	-	-	2018-02-18, 12:23:00	-
SHINJUKUGOEN.jpeg	-	-	-	2018-02-18, 14:31:50	-
SHINJUKUGOEN (2).jpeg	-	-	-	2018-02-18, 14:36:44	-
MIKKELER.jpeg	-	-	-	2018-02-18, 20:01:31	-
MIKKELER (2).jpeg	-	-	-	2018-02-18, 20:01:32	-
MIKKELER (3).jpeg	-	-	-	2018-02-18, 20:01:44	-
IMG_4190.jpeg	-	-	-	2018-03-02, 16:39:09	-
MITSZUKI.jpeg	34,995875	135,7678083	35,62154696	2018-03-03, 07:01:18	-
FUN.jpeg	34,88934722	135,7991472	28,12298387	2018-03-03, 20:59:11	-
LIEBE.jpeg	35,66888889	139,7057806	37,4981203	2018-03-11, 16:10:54	-
ROADTRIP.jpeg	35,925125	139,4113306	33,51100244	2018-03-12, 12:35:24	-
IMG_4811.jpeg	35,68926944	139,7229472	41,87228261	2018-03-16, 01:11:51	-
MAYUKO.jpeg	35,72095	139,7709806	10,29290853	2018-04-01, 17:09:26	-
UDONYAMACHO.jpeg	35,64824167	139,7112583	21,54215976	2018-04-02, 20:42:22	-
IMG_5581.jpeg	35,64576389	139,7423389	32,48669202	2018-04-08, 17:33:21	-
IMG_7484.jpeg	-	-	-	2018-05-08, 19:26:45	-
IMG_4355.jpeg	35,65459444	139,6559139	40,51	2019-02-01, 16:38:35	-
MAYU AND ME HAPPY.jpeg	35,67098889	139,707825	28,16146298	2019-02-01, 21:48:47	-
MAYU AND ME HAPPY NR.02.jpeg	35,67098889	139,707825	28,16146298	2019-02-01, 21:48:48	-
OKOK.jpeg	35,72320278	139,7770222	23,61370717	2019-02-05, 16:19:41	3.442
THE SMOKINGAREA.jpeg	35,69087222	139,7037056	37,88501742	2019-02-08, 16:55:16	6.446
THE SMOKING AREA Nr.02.jpeg	35,69230278	139,7007444	31,33614956	2019-02-08, 18:15:22	-
THIS IS WHERE I KEEP MY CLOTHES.jpeg	35,661625	139,6658778	40,50999829	2019-02-08, 18:52:45	-
MY.jpeg	35,67240833	139,764175	18,40999985	2019-02-09, 16:29:14	13.426
DINNER.jpeg	35,65152778	139,6557	36,73279188	2019-02-09, 18:21:53	-
DREAMHOUSE Nr.02.jpeg	35,64991389	139,6503	35,08604845	2019-02-10, 15:09:29	11.601
IMG_1617.jpeg	35,65019167	139,6499639	39,34216081	2019-02-10, 15:10:08	-
IMG_1618.jpeg	35,64997222	139,6494	45,99436498	2019-02-10, 15:11:34	-
IMG_1621.jpeg	35,64846111	139,6470194	29,5847713	2019-02-10, 16:04:32	-
IMG_1622.jpeg	35,648475	139,6470333	29,42706252	2019-02-10, 16:05:33	-
IMG_1624.jpeg	35,64839167	139,6470333	34,16609598	2019-02-10, 16:06:38	-
IMG_1626.jpeg	35,64821944	139,6455833	36,98995816	2019-02-10, 16:13:14	-
END.jpeg	35,64836944	139,6458889	37,79482488	2019-02-10, 16:13:18	-
VITAMINC.jpeg	35,64714722	139,6492917	38,13949716	2019-02-10, 16:22:37	-
IMG_1630.jpeg	35,64449444	139,6503611	33,34461078	2019-02-10, 16:32:47	-
FAVHOUSE.jpeg	35,64399444	139,6504222	38,62785902	2019-02-10, 16:33:47	-
即席LIVING.jpeg	35,64384722	139,6503306	34,37206266	2019-02-10, 16:45:58	-
IMG_1636.jpeg	35,653825	139,6469722	45,91997528	2019-02-10, 18:21:41	-
NEWHOMES.jpeg	35,65417222	139,6473222	45,48974224	2019-02-10, 18:22:15	-
APARTMENTS I WILL NEVER RENT.jpeg	35,65417778	139,6472639	41,57279223	2019-02-10, 18:22:44	-
NIGHTWALK SEARCHING FOR THE NEW BEDROOM.jpeg	35,65495556	139,6502389	44,47315282	2019-02-10, 18:30:14	-
IMG_1642.jpeg	35,65528889	139,65065	41,03661444	2019-02-10, 18:31:33	-
IMG_1646.jpeg	35,65142778	139,6556694	34,78608075	2019-02-10, 20:21:20	-
AGAIN A NIGHTWALK.jpeg	35,64944167	139,6542361	33,27123582	2019-02-10, 22:25:39	-
IMG_1649.jpeg	35,65135556	139,6546333	37,82721202	2019-02-10, 22:29:09	-
SMOKING.jpeg	35,69121111	139,6994333	-	2019-02-11, 11:45:17	21.244
IMG_1652.jpeg	35,64903889	139,7079167	24,44566727	2019-02-11, 12:59:03	-
IMG_1653.jpeg	35,64898056	139,7078389	30,27373022	2019-02-11, 12:59:08	-
IMG_1654.jpeg	35,64901667	139,7077778	28,82105318	2019-02-11, 12:59:17	-
FACADE (2).jpeg	35,64918611	139,7075806	30,57084465	2019-02-11, 13:00:14	-
IMG_1656.jpeg	35,64944444	139,7070167	25,33928725	2019-02-11, 13:00:40	-
IMG_1657.jpeg	35,64846667	139,7059778	20,51317214	2019-02-11, 13:04:41	-
IMG_1663.jpeg	35,65086667	139,7053833	19,19593692	2019-02-11, 13:17:46	-
IMG_1664.jpeg	35,65086111	139,7053667	20,8562812	2019:02:11, 13:17:52	-
IMG_1666.jpeg	35,65372778	139,7046667	16,95360126	2019:02:11, 14:06:57	-
IMG_1675.jpeg	35,65801944	139,7005472	65,33982627	2019:02:11, 15:23:49	-

IMG_1681.jpeg	35,65746944	139,7018278	36,60049439	2019-02-11, 15:25:53	-
IMG_1684.jpeg	35,65778611	139,7025917	36,12800218	2019-02-11, 15:26:47	-
IMG_1690.jpeg	35,65817778	139,7030194	68,29229653	2019-02-11, 15:31:30	-
LINDA.jpeg	35,65605278	139,6530917	40,17845103	2019-02-12, 12:57:38	3.487
IMG_1699.jpeg	35,65531111	139,6565556	40,50999829	2019-02-12, 13:12:39	-
IMG_1700.jpeg	35,67015833	139,6894528	36,6331663	2019-02-12, 13:24:00	-
IMG_1701.jpeg	35,67054444	139,6909639	30,75855447	2019-02-12, 13:28:03	-
IMG_1702.jpeg	35,67068889	139,6908417	40,58389662	2019-02-12, 13:30:14	-
IMG_1704.jpeg	35,67002778	139,6961833	27,14485739	2019-02-12, 13:55:18	-
IMG_1705.jpeg	35,67055556	139,7026361	29,95930861	2019-02-12, 14:01:26	-
IMG_1708.jpeg	35,66976944	139,7024694	36,9391563	2019-02-12, 14:05:33	-
IMG_1711.jpeg	35,66964444	139,7030806	35,77000046	2019-02-12, 14:12:42	-
IMG_1716.jpeg	35,6688	139,7057639	35,73911667	2019-02-12, 14:55:39	-
IMG_1718.jpeg	35,668725	139,7053833	35,38982393	2019-02-12 , 14:58:36	-
IMG_1720.jpeg	35,66873889	139,7059028	43,34733578	2019-02-12, 15:18:25	-
IMG_1721.jpeg	35,66874722	139,7060556	52,95591566	2019-02-12, 15:18:36	-
IMG_1722.jpeg	35,66867778	139,7060083	52,04939741	2019-02-12, 15:18:49	-
IMG_1723.jpeg	35,66869722	139,7059944	49,90824456	2019-02-12, 15:18:56	-
IMG_1727.jpeg	35,66344444	139,7108	34,06287764	2019-02-12, 15:51:35	-
IMG_1728.jpeg	35,66234167	139,714875	31,75187302	2019-02-12, 16:02:38	-
IMG_1730.jpeg	35,66532222	139,7128444	40,39597321	2019-02-12, 16:03:42	-
IMG_1732.jpeg	35,66224722	139,7149972	59,08296582	2019-02-12, 16:08:04	-
IMG_1733.jpeg	35,66626667	139,7153778	29,4518397	2019-02-12, 16:15:46	-
IMG_1735.jpeg	35,66567222	139,7162778	33,42707442	2019-02-12, 16:28:36	-
IMG_1738.jpeg	35,66628333	139,7135	50,72626492	2019-02-12, 17:22:02	-
IMG_1740.jpeg	35,66632778	139,7135306	51,98254395	2019-02-12, 17:23:34	-
IMG_1748.jpeg	35,6615	139,6699972	42,21619798	2019-02-13, 00:53:05	8.081
IMG_1751.jpeg	35,65154722	139,6557472	36,43904114	2019-02-13, 13:29:05	-
IMG_1752.jpeg	35,65156111	139,6556861	36,41914367	2019-02-13, 13:43:59	-
IMG_1753.jpeg	35,65153056	139,6557167	36,26263492	2019-02-13, 13:44:02	-
IMG_1754.jpeg	35,65147778	139,6557	36,1891555	2019-02-13, 13:44:07	-
IMG_1755.jpeg	35,65149722	139,6556556	37,02205585	2019-02-13, 13:46:36	-
IMG_1760.jpeg	35,64823611	139,7115028	23,20120048	2019-02-13, 21:03:51	-
IMG_1761.jpeg	35,64810278	139,7114861	25,20424605	2019-02-13, 22:44:17	-
MAYU-CHAN.jpeg	35,64817778	139,7114722	23,09952607	2019-02-13, 22:53:07	-
WHAT I READ.jpeg	35,65149722	139,6557611	36,64936829	2019-02-14, 12:02:13	11.914
THE WAKE UP CALL.jpeg	35,65193611	139,6554111	40,53796872	2019-02-14, 12:40:37	-
THE UMBRELLASTAND.jpeg	35,65574722	139,6532889	40,50999829	2019-02-14, 12:52:44	-
IMG_1775.jpeg	35,65576111	139,653275	40,50999829	2019-02-14, 12:52:47	-
THE USUAL TOILET OF KONBINITY.jpeg	35,70704722	139,7689361	40,50999829	2019-02-14, 13:37:38	-
A CLOSED WRAPPING OF THE CHICKEN I LOVED.jpeg	35,70890556	139,7698833	13,24407959	2019-02-14, 13:41:46	-
THE CHICKEN I LOVED.jpeg	35,70921389	139,7697444	13,01731967	2019-02-14, 13:42:20	-
IMG_1784.jpeg	35,71563333	139,7678528	13,36216972	2019-02-14, 14:14:06	-
IMG_1785.jpeg	35,71563333	139,7678667	13,35238218	2019-02-14, 14:14:09	-
IMG_1787.jpeg	35,716125	139,7696222	10,92103641	2019-02-14, 14:18:35	-
IMG_1793.jpeg	35,718125	139,7699444	13,03259177	2019-02-14, 14:26:49	-
IMG_1796.jpeg	35,71967778	139,7704306	12,77999973	2019-02-14, 14:30:28	-
IMG_1800.jpeg	35,71958611	139,7716056	12,33431052	2019-02-14, 14:31:41	-
即席LIVINGROOM.jpeg	35,71840556	139,7722944	19,44682896	2019-02-14, 14:35:49	-
A SHOWER.jpeg	35,71845556	139,7720194	12,90998745	2019-02-14, 14:52:17	-
即席BATH.jpeg	35,71845556	139,7720194	12,90998745	2019-02-14, 14:52:22	-
即席BATH Nr.02.jpeg	35,71831389	139,7722944	13,27577113	2019-02-14, 14:53:17	-
WHERE I AM WORKING.jpeg	35,71827778	139,7722639	12,87094211	2019-02-14, 14:57:47	-
A LIVINGROOM.jpeg	35,72182778	139,7705222	4,567362312	2019-02-14, 15:24:35	-
MY GARDEN.jpeg	35,72259444	139,7702639	13,40420177	2019-02-14, 15:31:22	-
THE DREAMHOUSE.jpeg	35,72082222	139,77095	12,17723369	2019-02-14, 15:34:43	-
THE RAMEN.jpeg	35,71226111	139,7748861	12,91779232	2019-02-14, 16:13:17	-
THE GIFT FOR WHITE DAY.jpeg	35,65148611	139,6556389	36,2465718	2019-02-15, 12:08:15	9.964
IMG_1945.jpeg	35,65555556	139,6545111	31,55799421	2019-02-15, 13:21:27	-
THE TV-SNACK.jpeg	35,65573611	139,653275	38,59444427	2019-02-15, 13:24:49	-
BREAKFASTTABLE.jpeg	35,6559	139,6533806	40,52000046	2019-02-15, 13:35:23	-
IMG_1956.jpeg	35,65641667	139,7029889	35,44313433	2019-02-15, 14:19:58	-
IMG_1991.jpeg	35,62286667	139,7777722	7,414146422	2019-02-15, 15:47:14	-
IMG_2016.jpeg	35,62701111	139,771775	5,640524968	2019-02-15, 17:34:11	-
IMG_2020.jpeg	35,62748611	139,7787333	13,58216857	2019-02-15, 18:41:17	-
IMG_2023.jpeg	35,66056944	139,6986556	35,80443194	2019-02-15, 19:22:45	-
IMG_2026.jpeg	35,66045	139,6963361	-	2019-02-15, 19:35:00	-
IMG_2032.jpeg	35,66046944	139,6964417	-	2019-02-15, 19:38:33	-
IMG_2033.jpeg	35,66066667	139,6961222	-	2019-02-15, 19:38:43	-
IMG_2039.jpeg	35,65974444	139,6963361	38,12597123	2019-02-15, 21:15:05	-
即席BED (6).jpeg	35,65972778	139,6964278	45,38173941	2019-02-15, 21:15:11	-
即席BED (3).jpeg	35,660125	139,6963056	42,83552169	2019-02-15, 21:17:16	-
即席BED (2).jpeg	35,66044722	139,6963194	-	2019-02-15, 21:18:18	-
即席BED (4).jpeg	35,66069444	139,6961667	-	2019-02-15, 21:18:55	-
即席BED (5).jpeg	35,65950278	139,6958778	39,36505129	2019-02-15, 21:21:10	-
即席BED (7).jpeg	35,65925278	139,6958167	40,48481366	2019-02-15, 21:23:33	-
IMG_2057.jpeg	35,65864167	139,7093056	35,76715523	2019-02-16, 03:23:55	15.793
IMG_2062.jpeg	35,66504722	139,7030333	33,12546544	2019-02-16, 04:02:16	-
IMG_2065.jpeg	35,66903611	139,7055806	-	2019-02-16, 04:09:47	-
IMG_2077.jpeg	35,67073333	139,7048806	35,86845827	2019-02-16, 16:32:35	-
IMG_2078.jpeg	35,67051667	139,7061611	35,40184049	2019-02-16, 16:43:22	-
IMG_2093.jpeg	35,68905	139,7420056	26,91454545	2019-02-16, 22:26:20	-
IMG_2094.jpeg	35,68906389	139,7420667	26,91454545	2019-02-16, 22:26:27	-
即席BED.jpeg	35,66233889	139,7326806	48,18608095	2019-02-17, 05:50:13	27.535
即席BED (8).jpeg	35,66245278	139,7331694	47,64574816	2019-02-17, 11:23:26	-
IMG_2114.jpeg	35,66217778	139,7321472	48,28905109	2019-02-17, 12:04:16	-
IMG_2127.jpeg	35,69411111	139,7016917	52,74159621	2019-02-17, 14:55:46	-
THE TOMATO RAMEN.jpeg	35,66088611	139,668625	40,52	2019-02-17, 17:18:47	-
IMG_2133.jpeg	35,663025	139,6551806	40,71301248	2019-02-17, 20:28:54	-
IMG_2137.jpeg	35,65151667	139,6557167	36,98539736	2019-02-18, 14:34:37	11.605
IMG_2139.jpeg	35,65893056	139,6560528	40,20039748	2019-02-18, 15:34:22	-
IMG_2149.jpeg	35,67384444	139,7039806	35,25945281	2019-02-18, 20:04:55	-
IMG_2152.jpeg	35,67379444	139,70395	37,27887427	2019-02-18, 20:16:31	-
IMG_2157.jpeg	35,71831111	139,7659306	12,73999977	2019-02-19, 15:01:23	10.641
SHARING 即席KITCHEN.jpeg	35,71831944	139,7659139	12,73999977	2019-02-19, 15:01:25	-
THE BEER I HAD WHEN I TALKED WITH THE RAMENCHEF.jpeg	35,6557	139,6531667	35,48838423	2019-02-19, 19:34:33	-

THE 2ND BEER I HAD WHEN I TALKED TO THE RAMENCHEF.jpeg	35,65569722	139,6531667	35,69078014	2019-02-19, 19:36:03	-
MY FAV MOCHI.jpeg	35,65143333	139,6556556	39,53012658	2019-02-19, 22:03:58	-
IMG_2237.jpeg	35,65474722	139,6969917	15,41968465	2019-02-20, 15:10:21	17.835
IMG_2241.jpeg	35,647925	139,7023917	23,12999915	2019-02-20, 15:29:26	-
IMG_2255.jpeg	35,64801111	139,7091056	19,07642339	2019-02-20, 15:58:35	-
IMG_2279.jpeg	35,64836111	139,7113028	23,05626868	2019-02-20, 18:14:24	-
IMG_2281.jpeg	35,64806667	139,7079167	26,74830057	2019-02-20, 20:26:39	-
IMG_2296.jpeg	35,65140556	139,655625	39,91583085	2019-02-21, 14:56:13	15.785
IMG_2297.jpeg	35,65148611	139,6556694	36,79982785	2019-02-21, 15:18:00	-
IMG_2300.jpeg	35,65476944	139,65445	32,72479248	2019-02-21, 16:09:34	-
IMG_2304.jpeg	35,65616944	139,6553028	31,35295573	2019-02-21, 16:19:56	-
IMG_2318.jpeg	35,65795556	139,6606139	54,55942008	2019-02-21, 16:52:13	-
IMG_2323.jpeg	35,65826389	139,6629639	37,86023014	2019-02-21, 16:55:50	-
IMG_2325.jpeg	35,65900833	139,663925	42,31984604	2019-02-21, 16:58:09	-
IMG_2347.jpeg	35,65572222	139,6531972	35,98301698	2019-02-21, 23:24:09	12.642
IMG_2360.jpeg	35,66003056	139,7014	49,54467773	2019-02-23, 00:05:11	19.638
IMG_2361.jpeg	35,65870278	139,7094111	71,16989778	2019-02-23, 01:42:35	-
IMG_2362.jpeg	35,65832778	139,7088778	37,69240571	2019-02-23, 04:49:19	-
IMG_2365.jpeg	35,66035556	139,6962889	40,45000076	2019-02-23, 05:38:32	-
IMG_2366.jpeg	35,66044722	139,6963361	-	2019-02-23, 05:38:35	-
IMG_2368.jpeg	35,66193889	139,7278583	35,70000076	2019-02-23, 17:00:41	-
IMG_2369.jpeg	35,66193056	139,7278583	35,70000076	2019-02-23, 17:00:44	-
IMG_2370.jpeg	35,66191944	139,7279194	52,1400223	2019-02-23, 17:03:18	-
IMG_2378.jpeg	35,66015556	139,7293861	231,0452117	2019-02-23, 18:03:53	-
IMG_2389.jpeg	35,66006944	139,7290028	228,162201	2019-02-23, 18:23:57	-
IMG_2405.jpeg	35,66506944	139,7259056	34,18703242	2019-02-23, 19:09:24	-
IMG_2429.jpeg	35,664725	139,7060389	33,98965836	2019-02-24, 21:21:31	5.415
IMG_2441.jpeg	35,63438056	139,7120056	25,98528672	2019-02-25, 16:04:22	13.672
WORKING AREA OF KONBINITY.jpeg	35,63311667	139,7081306	20,24834442	2019-02-25, 16:33:23	-
THE GROUPCHAT.jpeg	35,65946667	139,6959389	42,44452663	2019-02-25, 23:29:27	-
IMG_2475.jpeg	35,6515	139,655625	35,49690892	2019-02-26, 14:54:55	18.510
IMG_2476.jpeg	35,65152222	139,6557611	36,73291016	2019-02-26, 14:56:15	-
MY CLOSET AGAIN.jpeg	35,65140833	139,6557472	31,38597228	2019-02-26, 15:04:48	-
ME AGAIN.jpeg	35,65141667	139,6557	28,89290162	2019-02-26, 15:17:59	-
ME.jpeg	35,65158056	139,6557167	26,16993831	2019-02-26, 15:27:00	-
THE 即席 LIVING.jpeg	35,65620556	139,6530611	36,15321352	2019-02-26, 16:20:41	-
IMG_2504.jpeg	35,65620556	139,653075	36,20455933	2019-02-26, 16:20:45	-
IMG_2505.jpeg	35,65618889	139,6530917	36,52243424	2019-02-26, 16:21:07	-
IMG_2508.jpeg	35,65856944	139,655975	42,96582139	2019-02-26, 16:28:53	-
ARUGAMAMA-STORY MATERIAL.jpeg	35,66299722	139,6551667	40,52023697	2019-02-26, 19:01:12	-
IMG_2527.jpeg	35,66245278	139,6557	41,73284531	2019-02-26, 21:33:47	-
IMG_2528.jpeg	35,66248333	139,6557167	41,6135712	2019-02-26, 21:33:51	-
IMG_2529.jpeg	35,66248056	139,6556861	41,71398926	2019-02-26, 21:35:00	-
IMG_2543.jpeg	35,66033889	139,6676472	39,96976854	2019-02-27, 01:08:29	20.176
IMG_2546.jpeg	35,66034722	139,6675417	40,11581039	2019-02-27, 01:14:09	-
MY LATE NIGHT KITCHEN.jpeg	35,66023611	139,6673139	40,34529114	2019-02-27, 01:25:26	-
IMG_2562.jpeg	35,651475	139,6557611	36,80533556	2019-02-27, 14:59:26	-
IMG_2566.jpeg	35,65815	139,65425	40,45000076	2019-02-27, 15:46:40	-
MY WORKSPACE.jpeg	35,66255833	139,6558083	46,64271107	2019-02-27, 16:20:19	-
MY FAV DRINK AT MY WORKSPACE.jpeg	35,66266389	139,6557611	39,58576201	2019-02-27, 17:02:01	-
IMG_2581.jpeg	35,65023889	139,6538694	33,85673338	2019-02-27, 19:03:39	-
IMG_2584.jpeg	35,65305	139,6525722	37,6764603	2019-02-27, 19:14:50	-
IMG_2585.jpeg	35,65299722	139,6526194	48,22461651	2019-02-27, 19:15:15	-
A MEETING.jpeg	35,66286389	139,6603861	40,62715531	2019-02-27, 21:09:56	-
MEETING THE ROOMATE I NEVER HAVE.jpeg	35,66286389	139,6604	40,45345685	2019-02-27, 21:34:47	-
FEELING ALONE.jpeg	35,65457778	139,6540833	38,2189522	2019-02-28, 02:24:28	16.850
IMG_2604.jpeg	35,64831944	139,7112889	23,05999946	2019-02-28, 17:55:27	-
IMG_2605.jpeg	35,64823056	139,7113028	23,05999946	2019-02-28, 18:03:38	-
MY ELEVATOR.jpeg	35,67389167	139,735275	28,29145433	2019-02-28, 19:34:30	-
MY BED SOMETIMES.jpeg	35,67398889	139,7350611	32,07249071	2019-02-28, 19:36:48	-
MY CRIB.jpeg	35,67391111	139,7351833	17,60805312	2019-02-28, 20:14:22	-
IMG_2665.jpeg	35,67306389	139,7378083	38,76554491	2019-03-01, 03:57:31	29.178
IMG_2666.jpeg	35,6731	139,7378833	38,44809341	2019-03-01, 03:57:37	-
IMG_2668.jpeg	35,67289444	139,7366167	-	2019-03-01, 03:59:09	-
IMG_2674.jpeg	35,67391111	139,7352306	22,01648714	2019-03-01, 04:17:13	-
IMG_2676.jpeg	35,67391667	139,7352306	21,76319122	2019-03-01, 04:20:25	-
IMG_2677.jpeg	35,67390833	139,7352444	21,74935912	2019-03-01, 04:21:11	-
IMG_2678.jpeg	35,67388056	139,7352611	21,99158861	2019-03-01, 04:21:19	-
IMG_2679.jpeg	35,67388056	139,7352611	21,99158861	2019-03-01, 04:21:21	-
IDK WTT.jpeg	35,67390833	139,7350472	23,53542901	2019-03-01, 04:35:11	-
即席BED (9).jpeg	35,67389167	139,7351389	23,4650135	2019-03-01, 04:35:16	-
即席BED (10).jpeg	35,67396111	139,7350778	24,53773118	2019-03-01, 09:50:42	-
IMG_2685.jpeg	35,67390556	139,7352611	22,89119542	2019-03-01, 09:51:30	-
IMG_2688.jpeg	35,67653611	139,7368	30,46472168	2019-03-01, 11:55:05	-
IMG_2690.jpeg	35,66702222	139,7349389	54,95458984	2019-03-01, 12:16:01	-
IMG_2692.jpeg	35,64404167	139,6998278	86,9798203	2019-03-01, 12:43:11	-
IMG_2693.jpeg	35,64435556	139,7011111	12,03458041	2019-03-01, 12:54:46	-
IMG_2694.jpeg	35,64438333	139,7012944	11,61477785	2019-03-01, 12:55:07	-
IMG_2697.jpeg	35,64726389	139,7020111	23,06	2019-03-01, 13:29:34	-
IMG_2698.jpeg	35,64448056	139,7012639	22,00211905	2019-03-01, 15:19:50	-
THE FLOWERS YOU PUT ON YOUR KITCHENTABLE (3).jpeg	35,64929167	139,7001639	33,90864256	2019-03-01, 17:00:02	-
IMG_2706.jpeg	35,652225	139,7024694	23,11295924	2019-03-01, 17:23:06	-
IMG_2709.jpeg	35,65308056	139,7038722	35,61870003	2019-03-01, 17:27:16	-
IMG_2710.jpeg	35,65310556	139,7039333	42,7586244	2019-03-01, 17:27:27	-
IMG_2712.jpeg	35,65356944	139,7050472	25,94744298	2019-03-01, 17:34:47	-
IMG_2714.jpeg	35,65354167	139,7050778	26,03601108	2019-03-01, 18:18:12	-
IMG_2718.jpeg	35,66168611	139,6999667	50,41841216	2019-03-01, 20:06:23	-
IMG_2721.jpeg	35,69209722	139,7600111	21,89414406	2019-03-01, 21:53:21	-
IMG_2740.jpeg	35,65951944	139,7003028	56,14009471	2019-03-02, 05:03:15	21.418
IMG_2742.jpeg	35,65898056	139,6983333	51,32450103	2019-03-02, 05:11:37	-
IMG_2759.jpeg	35,69181944	139,7603917	30,39981126	2019-03-02, 06:16:03	-
IMG_2763.jpeg	35,6918	139,7600861	30,8060059	2019-03-02, 06:16:27	-
IMG_2765.jpeg	35,69180556	139,7600556	30,4585332	2019-03-02, 06:16:40	-
IMG_2766.jpeg	35,6923	139,760025	27,70895765	2019-03-02, 06:20:24	-
IMG_2770.jpeg	35,69210556	139,7600556	20,93886948	2019-03-02, 06:34:21	-
IMG_2771.jpeg	35,6921	139,7600556	20,82309913	2019-03-02, 06:34:24	-

IMG_2772.jpeg	35,6921	139,7600556	20,82309913	2019-03-02, 06:34:28	-
IMG_2774.jpeg	35,69221111	139,7602833	24,15115562	2019-03-02, 09:47:01	-
IMG_2785.jpeg	35,68555	139,7656694	-	2019-03-02, 12:08:19	-
IMG_2790.jpeg	35,67213056	139,7627722	18,10282518	2019-03-02, 13:07:14	-
THE FLOWERS YOU PUT ON YOUR KITCHENTABLE (4).jpeg	35,67250556	139,7631694	18,21973229	2019-03-02, 13:17:52	-
THE FLOWERS YOU PUT ON YOUR KITCHENTABLE (5).jpeg	35,672325	139,7628778	18,22752761	2019-03-02, 13:18:05	-
THE FLOWERS YOU PUT ON YOUR KITCHENTABLE.jpeg	35,67198611	139,7623139	-	2019-03-02, 13:24:10	-
THE FLOWERS YOU PUT ON YOUR KITCHENTABLE (2).jpeg	35,671975	139,7622833	-	2019-03-02, 13:24:24	-
IMG_2816.jpeg	35,62789167	139,6884917	29,50570004	2019-03-02, 21:11:50	-
IMG_2820.jpeg	35,62821667	139,6849972	30,85044861	2019-03-02, 21:34:45	-
IMG_2821.jpeg	35,62914167	139,6856694	35,9909949	2019-03-02, 22:07:09	-
IMG_2822.jpeg	35,62931111	139,6856833	34,35352654	2019-03-02, 22:07:47	-
DREAM.jpeg	35,62890556	139,6871806	34,2953973	2019-03-02, 22:11:42	-
SMOKINGAREA (2).jpeg	35,62643333	139,6894694	34,38569754	2019-03-02, 22:25:53	-
THE NIGHT I MISSED THE PRIVATE APARTMENT.jpeg	35,62579722	139,6898028	33,33581543	2019-03-02, 22:29:28	-
MY SHIRTS FROM MY CLOSET.jpeg	35,62586111	139,689925	33,22000123	2019-03-03, 11:39:08	19.806
WINDOW.jpeg	35,62593333	139,6896667	33,22000123	2019-03-03, 12:38:12	-
WINDOWOPENING.jpeg	35,62572222	139,6895917	33,22000123	2019-03-03, 12:39:02	-
THE FLOWERS YOU PUT ON YOUR KITCHENTABLE (6).jpeg	35,62891667	139,6878056	33,22000123	2019-03-03, 12:50:23	-
SAUNA+BED.jpeg	35,64810556	139,710175	26,53122901	2019-03-03, 13:35:21	-
SAUNA+BED-LOCKER.jpeg	35,64807778	139,7102194	25,60928916	2019-03-03, 13:35:37	-
SAUNA+BED-WAITING DAILY.jpeg	35,647975	139,7100361	28,36063956	2019-03-03, 13:58:12	-
SAUNA+BED-WAITING DAILY (2).jpeg	35,64801111	139,7100667	28,20523139	2019-03-03, 13:58:22	-
THE HUNGOVER LIVINGROOM.jpeg	35,64654444	139,7095028	-	2019-03-03, 14:41:31	-
WAITINGFORTHELAUNDRY.jpeg	35,64209722	139,6962139	17,1496563	2019-03-03, 15:39:21	-
WASHINGMACHINE.jpeg	35,64213611	139,6961528	16,15847969	2019-03-03, 15:53:46	-
MAMA.jpeg	35,64205278	139,6961972	13,92004625	2019-03-03, 15:54:01	-
UMBRELLASTAND (2).jpeg	35,64619167	139,7062083	27,47902922	2019-03-03, 16:23:36	-
SHEEP.jpeg	35,64768333	139,7078389	19,06663026	2019-03-03, 16:28:07	-
FACADE.jpeg	35,64773056	139,7079472	18,25561277	2019-03-03, 16:28:35	-
IMG_2870.jpeg	35,64738889	139,7084056	23,97258187	2019-03-03, 16:30:31	-
THE FILTH IN ME.jpeg	35,669225	139,7068639	27,57041464	2019-03-03, 17:36:47	-
THE SAUNA+BED.jpeg	35,64782222	139,7100667	30,52931978	2019-03-03, 20:59:00	-
MY FAV DRINK IN MY FAV UDONSHOP AKA LIVINGROOM.jpeg	35,64817778	139,7114111	24,13061333	2019-03-03, 21:26:06	-
MY FAV UDON.jpeg	35,64818056	139,7112889	22,27138521	2019-03-03, 21:33:52	-
IMG_2895.jpeg	35,64264167	139,696975	19,18164253	2019-03-03, 22:13:48	-
BEEF.jpeg	35,64266667	139,6970361	21,09110266	2019-03-03, 22:13:53	-
NODDLELOVE.jpeg	35,64343611	139,6979222	22,80113539	2019-03-03, 22:15:10	-
THE LOVEHOTEL.jpeg	35,65925278	139,6958	40,35752102	2019-03-04, 02:41:10	26.448
POLICE.jpeg	35,65928333	139,6958306	40,35031892	2019-03-04, 02:41:58	-
LOVEHOTELBREAKFAST.jpeg	35,65923333	139,6957694	40,3403435	2019-03-04, 02:45:22	-
LOVEHOTELEQUIP.jpeg	35,65924444	139,6958	40,33774569	2019-03-04, 02:45:43	-
WARDROBE.jpeg	35,64657222	139,7071389	24,15607453	2019-03-04, 11:46:25	-
IMG_2969.jpeg	35,64714167	139,7092444	33,99158478	2019-03-04, 11:56:04	-
DREAM (2).jpeg	35,646575	139,7102972	-	2019-03-04, 11:57:58	-
REPLICA.jpeg	35,64649444	139,7100972	-	2019-03-04, 12:01:10	-
IMG_2972.jpeg	35,69068889	139,699875	35,52146151	2019-03-04, 12:18:15	-
INFO.jpeg	35,69521389	139,7007917	40,67317582	2019-03-04, 12:36:24	-
WATCHINGME.jpeg	35,69549167	139,7007139	39,67478941	2019-03-04, 12:36:32	-
BOOK+BED.jpeg	35,69554167	139,7008056	38,07284162	2019-03-04, 12:37:23	-
IMG_2978.jpeg	35,69592778	139,7008833	35,61000061	2019-03-04, 12:55:05	-
PHILIP.jpeg	35,69423333	139,7002722	-	2019-03-04, 13:20:05	-
IMG_2981.jpeg	35,69147222	139,7010806	-	2019-03-04, 13:33:51	-
SMOKINGAREA (3).jpeg	35,67133333	139,70305	52,00831768	2019-03-04, 13:42:13	-
SMOKINGAREA (4).jpeg	35,67131111	139,7030333	52,29555586	2019-03-04, 13:42:16	-
MOOD.jpeg	35,65799722	139,7003167	53,90703581	2019-03-04, 17:17:04	-
即席BED (11).jpeg	35,69502222	139,7008667	59,52024081	2019-03-04, 18:10:08	-
即席BED (12).jpeg	35,69502222	139,7008667	59,52024081	2019-03-04, 18:10:16	-
THE DOOR TO MY 即席BEDROOM.jpeg	35,69796389	139,6996306	55,39883041	2019-03-04, 19:56:59	-
IMG_3044.jpeg	35,69660833	139,6999056	57,78570938	2019-03-04, 19:58:24	-
IMG_3046.jpeg	35,69801389	139,6971139	56,81185145	2019-03-04, 21:06:35	-
BOOKSFROMBOOK+BED (2).jpeg	35,69797222	139,6994778	56,81185145	2019-03-04, 21:06:40	-
BOOKSFROMBOOK+BED.jpeg	35,69797222	139,6994778	56,81185145	2019-03-04, 21:06:46	-
VIEW.jpeg	35,69593056	139,7008833	56,02626421	2019-03-04, 21:07:00	-
SARDINES.jpeg	35,69516667	139,7003472	52,84111022	2019-03-04, 22:37:04	-
IMG_3053.jpeg	35,69516111	139,7003472	52,88210296	2019-03-04, 22:38:07	-
BOOK+BED (3).jpeg	35,69499722	139,7000722	-	2019-03-05, 12:31:25	10.904
BOOK+BED (2).jpeg	35,69536111	139,700425	53,09645839	2019-03-05, 13:00:33	-
IMG_3068.jpeg	35,69498056	139,7000722	-	2019-03-05, 13:00:41	-
BOOK+BED (4).jpeg	35,69497778	139,7000583	-	2019-03-05, 13:01:26	-
BOOK+BED (3)VIEW.jpeg	35,6955	139,7008222	55,23616412	2019-03-05, 13:02:31	-
GOODSLEEP.jpeg	35,69484722	139,7001194	-	2019-03-05, 13:02:46	-
BOOK+BED (5).jpeg	35,69565833	139,7007611	54,49605945	2019-03-05, 13:12:02	-
BREAKFAST (2).jpeg	35,69050556	139,6995389	-	2019-03-05, 13:12:12	-
BREAKFAST.jpeg	35,69552222	139,7015389	60,32408524	2019-03-05, 14:29:23	-
IMG_3100.jpeg	35,69900833	139,7028667	35,48025509	2019-03-05, 14:55:42	-
IMG_3101.jpeg	35,69910833	139,70285	38,33697508	2019-03-05, 15:05:52	-
INTERNET.jpeg	35,69581111	139,7019972	56,20186618	2019-03-05, 15:14:57	-
KONBINI.jpeg	35,69580833	139,702025	56,37722397	2019-03-05, 15:15:26	-
KONBINI (2).jpeg	35,69580833	139,702025	56,37722397	2019-03-05, 15:15:28	-
DRINKS.jpeg	35,69580556	139,702025	56,41403588	2019-03-05, 15:15:33	-
KONBINI (3).jpeg	35,69580833	139,7020417	56,33383559	2019-03-05, 15:15:44	-
DRINKS (2).jpeg	35,69580833	139,7020417	56,33383559	2019-03-05, 15:15:48	-
MAIL.jpeg	35,69580556	139,702025	56,38714981	2019-03-05, 15:16:59	-
UMBRELLASTAND.jpeg	35,69581111	139,7020111	56,24492263	2019-03-05, 15:17:13	-
COFFEEMACHINE.jpeg	35,69580833	139,7020417	56,29584882	2019-03-05, 15:17:32	-
IMG_3115.jpeg	35,69580833	139,702025	56,3562355	2019-03-05, 15:17:44	-
SMOKINGAREA.jpeg	35,6958	139,7019806	56,11587389	2019-03-05, 15:21:09	-
IMG_3119.Jjpeg	35,69546111	139,7025611	71,97516444	2019-03-05, 15:30:18	-
HIROSHIMA.jpeg	35,69412222	139,7017056	62,44036866	2019-03-05, 15:32:22	-
EQUIPPED.jpeg	35,69415	139,7002417	-	2019-03-05, 15:33:00	-
9H (6).jpeg	35,67388056	139,7352611	22,11042593	2019-03-05, 16:22:31	-
9H (5).jpeg	35,67387778	139,735275	22,29186441	2019-03-05, 16:48:14	14.682
HOME.jpeg	35,67386944	139,7352611	22,46009544	2019-03-05, 17:01:31	-
RULES.jpeg	35,66496667	139,7127694	33,39320755	2019-03-05, 17:33:11	-
TREAT.jpeg	35,66465833	139,7134556	27,29308986	2019-03-05, 17:42:23	-

IMG_3150.jpeg	35,66635556	139,7136833	50,13014981	2019:03:05, 18:04:19	-
SAYKO-CHAN.jpeg	35,66560278	139,7129222	48,65358734	2019:03:05, 20:54:21	-
FRENCH.jpeg	35,66557778	139,7129056	49,08878327	2019:03:05, 21:29:32	-
GOODBYE.jpeg	35,65886944	139,6955556	42,35261538	2019:03:05, 22:46:44	-
OSAKASTYLE.jpeg	35,65886944	139,6955556	42,35261538	2019:03:05, 22:46:47	-
IMG_3165.jpeg	35,658975	139,6955861	41,90045927	2019:03:06, 00:04:21	-
IMG_3172.jpeg	35,66041111	139,6962583	-	2019:03:06, 02:58:52	-
9H (4).jpeg	35,67391667	139,7352611	23,27791787	2019:03:06, 09:48:02	
MY FAV CAPSULE.jpeg	35,6739	139,7352306	22,71066475	2019:03:06, 09:48:25	-
9H (2).jpeg	35,67392222	139,7352444	22,69352532	2019:03:06, 09:49:04	14.682
9H.jpeg	35,67390833	139,7352139	22,76957703	2019:03:06, 09:49:19	-
ENTRANCE.jpeg	35,67385	139,7352444	22,15778923	2019:03:06, 09:51:28	-
9H (3).jpeg	35,67389167	139,7352611	22,18741036	2019:03:06, 10:23:56	-
9HKOHI.jpeg	35,67391111	139,7352444	22,41393472	2019:03:06, 10:39:58	10.904
MENSA (2).jpeg	35,67112222	139,7057194	32,58480074	2019:03:06, 14:04:43	-
LOSTPLANEMEETING.jpeg	35,67112222	139,7057194	32,58480074	2019:03:06, 14:04:46	-
MENSA.jpeg	35,67187778	139,7039028	31,45552062	2019:03:06, 14:04:56	-
GONE.jpeg	35,54550278	139,7695	18,54141683	2019:03:06, 19:27:29	10.904
AIRPORT.jpeg	35,54353056	139,780625	22,67453384	2019:03:06, 19:29:22	-
IMG_3226.jpeg	35,544675	139,7691333	6,097558027	2019:03:06, 19:53:59	-

PHOTO INDEX (Title)	GPS LATITUDE (Numbers)	LONGITUDE (Numbers)	ALTITUDE (Numbers)	CREATE DATE (Date, Time)	DAILY STEPS (Human)
123YEARS.jpeg	34,69029722	135,4934694	5,35181046	2022-11-02, 20:42:16	20.671
2HOURSOFWAITING.jpeg	35,72313333	139,6522056	44,45381927	2022-11-05, 21:19:05	-
2HOURSWAITGYOZAAA.jpeg	35,72324444	139,6518389	43,9773674	2022-11-05, 20:42:26	-
3D-MODELL.jpeg	33,595	130,1091917	18,05665356	2022-09-07, 15:18:35	17.872
3D_SCAN_PARTY_OSAKA (2).jpeg	-	-	-	2022-11-02, 21:43:08	-
3D_SCAN_PARTY_OSAKA.jpeg	-	-	-	2022-11-02, 21:43:10	-
635B6582-D29E-497D-95AD-AE1E8055F91F.jpeg	-	-	-	2022-09-19, 01:25:41	7.038
ABOUT.jpeg	35,68327778	139,6874556	46,4810257	2022-08-21, 16:21:07	17.170
AKADEMIE.jpeg	33,58333889	130,3843694	12,05362864	2022-09-03, 15:07:36	12.034
AKI-CHAN.jpeg	35,66921667	139,7077639	18,36598227	2022-11-07, 16:41:33	651
AKIRAWAKITA_SAN_MEETUPSIBUYA.jpeg	35,66072778	139,7046806	30,80249095	2022-08-27, 12:52:13	13.989
ALLASIA (2).jpeg	-	-	-	2022-11-03, 21:22:58	16.711
ALLASIA (3).jpeg	35,00254722	135,7636861	37,46007536	2022-11-03, 21:49:21	-
ALLASIA (4).jpeg	35,00255278	135,7635944	37,45994188	2022-11-03, 21:38:00	-
ALLASIA (5).jpeg	35,00251667	135,7637639	55,36983882	2022-11-03, 21:06:26	-
ALLASIA.jpeg	35,00254167	135,7638556	37,46032336	2022-11-03, 21:43:39	-
ALL_ASIA (2).jpeg	-	-	-	2022-11-03, 20:47:53	-
ALL_ASIA (3).jpeg	-	-	-	2022-11-03, 21:22:57	-
ALL_ASIA.jpeg	-	-	-	2022-11-03, 20:47:46	-
ANGEL.jpeg	35,67216389	139,6906444	19,95228959	2022-08-28, 13:34:55	14.399
ARRIVE_LEAVE_ARRIVE.jpeg	-	-	-	2022-08-15, 18:48:27	-
ART.jpeg	-	-	-	2022-11-04, 12:49:37	8.792
ASSISTKOZAIMAS.jpeg	34,69033056	135,4934528	5,360520362	2022-11-02, 22:29:26	-
AUSTRIANCULTURALFORUM.jpeg	-	-	-	-	-
BACKDDOORENTRANCE.jpeg	35,6594	139,6933139	32,31513595	2022-08-30, 15:10:10	19.622
BATH (2).jpeg	35,67214167	139,6907667	26,18916319	2022-08-31,12:50:34	-
BEDROOMVIEW.jpeg	35,67210278	139,690675	25,21419147	2022-08-27, 09:49:13	-
BEDROOMVIEW_DOGS.jpeg	35,67203889	139,6904917	27,07932281	2022-08-27, 10:18:26	-
BESTCUCUMBERS (2).jpeg	35,72316667	139,6522972	44,02486039	2022-11-05, 21:02:17	-
BESTCUCUMBERS.jpeg	35,72315278	139,6522361	44,94600326	2022-11-05, 21:02:22	-
BESTCURRY (2).jpeg	34,70981111	135,5131694	5,403665542	2022-11-02, 16:08:54	-
BESTCURRY (3).jpeg	-	-	-	2022-11-02, 16:14:28	-
BESTCURRY.jpeg	-	-	-	2022-11-02, 16:14:28	-
BESTICE.jpeg	35,67211667	139,6905833	25,18056104	2022-08-26, 23:05:41	6.502
BESTKOHI.jpeg	34,69034167	135,4934833	5,363541599	2022-11-03, 00:01:23	-
BESTSASHIMI.jpeg	35,66001111	139,6948556	16,71541729	2022-08-24, 21:28:15	-
BESTTREAT.jpeg	35,67808889	139,6768944	40,42915727	2022-08-23, 23:44:08	17.845
BESTUDONINTHEWORLD.jpeg	35,64841111	139,7111972	14,82023525	2022-08-23, 20:26:58	-
BKK.jpeg	33,51215	130,12935	2,088041309	2022-09-04, 17:29:16	12.821
BLESSED.jpeg	35,67011944	139,6893	24,88399697	2022-09-01, 02:12:29	7.922
BNA (2).jpeg	35,00022222	135,7683861	39,43769454	2022-11-05, 11:03:50	-
BNA.jpeg	-	-	-	2022-11-04, 12:49:35	-
BOBI.jpeg	33,53492222	130,1544639	14,76203656	2022-10-30, 16:40:47	-
BOLO.jpeg	35,67209167	139,6905056	28,26719093	2022-08-26, 21:55:25	-
BRAINFREEZE.jpeg	35,67214722	139,69075	27,02484513	2022-08-26, 23:05:09	-
BREKKI (2).jpeg	34,70897222	135,5053556	2,22091484	2022-11-02, 12:18:24	-
BREKKI (3).jpeg	33,53400833	130,1542056	4,26778984	2022-10-30, 15:02:09	-
BREKKI.jpeg	34,70879444	135,5052806	0,39141655	2022-11-02, 12:19:10	-
BROTZEIT.jpeg	35,67668611	139,6747444	46,39610283	2022-08-24, 17:29:44	-
BUS.jpeg	-	-	-	2022-08-16, 18:08:28	-
BYE_MOON (2).jpeg	35,66173611	139,6674806	39,8864937	2022-11-08, 18:57:22	-
BYE_MOON.jpeg	35,66211944	139,6675556	38,20174025	2022-11-08, 19:00:29	-
CARBO.jpeg	35,67825	139,6769417	39,66225052	2022-08-23, 01:50:18	-
CDC.jpeg	-	-	-	2022-11-02, 21:28:26	-
CHEEESSEE-NE.jpeg	35,67040556	139,6834417	35,23293493	2022-08-29, 21:52:15	-
CHICK (2).jpeg	35,67193333	139,6880806	28,0830269	2022-08-26, 16:55:55	-
CHICK.jpeg	35,66269722	139,7006222	16,64354706	2022-08-17, 01:02:10	8.945
COMME.jpeg	35,67198889	139,6905972	25,50895693	2022-08-30, 11:03:12	-
CONSTRUCTION.jpeg	35,72440278	139,7704472	21,32491684	2022-08-23, 15:42:33	-
COOKING (2).jpeg	35,66030833	139,6989139	39,53085326	2022-11-07, 18:53:19	-
COOKING.jpeg	35,65880556	139,7002556	-	2022-11-07, 18:53:20	-
CROATIA.jpeg	-	-	-	2022-08-15, 20:30:43	-
CROATIANDINNER.jpeg	35,67205	139,6906889	26,7245674	2022-08-31, 20:33:04	-
CURE.jpeg	35,6627	139,6963806	19,84028059	2022-08-25, 14:00:44	18.127
DELIRIUM.jpeg	35,6721	139,6906139	25,01203252	2022-08-30, 18:18:47	-
DINNER (2).jpeg	33,53232222	130,1516583	17,42642021	2022-09-05, 17:56:26	5.119
DINNER.jpeg	33,53245556	130,1515806	13,93087006	2022-09-03, 23:06:41	-
DINNEREVENING.jpeg	35,67499444	139,6681056	32,3456621	2022-08-18, 22:10:33	-
DOMUM_OSAKA (2).jpeg	34,69036389	135,4934833	5,560865398	2022-11-02, 23:03:03	-
DOMUM_OSAKA (3).jpeg	34,69036389	135,4934833	5,560865398	2022-11-02, 23:03:07	-
DOMUM_OSAKA (4).jpeg	34,69029167	135,4934389	5,35603333	2022-11-02, 22:39:14	-
DOMUM_OSAKA (5).jpeg	34,69033056	135,4934528	5,360520362	2022-11-02, 22:29:28	-
DOMUM_OSAKA (6).jpeg	-	-	-	2022-11-02, 21:28:21	-
DOMUM_OSAKA.jpeg	34,69035278	135,4934528	5,663339614	2022-11-02, 23:03:09	-
DOMUM_SCANNING_OSAKA (2).jpeg	-	-	-	2022-11-02, 21:44:37	-
DOMUM_SCANNING_OSAKA.jpeg	-	-	-	2022-11-02, 22:07:25	-
DOMUM_TEAM_OSAKA.jpeg	34,69039444	135,4934222	5,47943592	2022-11-03, 00:25:45	-
DRAGON (2).jpeg	33,53243889	130,1516417	14,28512382	2022-09-08, 22:05:21	-
DRAGON.jpeg	33,53243889	130,1516111	15,41659356	2022-09-08, 22:05:20	-
EDEKA60EUROBITTE.jpeg	-	-	-	2022-08-23, 18:02:31	-
FAIL.jpeg	34,6687	135,5022889	14,97469713	2022-11-01, 19:10:27	13.766
FAKE.jpeg	35,66022222	139,7015222	19,0313451	2022-08-19, 19:13:08	17.765
FAVBAR04 (2).jpeg	35,65837778	139,7091833	35,35300253	2022-08-30, 21:53:22	-
FAVBAR04.jpeg	35,65837778	139,7091833	35,35300253	2022-08-30, 21:53:20	-
FAV_UDON.jpeg	35,64823611	139,7112417	14,79835701	2022-11-10, 19:27:34	-
FENCING.jpeg	34,69031944	135,4934833	5,498538976	2022-11-02, 23:03:33	-
FILMSET.jpeg	35,658325	139,7088306	34,33737562	2022-08-30, 21:35:08	-
FINAL_HOME (2).jpeg	35,72400556	139,7703861	18,3419426	2022-11-09, 15:54:21	-
FINAL_HOME (3).jpeg	35,72536389	139,7705833	21,70251422	2022-11-09, 15:51:53	-
FINAL_HOME (4).jpeg	35,72536389	139,7705833	21,70251422	2022-11-09, 15:51:52	-
FINAL_HOME (5).jpeg	35,72584167	139,7707222	20,17093354	2022-11-09, 15:51:08	-
FINAL_HOME (6).jpeg	35,72590556	139,7707056	20,88586842	2022-11-09, 15:51:00	-
FINAL_HOME.jpeg	35,72480833	139,7705528	19,73692172	2022-11-09, 15:52:50	-
FISHYLIVER.jpeg	35,66011944	139,6949306	16,71541729	2022-08-24, 21:22:56	-

FISHYS.jpeg	35,62876389	139,7408611	-	2022-09-01, 11:44:29	-
FLIGHTMODE.jpeg	50,04803333	8,568375	-	2022-08-15, 19:02:35	-
FLOORPLAN□□BATH.jpeg	35,67894444	139,6743611	43,50585958	2022-08-18, 17:42:14	-
FROG.jpeg	35,00255278	135,7636556	40,20351793	2022-11-03, 21:06:12	-
FUKUDA-STUDIO_ARIGATO (2).jpeg	-	-	-	2022-11-02, 21:44:35	-
FUKUDA-STUDIO_ARIGATO.jpeg	-	-	-	2022-11-02, 21:52:56	-
FUTUREHOME.jpeg	35,67086667	139,7088778	26,83409882	2022-08-23, 18:29:28	-
GALLERY.jpeg	35,661275	139,7003944	22,56926728	2022-08-18, 00:28:28	-
GALLERYFUN.jpeg	35,667175	139,7065111	26,05498502	2022-08-23, 18:37:46	-
GAMEON (2).jpeg	35,65839444	139,7022083	19,99835014	2022-08-19, 19:46:52	-
GAMEON (3).jpeg	35,66243056	139,6969611	23,55303001	2022-08-27, 10:43:46	-
GAMEON.jpeg	34,70811111	135,5118417	8,25580477	2022-11-02, 15:58:59	-
GAMINGBAR.jpeg	35,67786389	139,6770028	49,11775592	2022-08-21, 15:35:27	-
GAMING_GLITCHBODIES_HATSUDA (2).jpeg	35,67788333	139,6770778	44,34065628	2022-08-22, 22:53:25	-
GAMING_GLITCHBODIES_HATSUDA (3).jpeg	35,6778	139,6770333	44,70841598	2022-08-22, 22:55:16	-
GAMING_GLITCHBODIES_HATSUDA (5).jpeg	35,67772222	139,6771083	43,17616659	2022-08-23, 00:05:43	-
GAMING_GLITCHBODIES_HATSUDA (6).jpeg	35,6778	139,6770333	44,10685351	2022-08-22, 22:55:19	-
GAMING_GLITCHBODIES_HATSUDA (7).jpeg	35,67780556	139,6770333	42,88542939	2022-08-23, 00:21:26	-
GAMING_GLITCHBODIES_HATSUDA.jpeg	35,67781944	139,6770167	42,66117093	2022-08-22, 22:43:47	-
GAMING_GLITCHBODIES_HATSUDAI (4).jpeg	35,67771667	139,6770778	41,14155959	2022-08-23, 00:05:32	-
GAMING_GLITCHBODIES_HATSUDAI.jpeg	35,67781944	139,6770167	42,50658037	2022-08-22, 22:43:42	-
GAMING_HATSUDAI.jpeg	35,67775833	139,6770778	57,51796336	2022-08-22, 22:54:31	-
GARDEN.jpeg	35,630275	139,7416222	207,4782639	2022-08-18, 13:31:02	-
GATE.jpeg	35,67885278	139,6744694	37,98566215	2022-08-18, 17:41:32	-
GEIDAI.jpeg	35,71795278	139,77275	32,16201401	2022-08-23, 16:17:54	-
GEIDAI_USED_To_SHOW_WORK_HERE.jpeg	35,71768889	139,7722639	17,63009263	2022-08-23, 16:16:47	-
GER (2).jpeg	35,66058611	139,6965472	25,24162674	2022-08-30, 14:04:42	-
GER.jpeg	-	-	-	2022-08-23, 18:02:27	-
GERMANY.jpeg	35,66048889	139,6978	22,15374183	2022-08-30, 16:27:43	-
GINKO.jpeg	35,67044167	139,6833028	34,55747605	2022-08-29, 21:50:08	-
GOLDFISH.jpeg	35,66024722	139,6950389	16,71541729	2022-08-24, 21:20:30	-
GORICE.jpeg	35,66523611	139,6941833	22,98711318	2022-08-25, 14:08:38	-
GORO-CHAN_LUNCH (2).jpeg	35,68391667	139,6895139	39,85070801	2022-08-21, 17:36:38	-
GORO-CHAN_LUNCH (3).jpeg	35,68370833	139,6897417	39,72579576	2022-08-21, 18:14:45	-
GORO-CHAN_LUNCH.jpeg	35,68391667	139,6895139	39,85070801	2022-08-21, 17:36:36	-
GOROSWORK.jpeg	35,68321667	139,6873944	46,4810448	2022-08-21, 16:21:02	-
GREATARTISTIKNOWFROMGEIDAI.jpeg	35,65944167	139,6644278	38,95230886	2022-08-28, 15:39:52	-
HAKATASTATION.jpeg	33,59053889	130,4218444	10,41131878	2022-09-01, 17:36:56	-
HALLOWEEN.jpeg	34,67054444	135,4995583	21,29004289	2022-11-01, 00:17:58	-
HALLOWEENWITHTHESWISSARTISTS (2).jpeg	34,66988056	135,50035	76,85636856	2022-11-01, 00:06:05	-
HALLOWEENWITHTHESWISSARTISTS (3).jpeg	34,67055833	135,4995583	16,88336564	2022-11-01, 00:17:41	-
HALLOWEENWITHTHESWISSARTISTS.jpeg	34,67055833	135,4995417	16,41907121	2022-11-01, 00:17:39	-
HANBAGA.jpeg	33,58811944	130,109925	2,398401259	2022-09-07, 15:50:54	-
HANGOVER (2).jpeg	35,66298333	139,6961667	26,22141464	2022-08-25, 14:01:17	-
HANGOVER.jpeg	35,646675	139,70935	19,33967608	2022-08-23, 19:50:05	-
HANS + TOILET.jpeg	35,67894444	139,6743611	43,71644399	2022-08-18, 17:42:19	-
HANS.jpeg	35,67501944	139,6681222	32,3456621	2022-08-18, 21:30:28	-
HATFORMAYU.jpeg	35,67207778	139,6905833	24,77077077	2022-08-31, 16:59:49	-
HATSUDAI_HOME.jpeg	-	-	-	2022-08-19, 00:51:22	-
HIGHLIFE.jpeg	35,6767	139,6771556	56,13551716	2022-08-23, 01:19:21	-
HOME (2).jpeg	-	-	-	2022-11-06, 12:49:43	-
HOME (3).jpeg	35,66418333	139,6934972	21,60761697	2022-08-19, 20:39:35	-
HOME (4).jpeg	35,65583889	139,7031111	19,65288188	2022-08-19, 18:05:37	-
HOME.jpeg	35,69529444	139,7001028	36,07480239	2022-11-12, 13:53:45	-
HOME2.jpeg	35,67213056	139,6905833	23,07625198	2022-08-31, 12:44:28	-
HOMESICK.jpeg	35,67209722	139,6906444	24,16194535	2022-08-30, 11:00:03	-
HOUSE.jpeg	33,59149167	130,1068889	5,370612256	2022-09-07, 15:30:41	-
HRDINNER.jpeg	35,6721	139,6905667	24,88990719	2022-08-31, 23:10:36	-
IMG_0004.jpeg	35,65978333	139,6955111	27,95585629	2022-08-30, 23:17:14	-
IMG_0012.jpeg	35,65966111	139,6954639	25,31966019	2022-08-31, 01:11:43	-
IMG_0018.jpeg	35,65979722	139,6955111	28,14675902	2022-08-31, 01:17:47	-
IMG_0023.jpeg	35,65968333	139,6955111	28,06785392	2022-08-31, 02:28:24	-
IMG_0024.jpeg	35,65964444	139,6955111	28,29674149	2022-08-31, 02:43:40	-
IMG_0037.jpeg	35,6721	139,6896972	29,81941211	2022-08-31, 15:17:23	-
IMG_0038.jpeg	35,672325	139,6889333	33,81808696	2022-08-31, 15:18:39	-
IMG_0039.jpeg	35,67233611	139,6889333	33,5695708	2022-08-31, 15:18:43	-
IMG_0040.jpeg	35,67419444	139,68625	34,74833869	2022-08-31, 15:25:34	-
IMG_0043.jpeg	35,67111111	139,6903083	23,74347441	2022-08-31, 16:50:52	-
IMG_0047.jpeg	35,67210278	139,6906583	28,16560748	2022-08-31, 19:17:14	-
IMG_0049.jpeg	35,67212222	139,6904139	26,46242906	2022-08-31, 23:10:15	-
IMG_0050.jpeg	35,67214167	139,6906278	24,7929878	2022-08-31, 23:10:21	-
IMG_0070.jpeg	35,66994722	139,6891778	24,42498161	2022-09-01, 02:10:58	-
IMG_0073.jpeg	35,67203056	139,6904917	26,15608405	2022-09-01, 02:35:53	-
IMG_0102.jpeg	35,62875	139,740875	-	2022-09-01, 11:44:27	-
IMG_0115.jpeg	34,81795556	134,7342694	15,17374323	2022-09-01, 15:03:54	-
IMG_0122.jpeg	-	-	-	2022-09-01, 15:29:58	-
IMG_0135.jpeg	33,59055278	130,4218611	11,78883838	2022-09-01, 17:51:57	-
IMG_0136.jpeg	33,51545	130,1400139	7,129105739	2022-09-01, 19:10:09	-
IMG_0137.jpeg	33,51546389	130,14	0,256071091	2022-09-01, 19:10:29	-
IMG_0138.jpeg	33,53448611	130,1684111	8,900053022	2022-09-01, 19:23:07	-
IMG_0139.jpeg	33,53441111	130,1683667	12,20065115	2022-09-01, 19:23:18	-
IMG_0140.jpeg	33,53434444	130,168275	10,12118339	2022-09-01, 19:33:16	-
IMG_0141.jpeg	33,53245833	130,1515806	13,90357018	2022-09-01, 21:33:22	-
IMG_0142.jpeg	33,53245556	130,1515806	13,90453911	2022-09-01, 22:34:11	-
IMG_0143.jpeg	33,53245833	130,1515806	13,88902664	2022-09-01, 22:39:31	-
IMG_0144.jpeg	33,53263611	130,1517333	11,47543143	2022-09-02, 05:43:45	8.711
IMG_0194.jpeg	33,53361389	130,1533056	6,453556889	2022-09-03, 11:16:02	-
IMG_0195.jpeg	33,53353056	130,1531667	6,941831977	2022-09-03, 11:16:27	-
IMG_0205.jpeg	33,59120833	130,3972167	5,578212752	2022-09-03, 13:15:18	-
IMG_0206.jpeg	33,59012222	130,3960111	4,647183869	2022-09-03, 13:19:24	-
IMG_0210.jpeg	33,58759444	130,39685	8,896214099	2022-09-03, 13:48:06	-
IMG_0213.jpeg	33,587925	130,3959194	9,852051726	2022-09-03, 14:24:13	-
IMG_0214.jpeg	33,58788056	130,3958139	9,900989523	2022-09-03, 14:25:30	-
IMG_0219.jpeg	33,58778333	130,3954472	9,698364931	2022-09-03, 14:40:32	-
IMG_0221.jpeg	33,58778333	130,3956139	9,766027218	2022-09-03, 14:41:03	-
IMG_0224.jpeg	33,587375	130,3955694	31,35268783	2022-09-03, 14:41:43	-

IMG_0226.jpeg	33,58706667	130,3924722	7,517901453	2022-09-03, 14:46:36	-
IMG_0227.jpeg	33,58703611	130,3924556	7,033432932	2022-09-03, 14:46:43	-
IMG_0228.jpeg	33,58626111	130,3913278	7,246962684	2022-09-03, 14:49:20	-
IMG_0229.jpeg	33,58504167	130,3874361	7,291220136	2022-09-03, 14:56:12	-
IMG_0230.jpeg	33,58503611	130,3874361	7,635720621	2022-09-03, 14:56:22	-
IMG_0231.jpeg	33,58495278	130,3879389	13,02077868	2022-09-03, 15:00:05	-
IMG_0232.jpeg	33,58495833	130,3879083	11,90945055	2022-09-03, 15:00:18	-
IMG_0233.jpeg	33,58502222	130,388	7,740332897	2022-09-03, 15:00:32	-
IMG_0257.jpeg	33,58282778	130,3815611	6,208129503	2022-09-03, 15:49:04	-
IMG_0258.jpeg	33,58284444	130,3815778	4,901104347	2022-09-03, 15:49:07	-
IMG_0259.jpeg	33,58284444	130,3815611	7,579739122	2022-09-03, 15:49:12	-
IMG_0260.jpeg	33,58284444	130,3815611	5,622880945	2022-09-03, 15:49:14	-
IMG_0261.jpeg	33,58284444	130,3815778	5,590863091	2022-09-03, 15:49:15	-
IMG_0262.jpeg	33,58284444	130,3815778	5,590863091	2022-09-03, 15:49:18	-
IMG_0264.jpeg	33,58383889	130,3792278	9,819581986	2022-09-03, 16:11:01	-
IMG_0265.jpeg	33,58383889	130,3792111	9,830558782	2022-09-03, 16:11:44	-
IMG_0266.jpeg	33,58383611	130,3792278	9,830630299	2022-09-03, 16:16:44	-
IMG_0267.jpeg	33,58381944	130,3792722	9,830697051	2022-09-03, 16:18:40	-
IMG_0268.jpeg	33,583875	130,3791667	9,830504423	2022-09-03, 16:19:20	-
IMG_0269.jpeg	33,58369167	130,3796083	9,831197729	2022-09-03, 16:31:40	-
IMG_0270.jpeg	33,58370278	130,3796222	9,831266396	2022-09-03, 16:31:46	-
IMG_0271.jpeg	33,583725	130,3795167	9,83106614	2022-09-03, 16:31:52	-
IMG_0272.jpeg	33,58373333	130,3794861	9,831041339	2022-09-03, 16:31:57	-
IMG_0273.jpeg	33,58412222	130,3796083	8,938198106	2022-09-03, 16:40:53	-
IMG_0288.jpeg	33,58370278	130,3784333	4,524716663	2022-09-03, 17:09:13	-
IMG_0290.jpeg	33,58550278	130,3788444	7,017652937	2022-09-03, 17:13:56	-
IMG_0291.jpeg	33,58550278	130,3788444	7,248164657	2022-09-03, 17:14:00	-
IMG_0294.jpeg	33,58923056	130,3767694	4,158922645	2022-09-03, 17:22:48	-
IMG_0295.jpeg	33,58925	130,3767083	4,3516227	2022-09-03, 17:23:05	-
IMG_0309.jpeg	33,53248611	130,1515361	19,18153493	2022-09-03, 19:54:42	-
IMG_0330.jpeg	33,53251944	130,1515056	16,38467218	2022-09-03, 22:44:19	-
IMG_0332.jpeg	33,53248611	130,1515806	16,36832466	2022-09-03, 23:03:40	-
IMG_0342.jpeg	33,53253611	130,1516417	13,90480613	2022-09-04, 11:13:34	-
IMG_0343.jpeg	33,51355278	130,1305694	3,762174606	2022-09-04, 15:37:01	-
IMG_0344.jpeg	33,51356389	130,1305694	6,780179982	2022-09-04, 15:37:04	-
IMG_0345.jpeg	33,51359444	130,1305694	7,382658023	2022-09-04, 15:37:10	-
IMG_0349.jpeg	33,50785556	130,1179972	11,07246313	2022-09-04, 16:18:36	-
IMG_0352.jpeg	33,50764722	130,1160139	13,11269024	2022-09-04, 16:24:09	-
IMG_0354.jpeg	33,50926944	130,1096944	7,890489808	2022-09-04, 16:29:07	-
IMG_0359.jpeg	33,51218889	130,1293194	2,179227828	2022-09-04, 17:45:48	-
IMG_0369.jpeg	33,53240556	130,1516278	13,66280937	2022-09-05, 00:40:29	-
IMG_0382.jpeg	33,53245556	130,1515806	13,90477563	2022-09-05, 14:10:08	-
IMG_0386.jpeg	33,53246667	130,15155	18,91781424	2022-09-05, 15:50:09	-
IMG_0387.jpeg	33,53245556	130,1515806	13,81281472	2022-09-05, 15:55:59	-
IMG_0388.jpeg	33,53245556	130,1515806	13,70570183	2022-09-05, 17:42:11	-
IMG_0389.jpeg	33,53245556	130,1515806	13,75614167	2022-09-05, 17:42:17	-
IMG_0391.jpeg	33,53226389	130,1514583	10,72884943	2022-09-05, 18:08:22	-
IMG_0392.jpeg	33,53226389	130,1514583	11,35763361	2022-09-05, 18:08:27	-
IMG_0393.jpeg	33,53207778	130,1513222	13,06688517	2022-09-05, 18:08:51	-
IMG_0394.jpeg	33,53208611	130,1513667	12,59352192	2022-09-05, 18:08:56	-
IMG_0397.jpeg	33,53234167	130,1516278	11,29934502	2022-09-05, 20:26:10	-
IMG_0398.jpeg	33,53258889	130,1517028	17,6468792	2022-09-05, 20:30:54	-
IMG_0399.jpeg	33,53245556	130,1515806	13,90477371	2022-09-05, 21:50:15	-
IMG_0401.jpeg	33,53245833	130,1515806	13,90477563	2022-09-05, 22:08:03	-
IMG_0404.jpeg	33,53245833	130,1515806	13,04603196	2022-09-05, 22:24:58	-
IMG_0405.jpeg	33,53245833	130,1515806	13,26219939	2022-09-05, 22:25:02	-
IMG_0406.jpeg	33,53245556	130,1515806	13,90476036	2022-09-05, 22:28:30	-
IMG_0411.jpeg	33,5325	130,1516111	13,90479851	2022-09-06, 01:26:45	-
IMG_0418.jpeg	33,53245833	130,1515806	13,90477563	2022-09-06, 15:50:28	-
IMG_0419.jpeg	33,51300556	130,1300667	1,849027634	2022-09-06, 17:10:57	-
IMG_0421.jpeg	33,512975	130,1300361	-0,297945023	2022-09-06, 17:27:24	-
IMG_0422.jpeg	33,512975	130,1300361	0,199674607	2022-09-06, 17:27:27	-
IMG_0428.jpeg	33,51299722	130,1299889	2,952726363	2022-09-06, 17:43:21	-
IMG_0430.jpeg	33,53448889	130,1547389	2,809965131	2022-09-07, 13:07:50	-
IMG_0431.jpeg	33,55543889	130,1653583	3,027921679	2022-09-07, 13:26:30	-
IMG_0432.jpeg	33,56087222	130,1588444	0,471403135	2022-09-07, 13:31:07	-
IMG_0434.jpeg	33,56863889	130,1425028	21,37917901	2022-09-07, 13:39:15	-
IMG_0435.jpeg	33,57282222	130,1259472	2,481596475	2022-09-07, 13:50:05	-
IMG_0436.jpeg	33,57281944	130,1259472	2,357221887	2022-09-07, 13:50:12	-
IMG_0437.jpeg	33,57282222	130,1259472	1,954631344	2022-09-07, 13:50:20	-
IMG_0440.jpeg	33,572825	130,1259611	1,686429978	2022-09-07, 13:58:01	-
IMG_0442.jpeg	33,59399722	130,1093306	2,869962694	2022-09-07, 14:23:39	-
IMG_0444.jpeg	33,59397222	130,1093444	3,269500328	2022-09-07, 14:37:55	-
IMG_0447.jpeg	33,59520833	130,1096028	5,075130695	2022-09-07, 14:52:52	-
IMG_0448.jpeg	33,59520833	130,1095889	5,067846507	2022-09-07, 14:52:55	-
IMG_0449.jpeg	33,59520833	130,1096028	4,95367441	2022-09-07, 14:52:59	-
IMG_0450.jpeg	33,59520833	130,1096028	4,727496052	2022-09-07, 14:53:01	-
IMG_0454.jpeg	33,59498889	130,1092222	19,444182	2022-09-07, 14:56:21	-
IMG_0455.jpeg	33,59498333	130,1090556	23,82726142	2022-09-07, 14:56:44	-
IMG_0457.jpeg	33,59485	130,1086111	30,00747099	2022-09-07, 14:57:57	-
IMG_0458.jpeg	33,59478333	130,1080944	27,84332204	2022-09-07, 15:01:41	-
IMG_0459.jpeg	33,59476389	130,1080639	28,00875357	2022-09-07, 15:01:52	-
IMG_0462.jpeg	33,59499722	130,1092528	18,58650299	2022-09-07, 15:18:54	-
IMG_0465.jpeg	33,59501389	130,1094361	12,46640411	2022-09-07, 15:19:40	-
IMG_0466.jpeg	33,59498889	130,1094972	10,45760668	2022-09-07, 15:20:24	-
IMG_0467.jpeg	33,59510833	130,1095722	7,894714809	2022-09-07, 15:20:48	-
IMG_0468.jpeg	33,59511111	130,1095722	7,762726926	2022-09-07, 15:20:54	-
IMG_0473.jpeg	33,59420278	130,1094972	2,375316443	2022-09-07, 15:25:37	-
IMG_0478.jpeg	33,58965278	130,1083056	4,216635457	2022-09-07, 15:32:10	-
IMG_0479.jpeg	33,58966389	130,1083056	3,689637495	2022-09-07, 15:32:12	-
IMG_0480.jpeg	33,58812778	130,1100472	6,291973603	2022-09-07, 15:34:19	-
IMG_0481.jpeg	33,58814167	130,1099694	6,703102117	2022-09-07, 15:47:29	-
IMG_0482.jpeg	33,58813889	130,109925	1,376704217	2022-09-07, 15:48:30	-
IMG_0483.jpeg	33,58803611	130,1101222	6,09365654	2022-09-07, 15:49:42	-
IMG_0485.jpeg	33,58515278	130,1081083	2,22056368	2022-09-07, 16:09:39	-
IMG_0488.jpeg	33,58518889	130,1079111	2,151434224	2022-09-07, 16:27:53	-

IMG_0489.jpeg	33,58518889	130,1079111	2,095481187	2022-09-07, 16:27:58	-
IMG_0490.jpeg	33,58518889	130,1079111	1,890319751	2022-09-07, 16:28:02	-
IMG_0493.jpeg	33,56084722	130,1590889	2,716845856	2022-09-07, 17:00:00	-
IMG_0500.jpeg	33,53437778	130,1681528	9,92159286	2022-09-07, 18:01:41	-
IMG_0519.jpeg	33,50226944	130,0709389	-4,820125582	2022-09-07, 19:25:35	-
IMG_0520.jpeg	33,50233889	130,0707556	-8,667049408	2022-09-07, 19:25:42	-
IMG_0523.jpeg	33,522575	130,167175	11,07760431	2022-09-07, 21:19:29	-
IMG_0524.jpeg	33,52249444	130,167175	6,751310345	2022-09-07, 21:23:14	-
IMG_0554.jpeg	-	-	-	2022-09-08, 12:16:45	6.950
IMG_0558.jpeg	33,53715	130,1599417	5,913679125	2022-09-08, 12:39:37	-
IMG_0561.jpeg	33,53715	130,1599417	5,893863682	2022-09-08, 12:47:44	-
IMG_0562.jpeg	33,53715	130,1599417	5,903752329	2022-09-08, 12:49:47	-
IMG_0572.jpeg	33,53245278	130,1515361	17,26089286	2022-09-08, 22:15:55	-
IMG_0573.jpeg	33,53249722	130,15155	9,261057854	2022-09-08, 22:16:24	-
IMG_0594.jpeg	33,57717778	130,0900889	5,398961069	2022-09-09, 10:36:23	14.576
IMG_0595.jpeg	33,57737778	130,0899667	8,816654205	2022-09-09, 10:44:09	-
IMG_0600.jpeg	33,57728889	130,0900889	9,944400786	2022-09-09, 11:03:58	-
IMG_0604.jpeg	33,59539167	130,1082167	50,33151054	2022-09-09, 11:34:23	-
IMG_0609.jpeg	33,58651389	130,3894806	5,247341151	2022-09-09, 16:13:47	-
IMG_0610.jpeg	33,58683333	130,3950361	9,651956559	2022-09-09, 17:39:46	-
IMG_0611.jpeg	33,58687222	130,3949889	9,441096305	2022-09-09, 17:42:44	-
IMG_0614.jpeg	33,58689444	130,3949889	9,621234891	2022-09-09, 17:46:12	-
IMG_0615.jpeg	33,58686111	130,3949889	6,469861036	2022-09-09, 17:47:08	-
IMG_0616.jpeg	33,58688611	130,3950361	6,555492397	2022-09-09, 17:51:56	-
IMG_0617.jpeg	33,58652222	130,394425	6,069179534	2022-09-09, 17:51:59	-
IMG_0618.jpeg	33,58681111	130,3950194	9,218090052	2022-09-09, 18:24:15	-
IMG_0675.jpeg	33,58660833	130,3977972	9,615624427	2022-09-10, 02:39:57	8.883
IMG_0677.jpeg	33,59316667	130,4047694	10,17078781	2022-09-10, 04:35:06	-
IMG_0678.jpeg	33,59316667	130,4047694	10,17078781	2022-09-10, 04:35:07	-
IMG_0679.jpeg	33,59405556	130,4049694	7,194013595	2022-09-10, 09:38:44	-
IMG_0680.jpeg	33,59404444	130,4049833	7,160678863	2022-09-10, 09:39:47	-
IMG_0681.jpeg	33,59403889	130,4049833	7,089966777	2022-09-10, 09:40:39	-
IMG_0686.jpeg	33,59405	130,4049694	7,183625228	2022-09-10, 09:43:32	-
IMG_0687.jpeg	33,59401389	130,4049389	7,242242818	2022-09-10, 09:43:57	-
IMG_0688.jpeg	33,59401667	130,4048	7,64373875	2022-09-10, 09:55:14	-
IMG_0689.jpeg	33,59403611	130,4047694	7,423230182	2022-09-10, 09:56:17	-
IMG_0690.jpeg	33,55711667	130,1992194	13,56705475	2022-09-10, 10:52:00	-
IMG_0691.jpeg	33,55711667	130,1992194	13,56705475	2022-09-10, 10:52:01	-
IMG_0693.jpeg	33,53901944	130,1730806	4,777555464	2022-09-10, 11:12:22	-
IMG_0694.jpeg	33,53731667	130,1636194	4,15572929	2022-09-10, 11:22:16	-
IMG_0695.jpeg	33,53729722	130,1632833	6,928068163	2022-09-10, 11:22:42	-
IMG_0713.jpeg	33,53168889	130,15175	5,101713177	2022-09-10, 19:42:53	-
IMG_0714.jpeg	33,53153333	130,1519472	2,864080907	2022-09-10, 19:46:38	-
IMG_0715.jpeg	33,53129444	130,1516417	3,206413747	2022-09-10, 20:08:41	-
IMG_0716.jpeg	33,531575	130,1519917	4,697991369	2022-09-10, 20:31:47	-
IMG_0721.jpeg	33,53153611	130,1519917	4,92145157	2022-09-10, 20:57:14	-
IMG_0733.jpeg	33,532425	130,1516111	14,88345147	2022-09-11, 10:06:55	8.652
IMG_0765.jpeg	33,53264722	130,1515667	17,32754325	2022-09-11, 11:10:20	-
IMG_0766.jpeg	33,53250833	130,1518389	13,80721856	2022-09-11, 11:54:00	-
IMG_0767.jpeg	33,53250833	130,1516278	15,05003849	2022-09-11, 12:52:25	-
IMG_0769.jpeg	33,52711111	130,1486194	2,609913173	2022-09-11, 14:48:16	-
IMG_0770.jpeg	33,51336389	130,130525	1,126963615	2022-09-11, 15:14:18	-
IMG_0771.jpeg	33,51336389	130,13025	4,591886533	2022-09-11, 15:20:20	-
IMG_0773.jpeg	33,51335556	130,1302639	6,54733085	2022-09-11, 15:29:03	-
IMG_0774.jpeg	33,51333333	130,1302806	1,613615037	2022-09-11, 15:46:15	-
IMG_0775.jpeg	33,51337778	130,1301889	1,601163863	2022-09-11, 15:51:03	-
IMG_0776.jpeg	33,51338333	130,1301889	1,037443176	2022-09-11, 15:51:08	-
IMG_0777.jpeg	33,51338333	130,1301889	0,980741514	2022-09-11, 15:51:12	-
IMG_0778.jpeg	33,51338611	130,1301889	0,083585771	2022-09-11, 15:51:14	-
IMG_0779.jpeg	33,51337778	130,1301889	-0,604219404	2022-09-11, 15:51:19	-
IMG_0786.jpeg	33,51980556	130,1392056	23,36190607	2022-09-11, 18:24:21	-
IMG_0787.jpeg	33,51982778	130,1393583	18,46267511	2022-09-11, 18:24:31	-
IMG_0788.jpeg	33,53245833	130,1515806	13,90359879	2022-09-11, 18:52:43	-
IMG_0801.jpeg	33,53246667	130,1513972	18,4784832	2022-09-12, 14:49:06	6.649
IMG_0802.jpeg	33,51319444	130,13025	3,075834275	2022-09-12, 16:17:00	-
IMG_0804.jpeg	33,53238333	130,1516111	13,89026451	2022-09-12, 20:33:18	-
IMG_0816.jpeg	33,36338056	130,2843333	159,6874046	2022-09-13, 10:13:19	8.712
IMG_0817.jpeg	33,36325	130,2841944	157,8867606	2022-09-13, 10:13:54	-
IMG_0818.jpeg	33,36325833	130,2841944	157,7593814	2022-09-13, 10:13:57	-
IMG_0819.jpeg	33,36326111	130,2841944	157,5499854	2022-09-13, 10:14:00	-
IMG_0820.jpeg	33,36328889	130,2841333	162,7045831	2022-09-13, 10:17:43	-
IMG_0821.jpeg	33,3633	130,28415	162,6657713	2022-09-13, 10:17:44	-
IMG_0822.jpeg	33,36334722	130,2841333	167,7413062	2022-09-13, 10:18:29	-
IMG_0824.jpeg	33,36336111	130,2841028	168,2204586	2022-09-13, 10:18:44	-
IMG_0825.jpeg	33,36330833	130,28415	164,611816	2022-09-13, 10:18:58	-
IMG_0826.jpeg	33,36333889	130,28415	163,9432337	2022-09-13, 10:19:03	-
IMG_0827.jpeg	33,36331944	130,2841333	163,6408241	2022-09-13, 10:19:06	-
IMG_0828.jpeg	33,36331667	130,2841194	163,4143413	2022-09-13, 10:19:08	-
IMG_0830.jpeg	33,36340278	130,2842861	112,426876	2022-09-13, 10:39:59	-
IMG_0831.jpeg	33,36345	130,2842556	161,3976713	2022-09-13, 10:40:14	-
IMG_0832.jpeg	33,36343056	130,28415	163,8957789	2022-09-13, 10:40:28	-
IMG_0833.jpeg	33,36328611	130,2842556	160,2403221	2022-09-13, 10:46:32	-
IMG_0834.jpeg	33,36328889	130,2842556	160,0371362	2022-09-13, 10:46:35	-
IMG_0835.jpeg	33,36335833	130,2843028	163,6878819	2022-09-13, 10:46:57	-
IMG_0836.jpeg	33,36340278	130,2843944	162,5706822	2022-09-13, 10:47:28	-
IMG_0837.jpeg	33,3634	130,2844083	162,8863692	2022-09-13, 10:47:37	-
IMG_0838.jpeg	33,3634	130,2844083	162,8863692	2022-09-13, 10:47:38	-
IMG_0839.jpeg	33,36345278	130,2843472	162,6906653	2022-09-13, 10:52:13	-
IMG_0840.jpeg	33,36345556	130,2843472	163,6068297	2022-09-13, 10:52:25	-
IMG_0841.jpeg	33,36333056	130,2844083	164,4319932	2022-09-13, 11:16:12	-
IMG_0842.jpeg	33,36336944	130,2844083	164,6013978	2022-09-13, 11:16:19	-
IMG_0843.jpeg	33,36347222	130,284425	162,9774018	2022-09-13, 11:18:47	-
IMG_0844.jpeg	33,36347222	130,2844083	163,1898074	2022-09-13, 11:18:50	-
IMG_0845.jpeg	33,363475	130,284425	163,0673655	2022-09-13, 11:18:54	-
IMG_0846.jpeg	33,45269444	130,276	408,8225966	2022-09-13, 11:47:47	-
IMG_0847.jpeg	-	-	-	2022-09-13, 11:59:20	-

IMG_0848.jpeg	33,45288056	130,276	407,2524072	2022-09-13, 12:01:58	-
IMG_0849.jpeg	33,45275556	130,2759389	407,228237	2022-09-13, 12:02:01	-
IMG_0852.jpeg	33,45278611	130,2758028	441,6567037	2022-09-13, 12:09:44	-
IMG_0853.jpeg	-	-	-	2022-09-13, 12:12:45	-
IMG_0854.jpeg	33,45319444	130,2762917	410,545925	2022-09-13, 12:13:06	-
IMG_0855.jpeg	-	-	-	2022-09-13, 12:20:35	-
IMG_0882.jpeg	33,53239167	130,1516278	3,468977449	2022-09-14, 12:38:33	11.696
IMG_0885.jpeg	-	-	-	2022-09-14, 14:30:47	-
IMG_0886.jpeg	33,58805833	130,3963611	23,63515854	2022-09-14, 14:56:39	-
IMG_0887.jpeg	33,58948611	130,3961806	11,24937153	2022-09-14, 15:45:33	-
IMG_0888.jpeg	33,58936667	130,3961806	14,46761131	2022-09-14, 15:49:30	-
IMG_0889.jpeg	33,58865833	130,3962694	11,41144465	2022-09-14, 17:49:32	-
IMG_0891.jpeg	33,58862222	130,3961333	11,5732336	2022-09-14, 17:49:36	-
IMG_0892.jpeg	33,58866111	130,3962694	11,23792267	2022-09-14, 18:28:38	-
IMG_0902.jpeg	33,58721111	130,3953083	9,842109683	2022-09-14, 20:53:21	-
IMG_0903.jpeg	33,58714167	130,3952944	9,523891452	2022-09-14, 23:42:52	-
IMG_0904.jpeg	33,58712778	130,3941028	9,699375145	2022-09-14, 23:58:04	-
IMG_0905.jpeg	33,58801667	130,4071361	25,44796371	2022-09-15, 02:14:09	11.601
IMG_0906.jpeg	33,58792222	130,4073333	10,95657826	2022-09-15, 02:15:32	-
IMG_0910.jpeg	33,59020278	130,4044333	17,40316412	2022-09-15, 10:14:05	-
IMG_0911.jpeg	33,59108611	130,4039306	6,486957553	2022-09-15, 10:15:39	-
IMG_0912.jpeg	33,59075278	130,4019611	6,310733182	2022-09-15, 10:18:31	-
IMG_0915.jpeg	-	-	-	2022-09-15, 11:13:04	-
IMG_0916.jpeg	33,53443611	130,1681833	9,624176498	2022-09-15, 11:53:48	-
IMG_0917.jpeg	33,5325	130,1517194	10,14388847	2022-09-15, 12:42:54	-
IMG_0918.jpeg	33,53235278	130,1515972	13,22909359	2022-09-15, 12:43:03	-
IMG_0919.jpeg	33,53241667	130,15155	5,988798146	2022-09-15, 12:47:14	-
IMG_0923.jpeg	33,53406389	130,1542972	5,309253542	2022-09-15, 13:28:49	-
IMG_0924.jpeg	33,51214722	130,1293333	0,821928039	2022-09-15, 14:11:38	-
IMG_0925.jpeg	33,51214722	130,1293028	2,642484663	2022-09-15, 14:15:41	-
IMG_0929.jpeg	33,51212222	130,1293028	3,49331474	2022-09-15, 14:17:12	-
IMG_0931.jpeg	33,51260833	130,1299889	2,724699034	2022-09-15, 14:49:50	-
IMG_0932.jpeg	33,51294722	130,1298222	3,96029472	2022-09-15, 15:43:52	-
IMG_0933.jpeg	33,51291389	130,1297917	2,516874314	2022-09-15, 15:43:54	-
IMG_0935.jpeg	33,51343611	130,1303556	0,437711716	2022-09-15, 16:58:09	-
IMG_0936.jpeg	33,51343611	130,1303722	1,118192687	2022-09-15, 16:58:14	-
IMG_0937.jpeg	33,5134	130,1303556	2,103292901	2022-09-15, 16:58:47	-
IMG_0938.jpeg	33,52185833	130,1315778	1,096036913	2022-09-15, 18:05:56	-
IMG_0939.jpeg	33,52187222	130,1315611	1,356168747	2022-09-15, 18:06:00	-
IMG_0955.jpeg	33,53245833	130,1515972	13,90479851	2022-09-16, 11:55:48	16.708
IMG_0956.jpeg	33,53246389	130,1515972	13,90254403	2022-09-16, 12:44:36	-
IMG_0961.jpeg	33,53233611	130,1516889	12,09890555	2022-09-16, 13:26:26	-
IMG_0964.jpeg	33,51415	130,1310111	6,263944637	2022-09-16, 17:57:30	-
IMG_0966.jpeg	33,52196111	130,1322167	9,740201951	2022-09-16, 18:32:14	-
IMG_0967.jpeg	33,52196111	130,1322472	11,60543634	2022-09-16, 18:32:22	-
IMG_0972.jpeg	33,53246389	130,1515667	12,26052667	2022-09-17, 02:35:55	9.197
IMG_0974.jpeg	33,53243889	130,1515667	13,24960137	2022-09-17, 11:39:19	-
IMG_0976.jpeg	33,53715556	130,1599417	5,917903899	2022-09-17, 14:25:27	-
IMG_0979.jpeg	33,537175	130,1599583	5,246379853	2022-09-17, 15:15:10	-
IMG_0981.jpeg	33,53823056	130,1548472	4,993912455	2022-09-17, 17:06:07	-
IMG_0996.jpeg	-	-	-	-	-
IMG_1005.jpeg	33,53237778	130,1516278	12,9944191	2022-09-18, 13:11:38	-
IMG_1006.jpeg	33,53241389	130,1516889	9,592435827	2022-09-18, 13:11:41	-
IMG_1014.jpeg	33,53240833	130,1514889	16,93478203	2022-09-18, 19:06:01	-
IMG_1015.jpeg	33,53239167	130,15155	16,02883721	2022-09-18, 19:14:38	-
IMG_1017.jpeg	33,53245278	130,1515972	13,07446099	2022-09-18, 19:38:01	-
IMG_1018.jpeg	33,53246667	130,151475	12,15090752	2022-09-18, 19:38:05	-
IMG_1028.jpeg	33,53245833	130,1515972	12,7891922	2022-09-18, 22:55:03	-
IMG_1045.jpeg	33,53246389	130,1516417	12,9350624	2022-09-19, 10:46:56	-
IMG_1046.jpeg	33,53245278	130,1517028	9,820157998	2022-09-19, 10:47:01	-
IMG_1049.jpeg	33,53247778	130,1515972	12,57272148	2022-09-19, 10:54:14	-
IMG_1050.jpeg	33,53243889	130,1516111	15,08407402	2022-09-19, 10:54:29	-
IMG_1051.jpeg	33,53243889	130,1516111	13,32064443	2022-09-19, 10:54:47	-
IMG_1052.jpeg	33,53242222	130,1516111	13,69752441	2022-09-19, 10:54:53	-
IMG_1054.jpeg	33,53243333	130,1515806	14,01114519	2022-09-19, 10:55:09	-
IMG_1059.jpeg	33,53245833	130,1515972	13,08548927	2022-09-19, 13:24:40	-
IMG_1060.jpeg	33,53188056	130,1558222	3,212252408	2022-09-19, 17:52:33	-
IMG_1061.jpeg	33,53188333	130,1558222	2,986242817	2022-09-19, 17:52:36	-
IMG_1063.jpeg	33,53180278	130,1559	3,563620108	2022-09-19, 17:52 58	-
IMG_1064.jpeg	33,52194722	130,1649944	7,054226675	2022-09-19, 17:59 10	-
IMG_1065.jpeg	33,52195	130,1649944	7,040890919	2022-09-19, 17:59 16	-
IMG_1075.jpeg	33,53256944	130,1516111	15,49595455	2022-09-20, 12:13 58	-
IMG_1077.jpeg	33,53241667	130,1517194	19,9267254	2022-09-20, 13:18 51	-
IMG_1081.jpeg	33,51296944	130,1301417	3,417997359	2022-09-20, 14:48 01	-
IMG_1086.jpeg	33,513175	130,1302028	1,650846483	2022-09-20, 15:52 53	-
IMG_1097.jpeg	33,53245556	130,1516111	12,90469742	2022-09-21, 01:51 02	11.877
IMG_1105.jpeg	33,50901111	130,1330417	35,59251074	2022-09-21, 12:23 14	-
IMG_1106.jpeg	33,50901111	130,1330417	35,57755308	2022-09-21, 12:23 17	-
IMG_1107.jpeg	33,50921944	130,1289056	40,94955254	2022-09-21, 12:28:20	-
IMG_1108.jpeg	33,50921944	130,1289056	40,23385432	2022-09-21, 12:28:22	-
IMG_1110.jpeg	33,508275	130,1254583	41,71169855	2022-09-21, 12:47:17	-
IMG_1111.jpeg	-	-	-	2022-09-21, 12:57:54	-
IMG_1112.jpeg	33,51000278	130,1293028	52,21279718	2022-09-21, 13:19:10	-
IMG_1113.jpeg	33,50998611	130,1292889	41,36446951	2022-09-21, 13:19:13	-
IMG_1129.jpeg	33,53245278	130,1516111	12,90482902	2022-09-21, 23:23:59	-
IMG_1130.jpeg	33,53245556	130,1516111	12,90482711	2022-09-21, 23:24:04	-
IMG_1131.jpeg	33,53245278	130,1516111	12,88818932	2022-09-21, 23:31:24	-
IMG_1146.jpeg	33,55944444	130,1996917	14,73568579	2022-09-22, 12:38:33	18.855
IMG_1147.jpeg	33,559425	130,1995694	12,88052177	2022-09-22, 12:38:46	-
IMG_1148.jpeg	33,55942222	130,1995861	12,94668387	2022-09-22, 12:38:49	-
IMG_1149.jpeg	33,55992222	130,1980889	12,79979792	2022-09-22, 12:45:22	-
IMG_1150.jpeg	33,56256111	130,1947333	7,349027636	2022-09-22, 12:46:06	-
IMG_1152.jpeg	33,58316667	130,1839	10,79782104	2022-09-22, 12:54:51	-
IMG_1155.jpeg	33,62206667	130,1867056	9,374044412	2022-09-22, 13:10:38	-
IMG_1157.jpeg	33,62263611	130,18625	8,387411135	2022-09-22, 13:18:35	-
IMG_1161.jpeg	33,63039444	130,1845694	11,1653042	2022-09-22, 13:31:18	-

IMG_1163.jpeg	33,63116111	130,1841889	12,01767046	2022-09-22, 13:32:53	-
IMG_1164.jpeg	33,63121111	130,1841444	11,84147128	2022-09-22, 13:32:58	-
IMG_1165.jpeg	33,63123333	130,1841278	12,1939577	2022-09-22, 13:33:00	-
IMG_1166.jpeg	33,63233889	130,1833639	-1,84787941	2022-09-22, 13:36:04	-
IMG_1168.jpeg	33,63776667	130,1943667	9,023275379	2022-09-22, 13:54:45	-
IMG_1169.jpeg	33,63776389	130,1943667	4,788106919	2022-09-22, 13:54:48	-
IMG_1170.jpeg	33,64205556	130,2014611	9,359523773	2022-09-22, 14:35:24	-
IMG_1181.jpeg	33,642075	130,2017056	16,71438217	2022-09-22, 14:45:40	-
IMG_1182.jpeg	33,64243056	130,2010333	2,397365572	2022-09-22, 15:26:00	-
IMG_1183.jpeg	33,64244167	130,2010639	2,827846525	2022-09-22, 15:26:08	-
IMG_1184.jpeg	33,64256389	130,2014778	1,328212739	2022-09-22, 16:08:20	-
IMG_1185.jpeg	33,64254722	130,2014917	7,055828465	2022-09-22, 16:09:08	-
IMG_1186.jpeg	33,64254444	130,2014917	7,056055176	2022-09-22, 16:09:10	-
IMG_1187.jpeg	33,63928889	130,1976611	7,771993635	2022-09-22, 16:33:37	-
IMG_1188.jpeg	33,639325	130,1976917	8,581930145	2022-09-22, 16:33:41	-
IMG_1195.jpeg	33,59338056	130,401275	14,4	2022-09-22, 18:05:45	-
IMG_1196.jpeg	33,59245278	130,3987417	30,70693589	2022-09-22, 18:13:29	-
IMG_1197.jpeg	33,59180556	130,3984222	11,80416488	2022-09-22, 18:15:50	-
IMG_1198.jpeg	33,58865278	130,3962556	14,96958923	2022-09-22, 19:46:33	-
IMG_1200.jpeg	33,58861944	130,3962083	10,8037119	2022-09-22, 19:50:33	-
IMG_1201.jpeg	33,58858056	130,3959056	10,34298611	2022-09-22, 20:02:09	-
IMG_1203.jpeg	33,58706944	130,3953556	10,75731468	2022-09-22, 20:46:54	-
IMG_1204.jpeg	33,58837778	130,3987417	11,23031541	2022-09-22, 21:16:22	-
IMG_1205.jpeg	33,58916111	130,4000556	9,635773196	2022-09-22, 21:17:43	-
IMG_1206.jpeg	33,58905278	130,4001472	9,492698729	2022-09-22, 21:17:45	-
IMG_1207.jpeg	33,58415278	130,3166194	4,846401211	2022-09-22, 21:49:41	-
IMG_1263.jpeg	33,52973611	130,1571056	2,730859397	2022-09-23, 11:41:40	-
IMG_1264.jpeg	33,52993889	130,1562194	2,157282921	2022-09-23, 11:51:47	-
IMG_1265.jpeg	33,52993333	130,1562194	2,405314416	2022-09-23, 11:51:50	-
IMG_1266.jpeg	33,52993333	130,1562194	-3,492219926	2022-09-23, 11:55:56	-
IMG_1268.jpeg	33,52993889	130,1562194	-0,088350268	2022-09-23, 11:56:12	-
IMG_1270.jpeg	-	-	-	2022-09-23, 12:08:03	-
IMG_1271.jpeg	33,5299	130,1562194	0,041532516	2022-09-23, 12:08:37	-
IMG_1272.jpeg	33,52992222	130,1562194	0,663541794	2022-09-23, 12:08:40	-
IMG_1273.jpeg	33,52986944	130,1562194	-10,14120675	2022-09-23, 12:15:35	-
IMG_1274.jpeg	33,52990278	130,1562194	-1,966829301	2022-09-23, 12:16:46	-
IMG_1281.jpeg	33,19466111	130,0166639	31,4521419	2022-09-23, 15:11:55	-
IMG_1282.jpeg	33,19482778	130,0164944	14,80160144	2022-09-23, 15:21:27	-
IMG_1283.jpeg	33,18973056	130,0269611	19,94558336	2022-09-23, 17:03:02	-
IMG_1284.jpeg	33,18947222	130,0278333	27,94207695	2022-09-23, 17:35:40	-
IMG_1285.jpeg	33,18945278	130,0277556	26,94569112	2022-09-23, 17:35:48	-
IMG_1286.jpeg	33,18937222	130,0272222	13,87470209	2022-09-23, 17:36:55	-
IMG_1345.jpeg	33,51908056	130,1393583	6,977121353	2022-09-24, 13:32:28	9,085
IMG_1354.jpeg	33,53246667	130,1516417	12,90480423	2022-09-24, 22:32:17	-
IMG_1355.jpeg	33,53253889	130,1516278	15,6550579	2022-09-24, 22:32:24	-
IMG_1358.jpeg	33,53243333	130,1514583	19,5786419	2022-09-24, 23:48:12	-
IMG_1369.jpeg	33,53457778	130,1546472	5,907796859	2022-09-25, 11:26:20	14.748
IMG_1371.jpeg	33,53461111	130,1544806	2,459684372	2022-09-25, 11:29:28	-
IMG_1372.jpeg	33,53461389	130,1544944	1,1112957	2022-09-25, 11:29:31	-
IMG_1374.jpeg	33,53323611	130,1522972	23,66525078	2022-09-25, 12:02:08	-
IMG_1376.jpeg	33,53255556	130,1516417	15,16323661	2022-09-25, 12:22:07	-
IMG_1379.jpeg	33,53715	130,1599417	5,913681028	2022-09-25, 13:50:49	-
IMG_1380.jpeg	33,53715	130,1599417	5,913681028	2022-09-25, 14:25:53	-
IMG_1381.jpeg	33,53715	130,1599417	5,913681028	2022-09-25, 14:25:55	-
IMG_1382.jpeg	33,53715	130,1599417	5,913681028	2022-09-25, 14:31:35	-
IMG_1383.jpeg	33,53715	130,1599417	5,913681028	2022-09-25, 14:38:30	-
IMG_1389.jpeg	33,51395833	130,1377556	6,017937148	2022-09-25, 16:35:52	-
IMG_1390.jpeg	33,51424444	130,1379694	5,471268155	2022-09-25, 16:38:34	-
IMG_1391.jpeg	33,51338611	130,1303556	1,524381638	2022-09-25, 16:54:59	-
IMG_1392.jpeg	33,513375	130,1303417	2,558988569	2022-09-25, 17:15:07	-
IMG_1393.jpeg	33,51336667	130,1303556	2,757169736	2022-09-25, 17:15:14	-
IMG_1394.jpeg	33,52011389	130,1399222	4,539624129	2022-09-25, 19:14:29	-
IMG_1396.jpeg	33,52009444	130,1400139	4,400175062	2022-09-25, 19:16:38	-
IMG_1402.jpeg	33,51976389	130,1391444	4,859112744	2022-09-25, 19:52:52	-
IMG_1429.jpeg	33,51428333	130,1380611	5,937338325	2022-09-26, 10:05:21	-
IMG_1430.jpeg	33,53238611	130,1516417	12,29127692	2022-09-26, 12:00:05	-
IMG_1433.jpeg	33,5089	130,1004778	7,809232715	2022-09-26, 15:10:28	-
IMG_1434.jpeg	33,50896389	130,1005083	8,362396342	2022-09-26, 15:13:26	-
IMG_1435.jpeg	33,50895556	130,100525	8,215341656	2022-09-26, 15:13:29	-
IMG_1436.jpeg	33,50893333	130,1003583	10,16683769	2022-09-26, 15:24:51	-
IMG_1437.jpeg	33,508975	130,1005083	6,737455366	2022-09-26, 15:38:36	-
IMG_1438.jpeg	33,50910833	130,1003889	10,77694512	2022-09-26, 16:11:25	-
IMG_1439.jpeg	33,50898056	130,1005083	8,570813754	2022-09-26, 16:16:13	-
IMG_1440.jpeg	33,50895278	130,100525	8,570813754	2022-09-26, 16:27:43	-
IMG_1441.jpeg	33,50911667	130,1003583	14,09554862	2022-09-26, 16:58:00	-
IMG_1443.jpeg	33,50896389	130,1004028	7,910978319	2022-09-26, 17:04:11	-
IMG_1445.jpeg	33,508975	130,1004639	8,768639563	2022-09-26, 17:20:01	-
IMG_1482.jpeg	33,53256944	130,151475	22,42501641	2022-09-27, 11:46:35	16.120
IMG_1483.jpeg	33,59888889	130,4472972	-	2022-09-27, 14:09:23	-
IMG_1488.jpeg	-	-	-	2022-09-27, 15:47:38	-
IMG_1489.jpeg	-	-	-	2022-09-27, 16:45:53	-
IMG_1491.jpeg	35,77855278	140,3833472	57,63770673	2022-09-27, 17:13:09	-
IMG_1494.jpeg	35,77413889	140,3864139	41,20051195	2022-09-27, 17:27:23	-
IMG_1495.jpeg	35,79715	140,3163917	14,72778385	2022-09-27, 17:47:48	-
IMG_1496.jpeg	35,80376389	140,1304333	20,72149993	2022-09-27, 17:55:30	-
IMG_1500.jpeg	35,66127778	139,7032778	24,1466258	2022-09-27, 19:21:11	-
IMG_1501.jpeg	35,66114444	139,7033694	24,49142743	2022-09-27, 19:21:23	-
IMG_1502.jpeg	35,66127778	139,7030028	26,73521042	2022-09-27, 19:25:45	-
IMG_1503.jpeg	35,66128611	139,7030028	26,49726869	2022-09-27, 19:25:51	-
IMG_1504.jpeg	35,661475	139,7031111	25,72261236	2022-09-27, 19:36:41	-
IMG_1507.jpeg	35,65949167	139,7000111	18,55555527	2022-09-27, 19:46:42	-
IMG_1508.jpeg	35,65951944	139,7000111	18,31293871	2022-09-27, 19:46:59	-
IMG_1528.jpeg	35,65589444	139,6963056	39,73500442	2022-09-27, 21:44:45	-
IMG_1529.jpeg	35,65581111	139,6961667	42,30086136	2022-09-27, 21:44:51	-
IMG_1530.jpeg	35,65720833	139,695175	38,66954804	2022-09-27, 23:27:30	-
IMG_1531.jpeg	35,65726111	139,6952361	38,47991562	2022-09-27, 23:38:52	-

IMG_1532.jpeg	35,65721111	139,6951444	38,34621426	2022-09-27, 23:46:33	-
IMG_1543.jpeg	35,66013333	139,7024083	21,52024823	2022-09-28,01:17:37	-
IMG_1544.jpeg	35,66165833	139,7024833	19,45829636	2022-09-28, 01:20:00	-
IMG_1547.jpeg	35,66161667	139,7028667	23,56668243	2022-09-28, 01:20:50	-
IMG_1548.jpeg	35,6615	139,7031389	24,06997758	2022-09-28, 01:21:40	-
IMG_1549.jpeg	35,66169444	139,7029889	54,84887695	2022-09-28, 01:22:29	-
IMG_1550.jpeg	35,66154167	139,7030333	30,8344936	2022-09-28, 01:22:33	-
IMG_1551.jpeg	35,66135833	139,7030806	27,8264637	2022-09-28, 01:22:43	-
IMG_1556.jpeg	35,66110556	139,7029583	27,4683399	2022-09-28, 02:08:10	-
IMG_1557.jpeg	35,66112222	139,7029417	27,34331513	2022-09-28, 02:10:25	-
IMG_1558.jpeg	35,66113611	139,7029417	26,91748999	2022-09-28, 02:23:28	-
IMG_1559.jpeg	35,66109722	139,7029417	26,24074934	2022-09-28, 02:38:34	-
IMG_1560.jpeg	35,661125	139,7029417	26,3920002	2022-09-28, 02:38:37	-
IMG_1561.jpeg	35,66108611	139,7029583	26,98600578	2022-09-28, 03:02:58	-
IMG_1562.jpeg	35,66111111	139,7029417	26,95315362	2022-09-28, 03:03:06	-
IMG_1565.jpeg	35,66110278	139,7029583	26,94812012	2022-09-28, 03:08:17	-
IMG_1570.jpeg	35,66128889	139,7030639	25,38900376	2022-09-28, 12:07:31	-
IMG_1575.jpeg	35,66146111	139,7030333	25,77595329	2022-09-28, 13:04:33	-
IMG_1576.jpeg	35,66146111	139,7030333	25,77595329	2022-09-28, 13:04:38	-
IMG_1578.jpeg	35,66604167	139,7039944	23,79637908	2022-09-28, 13:26:19	-
IMG_1579.jpeg	35,66612222	139,7041778	30,97148895	2022-09-28, 13:26:36	-
IMG_1580.jpeg	35,667775	139,7058556	21,31544291	2022-09-28, 13:32:50	-
IMG_1581.jpeg	35,66779722	139,7058111	21,19360398	2022-09-28, 13:32:58	-
IMG_1582.jpeg	35,66773333	139,7057806	103,2042389	2022-09-28, 13:36:36	-
IMG_1583.jpeg	35,66768611	139,7057639	24,98915102	2022-09-28, 13:45:03	-
IMG_1584.jpeg	35,66777778	139,7057333	21,57512665	2022-09-28, 13:46:08	-
IMG_1585.jpeg	35,66782778	139,705825	22,20940399	2022-09-28, 13:46:16	-
IMG_1586.jpeg	35,66860556	139,7057333	-	2022-09-28, 13:48:47	-
IMG_1587.jpeg	35,66893056	139,7055972	25,69234275	2022-09-28, 15:03:35	-
IMG_1588.jpeg	35,6619	139,7025917	19,72818281	2022-09-28, 15:53:43	-
IMG_1589.jpeg	35,66295278	139,7029278	18,25522816	2022-09-28, 16:20:[illegible]4	-
IMG_1590.jpeg	35,6632	139,7032	19,16423533	2022-09-28, 16:21:15	-
IMG_1591.jpeg	35,66369167	139,7048333	25,35492764	2022-09-28, 16:24:37	-
IMG_1593.jpeg	35,66470833	139,7073528	33,30525172	2022-09-28, 16:34:23	-
IMG_1594.jpeg	35,66522222	139,7128139	35,9696217	2022-09-28 16:45:17	-
IMG_1595.jpeg	35,66545	139,7132417	39,26745605	2022-09-28, 16:49:38	-
IMG_1597.jpeg	35,66523333	139,7128306	36,0599289	2022-09-28, 16:55:09	-
IMG_1598.jpeg	35,66577222	139,7132556	34,72405134	2022-09-28, 16:57:05	-
IMG_1603.jpeg	35,66644722	139,7135917	36,25677874	2022-09-28, 17:08:12	-
IMG_1604.jpeg	35,66966944	139,7180028	35,32931988	2022-09-28, 17:41:13	-
IMG_1605.jpeg	35,66970833	139,7180028	34,99215247	2022-09-28, 17:41:22	-
IMG_1606.jpeg	35,67261389	139,7297833	27,59499337	2022-09-28, 18:05:36	-
IMG_1607.jpeg	35,67327778	139,7296917	30,11037238	2022-09-28, 18:11:37	-
IMG_1608.jpeg	35,67302222	139,7301778	34,90749935	2022-09-28, 18:19 39	-
IMG_1609.jpeg	35,67301944	139,7300722	34,90726283	2022-09-28, 18:19 43	-
IMG_1620.jpeg	35,673125	139,7297667	42,21375277	2022-09-28, 21:59 50	-
IMG_1621.jpeg	35,67300278	139,7298278	42,21391296	2022-09-28, 21:59:56	-
IMG_1622.jpeg	35,66173056	139,7028361	27,91490555	2022-09-28, 23:29:20	-
IMG_1623.jpeg	35,66178611	139,7027278	25,76235964	2022-09-28, 23:29:26	-
IMG_1625.jpeg	35,66099444	139,7029111	54,3494186	2022-09-29, 00:27:34	-
IMG_1627.jpeg	35,66106111	139,7029583	26,66230581	2022-09-29, 00:42:25	-
IMG_1629.jpeg	35,66111667	139,7029417	25,92267608	2022-09-29, 00:53:20	-
IMG_1639.jpeg	35,66149444	139,7023917	26,97563934	2022-09-29, 03:14:37	-
IMG_1640.jpeg	35,66030556	139,7013861	39,77208707	2022-09-29, 03:16:51	-
IMG_1641.jpeg	35,66050278	139,7000583	19,53154754	2022-09-29, 03:18:34	-
IMG_1642.jpeg	35,66050833	139,7000722	19,45323944	2022-09-29, 03:18:36	-
IMG_1644.jpeg	35,66074722	139,6982889	21,43954851	2022-09-29, 03:3[illegible]:42	-
IMG_1645.jpeg	35,66073889	139,6982278	21,25152586	2022-09-29, 03:3[illegible]:44	-
IMG_1648.jpeg	35,66128611	139,70305	25,7736969	2022-09-29, 04:21:15	-
IMG_1649.jpeg	35,66130556	139,70305	25,78001596	2022-09-29, 04:27:17	-
IMG_1652.jpeg	35,661675	139,7028972	24,26356887	2022-09-29, 11:44:32	-
IMG_1653.jpeg	35,66171667	139,7029111	24,72322847	2022-09-29, 12:11:50	-
IMG_1654.jpeg	35,66165278	139,7029417	24,66832159	2022-09-29, 12:54:34	-
IMG_1656.jpeg	35,66165278	139,7029583	24,68166922	2022-09-29, 13:15:16	-
IMG_1657.jpeg	35,66167778	139,7028972	24,74059871	2022-09-29, 13:23:43	-
IMG_1659.jpeg	35,66261389	139,6660167	49,50812909	2022-09-29, 14:27:44	-
IMG_1664.jpeg	35,66902222	139,705475	30,03340909	2022-09-29, 17:29:26	-
IMG_1666.jpeg	35,65723333	139,6951917	38,51179506	2022-09-29, 19:39:00	-
IMG_1668.jpeg	35,65721944	139,6951611	38,51199338	2022-09-29, 19:49:52	-
IMG_1671.jpeg	35,66268056	139,6659861	46,49959947	2022-09-30, 00:47:01	16.745
IMG_1681.jpeg	35,66282778	139,6693278	36,8499336	2022-09-30, 18:06:01	-
IMG_1689.jpeg	-	-	-	2022-09-30, 21:19:33	-
IMG_1690.jpeg	35,66265833	139,6659861	46,76369475	2022-10-01, 10:37:46	12.049
IMG_1691.jpeg	35,66265833	139,6659694	46,78727724	2022-10-01, 10:38:05	-
IMG_1692.jpeg	35,66266944	139,6659861	46,96917723	2022-10-01, 10:48:32	-
IMG_1693.jpeg	35,66266667	139,6659861	46,69688416	2022-10-01, 10:49:45	-
IMG_1696.jpeg	35,66183333	139,6661222	44,45405956	2022-10-01, 11:48:29	-
IMG_1698.jpeg	35,62903889	139,7404778	-	2022-10-01, 12:43:56	-
IMG_1699.jpeg	35,62899722	139,7402028	8,836025243	2022-10-01, 12:44:00	-
IMG_1700.jpeg	35,62909444	139,7406917	-	2022-10-01, 12:44:11	-
IMG_1703.jpeg	35,57216389	139,6640639	9,863609319	2022-10-01, 13:05:09	-
IMG_1704.jpeg	35,57051944	139,6645972	11,79323579	2022-10-01, 13:05:16	-
IMG_1705.jpeg	35,569675	139,66475	11,85056259	2022-10-01, 13:05:18	-
IMG_1706.jpeg	35,56486944	139,663375	10,33439599	2022-10-01, 13:05:35	-
IMG_1707.jpeg	35,56219167	139,6614083	10,435555	2022-10-01, 13:05:46	-
IMG_1708.jpeg	35,56107222	139,6603694	10,83755053	2022-10-01, 13:05:50	-
IMG_1712.jpeg	35,5317	139,6398611	6,868309024	2022-10-01, 13 07:00	-
IMG_1713.jpeg	35,52998333	139,6386556	7,711753846	2022-10-01, 13 07:04	-
IMG_1718.jpeg	35,32586389	139,2905278	27,48763312	2022-10-01, 13:20:23	-
IMG_1719.jpeg	35,30624722	139,245025	28,10184479	2022-10-01, 13:21:28	-
IMG_1721.jpeg	35,14908333	138,7846222	40,91481781	2022-10-01, 13:37:46	-
IMG_1723.jpeg	35,14998889	138,7816306	36,69857025	2022-10-01, 13:37:52	-
IMG_1725.jpeg	34,87940556	138,3167583	-0,50315469	2022-10-01, 13:52:24	-
IMG_1726.jpeg	34,87891667	138,3161306	-0,385207887	2022-10-01, 13:52:24	-
IMG_1727.jpeg	34,876025	138,3123778	-0,870828907	2022-10-01, 13:52:30	-
IMG_1728.jpeg	34,80429444	138,206375	33,44662913	2022-10-01, 13:55:11	-

IMG_1729.jpeg	34,80331667	138,2041167	33,5870916	2022-10-01, 13:55:14	-
IMG_1730.jpeg	34,80300833	138,2033222	33,9133689	2022-10-01, 13:55:14	-
IMG_1731.jpeg	34,80300833	138,2033222	33,9133689	2022-10-01, 13:55:15	-
IMG_1732.jpeg	34,80300833	138,2033222	33,9133689	2022-10-01, 13:55:15	-
IMG_1733.jpeg	34,80009722	138,1937556	37,70602156	2022-10-01, 13:55:27	-
IMG_1736.jpeg	35,17036389	136,8803417	6,986291886	2022-10-01, 14:32:23	-
IMG_1738.jpeg	35,32416111	136,6760111	12,48854172	2022-10-01, 14:40:17	-
IMG_1742.jpeg	34,98122778	135,8035722	41,99158957	2022-10-01, 15:03:04	-
IMG_1743.jpeg	34,9813	135,801575	22,83349795	2022-10-01, 15:03:07	-
IMG_1744.jpeg	34,98457778	135,76065	29,86997649	2022-10-01, 15:05:06	-
IMG_1745.jpeg	34,98546667	135,7599639	30,70903015	2022-10-01, 15:15:54	-
IMG_1746.jpeg	34,98546667	135,7599639	30,70903015	2022-10-01, 15:15:58	-
IMG_1749.jpeg	35,01217778	135,7657167	44,5881303	2022-10-01, 17:09:03	-
IMG_1750.jpeg	35,01214167	135,7662361	41,93980088	2022-10-01, 17:09:44	-
IMG_1751.jpeg	35,01212778	135,7681722	45,3893783	2022-10-01, 17:13:16	-
IMG_1752.jpeg	35,01124167	135,7714389	64,45113754	2022-10-01, 17:28:46	-
IMG_1753.jpeg	35,01110556	135,7717583	39,4480858	2022-10-01, 17:29:07	-
IMG_1754.jpeg	35,01065556	135,77205	37,06826401	2022-10-01, 17:30:28	-
IMG_1755.jpeg	35,01060556	135,77205	38,11184314	2022-10-01, 17:30:30	-
IMG_1756.jpeg	35,01014722	135,7720639	33,74221419	2022-10-01, 17:31:16	-
IMG_1757.jpeg	35,00934722	135,7720333	37,25362776	2022-10-01, 17:32:26	-
IMG_1758.jpeg	35,00842222	135,7718361	46,84127424	2022-10-01, 17:34:05	-
IMG_1759.jpeg	35,00843889	135,7719278	38,47158432	2022-10-01, 17:41:25	-
IMG_1767.jpeg	35,00506111	135,7704306	41,60311509	2022-10-01, 18:21:27	-
IMG_1768.jpeg	35,00506944	135,7704472	40,48232648	2022-10-01, 18:21:28	-
IMG_1771.jpeg	-	-	-	2022-11-02, 21:37:43	-
IMG_1775.jpeg	-	-	-	2022-11-02, 21:43:52	-
IMG_1779.jpeg	35,00510278	135,7705083	45,53816603	2022-10-01, 19:01:28	-
IMG_1780.jpeg	35,00510278	135,7705083	45,53816603	2022-10-01, 19:01:32	-
IMG_1781.jpeg	35,00386944	135,7714528	36,08529283	2022-10-01, 19:09:44	-
IMG_1785.jpeg	-	-	-	2022-10-01, 19:19:39	-
IMG_1786.jpeg	-	-	-	2022-10-01, 19:19:44	-
IMG_1787.jpeg	-	-	-	2022-11-03, 01:28:19	-
IMG_1788.jpeg	-	-	-	2022-11-03, 01:28:23	-
IMG_1789.jpeg	-	-	-	2022-11-03, 01:28:27	-
IMG_1796.jpeg	34,69148611	135,5082389	7,224000935	2022-10-01, 20:08:27	-
IMG_1797.jpeg	34,69148611	135,5082389	7,224000935	2022-10-01, 20:08:31	-
IMG_1798.jpeg	-	-	-	2022-10-01, 20:11:35	-
IMG_1799.jpeg	-	-	-	2022-10-01, 20:11:37	-
IMG_1800.jpeg	-	-	-	2022-10-01, 20:11:45	-
IMG_1802.jpeg	34,69253056	135,499725	11,18563461	2022-10-01, 20:16:09	-
IMG_1803.jpeg	34,692525	135,499725	13,35634995	2022-10-01, 20:16:13	-
IMG_1805.jpeg	34,68734444	135,4890583	2,416385653	2022-10-01, 20:34:16	-
IMG_1806.jpeg	34,68721389	135,4887389	2,995304106	2022-10-01, 20:34:20	-
IMG_1807.jpeg	34,68349167	135,4844056	10,57293893	2022-10-01, 20:59:52	-
IMG_1809.jpeg	34,68348611	135,4845278	3,524629118	2022-10-01, 21:40:29	-
IMG_1810.jpeg	34,68357222	135,4843611	6,168094624	2022-10-01, 21:51:00	-
IMG_1811.jpeg	34,68347222	135,4843889	6,041878926	2022-10-01, 21:51:04	-
IMG_1813.jpeg	34,68369722	135,4845278	6,430484769	2022-10-01, 22:11:52	-
IMG_1814.jpeg	34,68331944	135,4844806	-32,14782336	2022-10-01, 22:28:23	-
IMG_1815.jpeg	34,683375	135,4844972	6,26391983	2022-10-01, 22:28:26	-
IMG_1816.jpeg	34,68380833	135,4846028	4,162834646	2022-10-01, 22:47:37	-
IMG_1818.jpeg	34,68383056	135,4846028	6,768383034	2022-10-01, 23:55:38	-
IMG_1820.jpeg	34,67792778	135,4956361	-	2022-10-02, 03:43:02	16.302
IMG_1821.jpeg	34,67755556	135,495925	-	2022-10-02, 03:49:40	-
IMG_1822.jpeg	34,67767778	135,4960944	6,635780336	2022-10-02, 03:50:50	-
IMG_1823.jpeg	34,67770278	135,4961694	6,307769773	2022-10-02, 03:52:46	-
IMG_1824.jpeg	34,67771667	135,4964	21,31543349	2022-10-02, 03:52:57	-
IMG_1830.jpeg	34,67769167	135,4959111	10,35864449	2022-10-02, 04:24:05	-
IMG_1831.jpeg	34,67765833	135,4958639	11,56164932	2022-10-02, 04:24:40	-
IMG_1832.jpeg	34,67745833	135,4958944	35,46191798	2022-10-02, 04:25:02	-
IMG_1833.jpeg	34,67755556	135,4958639	9,056550896	2022-10-02, 04:25:51	-
IMG_1834.jpeg	34,67755556	135,4958639	9,056550896	2022-10-02, 04:26:16	-
IMG_1842.jpeg	34,67766667	135,4959722	10,38350391	2022-10-02, 12:04:41	-
IMG_1843.jpeg	34,67763056	135,4960167	8,312992096	2022-10-02, 12:04:49	-
IMG_1844.jpeg	34,67780278	135,4960028	12,95792104	2022-10-02, 12:06:17	-
IMG_1845.jpeg	34,67799444	135,4958194	14,17694473	2022-10-02, 12:39:55	-
IMG_1846.jpeg	34,67864167	135,4958639	20,82513808	2022-10-02, 12:41:04	-
IMG_1847.jpeg	34,67863333	135,4958639	15,26996232	2022-10-02, 12:41:08	-
IMG_1848.jpeg	34,67968333	135,4971	12,3409462	2022-10-02, 12:51:19	-
IMG_1849.jpeg	34,67968333	135,4971	12,3409462	2022-10-02, 12:51:20	-
IMG_1850.jpeg	34,68060556	135,4966583	2,814640045	2022-10-02, 12:54:08	-
IMG_1851.jpeg	34,68061944	135,49675	8,408817309	2022-10-02, 12:54:17	-
IMG_1852.jpeg	34,68093056	135,495575	31,90240864	2022-10-02, 12:56:38	-
IMG_1853.jpeg	34,68088611	135,4958028	9,121585859	2022-10-02, 13:05:21	-
IMG_1855.jpeg	34,68101944	135,4956667	13,05591201	2022-10-02, 13:06:59	-
IMG_1856.jpeg	34,681275	135,4951639	8,156460486	2022-10-02, 13:08:44	-
IMG_1857.jpeg	34,68145	135,4950861	6,378482815	2022-10-02, 13:09:04	-
IMG_1858.jpeg	34,68155	135,4951472	2,284488678	2022-10-02, 13:09:25	-
IMG_1859.jpeg	34,68170556	135,496825	25,40204242	2022-10-02, 13:11:55	-
IMG_1860.jpeg	34,68390278	135,4970389	22,2994423	2022-10-02, 13:18:43	-
IMG_1861.jpeg	34,68403889	135,4969944	19,65991211	2022-10-02, 13:20:22	-
IMG_1863.jpeg	34,68554444	135,4955	0,371402757	2022-10-02, 13:30:31	-
IMG_1866.jpeg	34,68601667	135,4949028	1,398746491	2022-10-02, 13:32:28	-
IMG_1867.jpeg	34,68631667	135,4944167	1,843753816	2022-10-02, 13:34:09	-
IMG_1868.jpeg	34,68639722	135,4944167	1,605960846	2022-10-02, 13:34:49	-
IMG_1872.jpeg	34,69215	135,496125	8,834476498	2022-10-02, 14:14:56	-
IMG_1874.jpeg	34,69244444	135,4976972	3,085565117	2022-10-02, 14:17:58	-
IMG_1880.jpeg	35,00945556	135,7752389	25,13302232	2022-10-02, 15:29:33	-
IMG_1881.jpeg	35,01006389	135,7752833	43,8443911	2022-10-02, 15:30:52	-
IMG_1882.jpeg	35,01088056	135,7757556	43,22603989	2022-10-02, 15:32:39	-
IMG_1883.jpeg	35,01111944	135,7757556	47,17226792	2022-10-02, 15:33:01	-
IMG_1888.jpeg	35,01355278	135,7783361	43,88121146	2022-10-02, 15:39:42	-
IMG_1889.jpeg	35,01378611	135,78	43,67280475	2022-10-02, 15:42:41	-
IMG_1890.jpeg	35,01183333	135,7775111	40,61782454	2022-10-02, 15:54:48	-
IMG_1891.jpeg	35,01195833	135,7726583	34,908993	2022-10-02, 16:00:12	-

IMG_1892.jpeg	35,00371111	135,7694083	44,62827527	2022-10-02, 16:46:00	-
IMG_1893.jpeg	35,00085556	135,7691944	26,7187157	2022-10-02, 17:00:36	-
IMG_1896.jpeg	35,00015556	135,7684778	39,96693803	2022-10-02, 17:28:21	-
IMG_1897.jpeg	34,99996944	135,7687528	36,68648914	2022-10-02, 17:28:43	-
IMG_1898.jpeg	35,00011944	135,7686306	36,57593427	2022-10-02, 17:29:21	-
IMG_1901.jpeg	35,00014167	135,7685556	31,95939254	2022-10-02, 17:42:14	-
IMG_1908.jpeg	35,01352222	135,7798167	43,91399349	2022-10-02, 21:10:16	-
IMG_1913.jpeg	35,00165833	135,7734083	42,22357351	2022-10-02, 22:10:52	-
IMG_1915.jpeg	35,00193056	135,7721417	38,27064876	2022-10-02, 22:12:55	-
IMG_1916.jpeg	35,002175	135,7711333	40,13144487	2022-10-02, 22:14:16	-
IMG_1918.jpeg	35,00264722	135,7704167	40,39142894	2022-10-02, 22:15:56	-
IMG_1919.jpeg	35,00224167	135,7693472	48,31809173	2022-10-02, 22:18:58	-
IMG_1920.jpeg	35,00224167	135,7693472	47,85833743	2022-10-02, 22:19:02	-
IMG_1921.jpeg	35,00221667	135,7692556	63,87478261	2022-10-02, 22:23:00	-
IMG_1926.jpeg	35,00225	135,7693028	44,73695758	2022-10-02, 22:29:49	-
IMG_1927.jpeg	35,00224722	135,7693472	44,15409851	2022-10-02, 22:32:03	-
IMG_1928.jpeg	35,0023	135,7692722	43,85489655	2022-10-02, 22:32:12	-
IMG_1929.jpeg	35,00226944	135,7692722	45,05077359	2022-10-02, 22:43:13	-
IMG_1930.jpeg	35,00028889	135,7682806	44,54116258	2022-10-02, 22:56:47	-
IMG_1932.jpeg	35,00018056	135,7684778	37,92345044	2022-10-02, 23:32:33	-
IMG_1941.jpeg	35,00020556	135,7684167	39,25131225	2022-10-02, 23:48:39	-
IMG_1942.jpeg	35,00021389	135,7684167	39,25799942	2022-10-03, 00:01:36	10.522
IMG_1944.jpeg	35,000175	135,7684333	39,15036775	2022-10-03, 00:24:07	-
IMG_1947.jpeg	35,000075	135,7686167	49,29922106	2022-10-03, 00:33:25	-
IMG_1948.jpeg	35,000125	135,7686917	33,33187486	2022-10-03, 00:39:50	-
IMG_1949.jpeg	35,00014167	135,7686306	34,38528059	2022-10-03, 00:39:53	-
IMG_1950.jpeg	35,00011111	135,7686167	38,18260194	2022-10-03, 00:42:49	-
IMG_1975.jpeg	35,00000278	135,7684778	36,99625837	2022-10-03, 01:17:29	-
IMG_1984.jpeg	35,00012222	135,768525	36,10757068	2022-10-03, 10:33:36	-
IMG_1986.jpeg	35,00021667	135,7684167	39,33729171	2022-10-03, 11:07:11	-
IMG_1987.jpeg	35,00021667	135,7684167	39,33729171	2022-10-03, 11:07:13	-
IMG_1988.jpeg	35,00226111	135,7708278	44,40084462	2022-10-03, 12:00:38	-
IMG_1989.jpeg	35,00198333	135,7743083	37,90336228	2022-10-03, 12:09:43	-
IMG_1991.jpeg	35,00198333	135,7743222	37,90338897	2022-10-03, 12:10:31	-
IMG_1992.jpeg	35,00211667	135,7743222	41,62636947	2022-10-03, 12:15:47	-
IMG_1995.jpeg	34,99468333	135,7679444	24,57741928	2022-10-03, 12:36:42	-
IMG_1996.jpeg	34,99469722	135,7679583	25,98348617	2022-10-03, 12:36:45	-
IMG_1998.jpeg	35,290875	136,2819833	103,1817892	2022-10-03, 13:55 24	-
IMG_2007.jpeg	-	-	-	2022-11-03, 14:32 36	-
IMG_2008.jpeg	-	-	-	2022-10-03, 14:36:03	-
IMG_2009.jpeg	34,692425	137,7099917	62,3350487	2022-10-03, 14:39:06	-
IMG_2028.jpeg	35,66266667	139,666	46,66447831	2022-10-03, 19:14:25	-
IMG_2029.jpeg	35,66168333	139,6674944	41,94815059	2022-10-03, 19:23:17	-
IMG_2032.jpeg	35,66300556	139,7010028	22,87824249	2022-10-03, 20:21:29	-
IMG_2033.jpeg	-	-	-	2022-10-03, 22:08:01	-
IMG_2034.jpeg	-	-	-	2022-10-03, 22:08:03	-
IMG_2035.jpeg	-	-	-	2022-10-03, 22:16:23	-
IMG_2036.jpeg	-	-	-	2022-10-03, 22:18:42	-
IMG_2038.jpeg	-	-	-	2022-10-03, 22:38:41	-
IMG_2041.jpeg	-	-	-	2022-11-06, 12:49:39	-
IMG_2051.jpeg	35,62858889	139,7383889	-	2022-10-04, 06:26:15	-
IMG_2052.jpeg	35,6282	139,7380222	10,75336265	2022-10-04, 06:26:19	-
IMG_2053.jpeg	35,545375	139,7687528	-	2022-10-04, 07:07:07	-
IMG_2055.jpeg	35,545375	139,7687528	-	2022-10-04, 07:07:11	-
IMG_2061.jpeg	35,54472778	139,7695167	-	2022-10-04, 07:49:20	-
IMG_2084.jpeg	-	-	-	2022-10-04, 14:16:06	-
IMG_2085.jpeg	-	-	-	2022-10-04, 14:16:15	-
IMG_2089.jpeg	-	-	-	2022-10-04, 14:18:40	-
IMG_2090.jpeg	-	-	-	2022-10-04, 14:18:42	-
IMG_2115.jpeg	50,04863611	8,572625	-	2022-10-04, 18:13:50	-
IMG_2116.jpeg	50,04800833	8,572847222	108,0066528	2022-10-04, 18:15:34	-
IMG_2117.jpeg	50,04566944	8,566847222	-	2022-10-04, 18:28:52	-
IMG_2848.jpeg	33,51423611	130,1382	5,618497843	2022-10-23, 14:55:22	-
IMG_2849.jpeg	33,51415	130,1380917	13,05489922	2022-10-23, 15:04:21	-
IMG_2850.jpeg	33,51328611	130,1301889	-5,23550606	2022-10-23, 15:13:43	-
IMG_2851.jpeg	33,51328611	130,1301111	3,99838066	2022-10-23, 15:13:51	-
IMG_2890.jpeg	33,58243889	130,3803556	-26,90140152	2022-10-24, 16:06:22	17.792
IMG_2891.jpeg	33,58243611	130,3802028	-0,256320953	2022-10-24, 16:06:24	-
IMG_2892.jpeg	33,58243056	130,3801889	4,726467131	2022-10-24, 16:06:28	-
IMG_2894.jpeg	33,58535833	130,3915861	22,71761705	2022-10-24, 16:25:14	-
IMG_2897.jpeg	-	-	-	2022-10-24, 16:48:42	-
IMG_2898.jpeg	-	-	-	2022-10-24, 16 59:07	-
IMG_2899.jpeg	-	-	-	2022-10-24, 17 13:51	-
IMG_2901.jpeg	33,58518889	130,3917694	8,802079208	2022-10-24, 17 23:19	-
IMG_2902.jpeg	33,58520556	130,3918139	8,654351235	2022-10-24, 17:24:46	-
IMG_2903.jpeg	33,58737222	130,3939806	16,42409896	2022-10-24, 18:06:01	-
IMG_2906.jpeg	33,58688611	130,39505	9,803916931	2022-10-24, 20:15:55	-
IMG_2916.jpeg	33,58660833	130,3939528	8,186061863	2022-10-24, 21:09:52	-
IMG_2917.jpeg	33,58710556	130,3953694	10,05112934	2022-10-24, 21:58:53	-
IMG_2919.jpeg	33,58706944	130,3953556	10,40636157	2022-10-24, 22:02:01	-
IMG_2921.jpeg	33,58713611	130,3954	10,65528583	2022-10-24, 22:51:07	-
IMG_2923.jpeg	33,58713056	130,3953556	10,12864208	2022-10-24, 22:51:45	-
IMG_2927.jpeg	33,58702222	130,3953389	10,29940795	2022-10-24, 22:59:02	-
IMG_2928.jpeg	33,58716944	130,3954167	10,80394553	2022-10-25, 00:17:53	12.774
IMG_2929.jpeg	33,58716667	130,3954306	10,7763729	2022-10-25, 01:28:48	-
IMG_2935.jpeg	33,58721667	130,3951417	10,79980278	2022-10-25, 02:04:05	-
IMG_2941.jpeg	33,58725278	130,3951111	10,810359	2022-10-25, 02:19:25	-
IMG_2942.jpeg	33,58667778	130,393875	7,904121628	2022-10-25, 02:33:30	-
IMG_2944.jpeg	33,59008056	130,3949583	5,367181778	2022-10-25, 11:47:56	-
IMG_2945.jpeg	33,58451389	130,3996278	7,829509757	2022-10-25, 12:11:52	-
IMG_2946.jpeg	33,58700556	130,3952639	8,723301887	2022-10-25, 12:32:29	-
IMG_2947.jpeg	33,5887	130,3964222	-	2022-10-25, 12:58:48	-
IMG_2959.jpeg	33,53409444	130,1541583	4,100797652	2022-10-25, 18:13:39	-
IMG_2961.jpeg	33,53423333	130,15425	6,543424624	2022-10-26, 07:15:05	15.504
IMG_2974.jpeg	33,54206111	130,1548	3,580656051	2022-10-26, 11:51:06	-
IMG_2975.jpeg	33,542	130,1548306	7,154935837	2022-10-26, 11:51:13	-

IMG_2976.jpeg	33,54140556	130,1548778	4,235441224	2022-10-26, 11:52:32	-
IMG_2977.jpeg	33,54140833	130,1548778	3,038297675	2022-10-26, 11:52:43	-
IMG_2978.jpeg	33,54140833	130,1548778	2,647184387	2022-10-26, 11:52:45	-
IMG_2981.jpeg	33,54290833	130,154525	2,463041305	2022-10-26, 11:57:10	-
IMG_2982.jpeg	33,54286667	130,1545417	4,479764951	2022-10-26, 11:57:30	-
IMG_2983.jpeg	33,54301389	130,154175	1,612211227	2022-10-26, 11:58:47	-
IMG_2984.jpeg	33,54298889	130,1541139	15,24807549	2022-10-26, 11:58:51	-
IMG_2985.jpeg	33,54306389	130,1540083	16,05727958	2022-10-26, 11:59:15	-
IMG_2987.jpeg	33,54289722	130,1544944	8,278287894	2022-10-26, 12:00:15	-
IMG_2988.jpeg	33,54287778	130,1544333	-3,011262894	2022-10-26, 12:00:45	-
IMG_2989.jpeg	33,54287222	130,1544639	-0,826082231	2022-10-26, 12:00:52	-
IMG_2990.jpeg	33,54287222	130,1544639	-0,826082231	2022-10-26, 12:00:53	-
IMG_2991.jpeg	33,57455833	130,1214611	3,01644707	2022-10-26, 12:50:41	-
IMG_2992.jpeg	33,574525	130,1215972	3,910245895	2022-10-26, 12:50:48	-
IMG_3003.jpeg	33,57457222	130,1215528	6,290861127	2022-10-26, 13:03:13	-
IMG_3004.jpeg	33,57453056	130,1213083	5,278157234	2022-10-26, 13:04:57	-
IMG_3005.jpeg	33,57446944	130,1214917	5,206571595	2022-10-26, 13:05:15	-
IMG_3006.jpeg	33,57446667	130,1214917	5,708158508	2022-10-26, 13:05:16	-
IMG_3007.jpeg	33,57447778	130,1214917	6,404386532	2022-10-26, 13:05:18	-
IMG_3009.jpeg	33,57448889	130,1213389	2,718595506	2022-10-26, 13:18:05	-
IMG_3010.jpeg	33,57453056	130,1215667	12,64083672	2022-10-26, 13:18:55	-
IMG_3012.jpeg	33,57446944	130,1214917	3,617069579	2022-10-26, 13:28:18	-
IMG_3013.jpeg	33,57448611	130,1214917	3,535428712	2022-10-26, 13:28:20	-
IMG_3014.jpeg	33,57454722	130,1212778	3,976748466	2022-10-26, 13:34:16	-
IMG_3015.jpeg	33,57455833	130,1215667	3,58621025	2022-10-26, 13:34:18	-
IMG_3017.jpeg	33,595225	130,1096194	7,033658989	2022-10-26, 14:14:32	-
IMG_3018.jpeg	33,59521944	130,1096028	7,02493098	2022-10-26, 14:14:36	-
IMG_3019.jpeg	33,59500556	130,1082611	27,53414727	2022-10-26, 14:24:53	-
IMG_3022.jpeg	33,59510556	130,1083361	35,87460131	2022-10-26, 14:25:32	-
IMG_3023.jpeg	33,59535278	130,1082167	38,38906667	2022-10-26, 14:29:49	-
IMG_3026.jpeg	33,59470278	130,1080944	30,78664969	2022-10-26, 14:34:53	-
IMG_3027.jpeg	33,59468333	130,1080778	29,30483818	2022-10-26, 14:35:03	-
IMG_3050.jpeg	33,53733333	130,1599889	5,70309257	2022-10-27, 13:37:39	11.507
IMG_3051.jpeg	33,53727778	130,1600028	5,777616513	2022-10-27, 14:18:12	-
IMG_3055.jpeg	33,52115556	130,139175	3,773345614	2022-10-27, 17:53:36	-
IMG_3093.jpeg	33,51358889	130,1305833	3,75472832	2022-10-28, 16:39:33	8.153
IMG_3094.jpeg	33,51354167	130,1305694	2,772855753	2022-10-28, 17:18:20	-
IMG_3141.jpeg	33,53412222	130,1541889	5,187690734	2022-10-29, 12:33:39	-
IMG_3145.jpeg	33,52988333	130,1472472	17,18209877	2022-10-29, 17:04:55	-
IMG_3149.jpeg	33,52929722	130,1475972	99,34884457	2022-10-29, 17:17:07	-
IMG_3150.jpeg	33,52975833	130,1473833	14,32131767	2022-10-29, 17:17:10	-
IMG_3151.jpeg	33,52976111	130,1474139	15,27230645	2022-10-29, 17:17:14	-
IMG_3158.jpeg	-	-	-	2022-10-29, 17:21:05	-
IMG_3159.jpeg	33,52995556	130,147125	19,28365968	2022-10-29, 17:39:21	-
IMG_3160.jpeg	33,52995	130,147125	19,94196858	2022-10-29, 17:39:30	-
IMG_3163.jpeg	33,51271111	130,1297917	2,833707822	2022-10-30, 10:57:01	-
IMG_3165.jpeg	33,51226944	130,1307667	3,113004684	2022-10-30, 13:39:14	-
IMG_3201.jpeg	33,590325	130,4196917	8,359523773	2022-10-31, 14:11:44	18.778
IMG_3202.jpeg	33,59031389	130,4196611	8,360744487	2022-10-31, 14:11:46	-
IMG_3204.jpeg	33,78995556	130,7324667	18,4314657	2022-10-31, 15:53:10	-
IMG_3205.jpeg	33,79093056	130,7337944	17,47448251	2022-10-31, 15:53:12	-
IMG_3219.jpeg	34,61344444	133,7313528	49,77133974	2022-10-31, 17:23:33	-
IMG_3220.jpeg	34,80424167	134,4179833	12,57421691	2022-10-31, 17:44:41	-
IMG_3221.jpeg	34,70873611	135,5037694	4,290484904	2022-10-31, 19:09:25	-
IMG_3223.jpeg	-	-	-	-	-
IMG_3225.jpeg	34,66939444	135,4993139	58,49197002	2022-10-31, 22:07:31	-
IMG_3226.jpeg	34,66946389	135,4980472	6,413578034	2022-10-31, 23:35:15	-
IMG_3230.jpeg	34,66979722	135,5002444	30,68732071	2022-11-01, 00:02:59	-
IMG_3231.jpeg	34,66981111	135,5002583	60,45984081	2022-11-01, 00:03:15	-
IMG_3232.jpeg	34,66989167	135,5004889	20,81161118	2022-11-01, 00:04:12	-
IMG_3233.jpeg	34,66988333	135,5002889	74,22383379	2022-11-01, 00:04:34	-
IMG_3235.jpeg	34,66985	135,5003972	38,51266099	2022-11-01, 00:05:27	-
IMG_3236.jpeg	34,66988889	135,5003806	70,49347903	2022-11-01, 00:05:37	-
IMG_3246.jpeg	34,67055	135,4995583	17,11066058	2022-11-01, 00:17:44	-
IMG_3248.jpeg	34,708825	135,5036167	1,349575043	2022-11-01, 14:16:36	-
IMG_3249.jpeg	34,708825	135,5036167	1,50674057	2022-11-01, 14:16:40	-
IMG_3250.jpeg	34,70870556	135,5034639	4,406032565	2022-11-01, 14:18:45	-
IMG_3251.jpeg	34,70870278	135,5034472	8,013942719	2022-11-01, 14:18:48	-
IMG_3252.jpeg	34,70857222	135,5034333	6,214199068	2022-11-01, 14:19:08	-
IMG_3253.jpeg	34,70836667	135,5033861	3,385979651	2022-11-01, 14:20:08	-
IMG_3254.jpeg	34,70835833	135,5034333	4,3110466	2022-11-01, 14:29:37	-
IMG_3257.jpeg	34,70844722	135,5033861	4,5437994	2022-11-01, 14:29:48	-
IMG_3258.jpeg	-	-	-	2022-11-01, 15:04:34	-
IMG_3259.jpeg	-	-	-	2022-11-01, 15:04:51	-
IMG_3260.jpeg	-	-	-	2022-11-01, 15:06:50	-
IMG_3261.jpeg	34,68171944	135,5169528	4,638004308	2022-11-01, 15:21:04	-
IMG_3262.jpeg	34,68171944	135,5169528	4,638031002	2022-11-01, 15:21:08	-
IMG_3264.jpeg	34,65515556	135,4324194	2,244937897	2022-11-01, 15:45:21	-
IMG_3288.jpeg	34,66869444	135,5022889	9,457546232	2022-11-01, 19:10:16	-
IMG_3292.jpeg	34,66896944	135,5014194	9,079494471	2022-11-01, 19:12:22	-
IMG_3296.jpeg	34,66737778	135,5001361	9,363834381	2022-11-01, 19:31:51	-
IMG_3327.jpeg	34,70877778	135,5034028	5,707057964	2022-11-02, 12:01:31	-
IMG_3331.jpeg	34,70827222	135,4978333	-39,09936523	2022-11-02, 14:20:17	-
IMG_3333.jpeg	34,70888056	135,4964917	3,028197457	2022-11-02, 14:29:49	-
IMG_3335.jpeg	34,71029167	135,4948889	11,54330444	2022-11-02, 14:35:32	-
IMG_3336.jpeg	34,71154722	135,4937583	3,071037237	2022-11-02, 14:38:55	-
IMG_3337.jpeg	34,71155278	135,4937444	3,425713279	2022-11-02, 14:38:59	-
IMG_3338.jpeg	34,71151389	135,4935	4,677376751	2022-11-02, 14:39:30	-
IMG_3342.jpeg	34,71190278	135,4936361	2,413724081	2022-11-02, 14:41:32	-
IMG_3345.jpeg	34,70732222	135,5075083	5,115077972	2022-11-02, 15:53:15	-
IMG_3350.jpeg	34,70989167	135,5130472	6,153568269	2022-11-02, 16:16:00	-
IMG_3351.jpeg	34,70836389	135,5123278	15,32101061	2022-11-02, 16:44:26	-
IMG_3352.jpeg	34,7079	135,5117944	7,828151705	2022-11-02, 16:45:20	-
IMG_3353.jpeg	34,70762222	135,51175	-15,93112564	2022-11-02, 16:45:55	-
IMG_3360.jpeg	34,69022778	135,4933611	3,89752998	2022-11-02, 18:11:26	-
IMG_3361.jpeg	-	-	-	2022-11-02, 18:35:48	-

IMG_3362.jpeg	34,6904	135,4936222	4,910630226	2022-11-02, 18:35:56	-
IMG_3367.jpeg	34,69026944	135,4935444	5,094986919	2022-11-02, 19:49:31	-
IMG_3373.jpeg	34,69028611	135,4936222	5,095082283	2022-11-02, 19:50:42	-
IMG_3374.jpeg	34,69039444	135,4935139	5,12884998	2022-11-02, 20:29:12	-
IMG_3402.jpeg	34,70875833	135,5037833	4,290016651	2022-11-03, 01:59:40	-
IMG_3449.jpeg	35,00773889	135,7677472	47,62649914	2022-11-03, 13:34:45	-
IMG_3473.jpeg	35,000725	135,7684639	43,73629372	2022-11-03, 22:10:53	-
IMG_3474.jpeg	35,00070278	135,7685861	41,62868883	2022-11-03, 22:11:02	-
IMG_3477.jpeg	34,9999	135,7680667	76,88412102	2022-11-04, 10:52:48	-
IMG_3479.jpeg	35,00003333	135,7682194	106,3340112	2022-11-04, 10:58:52	-
IMG_3480.jpeg	35,00001389	135,7681583	116,0461083	2022-11-04, 10:58:56	-
IMG_3490.jpeg	-	-	-	-	-
IMG_3492.jpeg	35,00006111	135,7687694	48,79598618	2022-11-04, 12:55:01	-
IMG_3493.jpeg	35,00692778	135,7691333	48,67122266	2022-11-04, 13:23:37	-
IMG_3494.jpeg	35,00660278	135,7734528	43,23513408	2022-11-04, 14:02:38	-
IMG_3495.jpeg	35,00647778	135,7733472	49,36528393	2022-11-04, 14:11:11	-
IMG_3506.jpeg	35,00906667	135,7716972	53,82400143	2022-11-04, 15:07:15	-
IMG_3508.jpeg	35,00385278	135,7706139	44,50587846	2022-11-04, 15:53:01	-
IMG_3509.jpeg	35,00424167	135,770325	42,56698226	2022-11-04, 15:53:05	-
IMG_3544.jpeg	35,72323611	139,6522361	44,06712829	2022-11-05, 19:15:08	-
IMG_3546.jpeg	35,72321667	139,6522528	43,6680879	2022-11-05, 19:15:22	-
IMG_3549.jpeg	35,72314167	139,6521611	44,5383263	2022-11-05, 20:36:37	-
IMG_3562.jpeg	35,72316111	139,6521444	44,0752754	2022-11-05, 21:19:14	-
IMG_3575.jpeg	35,72123056	139,6522361	43,46085741	2022-11-06, 13:44:35	-
IMG_3627.jpeg	35,65931667	139,6972194	31,64482307	2022-11-07, 21:49:37	-
IMG_3628.jpeg	35,65927222	139,6971583	31,54364396	2022-11-07, 23:06:45	-
IMG_3629.jpeg	35,71646111	139,6996	30,08304025	2022-11-07, 23:20:36	-
IMG_3630.jpeg	-	-	-	2022-11-07, 23:23:51	-
IMG_3680.jpeg	-	-	-	2022-11-08, 00:38:44	-
IMG_3681.jpeg	-	-	-	2022-11-08, 00:38:46	-
IMG_3687.jpeg	35,71978333	139,6532889	38,04860303	2022-11-08, 13:32 32	-
IMG_3693.jpeg	35,656425	139,7330167	17,90267182	2022-11-08, 14:28 43	-
IMG_3694.jpeg	35,65639444	139,7330167	10,92235565	2022-11-08, 15:11 09	-
IMG_3696.jpeg	35,66300278	139,7318278	35,8039017	2022-11-08, 15:55:49	-
IMG_3697.jpeg	35,66300278	139,7318278	35,8039017	2022-11-08, 15:55:51	-
IMG_3698.jpeg	35,64839444	139,7091056	29,98107149	2022-11-08, 16:13:33	-
IMG_3700.jpeg	35,65559722	139,7035222	26,37382319	2022-11-08, 17:08:02	-
IMG_3701.jpeg	35,65868056	139,6997528	-	2022-11-08, 17:14:58	-
IMG_3706.jpeg	35,66213889	139,6676472	41,67010309	2022-11-08, 19:00:55	-
IMG_3707.jpeg	35,66191111	139,6678917	40,60573199	2022-11-08, 19:13:17	-
IMG_3712.jpeg	-	-	-	2022-11-08, 20:23:08	-
IMG_3714.jpeg	35,7127	139,7037667	22,45736504	2022-11-09, 00:17:25	-
IMG_3715.jpeg	35,7127	139,7037667	22,45736504	2022-11-09, 00:17:28	-
IMG_3716.jpeg	35,71245278	139,7036583	25,66576192	2022-11-09, 00:17:31	-
IMG_3717.jpeg	35,71892222	139,6525417	44,61500548	2022-11-09, 00:47:27	-
IMG_3723.jpeg	35,728725	139,7764889	7,933650476	2022-11-09, 15:22:45	-
IMG_3724.jpeg	35,72873333	139,7763972	7,706687164	2022-11-09, 15:22:54	-
IMG_3725.jpeg	35,72873611	139,7763972	7,745140934	2022-11-09, 15:22:57	-
IMG_3726.jpeg	35,72876667	139,7761222	7,953964899	2022-11-09, 15:29:33	-
IMG_3728.jpeg	35,72871667	139,7758333	6,436977587	2022-11-09, 15:30:43	-
IMG_3729.jpeg	35,72873333	139,7758333	6,247035999	2022-11-09, 15:30:44	-
IMG_3730.jpeg	35,72841944	139,7723389	4,801899141	2022-11-09, 15:44:32	-
IMG_3741.jpeg	35,72387778	139,7703389	18,91041683	2022-11-09, 15:55:08	-
IMG_3742.jpeg	35,72375	139,770325	19,914801	2022-11-09, 15:55:21	-
IMG_3743.jpeg	35,72374444	139,770325	19,82386707	2022-11-09, 15:55:22	-
IMG_3744.jpeg	35,72220278	139,7704611	17,27492355	2022-11-09, 16:04:45	-
IMG_3745.jpeg	35,72269444	139,7698833	15,24410676	2022-11-09, 16:05:41	-
IMG_3746.jpeg	35,72223611	139,7704917	19,13038537	2022-11-09, 16:05:51	-
IMG_3749.jpeg	35,72186944	139,7705083	17,73648256	2022-11-09, 16:13:21	-
IMG_3750.jpeg	35,72156389	139,7707667	18,69694523	2022-11-09, 16:14:28	-
IMG_3752.jpeg	35,7214	139,7707833	17,89651626	2022-11-09, 16:15:54	-
IMG_3753.jpeg	35,72119444	139,7708444	17,64989107	2022-11-09, 16:16:29	-
IMG_3755.jpeg	-	-	-	-	-
IMG_3760.jpeg	35,71036944	139,7756194	-	2022-11-09, 19:07:28	-
IMG_3771.jpeg	35,73480278	139,6548	42,61936165	2022-11-10, 16:04:07	-
IMG_3772.jpeg	35,734825	139,6548167	42,15417722	2022-11-10, 16:04:13	-
IMG_3775.jpeg	35,64785278	139,7081139	17,29526736	2022-11-10, 18:27:10	-
IMG_3779.jpeg	-	-	-	-	-
IMG_3783.jpeg	35,64825	139,7112889	14,79750539	2022-11-10, 19 02:05	-
IMG_3789.jpeg	35,68855556	139,7002861	37,26564406	2022-11-10, 22 20:44	-
IMG_3790.jpeg	35,68855556	139,7002861	37,26564406	2022-11-10, 22:20:47	-
IMG_3798.jpeg	35,72033333	139,6754917	28,40547562	2022-11-11, 14:23:46	-
IMG_3807.jpeg	35,72050556	139,6529389	42,81850054	2022-11-11, 17:52:01	-
IMG_3820.jpeg	35,68901944	139,7068944	37,09116911	2022-11-12, 14:18:23	-
IMG_3822.jpeg	-	-	-	2022-09-23, 15:19:56	-
IMG_3823.jpeg	35,68071111	139,7012472	29,09519234	2022-11-12, 15:06:15	-
IMG_3824.jpeg	35,68045833	139,7018889	14,74315642	2022-11-12, 15:06:20	-
IMG_3825.jpeg	35,68015278	139,7018139	29,8295212	2022-11-12, 15:07:53	-
IMG_3826.jpeg	35,68028333	139,7019194	24,14763641	2022-11-12, 15:08:07	-
IMG_3827.jpeg	-	-	-	2022-09-23, 15:29:45	-
IMG_3828.jpeg	-	-	-	2022-09-23, 15:29:49	-
IMG_3829.jpeg	-	-	-	2022-09-23, 15:29:55	-
IMG_3831.jpeg	-	-	-	2022-09-23, 16:22:14	-
IMG_3834.jpeg	35,67686111	139,70195	29,49736787	2022-11-12, 15:15:21	-
IMG_3839.jpeg	-	-	-	2022-09-23, 17:06:28	-
IMG_3841.jpeg	-	-	-	2022-09-23, 18:06:46	-
IMG_6541.jpeg	35,67225556	139,6911	30,26973533	2022-08-31, 20:27:24	-
IMG_6622.jpeg	35,67239722	139,6908722	25,81286829	2022-09-01, 02:19:31	-
IMG_8858.jpeg	48,12148333	16,5604	176,8827781	2022-08-15, 15:18:17	-
IMG_8870.jpeg	48,11743056	16,57238056	196,014126	2022-08-15, 17:29:56	-
IMG_8878.jpeg	50,047925	8,573008333	108	2022-08-15, 19:06:09	-
IMG_8879.jpeg	50,047925	8,573008333	108	2022-08-15, 19:06:10	-
IMG_8880.jpeg	50,04805833	8,57495	108,3396072	2022-08-15, 19:27:44	-
IMG_8883.jpeg	-	-	-	2022-08-15, 20:28:39	-
IMG_8886.jpeg	-	-	-	2022-08-15, 21:34:16	-
IMG_8888.jpeg	-	-	-	2022-08-15, 21:57:55	-

IMG_8890.jpeg	-	-	-	2022-08-15, 22:01:17	-
IMG_8891.jpeg	-	-	-	2022-08-15, 22:02:44	-
IMG_8892.jpeg	-	-	-	2022-08-15, 22:17:52	-
IMG_8895.jpeg	-	-	-	2022-08-16, 02:41:53	-
IMG_8896.jpeg	-	-	-	2022-08-16, 07:24:52	-
IMG_8919.jpeg	35,54441389	139,7684778	118,8501663	2022-08-16, 17:42:50	-
IMG_8921.jpeg	35,54405556	139,7660056	-9,156852727	2022-08-16, 17:46:14	-
IMG_8922.jpeg	35,54463889	139,7655639	5,479438781	2022-08-16, 17:46:18	-
IMG_8931.jpeg	35,65958889	139,700225	19,46440891	2022-08-16, 18:36:01	-
IMG_8933.jpeg	35,66343611	139,7021778	20,29374505	2022-08-16 18:59:55	-
IMG_8934.jpeg	35,663475	139,7021639	20,23048021	2022-08-16, 19:23:05	-
IMG_8938.jpeg	35,65896111	139,6977083	26,18254854	2022-08-16, 21:05:32	-
IMG_8941.jpeg	35,65956944	139,696075	31,88960646	2022-08-16 22:43:07	-
IMG_8943.jpeg	35,66004444	139,69545	31,56227493	2022-08-17, 00:23:53	-
IMG_8951.jpeg	35,66264722	139,7006389	23,76726532	2022-08-17, 01:02:19	-
IMG_8954.jpeg	35,66326111	139,7015833	22,36355975	2022-08-17, 01:13:38	-
IMG_8959.jpeg	35,66327222	139,7016139	23,06759836	2022-08-17, 02:20:26	-
IMG_8960.jpeg	35,66326944	139,7016139	22,68038366	2022-08-17, 02:20:33	-
IMG_8974.jpeg	35,66326111	139,7015833	22,60865023	2022-08-17, 03:26:24	-
IMG_9023.jpeg	35,65960278	139,6955417	27,66371534	2022-08-17, 22:33:40	-
IMG_9056.jpeg	35,65855	139,7020722	22,19477843	2022-08-18, 14:19:29	-
IMG_9057.jpeg	35,65854167	139,7020556	20,89073561	2022-08-18, 14:20:08	-
IMG_9066.jpeg	35,66323056	139,7021639	18,2172938	2022-08-18, 15:01:00	-
IMG_9067.jpeg	35,66321111	139,7021778	17,90039433	2022-08-18, 15:01:05	-
IMG_9081.jpeg	35,67826389	139,6747583	43,76723205	2022-08-18, 18:27:21	-
IMG_9107.jpeg	35,67821111	139,6768944	41,9361763	2022-08-19, 06:48:43	-
IMG_9111.jpeg	35,67806667	139,6767889	39,46290972	2022-08-19, 13:58:47	-
IMG_9112.jpeg	35,67814167	139,6770028	39,63850782	2022-08-19, 14:53:35	-
IMG_9113.jpeg	35,67595556	139,6775361	42,11525341	2022-08-19, 15:07:04	-
IMG_9114.jpeg	35,67595278	139,6775667	41,66933059	2022-08-19, 15:07:08	-
IMG_9122.jpeg	35,67495833	139,6789389	38,71193311	2022-08-19, 15:09:35	-
IMG_9123.jpeg	35,67450833	139,6801444	40,09846885	2022-08-19, 15:11:11	-
IMG_9124.jpeg	35,67449444	139,6801917	43,67830209	2022-08-19, 15:11:14	-
IMG_9126.jpeg	-	-	-	2022-08-19, 15:16:31	-
IMG_9133.jpeg	35,66552778	139,7122639	28,74840547	2022-08-19, 16:14:16	-
IMG_9134.jpeg	35,66513333	139,7124639	47,45000461	2022-08-19, 16:20:07	-
IMG_9146.jpeg	35,65791389	139,7011861	19,55910764	2022-08-19, 17:55:55	-
IMG_9147.jpeg	35,657825	139,7013083	19,18718556	2022-08-19, 17:56:14	-
IMG_9163.jpeg	35,66543333	139,6925667	22,88685575	2022-08-19, 20:42:27	-
IMG_9168.jpeg	35,67777222	139,6785139	46,89864346	2022-08-19, 22:01:11	-
IMG_9186.jpeg	35,67818333	139,6770167	43,61598588	2022-08-20, 00:12:18	-
IMG_9195.jpeg	35,68135	139,7646944	5,742883182	2022-08-20, 07:23:59	-
IMG_9196.jpeg	35,68134722	139,7646944	5,622042822	2022-08-20, 07:24:01	-
IMG_9204.jpeg	35,76055833	139,7307889	6,362191989	2022-08-20, 08:03:40	-
IMG_9218.jpeg	36,35635	138,5871111	990,5004975	2022-08-20, 10:37:31	-
IMG_9223.jpeg	36,35674167	138,5870222	991,8114478	2022-08-20, 11:15:31	-
IMG_9225.jpeg	36,35673056	138,5870056	990,2446982	2022-08-20, 11:15:56	-
IMG_9226.jpeg	36,35673056	138,5870056	990,2446982	2022-08-20, 11:15:57	-
IMG_9227.jpeg	36,35671944	138,5870528	990,7000783	2022-08-20, 11:16:18	-
IMG_9231.jpeg	36,35671944	138,5870222	992,6832994	2022-08-20, 11:16:49	-
IMG_9233.jpeg	36,356725	138,5870361	991,6463331	2022-08-20, 11:18:00	-
IMG_9237.jpeg	36,35675833	138,5870528	991,0778739	2022-08-20, 11:19:03	-
IMG_9238.jpeg	36,35675833	138,5870528	991,0508452	2022-08-20, 11:19:04	-
IMG_9239.jpeg	36,35674167	138,5870667	990,9963459	2022-08-20, 11:19:12	-
IMG_9240.jpeg	36,35674722	138,5870667	991,6098917	2022-08-20, 11:19:14	-
IMG_9247.jpeg	36,35168889	138,5912333	997,816616	2022-08-20, 11:57:29	-
IMG_9251.jpeg	36,29891944	138,6193389	942,3919052	2022-08-20, 12:26:56	-
IMG_9256.jpeg	-	-	-	-	-
IMG_9270.jpeg	36,29883056	138,6193694	941,8424658	2022-08-20, 13:02:16	-
IMG_9271.jpeg	36,29878889	138,6193083	941,3523557	2022-08-20, 13:02:23	-
IMG_9274.jpeg	36,29881944	138,6193389	941,7671518	2022-08-20, 13:02:32	-
IMG_9280.jpeg	36,29879444	138,6193694	934,0333863	2022-08-20, 13:19:41	-
IMG_9281.jpeg	-	-	-	2022-08-20, 13:29:04	-
IMG_9284.jpeg	36,29878889	138,619475	943,2618772	2022-08-20, 13:30:39	-
IMG_9295.jpeg	36,29875278	138,6194917	947,0234987	2022-08-20, 13:36:49	-
IMG_9298.jpeg	36,29899167	138,6192167	942,4663727	2022-08-20, 13:51:04	-
IMG_9303.jpeg	36,29879722	138,6194167	940,3358147	2022-08-20, 13:56:54	-
IMG_9306.jpeg	-	-	-	2022-08-20, 14:16:32	-
IMG_9311.jpeg	36,29886667	138,6193556	942,4518048	2022-08-20, 14:48:33	-
IMG_9312.jpeg	36,29876667	138,6191111	943,1926877	2022-08-20, 14:48:39	-
IMG_9314.jpeg	36,29879722	138,6192333	943,4373178	2022-08-20, 15:02:58	-
IMG_9315.jpeg	-	-	-	2022-08-20, 15:25:48	-
IMG_9317.jpeg	-	-	-	2022-08-20, 16:17:51	-
IMG_9320.jpeg	-	-	-	2022-08-20, 16:56:40	-
IMG_9326.jpeg	-	-	-	2022-08-20, 18:09:24	-
IMG_9347.jpeg	35,68258333	139,6870417	43,12813187	2022-08-21, 16:03:16	-
IMG_9366.jpeg	35,68307778	139,6871806	46,48007968	2022-08-21, 17:01:40	-
IMG_9369.jpeg	35,68309444	139,6868278	44,53352354	2022-08-21, 17:03:33	-
IMG_9375.jpeg	35,68219444	139,6869806	43,37654498	2022-08-21, 18:53:27	-
IMG_9376.jpeg	35,68131667	139,6857917	43,81363501	2022-08-21, 18:56:40	-
IMG_9377.jpeg	35,67985556	139,6823417	42,31094896	2022-08-21, 19:06:07	-
IMG_9379.jpeg	35,68153333	139,6807861	38,01064629	2022-08-21, 19:12:06	-
IMG_9382.jpeg	35,68005833	139,6771556	43,72731377	2022-08-21, 19:20:29	-
IMG_9383.jpeg	35,67810833	139,6774	42,6809322	2022-08-21, 19:25:21	-
IMG_9384.jpeg	35,67805	139,6770167	42,4186071	2022-08-21, 19:26:11	-
IMG_9385.jpeg	35,67810833	139,6769722	40,67409597	2022-08-21, 19:26:35	-
IMG_9392.jpeg	35,66214444	139,6680444	40,95131215	2022-08-21, 20:59:44	-
IMG_9394.jpeg	35,67166389	139,6678611	42,52298074	2022-08-21, 21:52:38	-
IMG_9396.jpeg	35,67778333	139,6770167	43,00579452	2022-08-21, 22:23:47	-
IMG_9397.jpeg	35,67778889	139,6770472	42,56892395	2022-08-21, 22:45:43	-
IMG_9398.jpeg	35,67758056	139,6771083	41,48622509	2022-08-21, 22:47:45	-
IMG_9400.jpeg	35,67776389	139,6770167	40,72932817	2022-08-21, 23:04:54	-
IMG_9401.jpeg	35,67774167	139,6770333	42,64152911	2022-08-21, 23:17:28	-
IMG_9405.jpeg	35,67775	139,6770472	42,54421994	2022-08-22, 00:03:40	-
IMG_9407.jpeg	35,67775	139,6770333	42,61653139	2022-08-22, 01:19:46	-
IMG_9408.jpeg	35,67778056	139,6770472	42,98660655	2022-08-22, 01:30:29	-

IMG_9436.jpeg	-	-	-	2022-08-22 18:12:03	-
IMG_9437.jpeg	-	-	-	2022-08-22 18:15:43	-
IMG_9438.jpeg	35,69066111	139,7030333	40,77027827	2022-08-22 18:31:15	-
IMG_9439.jpeg	35,6903	139,7026667	39,71262038	2022-08-22 18:32:34	-
IMG_9440.jpeg	35,6903	139,7026667	39,91450013	2022-08-22 18:32:36	-
IMG_9449.jpeg	35,69102222	139,6988056	20,94874983	2022-08-22 19:12:51	-
IMG_9477.jpeg	35,67780556	139,6770167	42,44742583	2022-08-22 23:17:40	-
IMG_9510.jpeg	35,73099167	139,7689361	10,85647203	2022-08-23 15:27:05	-
IMG_9512.jpeg	35,72617222	139,7707222	20,31386948	2022-08-23 15:39:43	-
IMG_9513.jpeg	35,72605	139,7707222	23,73025135	2022-08-23 15:40:01	-
IMG_9514.jpeg	35,72585556	139,7706611	14,43850328	2022-08-23 15:40:23	-
IMG_9518.jpeg	35,72379167	139,7703389	13,04946517	2022-08-23 15:43:57	-
IMG_9519.jpeg	35,72232778	139,7708139	11,26119615	2022-08-23 15:55:20	-
IMG_9521.jpeg	35,72234444	139,7709806	25,56917953	2022-08-23 15:55:50	-
IMG_9522.jpeg	35,72244167	139,7709806	21,07674789	2022-08-23 15:56:17	-
IMG_9523.jpeg	35,72235	139,7710111	27,8694725	2022:08:23 15:56:39	-
IMG_9529.jpeg	35,72160833	139,7706139	26,69747544	2022:08:23 15:59:30	-
IMG_9531.jpeg	35,72115278	139,7708444	17,29488753	2022:08:23 16:07:42	-
IMG_9538.jpeg	35,71802222	139,77275	32,75747314	2022:08:23 16:18:02	-
IMG_9540.jpeg	35,71935556	139,7710583	18,712368	2022:08:23 16:27:20	-
IMG_9565.jpeg	35,64823611	139,7112583	14,78516103	2022:08:23 20:39:11	-
IMG_9570.jpeg	35,68213611	139,6964278	32,52969899	2022:08:23 21:37:00	-
IMG_9582.jpeg	35,67775	139,6770472	42,76954269	2022:08:24 15:39:48	-
IMG_9583.jpeg	35,68120278	139,6749722	35,75162751	2022:08:24 16:33:57	-
IMG_9590.jpeg	35,67671111	139,6747444	46,27480698	2022:08:24 17:45:02	-
IMG_9603.jpeg	35,66008056	139,6949	16,71541729	2022:08:24 21:43:[illegible]5	-
IMG_9604.jpeg	35,66019167	139,6950222	21,2754173	2022:08:24 22:24:23	-
IMG_9609.jpeg	35,65932778	139,6972056	26,7654173	2022:08:25 01:17:39	-
IMG_9614.jpeg	35,65932778	139,6972056	26,7654173	2022:08:25 02:13:33	-
IMG_9618.jpeg	35,65930556	139,6971889	26,7654173	2022:08:25 02:57:28	-
IMG_9626.jpeg	35,67773056	139,6770472	38,8854173	2022:08:25 11:13:49	-
IMG_9627.jpeg	35,67773333	139,6770472	39,03874208	2022:08:25 11:13:52	-
IMG_9630.jpeg	35,67778333	139,6770472	38,8854173	2022:08:25 11:28:36	-
IMG_9660.jpeg	35,67217222	139,6905667	20,78523635	2022:08:25 12:49:16	-
IMG_9661.jpeg	35,67211944	139,6905972	25,30167464	2022:08:25 12:51:37	-
IMG_9662.jpeg	35,67213056	139,6905972	25,14249557	2022:08:25 12:51:48	-
IMG_9663.jpeg	35,67213056	139,6906139	25,18567528	2022:08:25 12:52:00	-
IMG_9667.jpeg	35,67071667	139,6908556	25,32001981	2022:08:25 13:13:53	-
IMG_9668.jpeg	35,66437778	139,6950833	23,60000584	2022:08:25 13:24:19	-
IMG_9669.jpeg	35,66121944	139,6980583	22,98541731	2022:08:25 13:40:48	-
IMG_9670.jpeg	35,66121944	139,6980583	22,98541731	2022:08:25 13:40:53	-
IMG_9671.jpeg	35,66242222	139,696975	22,98430445	2022:08:25 13:55:39	-
IMG_9672.jpeg	35,66242222	139,696975	22,98477936	2022:08:25 13:55:48	-
IMG_9681.jpeg	35,66526111	139,6941694	23,2142657	2022:08:25 14:08:39	-
IMG_9690.jpeg	35,67217222	139,6907194	26,44216919	2022:08:25 17:01:27	-
IMG_9692.jpeg	35,67034444	139,6915889	28,07197464	2022:08:25 17:10:08	-
IMG_9693.jpeg	35,67012778	139,6914528	28,49446487	2022:08:25 17:10:26	-
IMG_9699.jpeg	35,67211667	139,6906583	25,28718951	2022:08:26 14:05:46	-
IMG_9702.jpeg	35,67202778	139,690675	24,07594682	2022:08:26 15:07:04	-
IMG_9708.jpeg	35,671875	139,6906444	25,12996294	2022:08:26 16:10:39	-
IMG_9709.jpeg	35,67187778	139,6906444	26,16688919	2022:08:26 16:10:45	-
IMG_9711.jpeg	35,67221111	139,6906583	23,06038285	2022:08:26 16:11:42	-
IMG_9713.jpeg	35,67223056	139,6906278	27,42360306	2022:08:26 16:14:20	-
IMG_9714.jpeg	35,67216944	139,6906444	25,598835	2022:08:26 16:16:18	-
IMG_9717.jpeg	35,67231389	139,689225	37,43690873	2022:08:26 16:25:43	-
IMG_9718.jpeg	35,67255	139,6885833	44,60634233	2022:08:26 16:26:47	-
IMG_9719.jpeg	35,67238889	139,6885083	36,20784385	2022:08:26 16:27:05	-
IMG_9720.jpeg	35,67229444	139,6882167	27,77232656	2022:08:26 16:27:41	-
IMG_9721.jpeg	35,67208056	139,6882944	30,38824715	2022:08:26 16:23:14	-
IMG_9722.jpeg	35,6716	139,6878194	25,53285601	2022:08:26 16:29:27	-
IMG_9732.jpeg	35,670875	139,6845083	27,4361763	2022:08:26 16:37:02	-
IMG_9736.jpeg	35,67221389	139,6883389	19,4198799	2022:08:26 16:56:56	-
IMG_9737.jpeg	35,67213889	139,6905222	26,76604651	2022:08:26 17:59:56	-
IMG_9745.jpeg	35,67340833	139,6876833	67,56526566	2022:08:26 20:15:20	-
IMG_9784.jpeg	35,6622	139,698625	40,27370071	2022:08:27 10:48:23	-
IMG_9785.jpeg	35,66114444	139,7047111	58,64543916	2022:08:27 10:55:35	-
IMG_9786.jpeg	35,66073333	139,7046806	30,82231243	2022:08:27 10:56:38	-
IMG_9789.jpeg	35,65975278	139,7024389	21,83300018	2022:08:27 12:55:31	-
IMG_9793.jpeg	-	-	-	-	-
IMG_9794.jpeg	-	-	-	-	-
IMG_9796.jpeg	35,64845278	139,7111194	14,81860161	2022:08:27 13:50:17	-
IMG_9797.jpeg	35,64845278	139,7111194	14,81860161	2022:08:27 13:50:19	-
IMG_9798.jpeg	35,64846111	139,7111806	14,81775284	2022:08:27 13:54:09	-
IMG_9799.jpeg	35,65974722	139,7000722	44,54094696	2022:08:27 14:27:19	-
IMG_9816.jpeg	35,67053889	139,6901556	23,75241736	2022:08:27 20:46:31	-
IMG_9820.jpeg	35,67209167	139,6905667	26,75954057	2022:08:27 22:18:18	-
IMG_9864.jpeg	35,66064167	139,6662611	42,70779184	2022:08:28 15:35:37	-
IMG_9866.jpeg	35,66048333	139,6658778	40,77269932	2022:08:28 15:36:42	-
IMG_9867.jpeg	35,65995833	139,6652361	36,13423884	2022:08:28 15:37:46	-
IMG_9869.jpeg	35,65955833	139,664475	38,14786674	2022:08:28 15:39:03	-
IMG_9872.jpeg	35,65935833	139,6644444	39,93385136	2022:08:28 15:40:16	-
IMG_9875.jpeg	35,65941111	139,66455	44,33693314	2022:08:28 15:41:43	-
IMG_9876.jpeg	35,65998333	139,6653444	36,96914053	2022:08:28 15:50:55	-
IMG_9881.jpeg	35,661775	139,667725	40,02270833	2022:08:28 16:05:30	-
IMG_9887.jpeg	35,66761111	139,706925	23,15814971	2022:08:28 16 55:06	-
IMG_9888.jpeg	35,66767222	139,7071083	22,78649521	2022:08:28 17 03:27	-
IMG_9896.jpeg	35,65965556	139,7024694	26,60234333	2022:08:28 17 55:07	-
IMG_9897.jpeg	35,65791667	139,7035528	17,15320617	2022:08:28 18:00:02	-
IMG_9898.jpeg	35,65297222	139,70935	17,5800089	2022:08:28 18:19:07	-
IMG_9901.jpeg	35,65298056	139,7096556	19,19155973	2022:08:28 18:20:20	-
IMG_9916.jpeg	35,66136111	139,6941083	33,8016106	2022:08:28 21:56:33	-
IMG_9917.jpeg	35,66224722	139,6939556	29,18153767	2022:08:28 21:57:58	-
IMG_9920.jpeg	35,66553056	139,6925056	23,46964882	2022:08:28 22:05:07	-
IMG_9921.jpeg	35,66606944	139,6920306	23,94816154	2022:08:28 22:06:17	-
IMG_9922.jpeg	35,66630278	139,6917583	44,49060343	2022:08:28 22:11:24	-
IMG_9924.jpeg	35,67205833	139,6905056	32,37581252	2022:08:28 22:35:34	-

IMG_9938.jpeg	35,67239444	139,6909639	26,75423051	2022:08:29 15:38:17	-
IMG_9939.jpeg	35,67256111	139,6907806	25,75343705	2022:08:29 15:38:21	-
IMG_9940.jpeg	35,693875	139,7043139	41,36488725	2022:08:29 19:55:21	-
IMG_9941.jpeg	35,67035278	139,6834417	25,32606887	2022:08:29 21:19:44	-
IMG_9942.jpeg	35,67036111	139,6835472	16,33644486	2022:08:29 21:20:09	-
IMG_9947.jpeg	35,67042222	139,6832583	28,9590225	2022:08:29 21:29:48	-
IMG_9959.jpeg	35,66056111	139,6966389	24,04519848	2022:08:30 14:02:45	-
IMG_9962.jpeg	35,65966667	139,6914056	10,83308793	2022:08:30 14:39:04	-
IMG_9964.jpeg	35,6605	139,6978306	22,93708609	2022:08:30 16:19:51	-
IMG_9965.jpeg	35,6605	139,6978306	22,93708609	2022:08:30 16:19:54	-
IMG_9977.jpeg	35,67219167	139,6906444	25,55702594	2022:08:30 18:17:25	-
IMG_9984.jpeg	35,65854722	139,7097944	34,65110396	2022:08:30 20:43:40	-
IMG_9987.jpeg	35,65833611	139,7089389	34,65007402	2022:08:30 20:58:53	-
IMG_9989.jpeg	35,65845833	139,7095028	34,65080259	2022:08:30 21:18:15	-
IMG_9994.jpeg	35,65826111	139,7027889	23,32201385	2022:08:30 22:08:38	-
IMG_9995.jpeg	35,65827222	139,7029889	24,76329804	2022:08:30 22:08:42	-
IMG_9997.jpeg	35,65920278	139,702575	21,40441132	2022:08:30 22:11:09	-
IMG_9998.jpeg	35,65991667	139,698625	22,12402724	2022:08:30 22:19:06	-
INDO_LAURIE.jpeg	35,00254722	135,7636111	40,20343777	2022:11:03 20:59:29	-
INSTRUCTIONS.jpeg	35,67885278	139,6744694	37,98566215	2022:08:18 17:41:31	-
ITALY (2).jpeg	-	-	-	2022:08:20 16:56:43	-
ITALY.jpeg	33,58268611	130,3828889	12,15886311	2022:09:03 15:09:47	-
ITOSHIMAHOME (2).jpeg	33,53409167	130,15425	5,617259118	2022:10:29 10:29:14	-
ITOSHIMAHOME (3).jpeg	33,534125	130,1541583	4,921771048	2022:10:28 19:59:26	-
ITOSHIMAHOME.jpeg	33,53402222	130,1542361	6,287714712	2022:10:29 10:29:33	-
IZAKAYA@HOME.jpeg	35,72061667	139,6531056	40,59011034	2022:11:11 21:39:44	-
IZAKAYASTORY (2).jpeg	35,67039167	139,6834556	28,12588693	2022:08:29 21:26:36	-
IZAKAYASTORY.jpeg	35,67041667	139,6832583	24,69448471	2022:08:29 21:26:09	-
IZAKAYASTORYBONES.jpeg	35,67053889	139,6835333	32,35050771	2022:08:29 21:41:35	-
IZAKAYASTORYSALADA.jpeg	35,67044167	139,6831806	28,95890045	2022:08:29 21:32:12	-
JESUS.jpeg	36,35633056	138,5870972	991,4487535	2022:08:20 10:38:17	-
JETLEG.jpeg	35,66326389	139,7016139	22,49165724	2022:08:17 03:38:25	-
KAFFEHAUSKULTUR (2).jpeg	33,58260278	130,3824611	11,73612891	2022:09:03 15:12:38	-
KAFFEHAUSKULTUR (3).jpeg	33,58252222	130,3824	12,21297837	2022:09:03 15:22:22	-
KAFFEHAUSKULTUR.jpeg	33,58261944	130,3824472	11,15549588	2022:09:03 15:12:32	-
KAWAI (2).jpeg	35,64877222	139,7008528	31,88015148	2022:11:10 18:06:44	-
KAWAI.jpeg	35,72053611	139,6531056	43,74094008	2022:11:11 15:18:16	-
KENGO.jpeg	35,659675	139,7025444	33,51738736	2022:08:27 12:55:59	-
KENGOAGAININSUN.jpeg	35,66017778	139,7024528	20,40191967	2022:08:28 17:54:12	-
KOLA.jpeg	35,67117222	139,6829833	28,49853516	2022:08:26 16:44:14	-
KURA.jpeg	33,53472778	130,1546167	7,148889884	2022:10:30 17:37:29	-
LAMPS.jpeg	35,72061944	139,6531222	45,09323116	2022:11:11 17:22:56	-
LEBEN.jpeg	33,58885278	130,3888389	9,105556494	2022:09:09 14:10:26	-
LEMONADE.jpeg	35,67671667	139,6747278	46,13014603	2022:08:24 17:23:46	-
LIVERorHEART.jpeg	35,67038056	139,6834111	33,64874461	2022:08:29 21:46:39	-
LONGTIMENOSEE.jpeg	-	-	-	2022:08:16 23:14:37	-
LOSTINTRANSLATION.jpeg	-	-	-	2022:08:30 19:53:23	-
LOT.jpeg	-	-	-	2022:11:03 20:12:08	-
LUNCH.jpeg	33,53220833	130,1518389	11,86599541	2022:09:05 14:18:08	-
LÄTZCHEN.jpeg	33,58787222	130,3958139	9,857494361	2022:09:03 14:26:31	-
MAN.jpeg	35,66164444	139,7007306	42,60350796	2022:08:17 00:59:30	-
MARIJANNA.jpeg	35,67208611	139,69075	25,94675569	2022:09:01 10:16:24	-
MATERIAL (10).jpeg	33,58460278	130,3867028	8,808652482	2022:09:03 15:03:58	-
MATERIAL (11).jpeg	33,5843	130,3863528	7,70334307	2022:09:03 15:04:39	-
MATERIAL (12).jpeg	33,58428611	130,3863361	8,419567271	2022:09:03 15:04:45	-
MATERIAL (13).jpeg	33,58393889	130,3860639	7,945287895	2022:09:03 15:05:23	-
MATERIAL (14).jpeg	33,51300556	130,1299278	-0,946931838	2022:09:06 17:43:13	-
MATERIAL (15).jpeg	33,59419722	130,1094972	2,989374336	2022:09:07 15:25:28	-
MATERIAL (16).jpeg	33,59419722	130,1094972	2,943221893	2022:09:07 15:25:31	-
MATERIAL (17).jpeg	33,59420278	130,1094972	2,788064539	2022:09:07 15:25:35	-
MATERIAL (18).jpeg	36,35708611	138,5872944	998,1055215	2022:08:20 11:20:35	-
MATERIAL (19).jpeg	36,35707778	138,5873111	997,7081021	2022:08:20 11:20:37	-
MATERIAL (2).jpeg	35,68393611	139,7157889	42,23387905	2022:11:12 14:39:29	-
MATERIAL (20).jpeg	36,35706667	138,587325	996,46593	2022:08:20 11:20:44	-
MATERIAL (21).jpeg	36,35706667	138,5873556	996,022	2022:08:20 11:20:45	-
MATERIAL (22).jpeg	35,67572778	139,6780083	31,71968461	2022:08:19 15:07:51	-
MATERIAL (23).jpeg	35,67568333	139,6780556	24,09303664	2022:08:19 15:07:46	-
MATERIAL (24).jpeg	35,67575	139,6779639	33,81392286	2022:08:19 15:08:00	-
MATERIAL (3).jpeg	35,72155	139,7707667	18,87478645	2022:11:09 16:14:33	-
MATERIAL (4).jpeg	35,67980556	139,7026528	33,33457381	2022:11:07 16:12:52	-
MATERIAL (5).jpeg	33,584975	130,3875278	7,661245597	2022:09:03 15:01:49	-
MATERIAL (6).jpeg	33,58476389	130,3871778	6,148432646	2022:09:03 15:02:31	-
MATERIAL (7).jpeg	33,584675	130,3869639	6,471572319	2022:09:03 15:02:58	-
MATERIAL (8).jpeg	33,58463611	130,3868417	7,648855774	2022:09:03 15:03:12	-
MATERIAL (9).jpeg	33,58464167	130,3867333	8,938856843	2022:09:03 15:03:46	-
MATERIAL.jpeg	35,68362778	139,7159417	32,51169147	2022:11:12 14:40:30	-
MAYU.jpeg	36,29895278	138,6193861	942,4281184	2022:08:20 12:27:12	-
MAYUS_FAV.jpeg	35,65880556	139,7002556	-	2022:11:07 18:59:01	-
MAYUUUMEET (2).jpeg	35,6603	139,6989139	21,44696999	2022:08:17 19:49:54	-
MAYUUUMEET.jpeg	35,6603	139,6989139	21,44696999	2022:08:17 19:49:54	-
MAYU_LUNCH.jpeg	35,72161944	139,677475	31,83833063	2022:11:11 13:09:16	-
ME (10).jpeg	35,67213333	139,6905972	21,42341998	2022:08:31 12:51:03	-
ME (2).jpeg	-	-	-	2022:11:03 01:28:47	-
ME (3).jpeg	33,53410833	130,1542806	5,290983209	2022:10:29 10:15:30	-
ME (4).jpeg	34,69031111	135,4934694	5,363740924	2022:11:02 23:02:51	-
ME (5).jpeg	-	-	-	2022:11:02 21:28:24	-
ME (6).jpeg	36,29881389	138,6193861	942,0392902	2022:08:20 12:35:53	-
ME (7).jpeg	35,65965	139,6955417	28,42357064	2022:08:17 22:40:48	-
ME (8).jpeg	35,66337222	139,701675	21,2551899	2022:08:18 00:52:24	-
ME (9).jpeg	35,67161944	139,6877444	38,42097853	2022:08:26 16:30:23	-
ME.jpeg	35,71979167	139,65335	38,10152057	2022:11:08 13:32:41	-
ME_HARAJUKU.jpeg	-	-	-	2022:11:07 16:50:58	-
MICHI.jpeg	35,65363056	139,7048028	26,6578903	2022:11:08 16:23:59	-
MILLIONS.jpeg	35,62900556	139,7407694	-	2022:09:01 11:43:08	-
MINI_HANBA.jpeg	35,671875	139,6907056	24,97426226	2022:09:01 02:29:04	-
MOCHICAFE (2).jpeg	33,53722778	130,159775	5,932828907	2022:10:28 13:27:55	-

MOCHICAFE.jpeg	-	-	-	2022:10:28 13:26:51	-
MONEY.jpeg	35,66713611	139,7070611	22,14199357	2022:08:28 17:06:34	-
MOVE.jpeg	35,63135833	139,7408	-	2022:09:01 12:13:57	-
MUJI.jpeg	33,53250833	130,1515056	15,54653741	2022:09:03 22:44:30	-
MURAYAMAHANGING.jpeg	35,68325833	139,6873778	46,48090362	2022:08:21 16:20:51	-
NACHTEIS.jpeg	33,53245833	130,1515806	13,90477754	2022:09:03 23:16:00	-
NANMADOL.jpeg	-	-	-	-	-
NATURE.jpeg	35,67099722	139,6865833	33,07448199	2022:08:26 16:33:23	-
NAVIGATION.jpeg	35,66925833	139,6802361	26,90144732	2022:08:19 15:27:14	-
NIGHTWALK (2).jpeg	35,67028333	139,6894833	25,38574673	2022:08:27 20:48:00	-
NIGHTWALK.jpeg	35,67020833	139,6894389	25,16948035	2022:08:27 20:48:15	-
NIGHTWALKERS.jpeg	35,672375	139,6907056	25,44522637	2022:09:01 02:19:47	-
NIKO.jpeg	34,70498611	135,5005333	0,281732797	2022:11:02 15:19:26	-
NOGATAVIEW.jpeg	35,72056944	139,6531056	43,53899768	2022:11:07 11:49:52	-
NOGATA_BED.jpeg	35,72068333	139,6531667	42,29951857	2022:11:06 11:23:03	-
NOGATA_HOME.jpeg	35,72046667	139,6530444	38,23114786	2022:11:05 15:32:09	-
NOGATA_WORK.jpeg	35,72061944	139,6531667	42,51973347	2022:11:07 10:51:03	-
NOMONEY.jpeg	35,667675	139,7071222	21,85371786	2022:08:28 17:08:19	-
NONONO (2).jpeg	35,68233889	139,6868583	41,53310011	2022:08:21 15:59:37	-
NONONO.jpeg	35,71716389	139,7748417	7,430507659	2022:08:23 16:33:59	-
NOSLEEP.jpeg	35,66326944	139,7016	22,34167672	2022:08:17 03:38:53	-
OBA_CHAN_CONSTRUCTION.jpeg	33,53483611	130,1546944	7,963903646	2022:10:30 17:38:59	-
ODEN.jpeg	35,71036667	139,7756194	-	2022:11:09 18:58:06	-
OFFICE.jpeg	35,69534167	139,7001028	36,67855456	2022:11:12 13:55:26	-
OHLEANDER.jpeg	35,669075	139,6681972	43,73019943	2022:08:21 21:48:59	-
OIRAN.jpeg	35,65980556	139,6955111	27,99126814	2022:08:31 00:32:57	-
OKONOMIYAKI.jpeg	35,66025833	139,6991417	21,4856682	2022:08:17 19:52:51	-
ONIGIRISNACK.jpeg	35,66225556	139,7022861	20,85343348	2022:08:28 17:51:23	-
ORANGEJUICE.jpeg	34,70872778	135,5051583	5,36219406	2022:11:02 12:17:36	-
OSAKA_wip (2).jpeg	-	-	-	2022:11:02 22:10:55	-
OSAKA_wip (3).jpeg	-	-	-	2022:11:02 22:10:48	-
OSAKA_wip.jpeg	-	-	-	2022:11:02 22:10:56	-
OURA.jpeg	-	-	-	2022:11:02 21:37:46	-
OYSTERS.jpeg	-	-	-	-	-
PARKS.jpeg	35,66283889	139,7023917	18,89857891	2022:08:28 17:50:28	-
PART.jpeg	35,65929722	139,6645056	40,79402545	2022:08:28 15:40:25	-
PARTY.jpeg	-	-	-	2022:08:20 16:21:39	-
PAUSE.jpeg	33,5852	130,1078944	1,881620421	2022:09:07 16:27:09	-
PIZZA.jpeg	35,66169444	139,7007139	40,98961638	2022:08:17 00:59:44	-
POSESSIONS.jpeg	35,67211944	139,6905361	24,21400839	2022:09:01 08:14:03	-
POTATO.jpeg	35,66025833	139,6991417	21,4856682	2022:08:17 19:52 48	-
POTENTIALHOME (10).jpeg	35,67084444	139,6857917	29,30946733	2022:08:26 16:34 54	-
POTENTIALHOME (2).jpeg	35,67023889	139,7088472	22,95586135	2022:11:07 16:51 41	-
POTENTIALHOME (3).jpeg	35,67451944	139,7048639	27,82537999	2022:11:07 16:27 34	-
POTENTIALHOME (4).jpeg	35,72144444	139,6522667	42,65864945	2022:11:06 14:03:31	-
POTENTIALHOME (5).jpeg	35,69074167	139,6987917	42,19950536	2022:11:06 22:17:52	-
POTENTIALHOME (6).jpeg	34,71009444	135,4951167	2,966849555	2022:11:02 14:34:52	-
POTENTIALHOME (7).jpeg	35,66673333	139,6717694	43,89526472	2022:08:21 20:48:56	-
POTENTIALHOME (8).jpeg	35,67072778	139,6848611	25,66210621	2022:08:26 16:36:26	-
POTENTIALHOME (9).jpeg	35,67224167	139,6882778	12,45808792	2022:08:26 16:56:49	-
POTENTIALHOME.jpeg	35,66923611	139,7077639	19,63828346	2022:11:07 16:41:28	-
POTENTIAL_HOME.jpeg	35,0083	135,7702944	47,68478011	2022:11:04 15:09:29	-
PROBS.jpeg	35,72056111	139,6531222	43,59432601	2022:11:11 17:03:11	-
RAIN.jpeg	35,67219167	139,6906139	26,68257523	2022:08:30 18:17:23	-
RAINAGAIN.jpeg	35,65992222	139,7056583	56,48052226	2022:08:30 20:20:30	-
RAMEN.jpeg	35,67778056	139,6784972	47,0314903	2022:08:19 21:56:53	-
REBECCA (2).jpeg	-	-	-	2022:11:03 01:28:43	-
REBECCA.jpeg	34,7075	135,5024722	2,784450576	2022:11:03 11:25:55	-
REBIINMIRROR.jpeg	35,66850278	139,70555	23,16257159	2022:08:28 16:38:20	-
RING (2).jpeg	35,66558056	139,6730639	42,01963043	2022:08:28 15:24:48	-
RING.jpeg	-	-	-	2022:11:02 21:37:38	-
RUKA.jpeg	35,64877222	139,7008667	32,02261292	2022:11:10 18:06:45	-
SAD (2).jpeg	35,659725	139,6955111	28,30129434	2022:08:30 23:19:44	-
SAD.jpeg	-	-	-	2022:08:18 14:21:42	-
SADNESS.jpeg	35,66327778	139,7016306	22,40073205	2022:08:17 03:38:33	-
SAFETY.jpeg	33,51991667	130,1396639	4,895660397	2022:10:23 14:10:50	-
SALT.jpeg	33,57703333	130,0895083	9,225772874	2022:09:09 10:32:53	-
SALTFACTORYPLAN.jpeg	33,57707222	130,0895083	8,986209869	2022:09:09 10:33:30	-
SALTFACTORYTREAT.jpeg	33,57706944	130,0900278	18,27557756	2022:09:09 10:51:31	-
SALTFACTORYWATER.jpeg	33,57718333	130,0900722	5,526714324	2022:09:09 10:49:46	-
SANDO.jpeg	35,67385833	139,6871944	26,94332834	2022:08:31 16:03:45	-
SAUNA.jpeg	33,53513611	130,1546167	22,12338066	2022:10:30 17:08:03	-
SCAI.jpeg	35,72189444	139,7705528	19,4824524	2022:11:09 16:07:58	-
SCAI_THE_BATHOUSE.jpeg	35,72188056	139,7705083	18,02411924	2022:11:09 16:13:11	-
SENTO (2).jpeg	33,50235278	130,0706472	8,367966903	2022:09:07 19:22:34	-
SENTO (3).jpeg	33,50234722	130,0706472	6,82085971	2022:09:07 19:23:11	-
SENTO (4).jpeg	33,50234722	130,0706472	7,042481544	2022:09:07 19:23:14	-
SENTO (5).jpeg	33,50234722	130,0706472	6,823704955	2022:09:07 19:23:21	-
SENTO (6).jpeg	33,50235	130,0706472	7,379042861	2022:09:07 19:23:27	-
SENTO.jpeg	-	-	-	2022:08:23 23:03:57	-
SENTOWITHTHEGIRLS.jpeg	33,50234167	130,0706333	6,521147581	2022:09:07 19:21:51	-
SHINKANSEN.jpeg	35,62912778	139,738725	-	2022:09:01 11:20:15	-
SHINKANSENLUNCH (2).jpeg	35,16739722	136,2073056	109,6070146	2022:11:05 12:20:39	-
SHINKANSENLUNCH (3).jpeg	35,13547778	136,1688222	111,5740492	2022:11:05 12:19:32	-
SHINKANSENLUNCH (4).jpeg	35,13401111	136,1660611	110,9385727	2022:11:05 12:19:28	-
SHINKANSENLUNCH.jpeg	35,21535833	136,2476056	110,8438378	2022:11:05 12:22:04	-
SIDE.jpeg	35,72323333	139,6521917	43,88783649	2022:11:05 21:02:10	-
SINKANSEN.jpeg	35,68121389	139,7674556	-	2022:08:20 07:51:36	-
SKIN.jpeg	35,66176667	139,6674944	37,94917681	2022:11:08 18:57:29	-
SLEEPY.jpeg	35,66191944	139,6999972	24,73091509	2022:08:17 00:51:11	-
SMOKINGAREA (10).jpeg	35,66190833	139,6677389	37,73392761	2022:08:28 15 28:28	-
SMOKINGAREA (11).jpeg	35,66926111	139,7056417	-	2022:08:23 18 04:33	-
SMOKINGAREA (12).jpeg	35,69129167	139,6993556	53,84852985	2022:08:22 19 10:00	-
SMOKINGAREA (13).jpeg	35,65834167	139,7010944	18,52531188	2022:08:19 18:21:43	-
SMOKINGAREA (14).jpeg	35,65834167	139,7010944	18,52531188	2022:08:19 18:21:43	-
SMOKINGAREA (15).jpeg	35,65865	139,7005472	21,8501873	2022:08:19 17:54:15	-

SMOKINGAREA (16).jpeg	35,67505	139,6681361	48,47945021	2022-08-18, 20:11:19	-
SMOKINGAREA (17).jpeg	35,67505556	139,6681361	48,46773149	2022-08-18, 20:11:20	-
SMOKINGAREA (18).jpeg	35,67505556	139,6681361	48,46773149	2022-08-18, 20:11:22	-
SMOKINGAREA (19).jpeg	35,67507222	139,6681222	49,2890206	2022-08-18, 20:11:23	-
SMOKINGAREA (2).jpeg	-	-	-	2022-11-04, 14:51:34	-
SMOKINGAREA (20).jpeg	35,67507222	139,6681222	49,2890206	2022-08-18, 20:11:24	-
SMOKINGAREA (21).jpeg	35,66671389	139,7061167	29,49297331	2022-08-28, 17:29:27	-
SMOKINGAREA (3).jpeg	-	-	-	2022-11-04, 14:51:29	-
SMOKINGAREA (4).jpeg	35,66187778	139,6677861	38,98701861	2022-11-08, 19:19:07	-
SMOKINGAREA (5).jpeg	34,71190556	135,4936361	2,582852967	2022-11-02, 14:41:29	-
SMOKINGAREA (6).jpeg	35,661625	139,7024528	19,27738473	2022-08-17, 17:15:40	-
SMOKINGAREA (7).jpeg	35,66163611	139,7022694	18,46625776	2022-08-17, 17:20:54	-
SMOKINGAREA (8).jpeg	35,66173611	139,7022389	22,68115234	2022-08-17, 17:22:35	-
SMOKINGAREA (9).jpeg	35,66295278	139,7022556	22,16700937	2022-08-16, 20:33:35	-
SMOKINGAREA.jpeg	35,000175	135,7684944	39,44387441	2022-11-03, 16:12:04	-
SMOKINGGAME.jpeg	35,66552778	139,7122639	28,78899381	2022-08-19, 16:14:13	-
SONY MEETING.jpeg	35,63116944	139,7422778	-14,95758821	2022-08-18, 13:29:18	-
SONY.jpeg	35,63081111	139,7430278	30,48357392	2022-08-18, 12:11:19	-
STEF.jpeg	33,58267222	130,3822028	10,89754503	2022-09-03, 15:46:53	-
SVINJA.jpeg	-	-	-	2022-08-20, 17:30:06	-
THE WEDDING.jpeg	-	-	-	-	-
THEBESTMEALOFMYLIFE (2).jpeg	35,04471944	135,7926167	71,61987522	2022-11-04, 18:02:02	-
THEBESTMEALOFMYLIFE.jpeg	35,04475278	135,7926778	72,06068626	2022-11-04, 18:02:10	-
TICKETING.jpeg	35,62904444	139,7385111	-	2022-09-01, 11:17:59	-
TOMATO.jpeg	35,62894444	139,7408	-	2022-09-01, 11:43:37	-
TOMATOJELLY.jpeg	35,64825556	139,7113333	14,78402137	2022-08-23, 20:17:23	-
TOMATOJELLYUNTOUCHED.jpeg	35,64833889	139,7111194	14,78389358	2022-08-23, 20:14:28	-
TOTORO.jpeg	33,59499444	130,1092222	18,67809791	2022-09-07, 15:18:43	-
TREAT.jpeg	-	-	-	2022-11-08, 00:39:09	-
TVDINNER.jpeg	35,67200833	139,690675	24,73213578	2022-08-26, 21:51:29	-
UDONWAITING.jpeg	35,64809444	139,7112111	17,62029551	2022-08-27, 13:22:27	-
USANIGIRI.jpeg	35,67734444	139,6767722	45,32880402	2022-08-23, 13:49:16	-
USED2BE_KITALABO.jpeg	35,71754722	139,7724444	17,11924743	2022-08-23, 16:17:17	-
USEDTODOINTERNSHIP.jpeg	35,66255833	139,7025139	19,14218797	2022-08-17, 17:37:33	-
USED_2BE_SMOKINGAREA.jpeg	35,71843056	139,7722472	18,73763657	2022-08-23, 16:15:34	-
VEGANLUNCH.jpeg	35,71413056	139,7769472	4,4	2022-08-23, 16:46:33	-
VIENNA (2).jpeg	35,72319722	139,6519306	44,03879926	2022-11-05, 21:01:35	-
VIENNA.jpeg	35,72319722	139,6519306	44,03879926	2022-11-05, 21:01:37	-
VINO.jpeg	35,65939722	139,6933139	24,53328133	2022-08-30, 14:16:48	-
VYNILBAR.jpeg	35,659325	139,6972194	26,7654173	2022-08-25, 02:57:49	-
WALK.jpeg	-	-	-	-	-
WEDDING CARD.jpeg	35,76634167	139,7254944	14,36987598	2022-08-20, 08:04:09	-
WEDDING READY (2).jpeg	35,67800556	139,6768944	40,27054569	2022-08-20, 06:42:48	-
WEDDING READY (3).jpeg	-	-	-	2022-08-20, 07:03:26	-
WEDDING READY.jpeg	35,67801389	139,6769111	40,82519801	2022-08-20, 06:43:05	-
WEDDINGAFTER.jpeg	-	-	-	2022-08-20, 16:21:50	-
WHY.jpeg	35,66833611	139,70575	33,51372528	2022-08-28, 16:39:51	-
WINTERISCOMING.jpeg	35,71034722	139,7756944	6,456142419	2022-11-09, 19:05:07	-
WORK (2).jpeg	35,72066111	139,653075	42,92372515	2022-11-11, 18:43:02	-
WORK (3).jpeg	35,72061667	139,653075	42,84241164	2022-11-11, 17:52:36	-
WORK (4).jpeg	35,72059722	139,6531361	43,86378861	2022-11-11, 17:24:54	-
WORK (5).jpeg	35,72055556	139,6530139	41,80769733	2022-11-11, 17:52:05	-
WORK.jpeg	35,72056944	139,6529833	41,89418417	2022-11-11, 17:52:10	-
WORKINGPLACE_NOGATAHOME (2).jpeg	-	-	-	2022-11-06, 12:49:39	-
WORKINGPLACE_NOGATAHOME.jpeg	35,72058611	139,6530611	42,71404867	2022-11-07, 10:51:23	-
YUSUKE AT OIRAN.jpeg	35,65971667	139,695525	21,08541729	2022-08-24, 23:54:11	-
YUSUKE.jpeg	35,65931667	139,6971889	26,7654173	2022-08-25, 02:57:36	-
ZAC.jpeg	33,58754722	130,3954167	9,598438489	2022-09-03, 14:40:23	-
ZDRELAC (2).jpeg	-	-	-	2022-11-03, 14:35:03	-
ZDRELAC (3).jpeg	-	-	-	2022-11-03, 14:34:59	-
ZDRELAC (4).jpeg	-	-	-	2022-11-03, 14:34:52	-
ZDRELAC.Jpeg	-	-	-	2022-11-03, 14:35:02	-
即席BATH (10).jpeg	-	-	-	2022-08-19, 23:28:00	-
即席BATH (11).jpeg	35,67809167	139,6768639	39,91295076	2022-08-19, 23:30:20	-
即席BATH (2).jpeg	35,70803889	139,6489417	46,29695513	2022-11-09, 23:47:20	-
即席BATH (3).jpeg	35,70804167	139,6489556	46,13185503	2022-11-09, 23:47:16	-
即席BATH (4).jpeg	35,70804167	139,6490028	45,58757182	2022-11-09, 23:47:43	-
即席BATH (5).jpeg	34,99995556	135,768325	37,2275047	2022-11-04, 11:37:03	-
即席BATH (6).jpeg	34,99998611	135,7683556	37,01363756	2022-11-04, 11:37:00	-
即席BATH (7).jpeg	35,69147222	139,7034	42,90127942	2022-08-22, 18:09:53	-
即席BATH (8).jpeg	35,68011389	139,6777028	44,01043046	2022-08-21, 19:19:27	-
即席BATH (9).jpeg	35,67885833	139,6745	44,27508915	2022-08-18, 17:39:50	-
即席BATH.jpeg	35,70800278	139,6489722	46,65688496	2022-11-09, 23:47:35	-
即席BATH_GARDEN.jpeg	35,67885833	139,6745	44,27508915	2022-08-18, 17:39:43	-
即席BED (2).jpeg	35,00022222	135,7684472	37,69936758	2022-11-04, 16:19:23	-
即席BED (3).jpeg	35,00015278	135,7680361	41,22652817	2022-11-04, 10:52:36	-
即席BED (4).jpeg	35,66326389	139,7016	22,44557952	2022-08-17, 15:06:52	-
即席BED (5).jpeg	35,66326944	139,7016	22,56113792	2022-08-17, 15:09:47	-
即席BED (6).jpeg	35,66346389	139,7021639	20,18602179	2022-08-16, 20:25:09	-
即席BED (7).jpeg	35,66494722	139,7028972	51,12023161	2022-08-19, 17:13:37	-
即席BED (8).jpeg	35,66327222	139,7016139	22,78204917	2022-08-17, 17:41:55	-
即席BED.jpeg	35,72058056	139,6531222	43,99443052	2022-11-08, 12:32:49	-
即席BED_VIW.jpeg	35,66326944	139,7015833	22,41456794	2022-08-17, 15:10:05	-
即席HOME (2).jpeg	-	-	-	2022-11-08, 00:10:59	-
即席HOME (3).jpeg	35,66182778	139,6688389	33,85182572	2022-11-08, 19:33:29	-
即席HOME.jpeg	35,72057778	139,6531667	43,3960762	2022-11-08, 00:17:19	-
即席KITCHEN (10).jpeg	35,65928611	139,697175	31,50924685	2022-11-07, 21:05:25	-
即席KITCHEN (11).jpeg	35,72131667	139,6523889	23,96016311	2022-11-06, 13:37:44	-
即席KITCHEN (12).jpeg	35,72133333	139,6524056	29,91164013	2022-11-06, 13:37:47	-
即席KITCHEN (13).jpeg	35,72136667	139,6523444	43,43221663	2022-11-06, 13:49:00	-
即席KITCHEN (14).jpeg	35,72136667	139,6523444	43,43221663	2022-11-06, 13:48:58	-
即席KITCHEN (15).jpeg	35,00647778	135,7733472	58,72881317	2022-11-04, 15:00:48	-
即席KITCHEN (16).jpeg	-	-	-	2022-11-04, 14:21:23	-
即席KITCHEN (17).jpeg	35,00664444	135,7733778	58,72873688	2022-11-04, 14:19:51	-
即席KITCHEN (18).jpeg	34,71200556	135,4933306	15,0725403	2022-11-02, 14:40:14	-
即席KITCHEN (19).jpeg	33,59036944	130,4197833	8,26144027	2022-10-31, 14:11:38	-

即席KITCHEN (2).jpeg	35,00563889	135,7762306	45,28609847	2022-11-03, 14:26:22	-
即席KITCHEN (20).jpeg	33,55	130,1624444	15,5118084	2022-10-28, 12:51:29	-
即席KITCHEN (21).jpeg	33,55001111	130,1624306	1,90023613	2022-10-28, 12:32:01	-
即席KITCHEN (22).jpeg	33,54996944	130,1624306	-0,484529495	2022-10-28, 12:23:22	-
即席KITCHEN (23).jpeg	33,54999167	130,1624306	0,793912888	2022-10-28, 12:23:20	-
即席KITCHEN (24).jpeg	33,55001111	130,1624444	2,26058769	2022-10-28, 12:19:04	-
即席KITCHEN (25).jpeg	33,54998889	130,1624306	1,050260543	2022-10-28, 12:14:35	-
即席KITCHEN (26).jpeg	35,68999444	139,7026528	-	2022-08-22, 18:57:01	-
即席KITCHEN (27).jpeg	35,67780278	139,6784972	46,87007145	2022-08-19, 22:01:06	-
即席KITCHEN (28).jpeg	35,67777222	139,6785139	46,89864346	2022-08-19, 22:01:09	-
即席KITCHEN (29).jpeg	35,67113611	139,6862806	48,04848099	2022-08-26, 16:34:00	-
即席KITCHEN (3).jpeg	35,00565833	135,7762139	41,22900012	2022-11-03, 14:10:20	-
即席KITCHEN (30).jpeg	35,670975	139,6862333	35,62935259	2022-08-26, 16:34:09	-
即席KITCHEN (4).jpeg	35,00565833	135,7762139	41,22900012	2022-11-03, 14:10:16	-
即席KITCHEN (5).jpeg	35,00568889	135,7763222	36,82040786	2022-11-03, 14:02:55	-
即席KITCHEN (6).jpeg	34,70876389	135,5052639	5,371450425	2022-11-03, 10:19:02	-
即席KITCHEN (7).jpeg	33,52009167	130,1396472	3,879362107	2022-10-23, 14:11:05	-
即席KITCHEN (8).jpeg	-	-	-	2022-11-08, 00:10:59	-
即席KITCHEN (9).jpeg	35,65880556	139,7002556	-	2022-11-07, 18:53:21	-
即席KITCHEN.jpeg	35,64833333	139,7112417	14,79102039	2022-11-10, 19:14:55	-
即席LEISURE (10).jpeg	35,71036944	139,7756194	-	2022-11-09, 19:10:32	-
即席LEISURE (11).jpeg	35,72468056	139,7705222	19,34969762	2022-11-09, 15:53:11	-
即席LEISURE (12).jpeg	35,72480278	139,7705528	19,35604454	2022-11-09, 15:52:54	-
即席LEISURE (13).jpeg	-	-	-	2022-11-03, 20:12:13	-
即席LEISURE (14).jpeg	-	-	-	2022-11-03, 20:11:51	-
即席LEISURE (15).jpeg	33,58705556	130,3953389	10,62925434	2022-10-24, 22:58:48	-
即席LEISURE (16).jpeg	33,58702222	130,3953389	10,29940795	2022-10-24, 22:59:00	-
即席LEISURE (17).jpeg	33,58702222	130,3953389	10,29940795	2022-10-24, 22:58:57	-
即席LEISURE (18).jpeg	34,999825	135,7688139	40,41164778	2022-11-04, 22:15:40	-
即席LEISURE (19).jpeg	34,999925	135,7688139	39,86181259	2022-11-04, 21:51:05	-
即席LEISURE (2).jpeg	35,67508056	139,70195	22,40654752	2022-11-12, 15:18:15	-
即席LEISURE (20).jpeg	35,00254722	135,7660667	47,70986558	2022-11-03, 20:11:43	-
即席LEISURE (21).jpeg	35,00257222	135,7660833	45,70797349	2022-11-03, 20:11:36	-
即席LEISURE (22).jpeg	35,00022222	135,7684028	40,4634056	2022-11-03, 18:37:56	-
即席LEISURE (23).jpeg	-	-	-	2022-11-04, 14:51:43	-
即席LEISURE (24).jpeg	-	-	-	2022-11-04, 14:51:39	-
即席LEISURE (25).jpeg	35,65929444	139,697175	31,50991821	2022-11-07, 21:05:19	-
即席LEISURE (26).jpeg	35,65931667	139,6972194	31,50908279	2022-11-07, 21:25:19	-
即席LEISURE (27).jpeg	35,67993889	139,7028194	29,13782263	2022-11-07, 16:12:35	-
即席LEISURE (28).jpeg	35,68289167	139,7021167	37,33351935	2022-11-07, 16:05:49	-
即席LEISURE (29).jpeg	35,00647778	135,7733472	58,72881317	2022-11-04, 14:12:08	-
即席LEISURE (3).jpeg	35,67625833	139,702025	35,40048675	2022-11-12, 15:15:56	-
即席LEISURE (30).jpeg	35,00648611	135,7733472	58,72881317	2022-11-04, 14:12:04	-
即席LEISURE (31).jpeg	35,00907222	135,7717583	39,31686019	2022-11-04, 15:07:01	-
即席LEISURE (32).jpeg	35,67776944	139,6770167	42,58137899	2022-08-21, 23:39:27	-
即席LEISURE (33).jpeg	35,67777222	139,6770333	42,6242485	2022-08-22, 01:07:14	-
即席LEISURE (34).jpeg	35,67779444	139,6770333	42,68794248	2022-08-22, 21:18:59	-
即席LEISURE (35).jpeg	35,67768611	139,6770639	27,36220169	2022-08-22, 21:38:49	-
即席LEISURE (36).jpeg	35,72231389	139,770875	34,02145002	2022-08-23, 15:55:40	-
即席LEISURE (37).jpeg	35,72202222	139,7702778	16,38314438	2022-08-23, 15:57:53	-
即席LEISURE (38).jpeg	36,35719722	138,5876611	989,792543	2022-08-20, 11:21:25	-
即席LEISURE (39).jpeg	35,65977778	139,7020111	19,63439994	2022-08-19, 19:15:22	-
即席LEISURE (4).jpeg	35,65674722	139,7046194	17,84402084	2022-11-12, 16:59:45	-
即席LEISURE (40).jpeg	35,66924167	139,7051389	-	2022-08-19, 15:40:33	-
即席LEISURE (41).jpeg	35,67595556	139,6775972	42,5036201	2022-08-19, 15:07:15	-
即席LEISURE (42).jpeg	35,67595278	139,6775806	41,92818074	2022-08-19, 15:07:13	-
即席LEISURE (43).jpeg	35,66282778	139,7018583	18,67290497	2022-08-18, 15:08:56	-
即席LEISURE (44).jpeg	35,67825	139,6747444	43,8474034	2022-08-18, 18:27:24	-
即席LEISURE (45).jpeg	35,65959167	139,6646278	38,51052049	2022-08-28, 15:38:44	-
即席LEISURE (46).jpeg	35,66049444	139,6659083	41,51485292	2022-08-28, 15:36:37	-
即席LEISURE (47).jpeg	35,66018333	139,7024528	20,51380249	2022-08-28, 17:54:15	-
即席LEISURE (5).jpeg	35,67739444	139,7021472	42,33043672	2022-11-12, 15:13:59	-
即席LEISURE (6).jpeg	35,677425	139,7021639	37,46459201	2022-11-12, 15:13:47	-
即席LEISURE (7).jpeg	35,64831111	139,7112111	14,79828453	2022-11-10, 21:13:02	-
即席LEISURE (8).jpeg	35,64833333	139,7112417	14,79102039	2022-11-10, 19:14:52	-
即席LEISURE (9).jpeg	35,64841944	139,7111972	14,83008004	2022-11-10, 18:59:38	-
即席LEISURE.jpeg	35,67625556	139,7020111	35,22804907	2022-11-12, 15:15:59	-
即席LIVINGROOM.jpeg	35,66309444	139,702225	18,21562774	2022-08-18, 15:01:19	-
即席TOILET (2).jpeg	35,66209444	139,699325	35,46046832	2022-08-27, 15:10:43	-
即席TOILET.jpeg	35,678925	139,6743167	43,59486736	2022-08-24, 16:39:11	-

Date	Sleep Score	Total Sleep Score	REM Sleep Score	Deep Sleep Score	Sleep Efficiency	Restfulness Score	Sleep Latency Score	Sleep Timin Score	Total Sleep Duration	Total Bedtime	Awake Time
2022-08-17	81	100	97	97	96	65	75	1	33750	37200	3450
2022-08-19	82	100	90	100	79	70	91	2	38430	46080	7650
2022-08-21	79	100	95	100	88	56	70	1	35490	40740	5250
2022-08-23	63	67	56	92	76	63	78	1	23100	28140	5040
2022-08-25	59	36	34	100	95	95	89	1	15480	17280	1800
2022-08-26	81	96	100	100	90	78	67	1	30690	35040	4350
2022-08-27	47	21	1	84	69	70	78	59	10860	13740	2880
2022-08-28	80	99	82	100	93	66	81	1	31800	35820	4020
2022-08-30	65	56	64	100	90	77	81	5	20370	23040	2670
2022-09-01	61	51	42	97	95	74	70	15	19260	21420	2160
2022-09-02	81	91	83	100	96	67	91	17	29010	31860	2850
2022-09-03	61	52	40	100	97	69	72	15	19470	21180	1710
2022-09-04	83	98	96	100	96	73	75	13	31470	34440	2970
2022-09-05	75	91	67	99	88	61	75	9	29160	33660	4500
2022-09-07	77	93	77	100	88	61	70	20	29520	34020	4500
2022-09-08	67	67	49	100	93	71	72	14	23190	25920	2730
2022-09-09	49	36	23	97	30	68	81	35	15420	24720	9300
2022-09-10	59	37	52	93	100	90	70	6	15660	16440	780
2022-09-11	87	100	92	100	93	63	91	47	34470	38880	4410
2022-09-12	69	69	57	100	97	70	78	14	23640	25560	1920
2022-09-13	63	49	47	100	98	74	78	26	18660	20040	1380
2022-09-14	80	90	85	99	97	71	75	21	28890	31560	2670
2022-09-15	57	37	48	97	93	84	67	8	15720	17640	1920
2022-09-16	82	97	85	99	96	67	67	35	30900	33900	3000
2022-09-17	52	37	29	97	79	84	59	3	15810	19020	3210
2022-09-19	62	69	44	98	76	60	64	11	23640	28740	5100
2022-09-21	77	77	80	98	95	72	97	20	25530	28260	2730
2022-09-22	65	60	44	96	98	80	67	19	21270	22980	1710
2022-09-24	57	24	17	96	90	80	70	92	12390	14160	1770
2022-09-25	67	66	62	98	51	62	91	48	22920	32280	9360
2022-09-27	72	69	43	98	83	95	75	37	23580	27780	4200
2022-09-30	80	93	85	100	98	68	70	22	29550	31620	2070
2022-10-01	66	54	50	100	99	88	81	7	20010	21360	1350
2022-10-02	67	63	71	100	97	78	67	1	22170	24060	1890
2022-10-03	67	71	53	100	83	69	67	9	24090	28380	4290
2022-10-05	76	75	84	100	86	71	83	39	25170	29280	4110
2022-10-06	69	68	62	98	81	69	78	31	23430	27780	4350
2022-10-07	59	43	44	99	98	81	78	1	17340	18600	1260
2022-10-08	87	100	97	98	95	65	78	51	35370	39300	3930
2022-10-11	70	71	50	99	81	71	89	29	24180	28800	4620
2022-10-12	44	32	37	98	21	65	67	10	14370	25980	11610
2022-10-13	91	100	95	100	95	72	91	74	33780	37500	3720
2022-10-14	77	71	97	100	100	87	81	17	24240	25320	1080
2022-10-15	85	94	81	100	95	71	72	69	29760	33000	3240
2022-10-19	85	100	99	100	90	63	94	23	43830	49620	5790
2022-10-20	72	80	65	98	97	66	83	1	26370	28800	2430
2022-10-21	78	95	70	100	90	66	83	9	30090	34020	3930
2022-10-22	63	49	37	99	98	86	78	20	18600	20100	1500
2022-10-24	84	100	84	100	90	67	67	49	32640	37080	4440
2022-10-25	58	48	37	97	95	68	72	10	18510	20460	1950
2022-10-26	88	100	97	100	95	66	81	59	37380	41340	3960
2022-10-27	63	57	38	100	86	60	83	31	20730	24240	3510
2022-10-28	71	68	75	99	97	68	81	16	23370	25320	1950
2022-10-31	76	84	66	100	95	63	70	42	27420	30420	3000
2022-11-01	62	41	51	97	99	85	81	21	16590	17700	1110
2022-11-02	74	100	76	98	58	62	37	30	32580	43920	11340
2022-11-03	63	55	73	59	96	69	91	18	20220	22320	2100
2022-11-04	85	100	96	100	95	68	89	20	32190	35580	3390
2022-11-07	79	87	82	100	86	71	86	22	28020	32460	4440
2022-11-08	77	81	85	88	98	79	86	13	26550	28440	1890
2022-11-09	78	95	73	99	99	63	70	14	30000	31920	1920
2022-11-11	78	93	83	99	76	58	94	16	29610	36240	6630
2022-11-12	82	95	74	100	95	75	91	16	30120	33480	3360
2022-08-15											
2022-08-16											
2022-08-18											
2022-08-20											
2022-08-22											
2022-08-24											
2022-08-29											
2022-08-31											
2022-09-06											
2022-09-18											
2022-09-20											
2022-09-23											
2022-09-26											
2022-09-28											
2022-09-29											
2022-10-04											
2022-10-10											
2022-10-18											
2022-10-23											
2022-10-30											
2022-11-05											
2022-11-06											
2022-11-10											

REM Sleep Duration	Light Sleep Duration	Deep Sleep Duration	Restless Sleep	Sleep Efficiency	Sleep Latency	Sleep Timing	Bedtime Start	Bedtime End	Average Resting Heart Rate
7320	20130	6300	30	91	360	18990	2022-08-17T04:33:29+09:00	2022-08-17T14:53:29+09:00	66.78
6120	21090	11220	34	83	1080	23550	2022-08-19T01:10:22+09:00	2022-08-19T13:58:22+09:00	69.95
6570	16680	12240	36	87	270	19830	2022-08-21T03:25:17+09:00	2022-08-21T14:44:17+09:00	59.07
3840	14400	4860	33	82	450	14610	2022-08-23T04:11:13+09:00	2022-08-23T12:00:13+09:00	63.47
2400	3570	9510	12	90	1110	8910	2022-08-25T05:27:32+09:00	2022-08-25T10:15:32+09:00	76.28
9900	11190	9600	24	88	180	16590	2022-08-26T04:10:28+09:00	2022-08-26T13:54:28+09:00	78.72
0	6450	4410	34	79	1380	7380	2022-08-27T02:17:30+09:00	2022-08-27T06:06:30+09:00	56.71
5580	15180	11040	31	89	480	18000	2022-08-28T03:19:12+09:00	2022-08-28T13:16:12+09:00	55.66
4380	7350	8640	28	88	510	10830	2022-08-30T04:21:32+09:00	2022-08-30T10:45:32+09:00	87.35
2940	9960	6360	24	90	240	10470	2022-09-01T03:30:32+09:00	2022-09-01T09:27:32+09:00	76.65
5700	12990	10320	32	91	1050	16290	2022-09-02T01:39:28+09:00	2022-09-02T10:30:28+09:00	56.57
2820	6210	10440	28	92	300	10320	2022-09-03T03:32:30+09:00	2022-09-03T09:25:30+09:00	57.41
7170	15060	9240	28	91	360	17460	2022-09-04T01:45:32+09:00	2022-09-04T11:19:32+09:00	60.37
4620	16110	8430	36	87	1440	17940	2022-09-05T02:01:28+09:00	2022-09-05T11:22:28+09:00	63.23
5280	11940	12300	33	87	270	15900	2022-09-07T01:26:48+09:00	2022-09-07T10:53:48+09:00	59.63
3390	9210	10590	27	89	330	12510	2022-09-08T03:01:29+09:00	2022-09-08T10:13:29+09:00	56.06
1680	6990	6750	27	62	480	11460	2022-09-09T01:56:30+09:00	2022-09-09T08:48:30+09:00	55.84
3600	7140	4920	10	95	270	8100	2022-09-10T05:03:30+09:00	2022-09-10T09:37:30+09:00	91.04
6270	19350	8850	34	89	720	19890	2022-09-10T23:13:33+09:00	2022-09-11T10:01:33+09:00	58.51
3930	9780	9930	35	92	420	12570	2022-09-12T02:58:30+09:00	2022-09-12T10:04:30+09:00	53.96
3300	4740	10620	29	93	420	9930	2022-09-13T02:41:30+09:00	2022-09-13T08:15:30+09:00	55.77
5790	15180	7920	28	92	390	15930	2022-09-14T01:24:33+09:00	2022-09-14T10:10:33+09:00	67.58
3330	5790	6600	20	89	180	8220	2022-09-15T04:47:20+09:00	2022-09-15T09:41:20+09:00	76.41
5820	16830	8250	27	91	180	17220	2022-09-16T00:21:27+09:00	2022-09-16T09:46:27+09:00	61.48
2040	6870	6900	32	83	30	8760	2022-09-17T05:08:33+09:00	2022-09-17T10:25:33+09:00	78.0
3060	12960	7620	37	82	120	14430	2022-09-19T02:48:02+09:00	2022-09-19T10:47:02+09:00	58.82
5430	12750	7350	24	90	960	14460	2022-09-21T01:51:30+09:00	2022-09-21T09:42:30+09:00	70.63
3060	12270	5940	25	93	180	11550	2022-09-22T02:45:31+09:00	2022-09-22T09:08:31+09:00	62.67
1170	5070	6150	15	88	270	6810	2022-09-24T01:21:59+09:00	2022-09-24T05:17:59+09:00	74.91
4260	11550	7110	34	71	1050	16440	2022-09-25T00:09:01+09:00	2022-09-25T09:07:01+09:00	73.78
3000	13290	7290	29	85	390	14190	2022-09-27T01:07:59+09:00	2022-09-27T08:50:59+09:00	64.59
5790	10860	12900	28	93	240	15720	2022-09-30T01:18:02+09:00	2022-09-30T10:05:02+09:00	64.51
3450	7740	8820	28	94	510	10650	2022-10-01T04:15:00+09:00	2022-10-01T10:11:00+09:00	73.99
4860	6930	10380	19	92	210	11490	2022-10-02T05:10:02+09:00	2022-10-02T11:51:02+09:00	77.77
3630	11640	8820	27	85	1590	15420	2022-10-03T02:42:02+09:00	2022-10-03T10:35:02+09:00	62.92
5760	8640	10770	25	86	570	14400	2022-10-05T01:00:01+02:00	2022-10-05T09:08:01+02:00	61.03
4230	11640	7560	28	84	420	14100	2022-10-06T01:21:58+02:00	2022-10-06T09:04:58+02:00	61.81
3030	6090	8220	17	93	450	9210	2022-10-07T05:16:00+02:00	2022-10-07T10:26:00+02:00	90.83
7350	20970	7050	34	90	420	20340	2022-10-07T22:58:01+02:00	2022-10-08T09:53:01+02:00	70.42
3450	12390	8340	25	84	1110	14970	2022-10-11T01:11:30+02:00	2022-10-11T09:11:30+02:00	59.12
2580	4770	7020	34	55	180	10470	2022-10-12T04:00:31+02:00	2022-10-12T11:13:31+02:00	81.1
6600	17130	10050	27	90	1080	19680	2022-10-12T22:22:42+02:00	2022-10-13T08:47:42+02:00	64.2
7380	5940	10920	14	96	480	12570	2022-10-14T02:43:29+02:00	2022-10-14T09:45:29+02:00	82.95
5490	13740	10530	24	90	330	16620	2022-10-14T23:23:31+02:00	2022-10-15T08:33:31+02:00	63.15
8640	21300	13890	34	88	810	25350	2022-10-18T22:34:00+09:00	2022-10-19T12:21:00+09:00	63.7
4470	14100	7800	31	92	570	14430	2022-10-20T04:31:16+09:00	2022-10-20T12:31:16+09:00	69.97
4800	13380	11910	37	88	570	16560	2022-10-21T02:26:14+09:00	2022-10-21T11:53:14+09:00	57.95
2550	7560	8490	22	93	450	9960	2022-10-22T03:07:29+09:00	2022-10-22T08:42:29+09:00	78.52
5760	17340	9540	30	88	210	19410	2022-10-23T23:17:14+09:00	2022-10-24T09:35:14+09:00	59.18
2580	9120	6810	29	90	330	10080	2022-10-25T04:07:23+09:00	2022-10-25T09:48:23+09:00	73.85
7650	15480	14250	28	90	480	20880	2022-10-25T22:32:39+09:00	2022-10-26T10:01:39+09:00	57.86
2610	8640	9480	34	86	570	11280	2022-10-27T02:09:01+09:00	2022-10-27T08:53:01+09:00	56.75
5160	10080	8130	31	92	480	12660	2022-10-28T02:46:25+09:00	2022-10-28T09:48:25+09:00	77.04
4530	12450	10440	31	90	240	15270	2022-10-31T00:39:11+09:00	2022-10-31T09:06:11+09:00	57.17
3540	6480	6570	12	94	510	8760	2022-11-01T03:22:38+09:00	2022-11-01T08:17:38+09:00	74.28
5220	19770	7590	36	74	2280	23700	2022-11-01T22:43:28+09:00	2022-11-02T10:55:28+09:00	57.48
5010	12060	3150	32	91	1080	11310	2022-11-03T02:59:28+09:00	2022-11-03T09:11:28+09:00	74.32
7140	15180	9870	30	90	1140	17940	2022-11-04T00:58:28+09:00	2022-11-04T10:51:28+09:00	56.12
5580	12990	9450	31	86	600	17340	2022-11-07T00:51:36+09:00	2022-11-07T09:52:36+09:00	61.33
5820	16080	4650	35	93	630	14310	2022-11-08T02:36:30+09:00	2022-11-08T10:30:30+09:00	71.76
4980	16530	8490	39	94	270	15840	2022-11-09T02:04:32+09:00	2022-11-09T10:56:32+09:00	65.15
5700	15870	8040	40	82	810	17100	2022-11-11T01:34:59+09:00	2022-11-11T11:38:59+09:00	68.06
5100	14520	10500	34	90	720	16230	2022-11-12T01:46:01+09:00	2022-11-12T11:04:01+09:00	57.51

Date	Lowest Resting Heart Rate	Average HRV	Temperature Deviation (°C)	Temperature Trend Deviation	Respiratory Rate	Activity Score	Stay Active Score	Move Every Hour Score	Meet Daily Targets Score	Training Frequency Score	Training Volume Score
2022-08-17	57.0	51	-0.28	-0.06	17.125	80	92	100	43	71	88
2022-08-19	57.0	61	-0.07	-0.01	17.125	93	100	100	78	100	98
2022-08-21	52.0	86	-0.02	0.05	16	99	100	100	95	100	99
2022-08-23	52.0	86	0.41	0.24	17.25	94	96	100	78	100	100
2022-08-25	65.0	26	-0.23	0.18	18.875	92	84	95	78	100	100
2022-08-26	69.0	32	-0.36	-0.03	17.125	87	82	95	60	100	99
2022-08-27	52.0	106	0.08	-0.05	17.5	89	68	95	78	100	99
2022-08-28	50.0	96	-0.2	-0.02	16	94	96	100	78	100	99
2022-08-30	74.0	16	0.32	0.15	19.5	92	75	100	95	100	100
2022-09-01	63.0	31	-0.53	-0.03	19	83	63	78	100	100	99
2022-09-02	51.0	114	-0.15	-0.08	16.375	93	68	78	100	100	98
2022-09-03	53.0	81	-0.44	-0.18	16.5	96	86	100	95	100	97
2022-09-04	54.0	63	-0.14	-0.09	16.375	97	93	100	95	100	97
2022-09-05	54.0	76	-0.25	-0.08	16.25	92	66	100	95	100	97
2022-09-07	53.0	78	-0.43	-0.24	16.625	94	100	100	78	100	100
2022-09-08	52.0	89	-0.66	-0.36	15.375	86	77	95	60	100	100
2022-09-09	52.0	114	-0.64	-0.42	16	91	79	100	78	100	100
2022-09-10	83.0	16	-0.42	-0.35	19.75	93	92	100	78	100	100
2022-09-11	50.0	108	-0.2	-0.15	15.75	80	64	100	43	96	98
2022-09-12	50.0	100	-0.52	-0.14	15.25	86	76	100	60	100	98
2022-09-13	51.0	85	-0.82	-0.3	15.5	89	69	100	78	100	97
2022-09-14	57.0	58	-0.04	-0.18	16.5	92	85	100	78	100	97
2022-09-15	66.0	25	-0.21	-0.03	15.875	96	85	100	95	100	97
2022-09-16	54.0	83	0.1	0.14	15.875	95	84	100	95	100	99
2022-09-17	67.0	34	0.15	0.25	17.375	91	77	95	95	100	99
2022-09-19	54.0	86	-0.05	0.26	16.125	85	58	78	78	100	97
2022-09-21	56.0	55	0.11	0.14	17.125	93	70	95	95	100	97
2022-09-22	54.0	87	0.22	0.28	15.625	93	68	100	95	100	99
2022-09-24	61.0	38	0.39	0.47	19	97	90	100	95	100	98
2022-09-25	57.0	49	0.13	0.46	18.25	97	86	95	100	100	99
2022-09-27	55.0	74	0.0	0.35	16.375	92	75	100	100	100	100
2022-09-30	55.0	73	-0.49	-0.15	15.375	75	72	100	100	100	100
2022-10-01	65.0	45	-0.12	-0.13	17.375	73	75	100	100	100	100
2022-10-02	69.0	36	-0.14	-0.01	17.75	71	74	95	100	100	100
2022-10-03	54.0	85	-0.12	0.05	16.375	85	100	100	100	100	100
2022-10-05	53.0	80	-0.1	0.27	15.75	97	82	100	100	100	99
2022-10-06	52.0	67	-0.29	0.1	15.875	98	97	100	100	100	100
2022-10-07	77.0	23	0.11	0.08	17.75	95	87	100	100	100	100
2022-10-08	57.0	53	0.2	0.24	16.125	100	98	100	100	100	99
2022-10-11	54.0	86	-0.5	0.08	15.5	95	78	100	95	100	99
2022-10-12	73.0	28	0.0	0.01	18.5	97	88	100	95	100	99
2022-10-13	54.0	79	-0.16	0.01	16	97	94	100	95	100	100
2022-10-14	75.0	22	0.07	0.13	17.5	95	97	100	95	100	100
2022-10-15	55.0	74	0.05	0.19	15.75	94	75	95	95	100	99
2022-10-19	53.0	75	0.28	0.32	16	84	85	100	60	96	81
2022-10-20	59.0	55	0.41	0.47	16.375	81	82	100	43	96	89
2022-10-21	51.0	104	0.01	0.41	15.375	84	94	100	43	96	95
2022-10-22	53.0	33	-0.46	0.09	18.125	92	93	100	78	100	97
2022-10-24	50.0	113	-0.14	-0.06	16.125	95	76	100	95	100	98
2022-10-25	64.0	43	0.28	0.25	18	98	94	100	95	100	98
2022-10-26	51.0	107	0.18	0.34	16.125	95	79	95	95	100	96
2022-10-27	51.0	90	0.05	0.34	16.25	93	83	100	100	100	98
2022-10-28	65.0	39	0.46	0.41	17	89	71	100	100	100	97
2022-10-31	52.0	95	-0.19	0.3	15.375	98	88	100	100	100	97
2022-11-01	67.0	26	-0.51	0.0	17.75	99	100	100	100	100	97
2022-11-02	50.0	82	-0.36	-0.2	16	96	95	100	100	100	99
2022-11-03	52.0	43	-0.32	-0.2	17.375	91	83	100	100	100	100
2022-11-04	51.0	112	-0.02	-0.04	15.75	88	86	100	95	100	100
2022-11-07	53.0	69	-0.35	-0.08	15.5	90	69	100	78	100	99
2022-11-08	59.0	48	0.18	0.07	15.5	92	87	100	78	100	100
2022-11-09	57.0	60	0.06	0.18	15.25	93	96	100	78	100	100
2022-11-11	53.0	63	-0.07	0.13	15.75	83	70	95	78	100	100
2022-11-12	52.0	106	-0.3	-0.02	15	97	87	100	95	100	100
2022-08-15						66	91	100	25	40	50
2022-08-16						75	74	100	43	71	76
2022-08-18						84	66	100	60	96	96
2022-08-20						83	55	95	78	100	97
2022-08-22						94	100	100	78	100	98
2022-08-24						94	100	100	78	100	99
2022-08-29						98	100	100	95	100	99
2022-08-31						94	97	100	100	100	100
2022-09-06						89	73	95	78	96	95
2022-09-18						87	70	95	95	100	98
2022-09-20						97	92	100	95	100	97
2022-09-23						92	78	100	95	100	99
2022-09-26						96	82	100	100	100	99
2022-09-28						90	79	95	100	100	100
2022-09-29						90	92	100	100	100	100
2022-10-04						91	44	95	100	100	100
2022-10-10						97	95	100	95	100	96
2022-10-18						88	92	95	78	96	75
2022-10-23						90	100	100	78	100	96
2022-10-30						97	87	100	100	100	96
2022-11-05						95	74	100	95	100	99
2022-11-06						94	100	100	78	100	99
2022-11-10						91	97	100	78	100	100

Activity Burn	Total Burn	Steps	Equivalent Walking Distance	Inactive Time	Rest Time	Low Activity Time	Medium Activity Time	High Activity Time	Non-wear Time	Average MET	Long Periods of Inactivity
426	2450	8945	8403	25140	37020	21300	2460	0	480	1.46875	0
689	2667	17765	14546	9720	38100	16140	7440	60	14940	1.59375	0
768	2808	17170	15542	12360	39000	26220	6660	120	2040	1.65625	0
797	2799	17845	16942	26520	30240	13860	10020	60	5700	1.6875	0
811	2971	18127	15898	30960	17640	27240	7320	60	3180	1.8125	1
273	2199	6502	5630	27240	37980	11400	1560	60	8160	1.3125	1
601	2661	13989	12196	37500	13200	19200	5520	0	10980	1.625	1
575	2573	14399	11491	22680	35640	17220	5940	0	4920	1.53125	0
800	2934	19622	16132	31500	22920	20520	8940	0	2520	1.78125	0
277	1966	7922	6360	38940	29280	15060	2280	60	780	1.40625	2
323	2049	8711	7284	37260	28860	16860	3000	0	420	1.46875	2
547	2551	12034	11315	28260	26700	19320	4440	0	7680	1.5625	0
558	2561	12821	11387	24600	32400	21840	4140	0	3420	1.5625	0
230	2194	5119	4116	37800	32520	15240	780	60	0	1.34375	0
1365	3379	17872	26167	14640	27780	15420	10440	2760	15360	2.0625	0
321	2313	6950	5982	32400	30420	19380	1560	0	2640	1.40625	1
681	2835	14576	13503	33540	11160	28440	5460	60	7740	1.75	0
395	2326	8883	7743	23400	41040	18060	2880	60	960	1.40625	0
366	2364	8652	7097	38280	24960	16140	3000	60	3960	1.4375	0
427	2402	6649	7833	31440	26220	12840	3060	0	12840	1.46875	0
403	2437	8712	7624	35700	25080	18900	3060	120	3540	1.5	0
554	2624	11696	10805	30480	23040	23640	4200	180	4860	1.625	0
472	2465	11601	9751	27900	31140	20040	2760	0	4560	1.5	0
885	2978	16708	17659	32460	20760	24720	7680	660	120	1.8125	0
500	2476	9197	9581	30600	33600	15480	3840	0	2880	1.5	1
308	2301	7038	5861	40140	27720	16680	1860	0	0	1.40625	2
545	2561	11877	11307	35460	25680	21600	3480	120	60	1.5625	1
894	2924	18855	18907	22320	19500	13500	11040	120	19920	1.78125	0
446	2495	9085	8517	25980	18480	23160	2820	120	15840	1.53125	0
690	2716	14748	13845	25620	17160	16800	6780	180	19860	1.6875	1
702	2794	16120	14454	34620	19140	26520	5700	120	300	1.71875	0
752	2835	16745	14963	36780	22380	18900	8220	120	0	1.75	0
531	2592	12049	10790	34680	21600	21900	4380	0	3840	1.59375	0
648	2654	16302	13519	33060	27600	19500	6180	60	0	1.625	1
412	2321	10522	8632	16020	29340	10800	4200	0	26040	1.40625	0
555	2307	13635	13124	29340	28200	23640	5040	180	0	1.625	0
873	2734	20660	20625	21600	16680	37500	8460	540	1620	1.96875	0
368	2053	8902	8418	27480	35820	15300	3900	60	3840	1.4375	0
313	2018	6260	7037	17700	21240	17040	2700	60	27660	1.4375	0
753	2560	20070	17885	32700	20280	24540	8640	240	0	1.84375	0
411	2077	12400	9869	21060	42840	14880	4620	60	2940	1.46875	0
687	2483	17916	16145	24900	24180	29940	7260	120	0	1.78125	0
300	1899	9225	7104	18420	44400	7440	4500	0	11640	1.3125	0
179	1824	4606	3940	28380	24120	9660	1560	0	22680	1.3125	1
407	2150	9729	9127	29400	30420	22980	3540	60	0	1.53125	0
422	2123	10331	10039	29280	34440	18420	3840	60	360	1.5	0
481	2244	12099	11029	24000	31140	28140	3060	60	0	1.59375	0
664	2525	16399	14609	25560	17580	38220	4680	360	0	1.8125	0
657	2459	17792	15472	34020	20760	23940	7320	120	240	1.75	0
423	2083	12774	10365	24840	40560	16320	4680	0	0	1.46875	0
517	2253	15504	12820	31560	27840	22500	4440	60	0	1.59375	1
508	2294	11507	11507	28440	21600	27480	4080	180	4620	1.65625	0
311	2032	8153	7182	32640	27060	20580	1320	0	4800	1.4375	0
693	2508	18778	16516	27420	20460	31860	6600	60	0	1.78125	0
438	2105	13766	10923	14700	29640	16920	4620	0	20520	1.5	0
734	2523	20671	17849	22620	26340	27960	7980	60	1440	1.8125	0
554	2278	16711	13621	29640	29940	20220	6600	0	0	1.625	0
295	1921	8792	7230	6900	24660	7740	3900	0	43200	1.375	0
526	2268	13230	12511	38280	25800	14640	7620	60	0	1.625	0
582	2322	14195	14000	27480	30480	21120	7320	0	0	1.65625	0
656	2388	18171	15853	22980	28620	19680	8640	0	6480	1.6875	0
346	2036	9537	7952	31440	35640	16080	3180	60	0	1.4375	1
525	2101	16869	13202	7800	25320	9060	8100	0	0	1.8125	0
509	2556	12066	10255	26580	8760	16800	4380	180	29700	1.5625	0
388	2384	9440	7672	24000	26520	13980	3540	60	18300	1.4375	0
662	2817	15327	13080	36420	17700	24300	5400	120	2460	1.71875	0
361	2502	8232	6440	44880	4260	24180	1020	0	12060	1.53125	1
363	2417	8921	7117	16800	420	14760	2760	60	51600	1.5	0
386	2454	7365	7538	19920	4620	19080	2460	0	40320	1.5	0
611	2711	14761	12329	15360	180	21900	5400	0	43560	1.6875	0
455	2571	10112	8608	22260	1380	23340	2580	60	36780	1.59375	0
273	2273	6409	5364	34200	16980	15180	840	0	19200	1.40625	1
141	2102	3201	2394	33840	18720	9780	180	60	23820	1.3125	1
602	2663	11844	12459	24480	19260	26400	4260	0	12000	1.625	0
435	2506	8649	8229	32160	9840	20040	3240	120	21000	1.5625	0
463	2527	10110	9099	29820	10740	22920	2760	120	20040	1.5625	0
777	2872	19614	15961	31740	11580	22020	7980	120	12960	1.78125	1
690	2697	16936	14255	25620	27720	17880	7560	120	7500	1.65625	0
459	2481	10620	9188	51180	14580	16920	3660	60	0	1.53125	1
363	2089	8451	8421	23700	8940	16020	3480	0	34260	1.53125	0
370	2122	10199	8434	25440	18060	22080	2220	0	18600	1.53125	1
100	1687	2596	2300	11400	35220	6960	360	0	32460	1.1875	0
469	2228	12832	11165	26820	14400	22140	3900	0	19140	1.59375	0
331	2062	9935	7882	33180	10800	15900	3120	0	23400	1.5	0
379	2122	10086	8785	33060	4500	16680	3720	0	28440	1.53125	0
466	2157	13813	11365	20520	31500	17460	4860	0	12060	1.53125	0

Date	Readiness Score	Previous Night Score	Sleep Balance Score	Previous Day Activity Score	Activity Balance Score	Temperature Score	Resting Heart Rate Score	HRV Balance Score	Recovery Index Score
2022-08-17	94	87	None	90	None	94	100	None	99
2022-08-19	78	88	63	75	78	100	100	81	62
2022-08-21	87	83	85	80	87	100	89	90	100
2022-08-23	74	53	84	100	89	66	93	93	34
2022-08-25	63	46	70	93	93	97	42	76	23
2022-08-26	71	87	80	76	77	92	24	68	91
2022-08-27	68	20	61	94	87	98	92	88	44
2022-08-28	83	85	71	78	82	98	86	93	92
2022-08-30	58	55	68	96	79	78	1	74	44
2022-09-01	63	47	63	91	87	87	64	61	35
2022-09-02	84	87	71	83	90	100	90	85	100
2022-09-03	77	46	66	84	91	90	97	88	82
2022-09-04	88	91	76	86	87	100	100	90	100
2022-09-05	86	75	81	90	83	97	100	92	81
2022-09-07	88	79	73	91	92	90	99	95	100
2022-09-08	73	58	73	1	74	83	96	97	100
2022-09-09	76	22	65	92	78	84	97	100	100
2022-09-10	57	42	58	78	73	91	1	89	75
2022-09-11	87	99	69	97	76	98	91	93	100
2022-09-12	81	62	70	84	79	88	92	95	100
2022-09-13	77	50	67	67	81	79	96	96	87
2022-09-14	82	85	73	85	82	100	88	94	71
2022-09-15	62	37	66	84	82	98	33	87	49
2022-09-16	87	89	73	91	82	97	100	89	100
2022-09-17	54	25	66	64	72	92	28	84	37
2022-09-19	80	47	67	97	81	100	100	87	100
2022-09-21	75	79	55	89	81	96	96	88	52
2022-09-22	73	53	56	80	79	86	100	91	62
2022-09-24	59	36	47	88	83	72	64	87	23
2022-09-25	72	57	51	92	85	93	90	84	69
2022-09-27	77	68	56	88	86	100	100	86	73
2022-09-30	79	85	57	85	70	88	100	90	83
2022-10-01	59	55	58	73	63	100	37	87	41
2022-10-02	58	57	60	84	66	100	13	77	63
2022-10-03	74	57	65	80	63	100	100	86	70
2022-10-05	75	76	52	69	73	100	100	87	86
2022-10-06	71	61	55	83	71	95	97	88	52
2022-10-07	46	39	52	74	61	95	1	74	26
2022-10-08	80	100	67	95	66	88	92	73	72
2022-10-11	82	63	73	94	73	88	100	83	100
2022-10-12	51	7	64	70	65	100	1	66	100
2022-10-13	87	100	76	99	69	100	100	77	92
2022-10-14	65	78	78	83	64	99	1	57	100
2022-10-15	84	96	84	100	72	100	100	67	64
2022-10-19	98	95	None	98	None	81	100	None	100
2022-10-20	70	67	None	91	None	70	77	None	51
2022-10-21	91	80	100	90	81	100	93	91	90
2022-10-22	79	48	100	94	80	89	100	82	17
2022-10-24	92	94	91	100	85	100	91	91	91
2022-10-25	64	37	82	74	78	81	39	87	38
2022-10-26	93	100	92	95	78	89	95	92	100
2022-10-27	83	48	87	82	76	100	96	95	100
2022-10-28	61	65	85	87	76	66	32	90	54
2022-10-31	89	76	86	90	78	99	99	93	100
2022-11-01	62	46	74	80	71	88	19	80	64
2022-11-02	85	72	83	98	75	93	91	86	100
2022-11-03	70	48	78	83	68	94	99	78	19
2022-11-04	89	96	86	84	66	100	96	88	100
2022-11-07	83	83	68	88	80	93	100	90	83
2022-11-08	73	78	72	76	79	89	70	87	47
2022-11-09	81	81	78	86	76	100	84	87	79
2022-11-11	86	80	86	96	76	100	100	86	76
2022-11-12	92	90	90	93	80	95	100	91	100
2022-08-15									
2022-08-16									
2022-08-18									
2022-08-20									
2022-08-22									
2022-08-24									
2022-08-29									
2022-08-31									
2022-09-06									
2022-09-18									
2022-09-20									
2022-09-23									
2022-09-26									
2022-09-28									
2022-09-29									
2022-10-04									
2022-10-10									
2022-10-18									
2022-10-23									
2022-10-30									
2022-11-05									
2022-11-06									
2022-11-10									

**TheCityAsAHouse. This is it.
The end of my experience.
I hope you enjoyed it and could live it through me.**

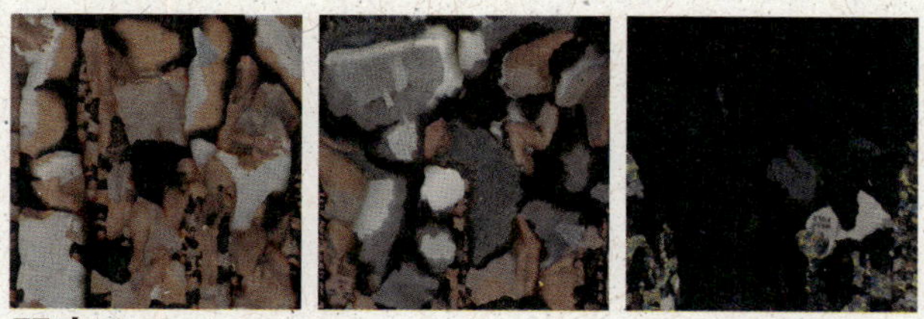

即席
BATH

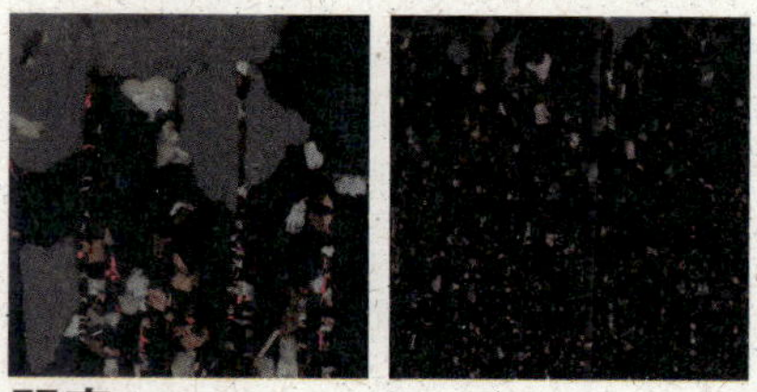

即席
KITCHEN

即席
LEISURE

即席
BED

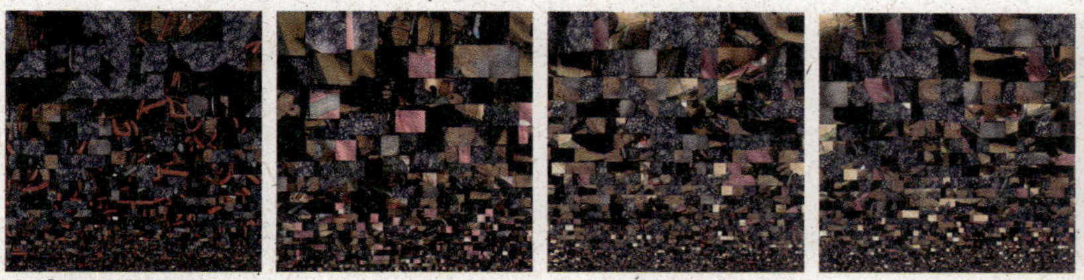

お祖母ちゃん
OBACHAN MATSUZAKI

水野遼
RYOICHIMIZUNO

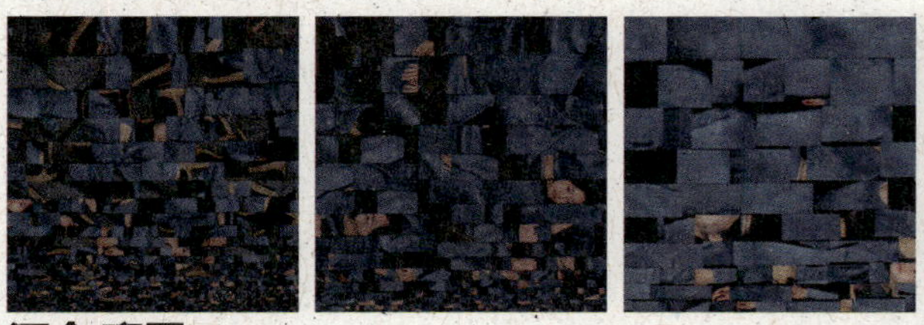

河合 瑠夏
RUKAKAWAI

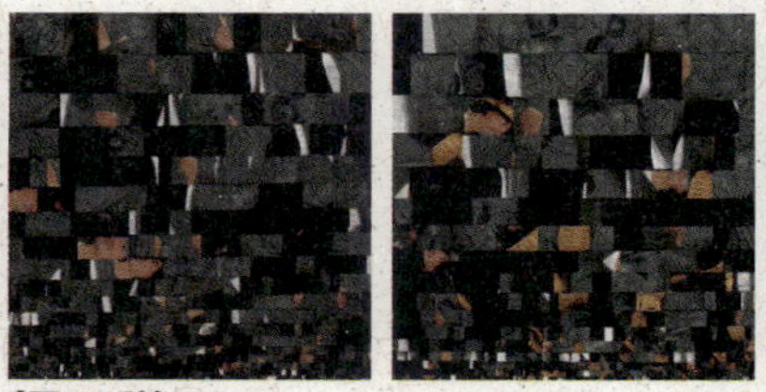

福田謙二
KENJIFUKUDA

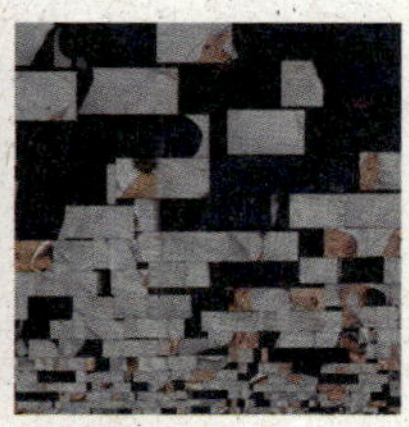

西晃平
KOHEINISHI

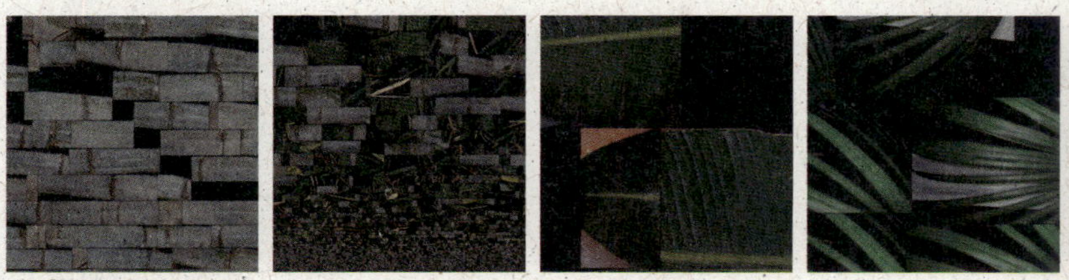

お祖母ちゃん
ITOSHIMA BAMBOO

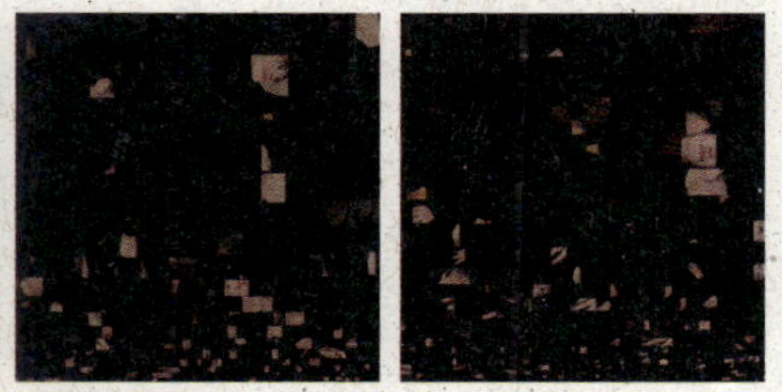

福田麻浪
MANAMIFUKUDA

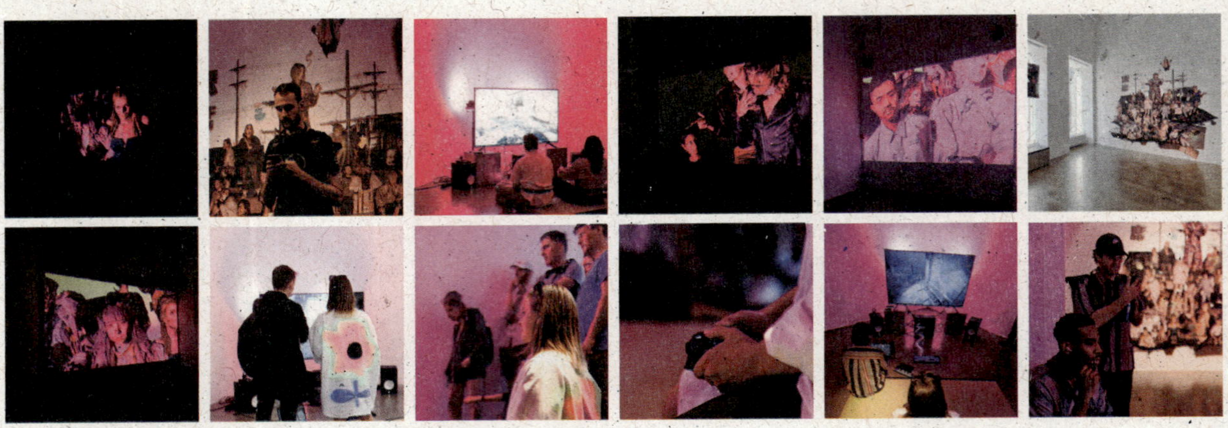

TheCityasAHouse, Bildrecht, 2022 ©Joanna Pianka

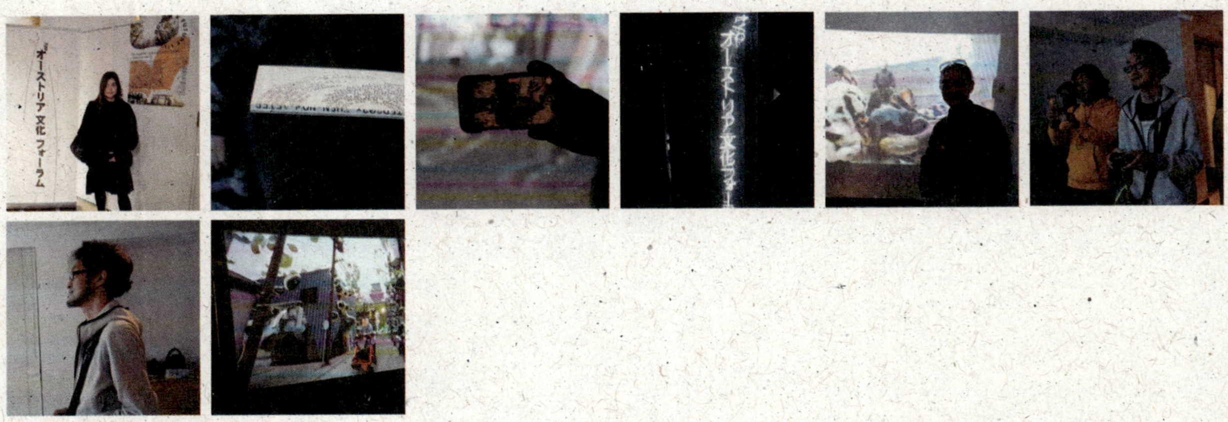

DOMUM, オーストリア文化フォーラム/糸島市
Austrian Cultural Forum Tokyo, JPN (irl), 2022 ©Kazuhiro Ichikawa

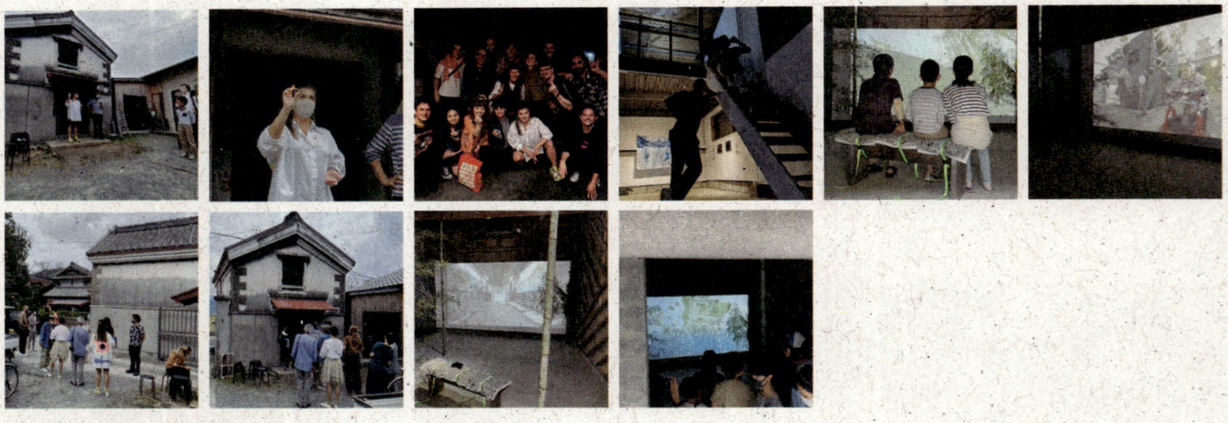

DOMUM Studio Kura 絵画教室, Itoshima,Fukuoka-ku, JPN (irl)

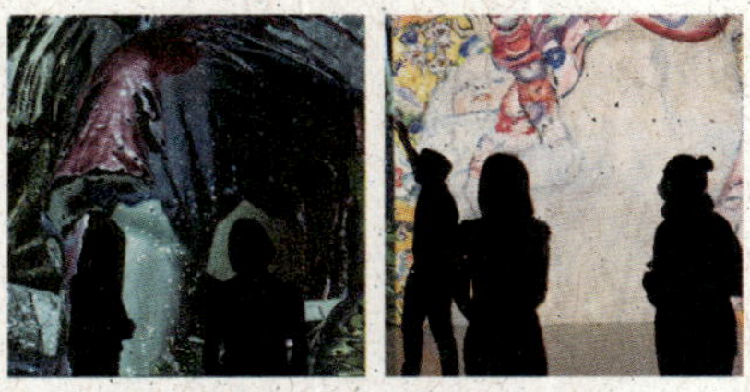

Close-ups from works by Rebecca Merlic and detail from Gustav Klimt's, "The Bride," 1917/18, Klimt Foundation, Deep Space 8K, Ars Electronica Center in Linz, AT (irl) © Robert Bauernhansl

OFFLINE EXHIBITIONS

09/2020	VIENNA DESIGN WEEK, Vienna, AUT
09/2020	DUTCH DESIGN WEEK, NL
01/2021	Symposium on Applied Paradox: Paradox in the Body, City of Munich's Department of Arts and Culture. with Dr. Ulf Hengstmann, Dr. Nelly Ben Hayoun-Stépanian, Franz Nahrada, H.E. Tomas Čepaitis
08/2021	TheCityAsAHouse 都市が家になるとき solo show, hosted by ARS ELECTRONICA, Bildraum 07, Bildrecht, Vienna, AUT (irl)
09/2021	VIENNACONTEMPORARY
11/2021	VIENNA ART WEEK, DESSOUS, Vienna, AUT (irl)
11/2021	CYLAND, CYFEST 13, St. Petersbourg, RUS (irl)
03/2022	DER STANDARD-Shortlisted Cover 10.000 Ausgabe 2nd place, "TheCityAsAHouse" von Rebecca Merlic
04/2022	Deep Space: Gustav Klimt's Images of Women— A Dialogue with the Portraits of Women by Rebecca Merlic, Belvedere, VIE, ARS ELECTRONICA CENTRE, Deep Space 8K, Linz, AT (irl)
10/2022	Studio Kura 絵画教室, Itoshima, Fukuoka-ku, JPN (irl)
11/2022	オーストリア文化フォーラム /Austrian Cultural Forum Tokyo, JPN (irl)

ONLINE EXHIBITIONS

07/2020	Solo exhibition (shortlisted Artist, Game Art, Techno-Tribalism)
08/2020	ADAF. Athens Digital Arts Festival, Athen, GR
09/2020	ARS ELECTRONICA, Garden, VENT Gallery Wien/Linz, AUT
09/2020	JAPANREVISITED202X Austrian Cultural Forum Tokyo, JPN

AWARDS

2020	Preisträgerin Preis für digitale Medien, Stadt Linz Frauenbüro, ARS ELECTRONICA
2021	Best Austrian Animation: Experimental short category winner Marianne von Willemer Preis (winner)

Babies Are Born	303
Humans Die	304
Persons Are Hired	408
Persons Move	1.251
Marriages Take Place	238
People Get A Divorce	65
Traffic Accidents Happen	102
Humans die by Traffic Accidents	0.5
Ambulance Dispatches Happen	2.075
Fires Occur	13.2
Fire Engines Dispatch	89
People Call The Police	3.894
Crimes are reported	439
Humans get arrested and a human dumps	115
Gram of Trash every Day in the Metropolitan Area of Tokyo.[2]	943
Books are borrowed	307.000

Reality Check

A big thank you to:
Vivien Schreiber (post processing)
Manuel Riegler (sound production)
Mayuko Horiuchi, Philip Wolfsohn, Max Unterfrauner, Manuela Hillmann, Martin Eichler, Jaka Patafta, Sarah and Deborah Merlic and my mother.

DOMUM
Austrian Cultural Forum Tokyo, JPN
FUKUOKA
Studio Kura, Oba-chan Matsuzaki
OSAKA
Manami Fukuda 福田麻浪, Kenji Fukuda 福田謙二, Kohei Nishi 西晃平, Ryoichi Mizuno 水野遼一
KYOTO
Ruka Kawai 河合 瑠夏
Assistance:
Philip Wolfsohn
(Best bamboo cutter)

Published by:
VfmK Verlag für moderne Kunst GmbH
Schwedenplatz 2/24,1010 Vienna, AT
hello@vfmk.org, www.vfmk.org

ISBN 978-3-99153-037-4

Print
Quatro Print
First edition, August 2023

Distribution
Europe: LKG, www.lkg-va.de
UK: Cornerhouse Publications, www.cornerhousepublications.org
USA: D.A.P., www.artbook.com

Bibliographic information published by the Deutsche Nationalbibliothek
The Deutsche Nationalbibliothek lists this publication in the Deutsche Nationalbibliografie; detailed bibliographic data is available in the Internet at dnb.de

Editor
Rebecca Merlic
Texts
Gerfried Stocker, Michaela Wimplinger, Manuela Hillmann, Helen Starr, Franz Smola, Dominik Strzelec, Andreas Spiegl and me.
Translation
Philip Wolfsohn, Mayuko Horiuchi
Design
Studio Es, Vienna
Photography
Rebecca Merlic, Anna Manabe, Joanna Pianka, Kazuhiro Ichikawa, Robert Bauernhansl
Proof Reading
Scott Clifford Evans

Gavin H.Whitelaw, ‚Konbini Morphology', in Christian Fruneaux, and Edwin Gardner (eds.), TOKYO TOTEM, Collingwood, VIC, CSIRO Publishing, 2004, p. 99.
[1] Maiko Arrieta Aoki, ‚Omoiyari', in Christian Fruneaux, and Edwin Gardner (eds.), TOKYO TOTEM, Tokyo, JPN, flick studio, 2015, p. 250.
[2] Kurashi to Tokei 2016" くらしと統計 2016, www.toukei.metro.tokyo.jp/kurasi/2016/ku-01.htm
LOG/OUT MAGAZINE VER 1.0 Mitsuhiro Sakakibara / RAD (Research for Architectural Domain), 2015 Booklets, 61 pages, Dimension Variable, ISBN 978-4-90827-901-0